›dge Studies in the Modern World Economy

›eralism in the Emerging Economy of India
›litical economy of international trade, investment and finance
›y Byasdeb Dasgupta, Archita Ghosh and Bishakha Ghosh

Foreign Direct Investment in Europe
›by Prana Krishna Biswas and Robert Dygas

›mic Policy and the Covid-19 Crisis
›acroeconomic response in the US, Europe and East Asia
›by Bernadette Andreosso-O'Callaghan, Woosik Moon and Wook Sohn

›trial Development
›tates build capabilities and deliver economic prosperity
›lydesdale

›g and Effecting Long-Term Care in China
›a Ching Yuen Luk, Hui Zhang and Peter P. Yuen

Trade and Investment in Europe
by Prana Krishna Biswas and Robert Dygas

›al Perspectives on Economics of Education
by Silvia Mendolia, Martin O'Brien, Alfredo Paloyo and Oleg Yerokhin

›-Owned Enterprises in the Global Economy
Bałtowski and Grzegorz Kwiatkowski

›nore information about this series, please visit: www.routledge.com/
›ledge-Studies-in-the-Modern-World-Economy/book-series/SE0432

State-Owned Enterprise: Global Economy

State-owned enterprises (SOEs) combine econo
their position on the market with non-econom
the state owner. In many of the world's major ec
portant role, and in some, such as China, India,
outright dominant. At the same time, the existen
by economic theory and the current figures on S
ble in the literature are questionable in terms of th
and thus they do not allow for a proper cross-cou
this research gap.

It focuses on the scope and importance of SO
largest economies, primarily on a variety of quant
the results of an extensive and unique empirical
largest economies over the period from 2009 to
that the average share of SOEs – measured by op
assets – in the group of the largest 100 enterprises
try is nearly 30%, while in the Top 20 group it is
authors present an econometric analysis showing th
scope of SOEs and the various economic and non-
the studied set of countries. The book also contain
selected key issues, such as the functions of SOEs
mies, the role of SOEs in capital markets and the p
foreign capital.

This work is addressed to academic economists
nomics and economic policy, as well as researchers
international organisations and think-tanks.

Maciej Bałtowski is Professor of Economics an
and Regional Policy Department at the Facult
Curie-Sklodowska University, Lublin, Poland.

Grzegorz Kwiatkowski is a lecturer of Economi
nomics, Maria Curie-Sklodowska University, Lubli

Rout

Neoli
The p
Edited

Asian
Edited

Econ
The r
Edite

Indu
How
Greg

Agei
Sabri

Asia
Edite

Criti
Edite

Stat
Maci

For
Rou

State-Owned Enterprises in the Global Economy

Maciej Bałtowski and
Grzegorz Kwiatkowski

Routledge
Taylor & Francis Group
LONDON AND NEW YORK

First published 2022
by Routledge
4 Park Square, Milton Park, Abingdon, Oxon OX14 4RN

and by Routledge
605 Third Avenue, New York, NY 10158

Routledge is an imprint of the Taylor & Francis Group, an informa business

British Library Cataloguing-in-Publication Data
A catalogue record for this book is available from the British Library

Library of Congress Cataloging-in-Publication Data
Names: Bałtowski, Maciej, author. | Kwiatkowski, Grzegorz, author.
Title: State-owned enterprises in the global economy / Maciej Bałtowski, Grzegorz Kwiatkowski.
Description: 1 Edition. | New York, NY : Routledge, 2022. | Series: Routledge studies in the modern world economy | Includes bibliographical references and index.
Identifiers: LCCN 2021059255 (print) | LCCN 2021059256 (ebook) | ISBN 9781032155203 (hardback) | ISBN 9781032155210 (paperback) | ISBN 9781003244462 (ebook)
Subjects: LCSH: Government business enterprises—Case studies. | Economic policy—Case studies.
Classification: LCC HD3850 .B235 2022 (print) | LCC HD3850 (ebook) | DDC 338.6/2—dc23/eng/20211203
LC record available at https://lccn.loc.gov/2021059255
LC ebook record available at https://lccn.loc.gov/2021059256

ISBN: 978-1-032-15520-3 (hbk)
ISBN: 978-1-032-15521-0 (pbk)
ISBN: 978-1-003-24446-2 (ebk)

DOI: 10.4324/9781003244462

Typeset in Bembo
by codeMantra

The data that support thew findings of this book are available from the corresponding author, GK, upon reasonable request, with the limitations due to legal restrictions.

This work was supported by the National Science Centre of Poland under Grant no. 2017/25/B/HS4/01103 "The Phenomenon of 'The Return of State-Owned Enterprises' in Contemporary Economy: Identification, Characteristics, and Consequences for the Economic Theory and for the Theory of Economic Policy".

Contents

Figures

Tables

Introduction

For years, the attitude of economists towards state-owned enterprises (SOEs) has been ambivalent. On the one hand, the existence of SOEs has been largely ignored by both mainstream and Keynesian economics. In the world's most popular textbooks, which have shaped the way of thinking about the economy of successive generations of economists worldwide, such as *Economics* by Paul A. Samuelson and William D. Nordhaus, *Principles of Economics* by N. Gregory Mankiw or *Economics* by Paul Krugman and Robin Wells, there are no chapters or more extensive passages devoted to the place and importance of SOEs in the economy. Although Samuelson and Nordhaus do refer to the role of SOEs several times, they treat this subject always marginally. Only when analysing the Chinese economy and the socialist system do they discuss the issue a little more extensively. Mankiw, Krugman and Wells write about SOEs solely in the context of addressing the problems with the existence of monopolies in the economy. The subject of SOEs is treated in a similar way in the increasingly popular textbook *The Economy (CORE Economics)*, created jointly by many scholars from around the world. The publication, whose mission is to radically change the way economists are educated, merely mentions SOEs and does not discuss their role in the economy or the principles of their operation in more detail.

Similarly, in economic policy concepts based on economic theory, the role of SOEs and state ownership is underestimated. Ownership policy tools are either completely ignored or treated perfunctorily as elements of industrial policy that are of minor importance. An example is an approach of Vito Tanzi (2011), who, in classifying the ways of state influence on the economy, distinguished fiscal tools (taxes, subsidies) and regulatory tools (laws, prohibitions and orders) as the basic ones, while he assigned the influence through ownership to the group of "other" less significant economic policy instruments.

On the other hand, a general picture of the economic reality shows that SOEs - special types of economic entities - have existed in all economies for hundreds of years and play a very important role in many of them. Economists should therefore not ignore this fact, not only for historical reasons. Obviously, this is not an original view. Many economists notice a "mismatch between doctrines and reality" (Florio, 2014) as regards SOEs. However, central to

DOI: 10.4324/9781003244462-1

contemporary research on SOEs is the profound shift in the balance of power in the global economy over the past 20–30 years. At a time when the patterns of economics were shaped by the books by Samuelson or Mankiw, Western-type economies, ideally private and competitive, seemed to be an irreplaceable source of wealth and, consequently, the well-being of citizens, while in the economy of the US, the most important in the world for decades, SOEs have always played a completely marginal role.

Today the situation is fundamentally different. The hypothesis of the superiority of a market capitalist economy based on private enterprises over an economy with an extensive SOE sector, especially in terms of development opportunities, would be difficult to prove conclusively. China, treated for decades as an economic Third World, has become a power comparable only with the long-standing hegemon, i.e. the US (Kołodko, 2020). And among the world's major economies, countries such as India, Indonesia and Brazil are gradually beginning to take the places historically held by the UK, France and Italy. Using our calculations and measures, presented in detail in the following chapters, we will briefly mention some numerical comparisons. In 2018, the share of SOEs in the set of the 100 largest companies in the US accounted for 0.6%, while in China - 85%, i.e. 140 times more! The only SOE in the Top 100 US non-financial companies is ranked 36. In China, meanwhile, the top seven positions on the list of the largest companies are occupied by SOEs, with 78 in the Top 100. The average share of SOEs in the group of four traditional economic powers (the US, Japan, Germany, the UK) is 5.3% and in the group of four BRIC (Brazil, Russia, India and China) countries, it is 55.7%, so over ten times more.

These hard facts do not escape the attention of economists. During the last 20 years, there has been a markedly increased interest in the studies on the place and role of SOEs in the economy. Research reports and expert analyses presented by international organisations such as the Organisation for Economic Co-operation and Development (OECD) and the International Monetary Fund (IMF) are particularly important. OECD reports on SOEs and state ownership, published widely and systematically for more than 15 years, have contributed both to the dissemination of knowledge on contemporary SOEs and to significant promotion of economic research on these issues. This has resulted, especially after the financial crisis of 2008–2009, in a significant increase in the number of scientific publications on SOEs. Bruton et al. (2015) showed a marked increase in the number of publications on SOEs in the most serious economics journals between 2007 and 2014. Its symptom in recent years is the appearance on the publishing market of two comprehensive works containing the sum of current scientific knowledge on the place, significance and functions of SOEs in the modern economy: *The Routledge Handbook of State-Owned Enterprises* (2020) and *The Oxford Handbook of State Capitalism and the Firm* (Forthcoming 2022).

However, the empirical base of these publications is far from perfect. The authors of the *The Routledge Handbook of State-Owned Enterprises*, rightly state: "The empirical literature on SOEs is voluminous but disjointed" [...], "Global analyses are uncommon", [...] "[the] dataset is far from exhaustive" (Bernier et al., 2020, p. 6). This weakness of the empirical base on SOEs, undoubtedly essential for in-depth studies on SOEs and consequently for the understanding of the contemporary economy, is mainly due to the fact that related research is for several reasons an extremely unrewarding and difficult field of economic analysis.

First, the set of economic entities generally referred to as "state-owned enterprises" is blurred. Distinguishing SOEs from the set of all enterprises in the economy, i.e. separating SOEs from private enterprises, as well as separating SOEs from other, non-commercial state entities must always be based on somewhat arbitrary decisions. In the case of comparative, multi-country studies, this leads to very serious methodological problems related to data reliability. We examine this issue in detail in Chapter 3.

Second, researchers dealing with SOEs must constantly identify the discrepancies between what is formal, recorded or declared in official statistics and documents and what is actual, existing in everyday life (Baltowski and Kozarzewski, 2016). And take account of it in their analyses - starting with defining and distinguishing SOEs, through their economic functions to problems of corporate governance and state ownership policy principles. At the same time - and this is a factor that raises additional problems - these discrepancies vary greatly from country to country. They are small in stabilised economies based on the rule of law and very significant in important economies with a lower level of institutionalisation and a very high share of SOEs, such as China, Russia or Egypt.

Third, and to some extent due to both of the above reasons, there is no globally relevant, useful for comparative research, uniform statistical data available. Although in the world statistics (and in the statistics of international organisations), as well as in the statistics of individual countries, it is possible to find data concerning "state-owned enterprises", this general term in different data sets (and in different countries) covers various specific entities. These are either only companies with 100% state ownership or companies with majority ownership and in some cases even with minority state ownership or controlled indirectly by the government. This seriously hinders cross-country analyses.

The authors hope that these fundamental methodological problems the researchers of SOEs are always faced with have been overcome in the book at least satisfactorily, that is in a manner that, with all natural deviations from the ideal, leads to reliable and indisputable results that allow comparative and synthetic analyses for a large group of countries. To date, there is no empirical analysis of SOEs in the world literature, covering a large set of the world's largest economies and based on a uniform research procedure.

The research results presented in this book, primarily in the quantitative dimension, but also concerning the role and functions of SOEs in various economic systems, will enable a better understanding of the phenomenon of SOEs and, consequently, will contribute to clarifying the ambiguity mentioned at the beginning concerning the approach to SOEs of economic theory as well as economic policy practice.

We are careful not to repeat the contents of *The Routledge Handbook of State-Owned Enterprises* and other serious publications on SOEs in this book. In particular, we completely ignore the issues of efficiency of SOEs and comparisons of their performance to private enterprises, and we pay little attention to the issues of SOEs' governance and state ownership control, which have been widely analysed in the literature. We concentrate on quantitative and structural issues concerning SOEs in the contemporary economy, which, in our view, have not been given due consideration in the literature.

★ ★ ★

This book has two major objectives. The first is to determine the condition, share and significance of SOEs in the contemporary economy and more specifically in a set of 32 world's largest economies (divided into groups of developed market and emerging market economies) and additionally in five economies of the post-communist countries. The second is to conduct an in-depth cross-country analysis concerning SOEs and to show diverse development trends and changes in the presence of SOEs in the various groups of economies after the financial crisis of 2008–2009.

The book consists of seven chapters. The first chapter presents a historical overview of the development of SOEs, both in the developed countries of the West and in such large and now globally important economies as those of China, India, Russia, Brazil and Indonesia. We seek to demonstrate that the place and functions of contemporary SOEs in the economy are largely determined by the origin of SOEs and their cultural and historical backgrounds.

The second chapter is devoted to the relationships between states (governments) and SOEs. We analyse the types of government-SOE relationships and discuss the functions of contemporary SOEs, drawing attention to the fundamental differences in this respect between SOEs in developed and developing countries. We focus on the key issues necessary to understand the place and role of SOEs in the contemporary economy. At the same time, we present our original views and statements, using the results of our empirical research and former studies regarding certain issues that seem insufficiently explored in the literature.

The third chapter covers methodological issues related to the empirical research and its results contained in this book. We precisely formulate research objectives, discuss the basic research assumptions and define indicators that describe various dimensions of the SOE shares in the economies considered. We present data sources and an original, specially designed procedure for the preparation of empirical data.

The next two chapters provide detailed findings for each of the countries analysed. The share of SOEs in different groups of the largest non-financial companies in 2009, 2013, 2018 (divided into majority SOEs and minority SOEs) is presented, a narrower group of the largest SOEs is characterised in detail. Finally, the share of SOEs in six key (strategic) sectors is estimated. The fourth, most extensive chapter of this book consists of 32 sub-chapters relating to 32 world's largest economies, and the fifth chapter covers analogous data for five post-communist economies.

Chapter 6 contains the most important research results presented in aggregate terms (for the four groups of distinguished economies) and in the form of a cross-country analysis. The basic aggregate data on the shares of SOEs in the groups of the largest enterprises are also presented in dynamic terms for 2009, 2013 and 2018, which made it possible to capture the directions and dynamics of changes in the scope of SOEs in the countries analysed after the 2008–2009 financial crisis.

In Chapter 7, we discuss selected problems of the SOE presence in the economy in the light of our findings. First, the problem of the scale, scope and types of listed SOEs, so state-private entities whose shares are listed on stock exchanges and which are still actually controlled by governments are considered and, second, the problem of foreign SOEs, i.e. the entities operating in a country that are controlled by governments of other countries. The empirical research on foreign SOEs in the world's largest economies presented in the book is probably pioneering in world literature. Third, we present the results of a basic econometric analysis showing, among others, the relationships between the share ratios of SOEs and various economic and non-economic characteristics for 37 countries and distinguished groups of countries. Based on the cluster analysis, we divide the studied economies into five groups according to the scope of SOEs.

* * *

The book is the result and culmination of our long-term - in the case of Maciej Baltowski almost 30 years - studies on SOEs. They concerned SOEs in the socialist economy, SOEs during the economic transition of post-communist countries and SOEs in the contemporary global economy. This research, conducted at Maria Curie-Sklodowska University in Lublin, Poland, has been financially supported by the National Science Centre for four years (grant No. 2017/25/B/HS4/01103).

This book owes a great deal to Piotr Kozarzewski, our friend and colleague, a researcher of transformations in post-communist countries. Professor Kozarzewski was the first reader of the draft versions of the subsequent chapters of the book and his comments and remarks significantly influenced its final form.

We would like to thank Professor Katarzyna Szarzec from the Poznań University of Economics and Business for her help in compiling the statistical data and for critical comments on some parts of the book.

We would also like to thank our junior colleagues for the fruitful cooperation - Marlena Gołębiowska, Jakub Mroczek and Stefan Sękowski,

PhD students of Professor Maciej Baltowski - whose help in collecting and processing statistical data, as well as their substantive assistance in certain areas, was very important.

Maciej Baltowski, Grzegorz Kwiatkowski
November 2021

Bibliography

Baltowski, M., & Kozarzewski, P. (2016). Formal and Real Ownership Structure of the Polish Economy: State-Owned Versus State-Controlled Enterprises. *Post-Communist Economies*, *28*(3), 405–411, Routledge.

Bernier, L., Florio, M., & Bance, P. (Eds.). (2020). *The Routledge Handbook of State-Owned Enterprises*. London; New York: Routledge.

Bruton, G. D., Peng, M. W., Ahlstrom, D., Stan, C., & Xu, K. (2015). State-Owned Enterprises around the World as Hybrid Organizations. *Academy of Management Perspectives*, *29*(1), 92–114.

Florio, M. (2014). The Return of Public Enterprise. *CISL Working Paper*, 1. Milan: Centre for Industrial Studies.

Kołodko, G. W. (2020). *China and the Future of Globalization: The Political Economy of China's Rise*. London; New York: Bloomsbury Publishing.

Tanzi, V. (2011). *Government Versus Markets: The Changing Economic Role of the State*. New York: Cambridge University Press.

Wright, M., Wood, G. T., Cuervo-Cazurra, A., Sun, P., Okhmatovskiy, I., & Grosman, A. (forthcoming 2022). *The Oxford Handbook of State Capitalism and the Firm*. Oxford: Oxford University Press.

1 Origin and history of the state-owned enterprise sector

Over the last 20–30 years, states have rarely created new SOEs. The existing SOEs usually have their origins in the distant past. They appeared in economies through a variety of processes 50, 100 or even more years ago, and their provenance and history still largely determine their functioning and roles in the economy. Knowing and understanding the origins of SOEs is important for knowing and understanding contemporary SOEs and the contemporary economy.

In this chapter and throughout the book, we will not limit the analysis to the developed Western countries, as is usually done by the authors dealing with the origins of SOEs (Toninelli, 2000; Bognetti, 2020). Today, the most important and also the most cognitively interesting is the existence and functioning of SOEs in such large and globally significant economies as those of China, India, Russia, Brazil and Indonesia, as well as in some smaller but nevertheless important economies, such as those of Poland, Egypt, Thailand and Saudi Arabia.

1.1 Before the First World War

Economic activities conducted by or on behalf of the state have a history as long as that of statehood itself. For centuries, from Ancient Egypt to the Chinese state of the Qing dynasty, state enterprises have enjoyed special privileges from rulers and have often benefited from legally guaranteed monopolies in many areas of the economy. However, the origins of modern state-owned enterprises (SOEs) need to be sought in the more recent past – around 150 years ago in the case of the developed Western countries and some Eastern countries, around 100 years ago in the case of countries that appeared on the world map after the First World War and only around 75 years ago in the case of post-colonial and post-communist countries.

In the second half of the 19th century, together with the formation of the modern arrangement of European states, various forms of economic activities carried out by governments developed. These early state enterprises, which are better described as economic government entities (EGEs), were fundamentally different from the modern ones. EGEs were generally elements

DOI: 10.4324/9781003244462-2

of state administration, departments of specific ministries or even separate ministries. Their assets were the assets of the state, and, in economic and financial terms, EGEs were directly linked to the budget. It was only after the First World War, starting with the developed Western countries, that they gradually adopted the legal and organisational form of enterprises, meaning economic entities independent (at least partly) of governments, having financial independence of the budget.

The motives of governments to undertake (or to develop former) economic activities from the second half of the 19th century onwards varied in different countries. Three of these motives seem to be the most important and most common globally. First, EGEs were used as tools in the unification processes associated with the formation of nation states (Millward, 2011). Second, they took control – due to political plans – of the sectors of the economy considered strategic. Third, they supported the industrialisation of the country in the absence of private capital.

A special, exemplary role for the further development of the business of governments was played by EGEs in two industries that were very important back then: post and railways. From the beginning of their existence, that is, from the 17th to the 18th century, postal companies were usually owned by the state (rulers), and from the second half of the 19th century, they developed dynamically, becoming modern, network enterprises, providing services to the public nationwide. In most countries, railway companies were established from the mid-19th century onwards as regional ventures, usually with private capital, and to a lesser extent with public (government) capital. Railway lines formed access networks to major cities and then connected individual cities. It was only at the end of the 19th century, and in some countries much later, that large, nationally uniform, state railway companies were established, through major state investments, and often through nationalisations.

Italy and Germany are the best examples of countries where the development of EGEs was connected with the national and economic unification processes in the second half of the 19th century. The state-owned post played an important role in these processes, providing the same services throughout the country at uniform prices, set by the government. In Italy, the nationwide postal administration was established in 1862, even before the unification process was completed. In the German empire, the establishment of the nationwide post in January 1872 was one of the first economic decisions of the government. In Italy, a tool used to unify the state, especially in terms of evening out regional differences, and a driver of economic development was also the central support for industrialisation policies. Whereas in Germany, where there was a strong and rich private commercial and industrial sector, and regional differences were not so significant, the government was not directly engaged in industrialisation processes.

In Italy, the national state railway, *Ferrovie dello Stato*, was established in 1905, following the nationalisation of five regional railway companies. In Germany, until the end of the First World War, the rail network was divided into nine national railway systems, operating more or less within particular major Reich states and typically owned by the states (*Länder*).

In France, in the last decades of the 19th century, EGEs grew slower than in Italy, which largely resulted from historically grounded statist traditions. The French state influenced the economy more by concessions and by controlling the private sector than by its own economic activity, although the latter was not missing. In 1879, the French government created a uniform administration of postal and telegraph services. In the same year, the French Ministry of Post and Telegraphs was created. Shortly after, the state extended its monopoly to the telecommunications sector (telegraph and telephone), on the grounds of state security. In the case of railways, the system of six regional railways (state-owned and private), formed in the 1860s, survived in its basic outlines in France until 1938, until the time of nationalisation.

In the UK, state ownership was historically less important than, for example, in France. In the second half of the 19th century, the UK was a highly developed country, according to the standards of those times, with a large amount of private capital. Under such circumstances, the motive to promote industrialisation, typical of the development of SOEs in many continental European countries, was irrelevant. Yet, due to the UK's ambitions to become a power, the strategic motive was important. As early as in 1869, the Telegraph Act created a state monopoly in telegraphic communication. At the same time, private telegraph companies existing then were nationalised. Much later, in 1912, the British government effectively nationalised the National Telephone Company, the largest private telephone company. In 1913, owing to Winston Churchill, the then First Lord of the Admiralty, the government acquired a majority stake in the thriving private oil company, Anglo-Persian Oil Company (APOC), a forerunner of the modern petrochemical giant – British Petroleum (BP). APOC, and from 1954, after the name change – British Petroleum – an SOE with mixed state-private capital, was controlled by the British government until the 1970s.

In the second half of the 19th century, the Royal Mail, established by Charles II in 1660, was a large and relatively mature EGE, a model for postal companies in many countries. The railway industry in the UK was in private hands for a very long time. It was not until the end of the Second World War, after the merger of four separate railway companies, that a national state enterprise – British Rail – was established.

In Spain, in the late 19th century, the scope of state ownership was small. EGEs existed only where they were justified strategically (defence), fiscally (tobacco monopoly and mines) or where they provided public services, such as postal and later telegraph services (Comín, 2008, pp. 695–696). The Spanish post has a tradition of more than 300 years as a state entity, while the Spanish railways as a uniform national SOE were only established in 1941, after the nationalisation of private entities that existed earlier, which generally operated on a concessionary basis.

In the US, the scope of state ownership declined systematically from the mid-19th century, both at the federal and at the state level, which clearly distinguished the US from other countries of the West. As C.J. Milhaupt and M. Pargendler (2017, p. 487) rightly noted, "the United States is exceptional in its traditional hostility to government ownership of enterprise". The history of the US post dates back to the end of the 18th century. In 1872, the US Postal Service was given the status of a government department. The railway sector, quite fragmented, was largely private.

In Canada, in the last decades of the 19th century, EGEs (traditionally referred to as crown corporations) were created in relatively large numbers, especially where there was no private capital. At the provincial level, SOEs that still exist today emerged in the energy (e.g. Ontario Hydro, 1906) and telecommunications (SaskTel, 1908) sectors. Shortly after the Confederation of Canada was formed of four provinces in 1867, the Post Office Department of the Canadian government, commonly referred to as the Royal Mail Canada, was established, which meant the creation of a national postal company. Meanwhile, the ownership of the railways was transferred from the provinces to the new central government.

Australia, today a country with a negligible share of SOEs, used to be a country with an extensive and active role of the state in the economy for a long time. In the last years of the 19th century, when the foundations of the Australian statehood were being formed, "governments played a significant role in the lives of citizens, and the statutory corporation and government business enterprises collectively, assumed critical roles in the development of a robust and well-functioning state" (Aulich & Wettenhall, 2019, p. 19). One of the historical sources states that "the Government fed, clothed and employed everyone. It cleared and cultivated farms; it bred and reared flocks; it built and ran mills; it discovered and developed mines" (Bland, 1945, p. 203). The Australian Post, initially in the form of the Postmaster-General's Department of the federal government, was established in 1901, as the successor to colonial post services. It was not until 1989 that this company was corporatised from an EGE form into the Australian Post Corporation. In Australia, the rail network developed within provinces, initially with private capital.

In China, in the very long history of this state, state ownership has always been important. For centuries, state entities have benefited from the legally guaranteed monopolies in many areas of the economy, which was to generate state revenue, and their existence has always been associated with the pursuit of various military and modernisation purposes. In the second half of the 19th century, a form of an enterprise involving cooperation of the state and private capital emerged, the purpose of which was to modernise the Chinese economy and catch up with the Western European countries (Sheng & Zhao, 2012, pp. 230–240).

The Chinese postal service, as a uniform enterprise, was established much later than its counterparts in the European countries, as it was only in 1912. The Qing dynasty ruling in China was sceptical about the introduction of railways, but the defeat in the First Sino-Japanese War caused a change in position – the government was forced to grant concessions to foreigners to build railways.

In Japan, the accelerated industrialisation of the economy in the second half of the 19th century was associated with nationalisations and the creation of new EGEs (in the form of industrial factories and shipyards). In the late 19th century, nationalisation pressures grew, mainly for military reasons. The state monopoly was extended to telephone services, tobacco production and distribution; a state-owned Yawata Steel Works was established. However, fiscal problems and organisational failures in the functioning of EGEs soon contributed to a change in the attitude – state-owned entities were privatised, often for part of their value. This was the way large industrial conglomerates (*zaibatsu*) were created, which supported the functioning of the Japanese economy in subsequent decades (Grabowiecki, 2006, p. 8) and which – formally private – showed a significant degree of informal dependence on the government.

The nationwide postal network in Japan was established in 1872, and the Japanese post existed as a government agency for many decades. The nationwide rail network – Japanese Government Railways – was established in 1906, following the nationalisation of 17 private railway companies. Local railways still remained in private hands.

In Russia, EGEs played a major role long before the 1917 Revolution. Since the time of Peter the Great, mines, factories, banks, forests, post and later also telegraph companies were owned by the state. Iron railways were created, as in many other countries, in various ownership configurations, largely as private joint-stock companies. As they developed, due to the strategic importance of railways, the state gradually took control over them using various methods (concessions, nationalisations, own investments), until the end of the 19th century, when all major railways went into the hands of the government. They were controlled by the Ministry of Communications, established in June 1865.

1.2 From the First to the Second World War

After the First World War, together with the development of the modern republic state, based on the constitution and codified law, in the developed Western countries, a need and expediency emerged to separate the economic activities carried out by the state from the budget. This was to be achieved by commercialising (corporatising) the existing EGEs, thus making the principles of their operation more similar to the private enterprise model – more effective and efficient, as the practice had shown. Australia was a pioneer of this kind of solutions, where in the early 20th century, EGEs were transformed into economic entities separate from the administration, where the influence of the government was legally established and limited, and whose employees were not public servants (Aulich & Wettenhall, 2019, pp. 19-21).

In Western Europe, SOEs in the form of commercialised EGEs appeared quite widely only in the 1920s. In accordance with the public corporation model – they enjoyed a considerable degree of legal, organisational, material and financial autonomy. They were no longer linked to the budget based on gross results, like other budgetary units, but based on net results, and the state owner exercised general control over the enterprise and determined the principles of profit distribution. In 1923 in France, a certain degree of financial and material autonomy was granted to various public entities, including the railways. In the UK, starting from 1926, state companies were run as separate legal entities, with a significant degree of organisational, material and financial autonomy. In Germany, too, railway companies, as well as the post, were commercialised – whilst retaining state ownership, they became independent entities with their own budgets (Wagenroth, 2000, pp. 109-115).

In Italy, starting from the beginning of the 20th century, a policy of gradual subordination of various areas of the economy to the state was followed. The state monopoly of telephone, postal and telegraph services was introduced. Following the nationalisation of private insurers, the state insurance monopoly INA (*Istituto Nazionale delle Assicurazioni* - National Insurance Institute, 1912) was established. The fascist government initially moved away from this kind of policies and started a privatisation programme involving important SOEs, but this was only an episode undertaken to gain support among large-scale entrepreneurs. Still in the 1920s, private entities were renationalised or SOEs were created, among others in the oil & gas or airline sectors, and a bit later – the financial sector (Bognetti, 2020, p. 30).

The collapse of the economy after the Great Depression contributed to the intensification of nationalisation policies. In 1933, a state-owned holding company was established – IRI (*Istituto per la Ricostruzione Industriale* - Institute for Industrial Reconstruction) – whose original task was to temporarily take over the shares in private industrial companies threatened with bankruptcy. In 1937, it was transformed into a permanently operating state-owned entity. IRI quickly became a mega-holding company, controlling a huge part of the economy, including the then strategic sectors, such as steel, shipbuilding or telecommunications sectors, as well as the banking sector. Some scholars believe that in the 1930s, Italy was the second only to the Soviet Union in terms of the level of state ownership in the economy (Amatori, 2000, p. 188).

In Germany, in 1920, as a result of a merger of the regional rail networks of nine Länder, German State Railways (*Deutsche Reichseisenbahnen*) was created, and four years later, after being converted into a company separate from the administration, they took the name of German Railways. The company was the largest employer in the Weimar Republic, employing 700,000 people by the end of the 1920s.

Since the 1920s, a greater state ownership involvement in industrial sectors could be noted. Several powerful state-owned industrial holding companies were established, including VIAG (1923) controlling companies in the electrical and aluminium industries, and VEBA (1929) in the energy and mining sectors. After the Great Depression, there were also cases of rescue nationalisations, for example, in the steel industry (partial nationalisation of *Vereinitge Stahlwerke* in 1932) or the aviation sector.

During Nazi rule, private companies were nationalised only occasionally. Instead, enterprises for special projects were created, such as *Reichswerke Hermann Göring* to provide supplies of cheap raw materials and semi-finished products for the industry, or *Volkswagenwerke* to produce passenger cars widely available to citizens. The assets of Jewish enterprises were taken over mainly by private entities, which acquired them at negative prices – through various pressures from the authorities.

In France, after the First World War, there was a noticeable expansion of SOEs. In 1924, the French government with private capital created *Compagnie française des pétroles*, the forerunner of the modern petrochemical giant Total, which was controlled by the state as long as until 1991. Between 1936 and 1937, after the left-wing Popular Front came to power, widespread nationalisation was carried out, among others in the aviation and arms industries, as well as in the railway industry (Amatori, 2017, p. 10). During the Great Depression, some large private companies (such as *Air France* – airlines and SNCF – French railway company) obtained government loans, which later on – when the companies were unable to repay them – were converted into state shares.

In the UK, the situation was similar to that of Italy and France, but the scale of expansion of state ownership was smaller. In the 1920s, particular industries or individual companies, mostly related to the broadly understood public services, as well as radio stations, were nationalised. In the 1930s, the state nationalised urban transport in London (1933) and deposits of oil and hard coal (1934 and 1938).

In Spain, a moderate increase in the importance of SOEs could be observed since the beginning of the 20th century. After the First World War, SOEs in Spain played "a limited but significant role" (Bognetti, 2020). It was the time when *Compañía Telefónica Nacional de España* (1924), among others, was created. The oil industry (1927–1930) and the *Iberia* airlines, privatised before the Second World War, were temporarily nationalised.

General Franco's plans for the industrialisation and military consolidation of the economy coincided with the spirit of interventionism prevailing after the Great Depression. Some public services were nationalised, for example, railways in 1941, airlines again in 1944 and also the telecommunications sector in the following year. An important stage of the state ownership interference in the economy was the creation of the National Institute of Industry (*Instituto Nacional de Industria,* INI) in 1941, a state-owned business group modelled on the Italian IRI, but with a smaller scale of operation.

In the US, traditionally reluctant about state ownership, the situation changed somewhat as a result of the Great Depression. President F.D. Roosevelt's economic programme – New Deal – assumed the departure from the classical liberal economic policy towards an increased state activity, both in the regulatory (public works, regulation of labour markets, etc.) and in the ownership sphere. When it came to the ownership function, the most important event was the creation of a large, still existing SOE, the Tennessee Valley Authority, in 1933. Its main purpose was to build energy infrastructure, produce electricity, prevent floods and support the overall economic development of the region affected by the crisis.

In Japan, in the 1930s, during preparations for the Second World War, the energy sector was nationalised. During the war itself, state-owned and state-private companies were created, such as Teikoku Oil, established in 1941, which was a merger of several oil exploration companies.

In Brazil, from the beginning of the 20th century, the state introduced price controls in certain sectors, which resulted in a decline in the profitability of private companies, and, consequently, in them often being taken over by state entities. The government granted concessions to private companies to deliver goods or services, making provisions in the contracts giving the state company ownership interests, if the concessionaire would fail to meet certain conditions. At the end of the 1930s, due to the militarisation needs of the country, a protectionist policy was widely applied, and one of its manifestations was the so-called import substitution industrialisation, largely implemented with the use of specially established SOEs.

In Russia, where a communist system was introduced after the First World War, the situation was specific. From the very beginning, deep ownership changes were a fundamental and unquestionable objective of the reconstruction of the economy. The progress of nationalisation, generally carried out using non-legislative and forceful methods, was spectacular. The activities of the state in terms of green field investments were also very intensive. By the end of 1920, among approximately 38,000 enterprises employing more than 10 people, 95% were owned by the state.

In Central and Eastern Europe, under the Austro-Hungarian monarchy, EGEs, including post and railways, were relatively numerous. After the First World War, they were taken over by the governments of the new states – Austria itself, Hungary, Czechoslovakia and partly also Romania. In Poland, the largest country of the region, the reborn state consisted of parts of three partitions – Russian, German and Austrian. Initially, there were three postal and railway systems (in the former Russian partition the track gauge was wider than in the other two parts) and three legal systems governing the operation of enterprises. The government was very active in influencing the economy, both by mitigating these differences, maintaining profitable monopolies, and by creating several new SOEs, mainly in the industry.

1.3 From the Second World War to the end of the 1970s

The need to rebuild economies after the Second World War, and the subsequent formation of the modern welfare states dominated by Keynesian economics as the basis for the economic policy, entailed the choice of the interventionist development model and, indirectly, the growth in the importance of state ownership. The widespread use of SOEs was treated as a condition for overcoming market failures, fulfilling fast-growing public-service tasks and allocating resources, corresponding to the socio-economic objectives formulated by the state. Such views in the developed economies of the West (mostly in the UK, but also in Italy, France and Canada) brought about the waves of nationalisations and the creation of new SOEs.

After the collapse of the colonial system, the governments of the newly emerging countries took over and nationalised enterprises previously owned by the colonial administration or private capital from European countries. Post-colonial countries, including large and important ones, such as India and Indonesia, often adopted the elements of the communist ideology and bound themselves in alliances with the USSR, which also meant the implementation of the principles of the socialist economy, especially the strengthening of state ownership at the expense of private ownership.

The processes of replacing private ownership with state ownership took place on an even greater scale in the states of the newly formed communist bloc – in China and the smaller countries of Central and Eastern Europe and Asia. The economic importance of SOEs increased also in Japan and Brazil.

In the 1960s, the share of SOEs in the economy, measured by their contribution to GDP or by their share in the employment in the business sector, reached 20% in the developed Western European countries, such as the UK, France, Austria and Italy. In the major developing countries, such as India and Indonesia, it was often 40%–60%, while in the communist countries 80%–90%. Only the US consistently maintained an almost completely private economy, where the share of SOEs was very low.

1.3.1 Developed countries of the West

In the UK, the experience of the Great Depression of the 1930s weakened the confidence in the effectiveness of the market mechanism, while the needs of the post-war reconstruction intensified the pressures to expand state ownership. In such circumstances, the Labour government of Clement Attlee pursued extensive nationalisation programmes, covering approximately 20% of the British economy in the first four post-war years. The former private business owners received adequate compensations. In 1946, the nationalisation extended to the Bank of England, which had been a private joint-stock company since its establishment in 1694. In 1948, four large railway companies that had existed since 1921 were nationalised and merged into a SOE – British Rail. Until 1950, the mining, energy, telecommunications and transport sectors were dominated by SOEs. In the early 1950s, the British Transport Commission, a holding of state-owned transport companies, employed over 800,000 people and was the largest employer in the UK. State-owned mines employed around 700,000 people, while the UK post almost 350,000.

The period of strong state interventionism, including ownership interventionism, lasted until the end of the 1970s in the UK. Gradually, however, a conviction grew, among both academics and the political class, that SOEs were less effective than private companies, which was confirmed by empirical studies, as well as by real-life experience. The country was paralysed by labour protests and strikes, inflation was around 20% annually, there were interruptions in the power supply, the state health service was terrible.

In Italy, likewise, the public mood after the Second World War favoured statist economic policies. The state-owned holding company, IRI, established before the war, grew and played an increasingly important role in the post-war economic development. Further state-owned companies were created, partly using IRI resources, in particular sectors, e.g. machinery production (*Finmeccanica*, 1948) or electrical engineering (*Finelettrica*, 1952). Most of the enterprises within these groups were characterised by overstaffing.

In 1953, in the oil & gas sector, the ENI (*Ente Nazionale Idrocarburi*) group was established, which after years of rapid, protectionist development became the largest Italian non-financial company, being constantly under the government control. In subsequent years, further state-owned business groups were created: EFIM (manufacturing – 1962), EGAM (mining and metallurgy – 1958) and ENEL (power industry – 1962).

As a result, in the second half of the 1960s, an economic system based on state-owned mega-corporations was formed in Italy. These corporations conducted their own economic activities but also held stakes in other, also partly private, entities. Their characteristic feature was their vertical integration, i.e. merging of enterprises from successive phases of the production process.

In France, the nationalisation processes, started in the late 1930s, were continued after the Second World War. Additionally, taking over of private companies was treated as a form of punishment for the collaboration of their owners with the German occupier – as was the case with the *Renault* car company. During this period, the state gained much control over the air transport, power industry, hard coal mining and, to a lesser extent, banking and insurance sectors.

In the Federal Republic of Germany, SOEs initially seemed to be a solution to the problem of high unemployment. Over time, however, this policy was abandoned. By the end of the 1950s and beginning of the 1960s, Germany was a pioneer of post-war privatisation processes, which resulted from basing the economic policy on the principles of Ordoliberalism. The privatisation processes – largely through the stock exchange – were driven by the fact that SOEs needed capital for investments, and this type of privatisation made it possible to obtain it. An additional objective was to stimulate the development of the capital market, which was a success, as small shareholding grew rapidly in a short time.

In Spain, the plans for industrialisation and military consolidation in the spirit of interventionism were continued. The statist tendencies weakened from the mid-1960s – since then, private enterprises were attributed a greater role in the industrialisation of the country. The pressures of the World Bank, supporting the development of the Spanish economy, were significant. The bank opted for a reduction in the role of the INI group in the economy. Since the mid-1970s, after the death of General Franco, the role of SOEs grew again. They were given two objectives: restructuring of the industry and counter-cyclical activity, for maintaining the employment level in times of adverse economic conditions.

In Norway, immediately after the Second World War, the state ownership of enterprises, as in the UK, Austria and Italy, was gaining importance. The state took over the assets existing in the country, which were owned by the Germans during the war, including 44% of the shares in the *NorskHydro* group, dealing with the production of aluminium and generation of power. New SOEs were created in the areas where natural resources occurred – e.g. coal mines in Spitsbergen.

When large deposits of oil and gas were discovered in the Norwegian Continental Shelf, the state became directly engaged in the mining of these resources. In 1972, an SOE – Statoil – was founded, whose mission was precisely to exploit and process energy sources. The financial and organisational success of Statoil in the 1970s encouraged the state to begin the process of creating further such entities. Among others, SOEs responsible for telegraph and railway services were established based on the former ministerial departments.

In Canada, the state sector grew significantly during and after the Second World War. In 1944, important regional power companies were established – Hydro-Québec and SaskPower. Many state-owned entities were created in the financial sector to support individual sectors of the economy, including Farm Credit Corporation, Business Development Bank of Canada and Export Development Corporation.

In the following years, further energy SOEs and some smaller entities were established at the federal and provincial levels, and in 1975, the Petro-Canada group was founded, which was to become the state-owned oil giant. It was not until 1981 that the Canadian legal form of a crown corporation was adopted by the Canadian post, which was by then a government department, thus an EGE. In the beginning of the 1980s, around 300 crown corporations were operating at the federal level and more than 200 at the provincial level. They employed more than 250,000 people. In contrast to the US, Canada was even referred to as the "public enterprise country" (Stanbury, 1989, p. 273).

In Australia, as in many other countries, after the Second World War, the use of SOEs grew and they were present in many sectors of the economy. At the state as well as the federal level, SOEs dealt with banking, railways, air and sea transport, telecommunications, insurance, running airports and producing electricity.

1.3.2 Other countries

In China, immediately after the Communist Party took power in 1949, a seven-year process of intensive, systematic nationalisation of the economy began. It was carried out using legal methods, as well as through massive confiscations of assets, including the assets of companies with foreign capital (Chen, 2013). At the same time, as in other socialist countries, the process of replacing market mechanisms with central planning continued.

In India, the history of the SOE sector started in 1947, together with the regaining of independence. The state inherited several large, important SOEs, mainly of an EGE nature from the British administration. The colonial experience caused the foreign capital to be largely mistrusted. Due to the shortages of human, physical and financial capital and a poorly developed private sector, SOEs were seen as the best tool to support the development of strategic industries in the economy (the so-called commanding heights of the economy).

The state created new companies or took over the existing private companies (e.g. private airlines were nationalised and the state-owned Air India was established), which was facilitated by the gradually introduced system of licences and permits, the so-called *Licence Raj*, which significantly increased the costs of conducting private business.

In Indonesia, after regaining independence in 1945, the capitalist system was associated with colonialism and exploitation, and the trust in market mechanisms and private capital among the economic elite of the country was low. Indonesia's constitution included provisions that companies in strategic industries (such as the natural resources sector) must be owned by the state. The Indonesian state gradually took over (partly with financial compensation) almost all companies that used to be owned by the Dutch government, as well as the vast majority of private Dutch companies operating in the country. In 1964, all Malaysian, British and American companies operating in Indonesia were nationalised.

As indigenous entrepreneurship was underdeveloped and there was no domestic capital, the state started creating and developing SOEs in areas such as banking (*Bank Negara*, 1946), trade (*Pantja Niaga*, 1947), exploration of oil (*Pertamina*, 1947) and industry (*Semen Gresik*, 1952). State-owned fertiliser factories and construction companies to build affordable houses for the poorer segments of the society were established.

In the mid-1960s, the SOE sector in Indonesia was very numerous, comparable to that of the socialist countries at the time, and included more than 800 significant entities. Its main objective was not to make a profit but to implement specific government programmes. From the late 1960s, after the military coup, the new government pursued an economic policy that was more market-oriented and open to international exchange. Reforms were initiated to increase the role of private ownership in the economy, and some SOEs were privatised.

In South Korea, in the first years of independence, several companies were nationalised, including all operating in the power and railway sectors. In 1950, drawing on the assets of the former Japanese mining companies, the Korea Coal Corporation was founded, and a few years later, the Korea Development Bank was established to coordinate the financing of the industrial reconstruction of the country.

The importance of SOEs in the economy of South Korea increased significantly in the 1960s when the economic policy that focused on export-oriented manufacturing industries was implemented. The tools supporting the development of selected industries included chaebols, i.e. large industrial conglomerates controlled by narrow groups of rich families informally linked to the authorities, as well as SOEs, usually newly created, such as Korea Electric Power Corporation (KEPCO), Korea Oil Corporation, Korean Air and Pohang Iron and Steel Company (POSCO). A major role in controlling the economy was also played by state-owned banks. In the early 1960s, the state had a large share in the banking sector, and over time, it took over subsequent banks (Ginting & Naqvi, 2020).

From the beginning of the 1970s, the government was developing the refining, steel and fertiliser industries. Both regulatory measures (barriers to entry allowing selected entities to obtain high, monopolistic profits) and ownership measures (e.g. re-investing all SOEs' profits from specific industries) were used.

Japan not only missed the phase of widespread post-war nationalisation, but the country underwent reverse processes, caused by the American occupation (1945–1952). In 1950, the already mentioned Teikoku Oil was privatised. In 1951, the energy sector, where the state had so far played an important role, was privatised and organised according to the American model. The US administration also commercialised those government departments (EGEs) which previously provided market goods and services (Beder, 2006). Based on the decision of the Supreme Command of the Allied Powers, independent state enterprises were established: Japan Tobacco and Salt (1948), Japanese National Railways (1948) and Nippon Telegraph and Telephone (1952).

In Brazil, from the end of the 1930s, a strong protectionist economic policy had been pursued, an important element of which was so-called import substitution industrialisation, which, in its essence, meant the involvement of state capital. The following companies were established then: *Companhia Siderúrgica Nacional* (steel industry, 1941), *Fabrica Nacional de Motores* (automotive industry, 1943) and *Campanhia Vale do Rio Doce* (mining, 1942), which over the years became the company ranking among the largest miners in the world. In 1953, a petrochemical company *Petrobras* was established, which was granted a state monopoly on oil prospection, exploration and processing. In subsequent years, *Petrobras* gradually took over private refineries and new deposits, making the company one of the largest petrochemical companies in the world (Mussachio & Lazzarini 2014a, pp. 82-85).

In Argentina, the government of Juan Peron, pursuing a corporatist policy, took control over the main companies in the telecommunications sector (*La Empresa Nacional de Telecomunicaciones* and *International Telephone and Telegraph*) and in the railway sector (a *Ferrocarriles Argentinos* company was created by combining the companies taken over from the British and the French and the existing state-owned railways). A number of banks and the merchant fleet were nationalised. New SOEs were established in the power industry and metallurgy. An agency, IAPI (*Instituto Argentino de Promoción del Intercambio*), was established to centralise foreign trade under the aegis of the state.

In subsequent years, as in many other countries of the world, negative consequences of this solution began to reveal themselves. SOEs functioned quite inefficiently, which translated into the poor quality of infrastructure, low competitiveness of the economy and a deficit of the central budget, burdened with the losses from enterprises. The import-substituting industrialisation policy failed, contributing significantly to the debt crisis.

1.4 From the 1980s to the financial crisis of 2008–2009

The second half of the 1970s in the Western countries was the time of a gradual departure from the earlier interventionist economic policies. Stagflation, for which the Keynesian paradigm was unable to find an effective remedy, the weakening budgetary situation of many countries with extensive social programmes and often confirmed inefficiency of the SOE sector contributed to a turn towards liberal (monetarist) economic policy, focusing on de-regulation and de-statisation. For more than three decades in many economies of the world, both in developed and in developing countries, especially in those that implemented the IMF (International Monetary Fund) recovery programmes, wide-ranging privatisation processes were carried out. According to the 2003 OECD (Organisation for Economic Co-operation and Development) report, in the last two decades of the 20th century, companies worth approximately $1 trillion were privatised in 100 countries (OECD, 2003, p. 8). However, the IMF studies point to a non-obvious fact – between 1980 and 1990, the share of SOEs in the economies of 40 developing countries remained at a relatively stable level, with a slight decrease starting only from the 1990s (Haggarty & Shirley, 1997, Figure 1.1).

From the beginning of the 1990s, also in basically all countries of the former communist bloc, a departure from state ownership in the economy could be observed, although due to the immense scope of SOEs that had existed earlier, these processes were spread over many years. While in the countries that joined the EU at the beginning of the 21st century the scale of reducing state ownership was relatively large (Poland was an exception, to some extent), in countries such as Ukraine and Belarus, partly Russia and some Asian republics, the petrification of state ownership occurred.

In many countries, from Italy, through Poland, to India and Brazil, these were often partial or even pseudo-privatisations and did not mean a real change in ownership control. An analysis of several hundred privatisation processes carried out during this period in OECD countries showed that the government still maintained some degree of control in more than 60% of the formally privatised companies. This phenomenon has been referred to in the literature as reluctant privatisation (Bortolotti & Faccio, 2004).

1.4.1 Developed countries of the West

In Italy, a gradual dismantling of the SOE system in the economy, shaped in the previous decades, had begun in the late 1970s. In a broad public debate, with the participation of specially appointed research teams, it was emphasised that SOEs are generally characterised by overstaffing, low productivity and a lack of dynamism typical of private entrepreneurship. Attention was drawn to problems arising from the dependency of SOEs on politicians. At the same time, among other things, as a result of stronger European integration, economic law liberalisation progressed, leading to a reduction in the previously widespread preference for the SOE sector.

Privatisation and restructuring processes began on a massive scale in the textile, car and other industries. State-owned holding companies were either liquidated (EGAM 1978, EFIM 1992) or transformed into commercial law companies (ENI, ENEL, INA), where parts of their shares were introduced to public trading; however, these were often reluctant privatisations – the state still controlled these companies. In 1993, the Ministry of State Treasury Shares, and in 2002, the IRI holding company – a symbol of presence of the Italian state in the economy – after the privatisation of a large part of its subsidiaries (including Alfa Romeo and *Banca Commerciale Italiana*), ceased to exist.

In Germany, which, as mentioned before, did not experience deeper nationalisation processes and the expansion of SOEs in the 1950s and 1960s, the liberalisation prevailing at the end of the 20th century was more modest. In the 1990s, two giant SOEs – postal (*Deutsche Post*) and telecommunications (*Deutsche Telekom*) – were partially privatised. The privatisation was preceded by the transformation of these entities into joint-stock companies, and then with the gradual sale of shares. Usually, the state initially retained minority stakes.

Privatisation issues became more important together with the German reunification – there were more than 8,000 socialist SOEs in the former Federal Republic of Germany. A special trust agency – *Treuhandanstalt* – was set up, whose main task, properly accomplished, was a swift privatisation of East German companies. Consequently, in 1994, after four years of operation of the agency, only 140 SOEs remained in the hands of the state.

In France, the return to power of the Socialists in the early 1980s resulted in another wave of nationalisations, which contrasted with the policies pursued by other developed countries at that time. A deeper nationalisation of the banking sector and parts of heavy industry was one of the focal points of the economic programme of President Francois Mitterrand. Under the Nationalisation Law of 11 February 1982, the French state took over dozens of banks and five large industrial groups (*CGE, Péchiney–Ugine–Kuhlmann, Thomson–Brandt, Rhône-Poulenc, Saint-Gobain*). In the following years, nationalisation also covered other industrial, transport, arms and nuclear power companies.

Yet, the results were far from what was expected. The state sector was characterised by overstaffing, a significant role of trade unions and low employee turnover (the employment in the SOE was seen as a job for life). State-owned banks chose to finance inefficient projects arising from the political objectives of the authorities, industrial factories had low productivity and economic growth was slow for the greater part of the decade.

The change in this policy began in the second half of the 1980s. Privatisation processes began, initially quite timidly, primarily covering smaller SOEs. Successive governments, both right and left wing, gradually sold out parts of the state's shares and floated companies on the stock exchange, often without losing government control.

In the UK, after some not very successful attempts to repair SOEs under the New Public Management, Margaret Thatcher's government decided to carry out one of the most extensive and advanced privatisation programmes among those carried out in the world at that time. At the beginning of 1984, a plan was announced to immediately close 20 of the most unprofitable mines, with 70 more to follow. By 1990, 115 mines were closed, and four years later, the privatisation of the British hard coal mining was practically completed. In December 1984, the stock exchange debut of the state-owned telecommunications giant – British Telecom – became an outstanding success, with over two million people willing to buy its shares. In the entire decade of the 1980s, about 40 large SOEs employing a total of 900,000 people, including gas supply companies, airports, water supply companies and the icons of the British automotive industry – Rolls-Royce and Jaguar – were privatised.

The de-nationalisation processes were continued during John Major's government. In 1992, the privatisation of the energy sector was completed, which was followed by the liquidation of the Ministry of Energy. In 1994, the process of privatising British Rail began, and lasted until 1997. Most of the rail infrastructure was handed over to the newly established SOE – Railtrack (now – Network Rail) – and the passenger connections were taken over as franchises by some 25 private operators.

In Spain, together with the socialists coming to power in 1983 and with the plans to join the European Community, the government launched reforms and privatisation of the SOE sector, which covered mostly the industry (Seat, Enasa) and financial sectors. By the mid-1990s, the shares of around 70 enterprises were sold, although in most cases these were only partial privatisations. The state retained minority but controlling stakes in profitable listed companies, such as Endesa, Repsol and Argentaria (Comín, 2008, p. 698).

Another more intensive stage of privatisation began in 1996 when the power was taken over by the right-wing People's Party. This time the privatisation was mostly full, and covered all main state monopolies, including some large SOEs, such as *Repsol*, *Telefónica*, *Iberia*, *Aceralia*, *Endesa*, *Red Eléctrica de España* and *Tabacalera*. The direct involvement of the state in the municipal service sector was also reduced significantly (Albalate et al., 2020, p. 572).

In Norway, the inefficiencies of state ownership that manifested themselves at the end of the 1970s contributed – as in the case of other Western countries – to the emergence of privatisation pressures. The privatisation was accelerated by the political change in 1981 when the Conservatives came to power again. In subsequent years, partial privatisations of companies such as *Telenor* and *Statoil* were carried out, but without the government losing control over them.

In the second half of the 1980s – contrary to global trends – in some sectors of the Norwegian economy, especially in banking, the share of state ownership began to increase. In response to the previous turmoil in the financial sector, the state undertook rescue measures. What is distinctive, when compared with the US, for example, even after the economic situation stabilised, is that in some of these entities the Norwegian state still retained minority stakes, so a degree of control.

In Canada, during a decade, from the mid-1980s to the mid-1990s, such major crown corporations as Air Canada, Canadian National Railways, Alberta Liquor Control Board and Nova Scotia Power were privatised at the federal and provincial levels. SOEs were generally seen as inefficient, having problems with the circulation of information and difficult to be organised in a systemic way as to fulfil objectives set for them, which were gradually limited only to the efficiency at the microeconomic level (Stevens, 1993). In 1990, the privatisation of Petro-Canada began – the company had its debut on the stock exchange in July 1991. The government gradually reduced the level of shares in the company, but by 2004 retained 19% of them.

In Australia, neoliberal views found fertile soil in an individualised and relatively prosperous society (Aulich & Wettenhall, 2019, pp. 28–29). As regards state ownership, this translated into reforms in the SOE sector in the spirit of the New Public Management, whose main elements included commercialisation and/or privatisation of state entities. A large part of the banking sector, Qantas airlines, public services and telecommunications were privatised. Nevertheless, at the end of the 1980s, SOEs were still an important part of the economy – they were responsible for 7% of GDP, 9% of employment and 14% of gross fixed capital formation (Abbott & Cohen 2014, p. 432).

Privatisation processes were intensified when the Conservatives took power. Between 1996 and 2006, John Howard's government privatised SOEs of the total value of $61 billion (a large part of which was for the telecommunications company *Telstra*), reducing the state debt virtually to zero. A side objective of the privatisation was to create a "shareholder society", which was largely achieved. An OECD report (2006) shows that Australia was in the group of countries with the highest value of privatisation relative to GDP between 1990 and 2001. Similar transformations, although to a lesser extent, occurred at state levels, among others, in relation to public utility companies (Aulich & Wettenhall, 2019, p. 27).

1.4.2 Other countries

In China, the failure of the "Cultural Revolution" and the Great Leap Forward, as well as the general inefficiency and backwardness of the economy, forced major reforms, including the ones concerning the SOE system, started in 1978, after the death of Mao Zedong. A small part of SOEs was liquidated, others tried to introduce efficiency-improving solutions, such as the decentralisation of ownership control, possibility to retain profit in enterprises, possibility to export production and so on. Until the early 1990s, the reforms had a very limited impact on the ownership issues (Szamosszegi & Kyle, 2011).

In the early 1990s, the Chinese government began the implementation of a "socialist market economy" programme, which meant the gradual transformation of many SOEs from the EGE form into separate economic entities. The companies were given the possibility to decide on redundancies and to acquire other entities. From the mid-1990s, privatisation processes began. Many smaller SOEs were partially or fully sold, and, regardless of the above, fully private domestic companies and companies with dominant foreign capital kept growing.

Privatisation processes were hampered during the Asian crisis of 1997. Again, the reform of the SOE sector was promoted. This time, though, the changes were more profound. Many SOEs were converted into state-private joint-stock companies with a dominant participation of the government, but their shares were often listed on the Shanghai and Hong Kong stock exchanges. This meant that they were profit-oriented (or the value of the company increased) and kept standardised accounts from which information was made public.

Since the beginning of the 21st century, the system of Chinese SOEs has been undergoing continuous reforms through a series of small steps, characteristic of this country. The general objective of the reforms is to improve the efficiency of operation of SOEs, yet with the control over these entities strengthened, although exercised not only through direct ownership tools. SOEs used to be and still are seen as tools of the state applied to stabilise the economy, maintain the employment level and build a system of social protection (Lee, 2009).

In Japan, a government commission – Provisional Commission for Administrative Reform – was established in 1981, which prepared a series of reports that recommended in-depth privatisation. Some SOEs were to be fully privatised, while in others the state was to become a major or even minority shareholder with the levels of shareholding statutorily defined (Toyama, 1998).

The privatisation carried out in the second half of the 1980s covered companies such as Nippon Telephone and Telegraph (the government retained 51% of the shares) and Japan Tobacco and Salt. Japanese National Railways were divided into smaller, regional companies, and most of them were privatised. In subsequent years, the second wave of privatisation began (during the government of Prime Minister J. Koizumi), which covered, in particular, the gradual sale of Japan Post Holdings.

Privatisation processes in **South Korea** started in 1987, covered some 30 large entities and took the form of full or partial sales. The first group included, among others, financial entities: Kookmin Bank, Industrial Bank of Korea and Korea Exchange Bank. KEPCO, Korea Telecom and POSCO were partially privatised (Ginting & Naqvi, 2020). These plans, however, failed – only 13 entities were privatised due to low political motivation (ministries and agencies dealing with the privatisation had a vested interest in maintaining SOEs) and strong resistance within the companies (Lee, 2019, p. 33). The Asian financial crisis of 1997, followed by the IMF pressures associated with the implementation of the rescue package, led to further decisions to intensify the privatisation processes and to improve corporate governance.

In the post-crisis period, several SOEs were privatised, including such major entities as POSCO, Korea Communications and Korea Heavy Industries. With Roh Moo-Hyun coming to power in 2003, privatisation processes were halted, and the focus was again on the reforms of the SOE sector, adjusting the principles of operation to the requirements of the market.

In India, amid the greater openness of the economy in the 1980s, the inefficiencies of SOEs, resulting from the lack of competitive environment and autonomy in making strategic decisions, began to emerge. It was only at the end of the decade that slow processes of liberalisation began. The new industrial policy of 1991 "liberated" sectors previously reserved exclusively to SOEs, such as telecommunications, natural resources, energy, mining and steel. The support provided to loss-making SOEs by the state budget was reduced and selected companies with state's shareholding were listed on the stock exchange. Since 1997, special groups of the largest and most important SOEs, operating according to separate rules, having a greater scope of financial and administrative autonomy, were created – the so-called Maharatna, Navratna and Miniratna companies. At the turn of the 20th and 21st centuries – unlike in other countries – there were no deep privatisation processes carried out. Several significant enterprises were subject to reluctant privatisations. Such steps, to some extent, improved their functioning, without the state losing control.

In Indonesia, another stage of reforming the SOE sector began only in the mid-1980s, this time partly in a neoliberal spirit. SOEs were subject to detailed periodic assessments, the results of which were translated into structural reforms – changes in the legal form, takeovers, privatisations or liquidations of enterprises. Despite these actions, most Indonesian SOEs continued to make losses – the state ownership control was unclear and ineffective.

The Asian crisis of 1997 and the collapse of the Indonesian banking sector was a turning point. The costs of rescuing the sector strongly affected the state budget, which forced the government to undertake more radical economic reforms, including those concerning SOEs. A special ministry was created, which centralised the control of enterprises and several improvements in terms of state ownership control were introduced. These changes brought some effects; the financial situation of SOEs significantly improved. The economic importance of SOEs and their number remained high.

In Brazil, the processes related to the democratisation of the country began in the 1980s, and the new constitution generally reduced the influence of the state on the economy. The economic inefficiencies of SOEs that emerged and the financial pressures of international institutions fostered privatisation. Initially, mainly small companies and the companies previously taken over by the state were sold as part of rescue nationalisations. In the first half of the 1990s, the National Privatisation Programme was launched, covering relatively well-functioning entities in the steel (*Usiminas*), transport (*Embraer*) and petrochemical sectors. Thereafter, the companies involved in the provision of public services (energy – *Eletrobras*, telecommunications – *Telebras*), financial institutions and the companies in the mining sector (e.g. *Vale*) were privatised.

However, these were often reluctant privatisations – the Brazilian government retained residual shares in many companies which guaranteed a significant degree of control over formally private entities (Musacchio & Lazzarini, 2014b, p. 25).

In Argentina, Carlos Menem, elected president in 1989, pursued a liberal, free-market economic programme, the aim of which was to restructure and stabilise the economy, and its key element was an extensive privatisation programme. Shortly thereafter, 67 companies were privatised (around 90% of all large SOEs that existed then), including such significant enterprises as *Yacimientos Petrolíferos Fiscales* (YPF), Somisa, *Ferrocarriles Argentinos*, AyE, *Gas del Estado* and *Aerolíneas Argentinas* (Goldstein, 1998). The funds obtained from the privatisation were partly used to reduce public debt.

Yet, the inconsistent economic policy pursued in subsequent years, combined with an unfavourable arrangement of external factors, led the Argentinian economy to a deep crisis in 2001. As a result, again, several solutions strengthening the role of the state in the economy were adopted. In relation to the ownership policy, they included the nationalisation of companies such as *Correo Argentino* (2003) and rescue renationalisations of *Aerolíneas Argentinas* (2008) and the petrochemical giant YPF in 2012 (OECD, 2018, p. 34). In 2015, *Ferrocarriles Argentinos* were re-launched, which included the previously operating state-owned railway enterprises in various areas (infrastructure management, passenger and freight transport). The post-crisis measures also involved the creation of new state-owned entities, including the power company *Enarsa* (2003) and the water supply and sanitation services company *AySa* (2006).

In the USSR, until 1986, companies with employees could only be state-owned. It was only under the perestroika policy, initiated by M. Gorbachev, that small businesses were allowed to develop, and regulations were introduced that partially reduced the dependence of SOEs on the administration. These half-hearted reforms involving an attempt to build certain elements of economic rationality into the completely inefficient economic system failed to deliver the expected results. The main factor shaping the rules and directions for the SEOs to function was still the five-year plan and the centralised distribution of resources.

The legacy of the socialist economy largely determined the structure and functioning of the Russian economy in the 1990s, then already – formally – non-socialist. In the first half of the 1990s, intense privatisation processes occurred, covering mainly smaller, regional and local SOEs. But at the same time, drawing on the existing state assets, new, large SOEs such as *Gazprom* and *Rosneft* were established, often in the form of mixed ownership, although under state control.

It is also worth noting the occasional but meaningful cases of nationalisations of private enterprises, such as the takeover of the *Yuganskneftgaz* company by the state-owned group *Rosneft* or taking over of the shares in several private steelworks by *RusSpetsStal*.

1.5 After the financial crisis of 2008–2009

The financial crisis of 2008–2009 undermined the political and economic order that had been a source of progress and prosperity in the Western countries, as well as a developmental model and an optimal, as it seemed, socio-economic model for the whole world. The crisis also highlighted the shift in power in the global economy, in which China and other developing countries, whose economies are generally characterised by a very large share of SOEs, became increasingly important.

In many, mainly non-Western, countries, in response to the effects of the crisis and the new situation in the world economy, the value of the open economy, global trade and foreign capital were questioned, while at the same time protectionist and statist measures were increased. There were attempts to strengthen the autonomous economic policies pursued at the level of nation states and to formulate their new objectives in the form of protection of the domestic economy from external influences and replacing the market, unreliable in various respects, with the state. To achieve these new objectives, regulatory and fiscal instruments of the economic policy sometimes proved insufficient or ineffective. This is why some countries additionally started using ownership instruments that had not been used in practice on a larger scale for decades in the policy of re-statisating the economy. SOEs began to be treated not only as important tools of protective interventionism but also as synonyms of national, native capital, creating a barrier against external enemies – global corporations and financial markets.

Such interference of the "visible hand"[1] of the state in the sphere of the market and private ownership, reaching far beyond the areas resulting from the market failure, was generally referred to in the economic literature and journalism as state capitalism.[2] In a broad sense, referring to the macroeconomic level, contemporary state capitalism can be understood as a form of economic (socio-economic) system, which – largely based on the Chinese model – developed after the financial crisis of 2008–2009 in many countries, mainly in the Third World, former Asian Soviet republics (Spechler et al.,

2017) and some post-socialist countries as Hungary, and since 2016 also Poland (Baltowski et al., 2022). A researcher of this system writes that in the countries of state capitalism "the government sees itself as having a direct role to play in managing the economy and guiding the corporate sector" (Kurlantzick, 2016, p. 9).

A feature of such a notion of state capitalism, which is characteristic mainly of semi-authoritarian governments, is the impact of the state on the economy of a voluntarist nature, meaning the preference – both in the assumptions (principles) of the economic policy and in its practice – of political criteria over economic or social ones. Ian Bremmer (2010, p. 5) defines state capitalism as an economic system where the state functions as a "leading actor" and "the governments manipulate markets for political ends".

In a narrow sense, referring to the microeconomic level, state capitalism means a particular type of economic policy. It consists of the active influence of the state in the economy that extends beyond contextual standards inherent to liberal capitalism, mostly through ownership or quasi-ownership tools, and not – as in the traditional Western model – regulatory tools. Musacchio and Lazzarini (2012, p. 3) refer to this subject: "We define state capitalism as the widespread influence of the government in the economy, either by owning majority or minority equity positions in companies or through the provision of subsidized credit and/or other privileges to private companies".

In contemporary state capitalism, the relation of the state to the largest and most important SOEs, using them as tools of the economic policy, is crucial. J. Kurlantzick (2016, p. 9) believes that an essential feature of state capitalism is the government's control over the largest companies. He even provides a – debatable, in our view – the borderline threshold of state capitalism: "I identify state capitalists as countries whose government has an ownership stake in or significant influence over more than one-third of the five hundred largest companies, by revenue". Other authors point out that a distinguishing feature of state capitalism is the control and support of the state provided mostly to large corporations operating in global markets, the so-called "national champions" (Bower et al., 2011).

Such a notion of state capitalism developed a few years after the financial crisis mainly in authoritarian countries (such as Russia and China) and flawed democracies (such as Brazil and Poland[3]), which had an extensive SOE sector. Yet, also in the developed Western countries, increased ownership activity of governments could be observed at that time. This was expressed mostly in rescue nationalisations, carried out in many countries, of large and important enterprises, mostly from the financial sector, threatened with bankruptcy, that were "too big to fail". These included the US corporation Fannie Mae and the British Royal Bank of Scotland.

The spectacular, partial nationalisation of the US automotive icons – General Motors and Chrysler – had a widespread resonance. In June 2009, General Motors declared bankruptcy, and the most valuable assets were transferred to the "new" GM, in which the US government took a 61% stake. In 2013, after the successful restructuring process, the GM state-owned shares went public and the sale resulted in $39 trillion to the US government. The nationalisation, and later re-privatisation, of Chrysler was similar, although its scale was smaller.

In many countries, after the financial crisis, yet another government activity in the sphere of ownership policy emerged – again following the Chinese model. Using various methods, both legal and persuasive, state authorities took over parts of corporate control over private enterprises (parts of the bundles of property rights). The phenomenon that can be described as *property-rights-restricting government intervention* meant a partial "nationalisation" of private ownership – restricting the ability of private owners to exercise certain property rights and transferring those rights to the state or its authorities.

On the basis of the extraordinary activity of governments in the sphere of economic ownership observed in the post-crisis reality, views have appeared in the economic literature which can be described - using the title of the article by F. Flores-Macias and A. Musacchio (2009) - as the hypothesis of "the return of state-owned enterprises".[4] These authors wrote that "the global financial crisis of 2008–2009 has prompted many industrialised states worldwide to increase their stakes in private corporations". And further they asked "what should we expect of the state-owned enterprises (SOEs) that spring back into economic life?" M. Florio (in the article entitled "The Return of Public Enterprise") analysed the factors conducive to the growth of the importance of SOEs in the post-crisis economy, reaching the following conclusion: "We have identified five drivers about the return of public enterprises as active players in the economic arena, in contrast with the perception that privatizations would have led to their disappearance" (Florio, 2014, p. 10). D. McDonald (2020, p. 267) writes that "after three decades of privatization the world is witnessing a significant growth in state-owned enterprises (SOEs)".

Although this hypothesis is not supported by any empirical quantitative evidence (as shown in Section 6.4), there is no doubt that the turn of the first and second decades of the 21st century saw a fundamental expansion in the set of functions performed in the economy by SOEs in many countries of the world. Both the phenomenon of state capitalism (in the narrow sense) and the phenomenon of the return of SOEs mean, in essence, not an increase in the scope of SOEs in the economy but a wider than before use of them by the governments for various non-economic purposes. While in the Western countries it is possible to speak of activities in good faith in this respect, mainly to rescue the companies threatened with bankruptcy, and consequently to prevent social and economic problems, in other countries these are often activities in bad faith. This applies mainly to treating SOEs as sources of political rent, both an individual and a group rent. We discuss this subject in more detail in the next chapter, in Section 2.2.3.

1.6 Summary and conclusions

1 The scope and significance (as well as functions – as the next chapter will show) of contemporary SOEs, although varied greatly globally, in particular countries are largely determined by their genesis and history. Both the historical period, when the state ownership was formed, and the reasons or events that resulted in the emergence of SOEs in the economy are important. In the countries such as France, Russia and China, widespread state ownership (royal, imperial) has a centuries-old tradition. In many European countries, the development of SOEs occurred in the second half of the 20th century, as a result of industrialisation and national unification processes. In the post-colonial and post-communist countries, the current SOEs have their roots in the previous system. In turn, several countries with a currently large SOE sector experienced long episodes of statist policies in the 20th century, usually inspired by the experience of Soviet Russia. An overview of the origin (causes of emergence) of SOEs for the 15 economies analysed further with the currently largest share of SOEs (see Section 6.2) is presented in Table 1.1.

2 Historically, state companies generally took the form of EGEs and from the 1920s, as a result of corporatisation processes, EGEs were transformed into shareholding companies fully or partly owned by the government. Then, generally after the Second World War, listed SOEs – companies

Table 1.1 The origin of SOEs in the group of 15 large economies with currently the largest share of SOEs (X – strong feature, x – weak feature)

	Distant history	*Industrialisation/ national unification*	*Colonial/ socialist legacy*	*Episodes of statist politics*
Austria		X		X
Brazil	x	X		
China	X		x	
Egypt			x	X
France	X			X
India			X	X
Indonesia			X	X
Italy		X		X
Norway		X		X
Poland		x	X	X
Russia	x	x	X	
Saudi Arabia		x	X	
South Africa		x	X	
Thailand		X		X
Turkey	x	X		

Source: Own compilation.

with mixed private-state capital – emerged more and more often. Oftentimes they were created as a result of reluctant privatisations – after which the government had minority stakes, but still a significant degree of corporate control.

3 Among the countries with a long-standing stable statehood, state companies (royal, imperial, etc.) have been present for centuries and have traditionally played a significant role in the economy. The developed countries of the West (with the notable exception of the US), in general, increased the scope of the state domain from the second half of the 19th century up to the 1970s, by creating new SOEs, as well as through nationalisation processes, especially in the periods of increased industrialisation with a scarcity of private capital. In most cases, this did not automatically mean an increase in the SOEs' shares in the economy, as private companies were created on a larger scale and grew faster than SOEs. Exceptions to this rule, involving strong absolute increases in the shares of SOEs in the economy, could be observed in Italy in the 1930s and in the UK and some other countries after the Second World War, as well as in France in the 1980s.
4 SOEs in the developed countries of the West have existed for decades predominantly surrounded by private companies, in a stable institutional environment, in a system of liberal democracy and under the rule of law, which naturally affected their operating principles.
5 In many countries described as emerging markets, the SOE sector is largely a legacy of the colonial period. In the first decades of independence, the governments of these countries usually carried out extensive nationalisations and created new SOEs following – more or less consciously – the socialist ideology and the example of socialist countries. However, the SOE sector in this group of countries has always existed alongside the domestic and foreign private sector.
6 In post-socialist countries, including Russia and China, the situation was fundamentally different. The SOE sector, created in a short time by political decisions, concerning the nationalisation, as well as new state investments, covered 80%–95% of the economy, and 100% in the case of large and important companies. The autonomy of SOEs was very limited; for several decades they essentially had the nature of EGEs, directly subordinated to and managed by the government. There was no market environment, and the legal and institutional system of their operation was merely a formal staffage disrespected by the authorities. Almost all SOEs that exist in these countries today have non-market and non-capitalist roots, with all sorts of burdens and problems resulting thereof. Completely new SOEs were rarely created in the last 30 years.
7 After the financial crisis of 2008–2009, there was an increase in the ownership activities of the governments of many countries. In the developed countries of the West, this was mainly associated with the rescue nationalisations of private companies threatened with bankruptcy. In

developing economies, it has become common to use SOEs as the tools of economic policy and to expand the range of functions fulfilled by SOEs in the economy, especially towards predatory functions.

8 Within the developed countries we have analysed, three groups with well-defined paths of the SOE sector transformations in the past 60 years can be distinguished:

   1 Countries that maintained a high level of SOEs or reduced it slightly – Italy, France, Norway, Austria.
   2 Countries that significantly reduced the share of SOEs – Germany, Sweden, Japan.
   3 Countries where the share of SOEs sharply declined – the UK, Canada, Spain, Australia.

9 In the emerging market countries, the share of SOEs in the past 60 years has also declined, but at a slower pace. In India, Indonesia and Egypt we can speak of the SOEs' share in the economy stabilising at a high level.

10 In post-socialist countries, where the changes in the SOEs' share started 30 years ago, the situation varies. In China and Russia, as well as in smaller countries, such as Belarus, Kazakhstan and Ukraine, SOEs still play a dominant role in the economy. In Poland and Hungary, as well as in Slovenia, this role is significant. Other countries show a slightly smaller share of SOEs in the economy, although it is still the 15%-25% share.

Notes

1 In line with the famous report *State Capitalism. Visible Hand* (*The Economist*, 2012), which analysed various manifestations, varieties and effects of the increasing role of the state and – especially – SOEs in modern economies.
2 The term "state capitalism" itself has a long-standing history, starting from the economic system of Soviet Russia shortly after the October Revolution. After the Second World War, the term was used quite often, usually in a pejorative sense, in reference to hybrid and most often corrupt economies of the Third World countries (Petras, 1977).
3 See the Democracy Index compiled by the Economist Intelligence Unit (https://en.wikipedia.org/wiki/Democracy_Index).
4 The term "the return of state capitalism" has also been used in the literature (Bremmer, 2008; Musacchio & Lazzarini, 2014).

Bibliography

Abbott, M., & Cohen, B. (2014). A Survey of the Privatisation of Government-Owned Enterprises in Australia Since the 1980s. *Australian Economic Review*, *47*(4), 432–454.

Albalate, D., Bel, G., & Reeves, E. (2020). (Re) Municipalisation: A New Era for Ownership and Control of Local Public Service Delivery? In L. Bernier, M. Florio, & P. Bance (Eds.), *The Routledge Handbook of State-Owned Enterprises*. London; New York: Routledge.

Amatori, F. (2000). Beyond State and Market: Italy's Futile Search for a Third Way. In P. A. Toninelli (Ed.), *The Rise and Fall of State-owned Enterprise in the Western World*. Cambridge: Cambridge University Press.

Amatori, F. (2017). State and Enterprise: The Case of SOEs in Europe in the Twentieth Century. In D. Felisini (Ed.), *Reassessing the Role of Management in the Golden Age*. Cham: This Palgrave Macmillan.

Aulich, C., & Wettenhall, R. (2019). The Evolution of Public Enterprise in Australia: Disillusion and Dissolution. *Asia Pacific Journal of Public Administration*, *41*(1), 19–32.

Baltowski, M., Kozarzewski, P., & Mickiewicz, T. (2022). State Capitalism in Poland and Hungary: Populist Varieties. In M. Wright, G. T. Wood, A. Cuervo-Cazurra, P. Sun, I. Okhmatovskiy, & A. Grosman (Eds.), *Oxford Handbook on State Capitalism and the Firm*. Oxford: Oxford University Press.

Beder, S. (2006). Power Play: The Japanese Situation. In S. Beder (Ed.), *Power Play: The Fight to Control the World's Electricity*. Soshisha.

Bernier, L., Florio, M., & Bance, P. (Eds.). (2020). *The Routledge Handbook of State-Owned Enterprises*. London; New York: Routledge.

Bland, F. A. (1945). Planning the Modern State: An Introduction to the Problem of Political and Administrative Re-organization. Sydney: Angus and Robertson Limited.

Bognetti, G. (2020). History of Western State-Owned Enterprises: From the Industrial Revolution to the age of globalization. In L. Bernier, M. Florio, & P. Bance (Eds.) *The Routledge Handbook of State-Owned Enterprises*. London; New York: Routledge.

Bortolotti, B., & Faccio, M. (2004). *Reluctant Privatization* (No. 130.2004). Nota di Lavoro.

Bower, J. L., Leonard, H. B., & Paine, L. S. (2011). *Capitalism at Risk: Rethinking the Role of Business*. Boston, MA: Harvard Business Press.

Bremmer, I. (2008). The Return of State Capitalism. *Survival*, *50*(3), 55–64.

Bremmer, I. (2010). *The End of the Free Market: Who Wins the War Between States and Corporations?* New York: Portfolio/Penguin.

Chen, D. (2013). China's State-Owned Enterprises: How Much Do We Know? From CNOOC to Its Siblings. *SPP Research Paper* (6–19).

Comín, F. (2008). Public Enterprises in Spain: Historical Cycles and Privatizations. *Analise Social*, *43*(189), 693–720.

Flores-Macias, F., & Musacchio, A. (2009). The Return of State-owned Enterprises: Should We Be Afraid? *Harvard International Review*, *4*.

Florio, M. (2014). The Return of Public Enterprise. *CISL Working Paper*, 1. Milan: Centre for Industrial Studies.

Goldstein, A. E. (1998). The Politics and Economics of Privatization: The Case of Argentina. *Canadian Journal of Latin American and Caribbean Studies*, *23*(45), 55–87.

Ginting, E., & Naqvi, K. (Eds.). (2020). *Reforms, Opportunities, and Challenges for State-Owned Enterprises*. Mandaluyong: Asian Development Bank.

Grabowiecki, J. (2006). Keiretsu Groups: Their Role in the Japanese Economy and a Reference Point (or a Paradigm) for Other Countries. Institute of Developing Economies, Japan External Trade Organization. Tokyo.

Haggarty, L., & Shirley, M. M. (1997). A New Data Base on State-Owned Enterprises. *The World Bank Economic Review*, *11*(3), 491–523.

Kurlantzick, J. (2016). *State Capitalism: How the Return of Statism is Transforming the World*. New York: Oxford University Press.

Lee, J. (2009). State Owned Enterprises in China: Reviewing the Evidence. *OECD Occasional Paper.*

Lee, M. (2019). *SOE Reform and Privatization of Korea.* Retrieved from https://www.carecinstitute.org/wp-content/uploads/2019/09/CI-KSU-SOE-workshop-Session-5-3-Minchang-Lee_SOE-Reform-in-Korea-KGZ-26-Sep-2019.pdf

McDonald, D. (2020). Don't Get Too Excited: The Structural Limits of State-Owned Enterprises in Capitalist Economies. In L. Bernier, M. Florio, & P. Bance (Eds.), *The Routledge Handbook of State-Owned Enterprises.* London; New York: Routledge.

Milhaupt, C. J., & Pargendler, M. (2017). Governance Challenges of Listed State-Owned Enterprises Around the World: National Experiences and a Framework for Reform. *Cornell International Law Journal, 50*(3), 3.

Millward, R. (2011). Public Enterprise in the Modern Western World: An Historical Analysis. *Annals of Public and Cooperative Economics, 82*(4), 375–398.

Musacchio, A., & Lazzarini, S. G. (2012). Leviathan in Business: Varieties of State Capitalism and Their Implications for Economic Performance. *Available at SSRN 2070942.*

Musacchio, A., & Lazzarini, S. G. (2014a). *Reinventing State Capitalism: Leviatan in Bussines, Brazil and Beyond.* Cambridge, MA: Harvard University Press.

Musacchio, A., & Lazzarini, S. G. (2014b). State-Owned Enterprises in Brazil: History and Lessons. *Workshop on State-Owned Enterprises in the Development Process. Paris: OECD, April* (Vol. 4).

OECD. (2003). Privatising State-owned Enterprises: An Overview of Policies and Practices in OECD Countries (Vol. 961). Paris: OECD Publishing.

OECD. (2018). OECD Review of the Corporate Governance of State-Owned Enterprises: Argentina.

Petras, J. (1977). State Capitalism and the Third World. *Development and Change, 8*(1), Wiley Online Library.

Sheng, H., & Zhao, N. (2012). *China's State-Owned Enterprises: Nature, Performance and Reform.* Series on Chinese Economics Research (Vol. 1). Singapore: World Scientific Publishing.

Spechler, M. C., Ahrens, J., & Hoen, H. W. (2017). *State Capitalism in Eurasia.* Singapore: World Scientific Publishing.

Stanbury, W. T. (1989). Privatization in Canada: Ideology, Symbolism or Substance? In W. Block, R. Schultz, & W. T. Stanbury (Eds.), *Privatization and State-Owned Enterprises.* Dordrecht: Springer.

Stevens, D. F. (1993). *Corporate Autonomy and Institutional Control: The Crown Corporation as a Problem in Organization Design* (Vol. 18). McGill-Queen's Press-MQUP.

Szamosszegi, A., & Kyle, C. (2011). *An Analysis of State-owned Enterprises and State Capitalism in China.* Washington, DC: U.S.-China Economic and Security Review Commission.

The Economist. (2012, January 21). State capitalism: The visible hand (Special Report).

Toninelli, P. M. (Ed.). (2000). *The Rise and Fall of State-owned Enterprise in the Western World.* Cambridge: Cambridge University Press.

Toyama, Y. (1998). Privatization of Public Enterprises and its Problems in Japan. *International Journal of Social Economics, 25*(2–4), 388–398.

Wengenroth, U. (2000). The Rise and Fall of State-Owned Enterprise in Germany. In P. A. Toninelli (Ed.), *The Rise and Fall of State-owned Enterprise in the Western World.* Cambridge: Cambridge University Press.

2 State as an owner

In this chapter, we analyse some issues - the most important, in our view - concerning the relationship between the state (government) as an owner and state-owned enterprise (SOEs). The literature on this subject is rich and these issues are somewhat beside the main objective of this book, which is to empirically analyse the scope of SOEs in the contemporary global economy in recent years. Therefore, it is not our intention to extend or change theoretical perspectives concerning them, but we focus on the matters that are crucial for the considerations in the further parts of the book. At the same time, we present our original views and statements, using the results of our empirical research as well as previous studies on SOEs and the state ownership function in the modern economy.

2.1 Types (kinds) of SOEs

2.1.1 Introductory remarks

It is true, as the authors of the World Bank Report (2015, p. 12) claim, that "the SOE landscape has become increasingly diverse. [...] With the growing complexity of state participation in the economy, there is no longer a uniform definition, and especially because the definition of an SOE has always been country-specific". A cross-country analysis reveals a surprising multitude of types, kinds and formulas of operation of contemporary SOEs, generally understood as economic entities subject to corporate control by the government, while this control can be exercised directly or indirectly, using ownership and non-ownership tools (the definition of an SOE adopted in this book is presented in detail in Section 3.1.2). This multitude means that SOEs can be classified according to different criteria, each time arising from the purpose and problem of the analysis being carried out.

When considering the issue of "SOEs and the state", the primary criterion for the classification of SOEs must be the extent or "strength" of their dependence on the government, meaning the formal dependence, resulting from the law and the principles of operation of SOEs[1] (the differences between formal and actual dependence, resulting from the practice of the

DOI: 10.4324/9781003244462-3

relationship between the government and SOEs and the institutional setup of the state, is further analysed in Section 2.3). Thus, adopting this criterion, three main types of SOEs can be distinguished. We mentioned them in the previous chapter while analysing the origin and historical development of SOEs. Here, we present them in more detail, highlighting the differences between them. These three types are:

1. Economic government entities (EGEs) - entities directly linked to the government that are parts of public administration (once ministries or departments, now most often departments) or separate government agencies. They usually provide public services, have a certain degree of organisational and decision-making autonomy, keep separate accounts, but do not have financial or legal autonomy.
2. Statutory corporations - 100% state-owned entities operating under special statutory laws, typically similar to private corporations. They are financially and organisationally separate from the government, and usually perform specific tasks defined by the state.
3. Corporate (private) law companies - entities over which the government directly or indirectly exercises actual corporate control with varying degrees of formal ownership. They operate under the general provisions of the law of the country, similar to private-owned companies.

This division should be seen as a general scheme, trying to cover the various types of SOEs found in individual countries. When analysing the types of SOEs (as well as their functions, as discussed further in Section 2.2) in various countries of different political systems and varying institutional maturity, we encounter specific solutions determined by historical circumstances or cultural contexts. Therefore, the following considerations should be treated as stylised facts, so essentially true generalisations resulting from empirical research, which may, however, show some inaccuracies in the details.

The boundaries between these three SOE types, as well as between SOEs and other state entities and units, are not only ambiguous in terms of the substantive autonomy of these entities but they are also differently established in different countries. They derive from legal provisions, national public statistics systems, but also traditional solutions, which introduce their natural but specific division. For example, in the UK, the borderline between EGEs and non-departmental public bodies, which are not commercial, is vague. The term "statutory corporation", found in the legal systems of many countries, covers divergent groups of business entities. Sometimes, as in Russia, some statutory corporations perform simultaneously – in addition to their business activities – the functions of government agencies or even entities with the authority of the state regulator in a particular industry for all companies, both state-owned and private. In India, on the other hand, the actual features of statutory corporations, as a rule – 100% state-owned entities – are exhibited by some companies with mixed state-private capital.

As we wrote in the previous chapter, EGEs were a common type of SOEs around the world until the early 20th century. In communist countries, until the transformation period, almost all state enterprises could be referred to as EGEs. Nowadays, after the extensive corporatisation processes that started in the Western World almost 100 years ago and lasted for several decades, as well as after commercialisation processes in the post-communist countries, EGEs are relatively rare, present usually in the developing countries. One may say that this type of SOEs is a kind of "creature" from the past. Perhaps the largest EGE in the world is India Post – a postal operator with approximately 430,000 employees, which is in the Top 10 of global SOEs with the greatest number of employees. In legal and organisational terms, India Post is a Department of Posts in the Ministry of Communication in the government of India (China Post Group has over 900,000 employees and operates under the Company Law of the People's Republic of China (PRC)). A similar situation is found, for example, in Egypt, where postal services are provided by the National Postal Authority, and in Saudi Arabia, where Saudi Post is a government agency, functioning as part of the Ministry of Communications and Information Technology. It may be added that by 1995 the Indonesian post and by 2003 the Thai post were also EGEs and now, after the commercialisation, they are state-owned companies.

The two other distinguished SOE types, i.e. statutory corporations and corporate law companies, are much more widespread nowadays and can be found in many countries of the world, although they also adopt different specific legal and organisational solutions in different countries. We will present them in more detail in the following sections.

2.1.2 SOEs as statutory corporations

Statutory corporations, also referred to in some countries as public corporations, are common throughout the world. Sometimes this term, however, applies also to entities that do not run a commercial business (as the aforementioned English "departmental public bodies"). In Germany, for example, statutory corporations referred to as corporations under public law (*Körperschaft des öffentlichen Rechts*) range from non-commercial universities or Local Health Funds to public broadcasters operating in the media market.

In the UK, there were several statutory (public) corporations, such as British Railways and the National Coal Board operating for a long time, until the privatisation in the 1980s and 1990s. Currently, with the very low importance of SOEs in the UK economy, only a few entities have the form of public corporations, and the most important is the British Broadcasting Corporation (BBC).

In France, "public companies of an industrial and commercial nature" (*établissement public à caractère industriel et commercial* - EPIC) can operate in the areas where private commercial entities are active. Previously, the largest French SOEs, including *Électricité de France* and *Gaz de France*, at the beginning of the 21st century, operated as EPICs, which have been turned into companies governed by private law. Now, there are only a few commercial EPICs. **In Spain**, statutory corporations include public policy-oriented companies controlled by the Directorate of State Property and the Minister of Finance.

In Canada, statutory corporations operating under special legislative acts are quite common. As many as six among Canada's seven largest SOEs are 100% state-owned entities having the nature of statutory corporations (see Table 4.6.1). **In Ireland**, similarly, SOEs that are required "to operate on a commercial basis" usually function under specific acts and are 100% government-owned (see Table 4.13.1).

In the US, the difference between a government corporation (statutory corporation) and a government agency is not clearly defined. The purpose of government (federal) agencies is usually to regulate a certain area of the economy and not to run a profit-oriented business activity. But, for example, the largest US SOE, i.e. the US Postal Service, is an independent agency of the federal government responsible for providing postal services in the US. As rightly noted by M. Pargendler (2011, p. 2926) [government corporations] "are often no more than state agencies organized under a different, and more flexible, legal structure".

In Argentina, there are a few statutory corporations, usually with a high direct dependency on the state. An intermediate form between EGEs and statutory corporations are state enterprises (*Empresas del Estado*), entities separate from the state, in which, however, the state exercises its property rights not on the basis of general provisions of law but directly on the basis of government decisions, such as decrees.

In Japan, there are special public corporations (*tokushu hōjin*), which can be described as statutory corporations that are established through company-specific legislation. They carry out tasks delegated by the state and may receive direct capital transfers from the budget. These are generally entities of minor importance. The best-known example is the Japan Broadcasting Corporation (NHK - *Nippon Hōsō Kyōkai*).

In Indonesia, among the various types of SOEs, there are the so-called Perum (*Perusahaan Umum*) – state entities whose purpose is to make profits, but their commercial activities are associated with public purposes (e.g. providing drinking water at relatively low prices). They operate based on special legislation. The so-called special purpose vehicles also operate under special laws and rules. This is the form of, for example, the largest Indonesian petrochemical company Pertamina, which was defined as a statutory corporation until 2003.

In Russia, there are several state-owned corporations, each operating under a separate, special law. As we mentioned, Russian statutory corporations sometimes combine the functions of a commercial entity, operating in the market, and a government agency with regulatory powers over the entire sector. This creates room for abuse and negatively affects the quality of state ownership control of these entities. Among the most important Russian state-owned corporations are *Rustec* ("State Corporation for Assistance to Development, Production and Export of Advanced Technology Industrial Product") in the arms sector and *Rosatom* in the nuclear power sector.

In Poland, there are a few SOEs with 100% state ownership, operating under special rules – the public TV broadcaster, and the Polish Security Printing Works. The Polish Post (*Poczta Polska*) operates partly under a special law guaranteeing it a limited monopolistic position.

2.1.3 SOEs as corporate law companies

This type of SOEs today is the most common and important, occurring in various varieties and manifestations in all larger economies of the world. Among 532 SOEs of the 37 economies analysed further, approximately 75% are SOEs in the form of corporate law companies. They exhibit two basic features:

a they function on the same legal basis as private companies in a given country,
b the actual corporate control is exercised by the government, using both ownership and non-ownership tools.

This type of SOEs can be classified in several ways:

1 According to the criterion of the size of the state's share - into entities with a majority (over 50%) and minority (or to be more precise - non-majority) share of the state. Among the former ones, entities with full (100%) state ownership can be further distinguished.
2 According to the criterion of the type of dependency on the government - into SOEs that are directly dependent (the property rights to the SOE are exercised by a government body or a special entity, appointed for that purpose, subordinate to the government) and indirectly dependent (the property rights to the SOE are exercised through other state entities).
3 A relatively distinct group of SOEs, gaining importance in recent years, are listed SOEs (listed companies with state ownership). On a global scale, there is an interesting relationship here. In some countries, listed SOEs represent a majority of all SOEs (as is the case, for example, in China, Brazil, France, Italy, Saudi Arabia and Poland), and in other countries, there are no such SOEs (e.g. Ireland, the Netherlands, Slovakia). This issue is discussed in detail in Section 7.1.

In **Italy, France, Spain and Germany**, there is a large group of companies operating under the general commercial law, with mixed capital, in which the government is one of the owners. These companies are treated by law identically to fully private companies when it comes to access to finance and tax burdens.

Canadian SOEs, as we wrote above, typically take the form of statutory corporations, although there are also SOEs, especially smaller ones, operating under the Canada Business Corporations Act. In **Brazil**, commercial SOEs which derive revenues from market activities and finance their operations therefrom are common. The vast majority of large SOEs are listed SOEs. In **Argentina**, in addition to *Empresas del Estado* mentioned above, there are also state corporations (*Sociedades del Estado*), where government corporate control is exercised along the lines of private companies, through ordinary shareholders' rights (OECD, 2018, pp. 23–34).

In **Japan,** *tokushu gaisha* (special companies) are joint-stock companies under government ownership control, operating under the general provisions of the corporation law (Companies Act). They are generally commercially oriented. In many of them, the state is only one of the shareholders. This group includes such major players as Japan Post and Nippon Telegraph & Telephone. In **Korea**, similarly, there are the so-called market-type SOEs and, similar to them, quasi-market-type SOEs, operating like private entities. In **Indonesia**, there is a sizeable group of commercial companies, called Persero, which are fully or mostly state-owned and operate under the general commercial company law.

In **China, India, Saudi Arabia and Russia**, the countries with the relatively greatest importance of SOEs in the economy, there are large groups of companies with mixed state and private capital, which are usually listed companies. Formally they operate under the general provisions of law, but actually they enjoy special privileges from the authorities (easier access to capital in state banks, tax exemptions and redemptions, etc.) and often perform specific non-economic functions. A similar situation exists in **Poland, Romania and Hungary**.

2.2 Functions of SOEs

2.2.1 Introductory remarks

The functions of SOEs in the economy and the related question of the rationale for the existence of SOEs have long been the subject of economic and political studies. The literature on this subject is extensive and the reader can find the latest state of the art, for example, in *The Routledge Handbook of State-Owned Enterprises* (Bernier et al., 2020), especially in the chapters by M.G. Bird (Ch. 3), M. Sorrentino (Ch. 4) and M. Howlett and M. Ramesh (Ch. 31). The problem is also discussed at length in OECD (Organisation for Economic Co-operation and Development) reports, particularly in the 2018 report titled *Ownership and Governance of State-Owned Enterprises: A Compendium of National Practices.*

However, these analyses generally tend to suffer from two weaknesses, typical of both theoretical and empirical studies concerning contemporary SOEs. First, they focus - as the analyses of the origin and historical development of SOEs do, as we pointed out in the previous chapter - on the developed economies of the West (or the economies of OECD countries). They only rarely cover other economies that are increasingly important in the modern world, such as Chinese, Indian, Indonesian and Thai economies, where, paradoxically, the role of SOEs in the economy is much more important than in the Western countries, and the functions of SOEs are much broader and differently defined.

Second, they usually concern the rationales for and functions of SOEs presented in various documents by the state owner, which are often significantly different from the actual objectives of SOEs and the economic and politico-economic functions performed by them in practice. The actual, not the declared, functions of SOEs (as well as rationales) are in many cases concealed or disguised by the state. We consider this problem further, by presenting our understanding of the contemporary functions of SOEs.

It must be added that in a cognitive sense, it seems more reasonable to study the functions of SOEs rather than their rationales (and objectives), as it is very difficult and always subject to uncertainty to identify the real rationales and objectives of SOEs and to separate them from the formal, declared ones. The same analysis in the case of functions is easier because they manifest themselves in specific decisions and their material effects. This includes decisions made at the level of SOEs, as well as decisions - that are superior - made at the level of the government exercising property rights over SOEs. For this reason, the following analysis will focus on the functions actually fulfilled by SOEs.

The discord between declared and actual functions of SOEs, noticeable at the level of economic research, often manifests itself at the level of theoretical research in the form of mixing or insufficiently distinguishing the functions in normative and positive terms. Usually, researchers analyse desirable or even ideal situations having little to do with the actual operation of SOEs. For example, T. J. Putniņš, adopting a normative point of view, lists a whole catalogue of the proper, in his opinion, rationales for the existence of SOEs, from which their desired functions also derive. He writes that "the use of SOEs should be limited to circumstances in which a market failure exists. [...] Finally, under a welfare maximization objective, operating an SOE is only justified when the welfare loss of the market failure exceeds the costs, distortions, and inefficiencies associated with the SOE" (Putniņš, 2020, pp. 233–234). Notwithstanding the fact that these statements may be correct for the developed economies of the West, and may not necessarily be correct for other economies, the author ignores the fundamental fact - that SOEs, especially in these other economies, are entities of a special not only economic but also political-economic nature.

The normative approach, meaning showing and advocating solutions concerning the "proper" functioning of SOEs, has been promoted by the OECD for many years, mainly in the form of various types of good practices and guidelines addressed to governments. H. Christiansen, an OECD analyst, writes explicitly about "balancing commercial and non-commercial priorities of state-owned enterprises" as the right basis for their operation. This author expresses a strongly postulative and difficult-to-achieve recommendation that any functions of SOEs that go beyond market standards should result from legal regulations, and not subjective government decisions (Christiansen, 2013). Similarly, the basic OECD document on the state ownership control and SOE management rules has a normative (postulative) dimension. It includes statements that "the ultimate purpose of state ownership of enterprises should be to maximise value for society, through an efficient allocation of resources", that "the state should define the rationales for owning individual SOEs and subject these to recurrent review", that "the government should allow SOEs full operational autonomy to achieve their defined objectives and refrain from intervening in SOE management" (OECD, 2015, pp. 17–18).

This good advice (not to say - wishful thinking) concerning the rationales for and functions of SOEs in the economy, formulated by the OECD as recommendations to governments, is rarely reflected in reality. The actual condition of most economies of the world is definitely far from this ideal model. Good practices are followed in some developed countries of the West, either where the role of SOEs is not significant (as in the Netherlands and Belgium) or which have developed proper principles of state control over the years (Norway is usually - rightly - given as an example). But in the vast majority of countries, especially in emerging markets, where SOEs are very important, both the actual rationales and the functions fulfilled in the economy are far from the OECD recommendations and normative postulates formulated in theoretical studies.

Looking positively (descriptively) at SOEs on a global scale, we see a huge diversity of their actual economic and non-economic functions - it is difficult to find general patterns or schemes to systematise this phenomenon. It can only be noted that the expectations formulated by governments towards SOEs are strongly related to the political system and institutional maturity of a given country. In general, the further the country moves away from the model of a democratic country based on the rule of law, the more diverse non-economic objectives are formulated towards SOEs by the state owner and the wider the range of the functions that are actually performed by them.

2.2.2 Evolution of functions of SOEs over time

Both the declared and actually performed economic and non-economic functions of SOEs have evolved over time together with the functions of the state - from a limited state of the 19th century to a much broader, extended state of the 21st century. These changes were a result of diverse relationships between the state and the economy in various places and periods, economic and political crises, after which the role of the state has usually expanded, as well as prevailing economic concepts and intellectual trends. Particularly rapid changes took place since the end of the 20th century. This is why research and academic studies on the subject, which seemed right and accurate 30–40 years ago (e.g. Gillis, 1980; Floyd et al., 1984), today seem incomplete and anachronistic.

Naturally, the evolution of functions of SOEs over time is very difficult to capture and generalise on a global scale for the reasons we discussed in the previous chapter. While SOEs in the modern sense appeared in the economy of the West at the end of the 19th century, initially mainly as EGEs, in the post-colonial or post-communist countries it happened much later and, moreover, under different civilisational and developmental conditions. Thus, the following short overview of the evolution of functions of SOEs over time is only illustrative and simplified.

In the late 19th century, SOEs in many developed countries of the West were a tool of industrialisation when private capital was insufficient, and the rationale for a relatively wide presence of the state in many industries and mining also included military reasons. In countries such as Germany and Italy, nationally uniform public service products provided by state-owned entities contributed to the fulfilment of an important political task of unifying nation states or even building national identity.

After the First World War, the governments of many countries, to rescue private companies strained by the economic consequences of the war from bankruptcy, started to acquire or take over their ownership shares, which tended to entail the expansion of their functions towards non-economic ones. A bit later, in the 1930s, the increased economic activity of SOEs was a response to the weaknesses of the private sector, affected by the Great Depression. Once again, rescue nationalisation measures were undertaken, covering also the banking sector. In Russia, after the October Revolution (and in the other countries of the socialist bloc – 30 years later), guided by the ideological doctrine, the authorities assumed that SOEs were not only the basic elements of the economy but also socialist workplaces, whose function was to shape appropriate attitudes and behaviours of the people employed there. This was the origin of the extremely extensive social and welfare functions of SOEs in these countries. Similar processes, although to a lesser extent, took place in fascist Italy.

The reconstruction of economies after the Second World War, and the subsequent formation of modern welfare states, entailed increased responsibilities of the state. The choice of a statist-interventionist model of development was encouraged by the progressing dominance of Keynesian economics as the basis of economic policy. It was a common thought that only the widespread use of SOEs may be a condition for overcoming market failures, fulfilling fast-growing public service tasks and allocating resources in a way corresponding to the socio-economic objectives formulated by the state. Such views in the developed economies of the West (mostly in the UK, but also in France and Italy) brought about waves of post-war nationalisations and the creation of new SOEs. The economic functions initially attributed to them quickly developed mainly towards social functions; special privileges for SOEs' employees commonly appeared, such as guarantees of job stability, additional extra benefits and employee participation in the management process. In some countries, such as Italy, the performance of specific tasks of the economic policy and the protection of jobs, rather than making profits, were explicitly formulated objectives of the largest SOEs.

Many post-colonial and developing countries, fascinated by the successful industrialisation of the early period of the socialist economy, adopted a similar development model. At the level of SOEs, this meant an expansion of their functions (described further in detail) from economic to social and development functions, and then quickly and largely also to the predatory function - SOEs were treated as political spoils or as "private" property of those currently in power. The predatory function also developed with great intensity over the years in Russia and in all countries that adopted the socialist system after the Second World War.

Since the end of the 1970s, state ownership in the countries of the West began to be seen as highly inefficient. In many economies of the world, primarily highly developed ones, the UK being a spectacular example, deep privatisation processes were carried out, and SOEs that were not privatised underwent extensive recovery and restructuring processes. Their purpose was to bring the principles of operation of SOEs closer to private companies and to decrease the scope of non-economic functions that strongly burdened the efficiency of SOEs. Although there were exceptions - in France in the early 1980s, after F. Mitterand came to power, there was another wave of nationalisations.

In the developing countries, mainly those that implemented IMF (International Monetary Fund) recovery programmes, privatisation processes progressed but with a lower intensity than in the developed countries and more often without the loss of state control over SOEs, and, consequently, without the elimination of non-economic functions that accrued over the years. In Russia, China and other socialist countries of that time, there were, obviously, no privatisation activities until the end of the 1980s. On the contrary, SOEs not only retained a definitely dominant position in the economy, but their non-economic functions extended in the three main areas: social and welfare, tools of economic and social policy, and source of political rent. The situation changed fundamentally in the early 1990s, when these countries began the processes of political and economic transformations, a key element of which was the restructuring and privatisation of the SOE sector.

2.2.3 Contemporary functions of SOEs

The briefly outlined evolution of the functions of SOEs since the end of the 19th century is now only of historical importance. In the last 15–20 years, several phenomena have emerged simultaneously on a global scale (analysed in more detail in Section 1.5) which, taken together, had a significant impact on the change of the role and importance of the SOE sector in the economy, and consequently on its functions. In the global economy, China has visibly gained importance, as well as India and Indonesia, the countries where both the scope of SOEs and their functions, especially non-economic ones, are significantly broader than in the developed countries of the West. The financial crisis triggered a return of states to an active role in the economy, and the crisis-related rescue nationalisations meant, de facto, an expansion of the domain of the state and new functions of SOEs. The development of populist and authoritarian tendencies in many countries was associated with the wider use by governments of SOEs as the means of affecting the economy, which was motivated by the need for defending the domestic economy from the attempts of global corporations, which found the approval of the electorate, although often group and individual interests of those in power were behind such actions.

Due to the specific nature of SOEs as the entities subject - to a greater or lesser extent - to market competition, and at the same time very often used by state authorities to achieve various specific objectives, the contemporary functions of SOEs can naturally be divided into economic (related to their existence in the market environment) and non-economic (related to the expectations of the state owner). Here, a methodological remark should be made. Any divisions of the functions of SOEs are not disjunctive, or at least not always, and they do not have to necessarily be disjunctive in all countries. Very often economic and non-economic functions intertwine. This division is not dichotomous.

This dual understanding of SOE functions is denominated by H. Mühlenkamp as the welfare approach and the public choice approach. He writes:

> According to the welfare approach, the economic rationale for public enterprises is (static or dynamic) market failure. Against this background, public enterprises are seen as a means to counter market failure, most notably in cases of natural monopolies or negative externalities. Without market failure there is no reason to have public enterprises.

By contrast, in the public choice approach, the functions of SOEs derive from the will of politicians exercising actual control over SOEs:

> Politicians may simply be acting as "rent-seekers" [...] and use public enterprises as a device for their political agenda. From this point of view, public enterprises can act on a macroeconomic level to correct income distribution, employment rates, investment levels, the provision of capacity, and so on. Such goals or outcomes could be classified as "socio-economic' or 'non-market output".
>
> (Mühlenkamp, 2015, pp. 537–538)

While adopting Mühlenkamp's division, we need to make one important addition arising from our observations of and research on SOEs, mainly outside the developing countries. Well, these non-market or non-economic functions of SOEs consist of two fundamentally different groups. One is related to acting of the state in good faith. The other, referred to below as the predatory function, is related to acting in bad faith (pursuing group interests). So, in essence, while observing the economic and non-economic behaviour of SOEs in different countries of the world and various market situations, it is possible to speak of a catalogue of diversified, intertwined functions, falling between treating SOEs as a means to counter market failure and using them as an instrument for the pursuit of political goals, while these political goals, in extreme, but not at all rare cases, are formulated in bad faith (see Kozarzewski, 2021, Section 6.1 on what is "good faith" and "bad faith" in the economic policy).

Using our research, the report of Ch. Richmond et al. (2019), based on empirical findings, as well as other studies related to the role of SOEs in the contemporary economy, mainly in the developed and post-communist countries (Heath & Normana, 2004; Putniņš, 2020; Kozarzewski, 2021), we distinguish the following set of functions that the contemporary SOE sector fulfils with different intensity in different countries or group of countries:

1 Market (economic) function,
2 Fiscal function,
3 Development function,
4 Social function,
5 Strategic function,
6 Predatory function.

The above sequence of functions is not random. In the subsequent positions of the list, the influence of the economic factor decreases, while that of the political factor increases.

Market (economic) function

The existence of market failures creates space for state interference, which can take the form of using regulatory tools, favoured by the economic theory, or the form of using ownership tools. These two ways of removing or reducing market failures are usually largely substitutable. For example, the elimination of disadvantages of a natural monopoly may involve either imposing price and product regulations on private entities while subsidising part of the costs or achieving similar economic effects using state-owned entities.

In the sphere of the provision of specific non-rivalrous and non-excludability public goods and services, too, there is an alternative: either the production and distribution of these goods and services are entrusted to private companies under the supervision and control of the state or they are carried out by special state entities. This mainly applies to infrastructure goods (once roads and bridges or water and sewage networks, nowadays, e.g. basic fibre optic networks), broadly understood power sector, as well as public services, such as health care or even food security.

However, the latter solution, which in both cases involves the use of SOEs, rather than regulations targeting private entities, from the political - in the negative sense – point of view, is far more appealing. For the government, or in fact, for the party in power, it creates greater opportunities to fulfil predatory functions than the first option. Of course, in the economies with well-developed institutional systems and transparent procedures of economic policy, these opportunities are realised to a lesser extent than in the less institutionalised economies, with various informal links between the political and economic spheres. Nevertheless, there is always the danger that the economic functions of SOEs are merely a cover for predatory functions.

Finally, let us add that economic functions of SOEs without the danger that predatory functions will occur may also exist. There are empirical studies showing that the SOEs from the financial area - especially those operating under appropriate institutional conditions - may play a stabilising role in the business cycle (Bertay et al., 2015; Richmond et al., 2019), by means of increased investments during recessions and reduced investments during economic booms, as well as through maintaining employment levels during downturns (in the last case, economic functions are basically the same as social functions).

Fiscal function

This traditionally important function, which often used to be associated with state monopolies, treated as a source of stable and high budget revenues, is now losing importance. This is especially true in the developed countries with few state monopolies, where tax systems are generally neutral with respect to forms of business ownership, and the competition in the markets forces SOEs to act efficiently. However, there are still countries, especially emerging markets, where SOEs in selected industries have - deliberately maintained by the governments - their market positions that enable them to achieve above-average profits that add to government revenues.

Yet, at the same time, the opposite situations exist. State aid, limited and controlled in the EU countries, from the budget to SOEs is a common phenomenon in many, especially developing, countries. This means that it is not the SOEs that are the source of extraordinary budget revenues, but the other way around - the budget fuels SOEs. This includes not only subsidies for the performance of specific public or strategic tasks for the state, which is quite obvious, but also tax exemptions aimed at sustaining unnecessary employment or levelling out market opportunities, to generally less efficient SOEs. In many countries with large, economically and socially important SOE sectors, such as Poland and India, average wages in SOEs are significantly higher than in comparable private enterprises, which can be treated as a form of budgetary subsiding of these entities.

The answer to the question of why governments sustain the existence of SOEs through budgetary subsidies is not simple. It seems that it results from the priority of non-economic functions, including the predatory functions, where the ability to fulfil them is more important to governments than the costs to the budget.

Development function

From the second half of the 19th century onwards, SOEs were relatively frequently used to support economic development and industrialisation, especially where private capital was insufficient to operate on a larger scale. This function of SOEs, which can be described as acting in good faith, also occurs in many countries today, although with less intensity than in the past, caused by easier access to capital on a global scale and the development of direct foreign investments. Research shows that state activity in the economy can foster large infrastructure investments or the development of technological innovations, in the cases considered too risky by some private investors (Qi & Kotz, 2020).

Public entities supported by the state (or by the state financial sector) are able to undertake economic projects that are rational from the point of view of long-term objectives of the state, which seem unprofitable or bring too low rates of return to private capital (e.g. investments in the energy sector, internet networks or related to climate requirements). SOEs may also operate in the fields that are important for the development of the country, where there is a risk of adverse externalities, such as the extraction of hazardous, radioactive raw materials or the nuclear power industry (Sorrentino, 2020, p. 75). In such a case, the state takes on the possible, although usually little, risks associated with these activities. The fact that "the use of SOEs as a vehicle of industrialisation might do more harm than good due to the frequent failure of policymakers to identify correctly promising industries" (Szarzec et al., 2021) must be always taken into account.

It should be noted that the development function of SOEs, especially in relation to the less developed countries, is often analysed and presented in OECD studies (e.g. OECD, 2013, pp. 109–110).

Social function

Since their beginning, SOEs have been and continue to be seen as much more stable places of employment than private companies. In many countries, such as France, India and Poland, there are formalised or unwritten but respected rules on the sustainability of work, improving the position of SOEs' employees in relation to those employed in the private sector, and employment contracts are usually concluded for an indefinite period. Traditionally, in many countries, being employed in SOEs is associated with special social privileges, such as thirteenth salary (relatively more often than in private-owned enterprises, POEs) and sometimes even statutory guarantees of employees' participation in the SOE profits. Sometimes SOEs' employees have a civil servant status in the company, as was the case in many large SOEs in France until the 1990s.

Although such social functions are seen as natural and positive by the employees of SOEs, from the point of view of the economy as a whole, the situation is not clear. Employee privileges of a certain group of employees violate the principle of equality before the law and introduce social tensions. Unhealthy paradoxes often arise here. In many countries (Poland can be an example here) trade unions, whose historical, fundamental task has always been to defend employee rights against exploitation by the owners-capitalists, now have the strongest organisations precisely in SOEs, not in POEs. And the purpose of trade unions in SOEs has become not so much to defend employee rights (which are usually guaranteed and respected to a higher degree than in POEs anyway) but to bargain with the government for subsequent pay increases, privileges and bonuses (Böwer, 2017; Matuszak & Szarzec, 2019).

Strategic function

This function, sometimes close to the development function, covers various manifestations of SOEs' activities related to the fulfilment of the so-called raison d'etre or the national interest of a given state. This means that SOEs are involved in providing the state with (military, energy, etc.) security, as well as hard and soft power projection (Levesque, 2017). This non-economic function, usually found in the borderland between acting in good faith and acting in bad faith, is specific in that it is not common. It appears mainly in the countries aspiring to become superpowers, whether globally (such as China, Russia and India) or regionally (such as Indonesia, Egypt and Brazil), where simultaneously the scope of SOEs is high. It is consciously shaped by the state owner of SOEs. In practice, the scope of "strategicity" is determined highly subjectively by the government and may be outlined very broadly.

Usually, the strategic function applies to the SOEs operating outside their country of origin. The aim may be to institute SOEs into the politics of the country of origin, as exemplified by the acquisition of foreign companies in many countries of the world by Chinese SOEs. Chinese SOEs, especially the largest ones, openly become tools for pursuing strategic geopolitical interests of the state, by incorporating various countries and their economies into China's sphere of influence (Hooijmaaijers, 2019; Kastner & Pearson, 2021). This is particularly evident in the presence of Chinese SOEs in many countries of Asia (including Singapore, as discussed in Section 7.2.2) and East Africa, but also increasingly in Europe, where they are buying up equity stakes in companies or even entire companies. In turn, this gives rise to defensive reactions in many countries, in the form of using indigenous SOEs to counteract this phenomenon.

Predatory function

The existence of SOEs creates a temptation for the government to use them to act in bad faith, contrary to the imperative of the common good, always declaratively applicable in the public sector. We will refer to the functions of SOEs related to such activities, often concealed and even denied, as predatory functions. Paradoxically, the inherent relationship of predatory functions with the existence of SOEs leads to two completely opposite consequences. In some countries, such as the US, the UK and Australia, it is a disincentive to creating and maintaining SOEs, or even a justification for nationalisation measures. In other countries, on the other hand, which are systemically distant from liberal democracy, the predatory function of SOEs is an unwritten, even somewhat shameful, yet widely accepted by political authorities, rationale for the existence of SOEs. The above differentiation is important because it explains a fundamental discrepancy of the scale and functions of SOEs in the various groups of countries, analysed in detail in Chapter 6.

The predatory function, making a social loss in principle, encompasses various situations, when an SOE becomes the object of political rent. It seems that the state and its officials can obtain various kinds of political rents using SOEs much easier and less visibly (and probably less disruptive to the market mechanism) than using regulatory pressures.

Taking into account the type of beneficiaries, two varieties of such political rent associated with the existence of SOEs can be distinguished. In the first one, the beneficiaries are specific individuals or entities indicated by the SOE or state owner. The rent drawn from the SOE may take different forms: nepotism, employment in fictitious positions, employment with unusually high salaries, assignments to "friend" companies, financial support for certain cultural entities, etc.

The second type of political rent occurs when the beneficiary is collective, non-specific, most often in the form of a political party (political team) holding power in the country or, more broadly, in the form of a group of voters associated with the ruling party. Again, the rent drawn from the SOE may have different specific manifestations, determined both by the degree of audacity and arrogance of power and by the cultural and historical context of a given country. This may involve sponsoring party events, covering the costs of advertising (often unproductive) in the media favourable to the authorities, financing politically motivated business ventures. This may also be an opportunity to manipulate prices of "politically sensitive" commodities, such as petrol or electricity, supplied by SOEs (e.g. before parliamentary elections).

The political rent of the first type is inherent to the existence of SOEs in all countries of the world, although, of course, its scale (so the social loss) varies fundamentally in different economies - from negligible in Norway and Sweden to very significant in Russia and Brazil. The rent of the second type appears only occasionally in developed economies, while it has been traditionally and is still present in developing economies. In the post-communist countries, the corporate governance exercised by the state during the transformation period, created from scratch, generally did not have mechanisms to sufficiently prevent the emergence of political rents of either the first or the second type.

2.2.4 Determinants of the functions of SOEs in the economy

Our empirical research, covering the operation of more than 530 large and very large SOEs in 37 countries over an extended time, and also other studies of contemporary SOEs available in the literature indicate that there are two main determinants of the functions of SOEs in the economy. The first is a type of institutional, or more broadly, systemic environment in which the SOE sector exists. In the developed countries, with established democracies, adhering to the rule of law, with a mature institutional system, the functions of the SOE sector are fundamentally different than in the countries of emerging markets, most often with questionable democracies, which are institutionally immature. This dissimilarity manifests itself in two dimensions. In the former group, the set of actual functions fulfilled by SOEs is narrower than in the latter, while, at the same time, the functions of SOEs are by far much more codified, written down and performed on this basis.

The second factor, quite obvious, but underestimated, is the scope of SOEs in a given economy.[2] In general, the greater the scope of SOEs, the broader and more significant the functions of the SOE sector. In countries such as China, Indonesia and Russia (as well as Norway), SOEs constitute the backbone and strength of the economy. They affect budgetary revenues, internal market and foreign expansion, which means that they fulfil different and important functions in the economy. In the case of economies, where the number of SOEs is negligible (at the level of the largest enterprises), such as Australia, Ireland, the Netherlands, Spain, the UK and the US, the functions of the SOE sector are also insignificant.

Taking into account both these factors, the countries analysed here can be divided into developed market economies and emerging market economies (the details of the division are presented in Section 3.4.2), and these in turn into groups of countries with different scopes of SOEs. Therefore, among the developed market economies we can distinguish:

a countries with a major (exceeding 30%) share of SOEs in the economy: Norway, Italy, France and Austria,
b countries with a minor (10–15%) share of SOEs in the economy: Taiwan, Sweden, Singapore, Germany, Korea,
c countries with a low (5–10%) share of SOEs in the economy: Switzerland, Belgium, Japan, Canada,

(The group of developed market economies lacks countries with the share of SOEs of 15–30%. The developed countries with a negligible, less

Table 2.1 Intensity of various functions of SOEs in the developed and emerging market economies

Functions of SOEs	*Share of SOEs in the economy*					
	Developed market economies			*Emerging market economies*		
	Low	*Minor*	*Major*	*Significant*	*Major*	*Very large*
Market function	+	+	++	++	++	+++
Fiscal function	-	+	+	+	++	++
Development function	+	++	++	++	++	+++
Social function	-	+	++	++	++	++
Strategic function	-	+	++	+	++	+++
Predatory function	-	+	+	++	+++	+++

+++ very significant function.
++ quite significant function.
+ not very significant function.
- no function.

Source: Own compilation.

than 5%, share of SOEs in the economy listed above, are omitted in the analysis).

In turn, among the emerging market economies, there are:

a countries with a very large (exceeding 50%) share of SOEs in the economy: China, Saudi Arabia, Russia, Indonesia, Egypt,
b countries with a major (30%–50%) share of SOEs in the economy: Poland, India, Thailand, Brazil, Hungary,
c countries with a significant (15%–30%) share of SOEs in the economy: Argentina, the Czech Republic, Turkey, Bulgaria, Slovakia, Mexico, Romania, South Africa.

(Countries with a negligible share of SOEs are absent among the emerging market economies).

Table 2.1 contains our estimates of the intensity of various functions of SOEs in developed and emerging market economies.

2.3 State ownership policy

2.3.1 Introductory remarks

The relationship between the government of the state and SOEs, or to be more precise, the state's influence on SOEs, is referred to in the literature in various ways: as state ownership control (Kozarzewski, 2021), corporate governance of SOEs (OECD, 2005; Word Bank, 2014) or state enterprise ownership policy

(OECD, 2018, p. 16). We consistently use the term of the state ownership policy because, in fact, in the modern economies this influence of the state on SOEs is an element or a type of the economic policy of the state (government policies), and the influence on the economy through SOEs can often be treated, as mentioned above, as a substitute tool for regulatory pressures.

State ownership policy, above all in terms of improving its quality and effectiveness, is relatively extensively analysed in the literature, mainly in OECD and World Bank reports (Christiansen, 2011; World Bank, 2014; OECD, 2018), although it must be remembered that OECD reports generally cover member countries and other countries only exceptionally. In the following analysis, we mainly want to draw attention to the important issues, in our view, but relatively rarely discussed in the literature and the issues related to the results of our empirical research.

The objectives, principles and methods of state ownership policy follow directly from the functions of SOEs we discussed above. The ownership policy that is effective from the point of view of the state owner is the one that enables the functions attributed to SOEs to be properly fulfilled. Since the functions of SOEs are always dual in nature - economic and non-economic – this insurmountable dualism associated with the existence of SOEs can also be identified in the influence of the state on SOEs. Moreover, what the OECD and World Bank reports seem not to distinguish sufficiently - the ownership policy can be pursued both in good faith, transparently, according to written declarations, and in bad faith, disguised, when there are fundamental discrepancies between what is written in the government documents and the policy actually pursued.

2.3.2 Differences between developed and developing countries

In the developed countries of the West, for a century, the general directions and principles of the ownership policy have largely depended and still depend on the political orientation of the ruling party. While the approach of social democrats and socialists can be described as favourable to state ownership, conservatists and republicans were generally hostile to a significant role of the state in the economy and public ownership. It is well illustrated by the example of the UK, where during the post-war governments of Prime Ministers C. Attlee and later H. Wilson, processes of broad expansion of the state domain were carried out, while, during the governments of M. Thatcher and J. Major, privatisation processes were implemented. It was similar in Norway, where the cycles of nationalisation and de-nationalisation of enterprises occurred to the rhythm of political changes. In France, a wide wave of nationalisations in the early 1980s was the result of the socialists returning to power and was in clear opposition to the economic policies pursued at the time by other governments in the world, including the administration of R. Reagan in the US or M. Thatcher in the UK.

In the developed countries with a significant scope of the SOE sector, regardless of the political orientation of the ruling party, there are usually government documents containing guidance on the ownership policy and periodically published reports on the condition of SOEs. Norway, where the scope of SOEs and their economic importance is the highest among the developed countries, has long been a model example of proper relations between the government and SOEs. The Norwegian Ministry of Trade, Industry and Fisheries annually publishes the *State Ownership Report*, containing both the objectives and principles of the ownership policy (including the State's Principles for Good Corporate Governance), as well as detailed, diverse characteristics of each SOE overseen by the government. Similarly, in Singapore, where the property rights towards SOEs are exercised by the state holding company Temasek, which annually publishes an extensive report - *Temasek Overview* – the relationship of the government with SOEs can be considered exemplary.

Analogous documents, containing both the directions and principles of the ownership policy, as well as the current characteristics of the largest national SOEs, exist in many other countries of the West, like Germany (*Participation Report of the Federal Government*), France (*State Shareholder Report*), Sweden (*State Ownership Policy and Principles for State-Owned Enterprises, Annual Report for State-Owned Enterprises*) and the Netherlands (*The State as Public Shareholder*).

But in Italy, for example, there is no single coherent report concerning the functioning of the entire SOE sector. Every year, every unlisted SOE prepares a report for the Ministry of Economy and Finance, containing the company's management principles and main financial results together with forecasts. In contrast, Italian listed SOEs publish standard annual reports, as all listed companies do.

In the developed countries with the SOE sector of minor scope and economic importance, there is often no codified and written state ownership policy, exhaustive systemic solutions that would define the principles of operation of SOEs. This is the situation in the UK, Canada and the US. For example, in the US, there is a great diversity in the legal provisions and organisational arrangements concerning the objectives, principles of operation and relationships of individual SOEs with the state owner. This results from the fact that the vast majority of SOEs, both at the federal and at the state levels, are established individually, most often by separate laws adopted by Congress.

In the developing and post-communist economies, usually with a very large or major scope of SOEs, relatively voluntarist ownership policies, heavily subordinated to current political objectives, are typical. The most common reason is that clear, codified and respected principles of the government behaviour towards SOEs constrain those in power and limit the voluntarism of authorities. They hinder the implementation of an important attribute of power in these countries, which is the use of SOEs as political spoils, usually belonging to the current government. There are two possible solutions here.

The first consists in replacing specific principles and rules of the ownership policy with vague, ideologically charged statements about the role of

SOEs in the economy, with the systemic absence of detailed information on the largest and most important SOEs. The most prominent example of this kind of "ownership policy" is China. SOEs of national importance are controlled in this country by the SASAC (State-Owned Assets Supervision and Administration Commission) agency operating under the authority of the State Council of China. A document entitled *Guidelines to the State-Owned Enterprises Directly under the Central Government* is published on the SASAC website (en.sasac.gov.cn), which in fact has little in common with the documents bearing similar titles from the Western countries. The purpose of this document is the following: "These Guidelines are proposed to comprehensively implement the spirit of the 17th Communist Party of China National Congress and the Scientific Outlook on Development, and give the impetus to state-owned enterprises (SOEs) directly under the central government". Its main idea is summarised in the sentences:

> CSOEs [SOEs directly under the central government] should take Deng Xiaoping Theory and the Important Thought of Three Represents as the guiding principles, thoroughly apply the Scientific Outlook on Development, adhere to the demands of human-oriented policy and sustainable development strategy from the Central Government of China, enhance their awareness of social responsibility and sustainable development.

SASAC also does not publish the economic results of individual SOEs. Only summary, what is more, outdated information covering the entire group of 96 SOEs overseen by the agency is available.

The second solution, used in countries such as Poland, Russia and Indonesia, is that there are relatively detailed, formally correct government documents such as Corporate Governance Codes and Guidelines, concerning the systemic principles of the state ownership control and ownership policy. These documents often refer to the *Guidelines on Corporate Governance of State-Owned Enterprises* recommended by the OECD (OECD, 2015). But these documents are not respected, and the principles of the relationship of the government and SOEs included therein are not observed. They exist only on paper, while in practice, other principles and other - hidden - methods of interaction are applied that can be identified and recognised only by analysing specific actions and decisions of the state exercising property rights, in particular, concerning the staffing of managerial positions in SOEs.[3] In general, the state ownership policy is subordinated to the current interests of the government on the one hand and the predatory function (in such form of rent extraction or another) on the other, usually hidden behind a mask of public interest.

Of course, the state ownership policy cannot completely ignore the issue of efficiency of SOEs, especially when they operate in competitive industries. The experience of many countries shows that there are generally two different ways to increase the efficiency of SOEs related to government actions. The first is to deregulate the environment of SOEs, hardening the soft budget constraints and reducing policy burdens, such as guarantees of employment for the workforce or welfare packages. The second is to make the internal principles of operation of SOEs similar to those of private companies. This is about professionalising the management, increasing the autonomy of SOEs, introducing internal evaluation systems, linking management personnel remuneration to the results or even partially privatising SOEs without losing the state's strategic control over them.

State ownership control in the developed countries uses both solutions, and when it comes to the latter, it is implemented in many of them comprehensively and at an advanced level. In Germany, Norway, New Zealand and Austria, the method of managing most large SOEs, their efficiency and corporate culture are at a level that is close to similar POEs. The situation is different in the developing and post-communist countries. Systemic deregulatory measures targeting the environment of SOEs are usually difficult to carry out for political and social reasons. Therefore, as a rule, the second method is used there. In the vast majority of major economies from this group of countries analysed further, such as Indian, Russian and Indonesian, modern strategic management solutions, incentive remuneration systems and other types of measures bringing the operation of SOEs closer to private companies are widely applied in SOEs (World Bank, 2014; Böwer, 2017). But the effects are only partially satisfactory, as the externally determined, political conditions and burdens on the activities of SOEs still remain.

2.3.3 State ownership control models

State ownership control models (sometimes referred to as Ownership Arrangements) create institutional frameworks for pursuing the ownership policy. OECD reports have popularised research and analyses in this field, although the OECD itself does not present a uniform position. Initially, OECD studies distinguished three types of ownership models: centralised, decentralised (sometimes also referred to as a sectoral model) and dual (OECD 2005, Figure 2.1), and in subsequent publications, there were five (2018, Table 4) or four models (2019, Figure 5.1).

Historically, the first to emerge was the decentralised model which, for the largest SOEs, means ministerial control. Postal or railway companies, and later also energy and industrial companies, were first, as EGEs, elements of various ministries, and then, after corporatisation, they were usually overseen by these ministries. Similarly, in all socialist economies, the control over SOEs was distributed among various line ministries which was a starting point in the transformation period, while in some post-communist countries, they survived for many years by force of inertia. The most frequently indicated advantage of the decentralised model is its industry-specific professionalism of control. Yet, nowadays, when the control focuses on corporate governance issues and setting strategic objectives of the organisation, and the operational issues are decided at the level of the professional management board, the industry-specific competence of the control is less relevant.

Still, the decentralised model has fundamental disadvantages. Line (sectoral) ministries combine control functions for a certain group of companies with regulatory functions for the entire sector, meaning both private and public, which leads to an inherent conflict and allegations of bias in pricing and procurement decisions. Private entities may be discriminated against. Separate interest groups are easily formed around ministries, which is conducive to the predatory function. Besides, the principles of operation and evaluation of SOEs are not uniform nationwide, which can cause various social and political tensions. It also makes it difficult to run a comparable evaluation and reporting of the SOE sector as a whole in the country.

After the Second World War, other models of state ownership control models gradually developed, mostly the dual model, where the Ministry of Finance has additional responsibilities and powers alongside line ministries. They usually oversee the financial and operational performance of SOEs. In this sense, the dual model ensures government control - at a uniform level - over the financial condition of the entire SOE sector. Most frequently, the dual ownership model is that one ministry sets financial objectives and another ministry formulates operational strategy. Obviously, the division of the control functions (exercising property rights) between the Ministry of Finance and line ministries is key here. The solutions applied around the world vary. There are solutions where line ministries "are on the front foot" and solutions where there is the balance of control. Germany is a characteristic example, where for several decades government control over SOEs has been successfully exercised precisely in the dual model.

In recent years, the centralised model has been widely perceived as the best institutional formula for exercising property rights by the state. The authors of the OECD report, which generally recommends the centralised model, write explicitly about "the growing trend of centralising the state's ownership function" (OECD, 2018, p. 10). Its main advantage is the separation of government ownership control over SOEs from regulatory functions directed towards all entities in the economy. It is also important to be able to provide uniform standards of control over SOEs, regardless of their industry, position in the economy, etc. The aforementioned OECD report additionally introduces a "twin track" model, denoting a situation where there are two governmental bodies, independent of each other, controlling SOEs, each with its "own" group of SOEs. For many years, such a model was used, for example, in Poland, where the Ministry of Treasury had control over most of the SOEs, but SOEs in the mining and energy sector were overseen by the Ministry of Industry, operating completely independently of the Ministry of Treasury.

The centralised model may take two significantly distinct forms, basically forming - in our view - two separate models. The first, which can be described as a centralised ministerial model, is that the property rights over

SOEs are exercised by the government body, mostly a relevant department of the Ministry of Finance or Economy, and sometimes even a special ministry (e.g. in Indonesia - the Ministry of Public Enterprises, and Poland - the Ministry of Treasury, and from 2019 - the Ministry of State Assets).

The second, which can be described as a centralised agency model, is that the government establishes a specialised agency or a holding company to which it delegates the property rights to be exercised over SOEs. This model seems more sensible than the ministerial one for one reason. As part of the ownership control, risky business decisions often need to be made. Ministerial officials, as a rule, have problems with making these kinds of decisions, while specialised employees of an agency or a supervisory holding should be able to address such challenges better. Besides, the agency or holding may be headed by a professional, appointed by way of a competition process, while a ministry is always headed by a politician, often having little to do with business management or corporate governance.

It should be added that it is quite typical in the world for a small group of the largest and most important SOEs to be centrally controlled, with control of the others to be dispersed. For example, in South Africa, the government Department of Public Entities oversees eight main SOEs, while in Belgium, only five most important SOEs are centrally controlled.

Of the 32 world's largest economies analysed in this book, 20 have a centralised state ownership control model, and only 5 have a decentralised model. Table 2.2 provides details on the subject, as well as - calculated based on the results of our empirical research - average shares of SOEs in the countries covered by a given model.

Table 2.2 State ownership control models in 32 world's largest economies*

No.	*Ownership model*	*Number of countries*	*Countries*	*Average share of SOEs (%)*
1	Decentralised	5	Argentina, Egypt, Japan, Mexico, US	20.5
2	Dual	8	Brazil, Canada, Germany, Italy, Korea, Switzerland, Thailand, Turkey	24.3
3	Centralised - agency	9	Austria, China, France, Russia, Saudi Arab., Singapore, Spain, Taiwan, UK	36.3
4	Centralised - ministerial	10	Australia, Belgium, India, Indonesia, Ireland, Netherlands, Norway, Poland, South Africa, Sweden	25.0

* In some countries, especially the less institutionally mature ones, there are relatively frequent changes of ownership models, so the data given above (usually reflecting the situation of a few years ago) may be partly outdated.

Source: Own compilation.

If we separate a subset of 15 economies with the highest share of SOEs from the analysed set of 32 economies, only 1 of them has a decentralised ownership model, 3 have dual models and 11 have centralised models (5 - agency and 6 - ministerial).

2.4 Summary and conclusions

1. The cross-country analysis shows a very deep differentiation of the types and principles of operation of SOEs, both historically and geographically. Considering the relationship between the state owner and SOEs, three basic types of SOEs can be distinguished:

   a. EGEs - entities directly linked to the government that are parts of public administration,
   b. statutory corporations - entities operating under special statutory laws,
   c. commercial (private) law companies - operating under the general provisions of the law of the country.

2. While in the late 19th century, most SOEs of the time were EGEs, today SOEs of the last group definitely prevail in the world. Among them, listed SOEs, so the entities with a mixed state-private ownership structure, controlled by governments, are particularly important. Of the 532 largest SOEs from 37 countries in 2018 analysed further, as many as 47% are listed SOEs, 1/3 of which are minority listed SOEs.
3. In our discussion on the rationales for and functions of SOEs, we tried to avoid two weaknesses that are quite common in the literature. First, of being limited to analysing the economies of the highly developed countries, as today SOEs are most important in the developing and post-communist countries. Second, of basing the analysis on the declarative rationales for and functions of SOEs formulated by the state owner, rather than those actually fulfilled. The latter are hidden in the case of many countries. Their disclosure would often mean that governments use SOEs in bad faith, as sources of political rents of various kinds, or tools to pursue specific social or political, and not just economic objectives.
4. Based on our research and various empirical studies that exist in the literature, we distinguish six functions of SOEs, economic and non-economic, and in the contemporary economy: market (economic), fiscal, development, social, strategic and predatory function. Their sequence is not random - in the subsequent positions, the influence of the economic factor decreases, while that of the political factor increases. The intensity and importance of particular functions are fundamentally different in the groups of developed and emerging market economies.
5. In the emerging market economies, especially those where the scope of SOEs is large, all presented functions are fulfilled with considerable

intensity. The situation is different for the developed market economies. In as many as 6 of the 19 developed market economies we analysed, the share of SOEs in the economy is negligible, and, consequently, the functions fulfilled by SOEs - either economic or non-economic - are practically irrelevant. However, in the rest of the developed market economies, all functions are fulfilled generally with lower intensity than in the emerging market economies. The difference between the distinguished groups of countries is particularly evident in the case of the predatory function, meaning the government acting towards SOEs in bad faith.

6 Similarly, fundamental differences between developed and developing countries are found in the field of the state ownership policy, whose objectives, principles and modes of implementation - generally speaking - derive directly from the functions of SOEs. In the developed countries, the state ownership policy is largely codified and pursued transparently, whereas in the developing countries, usually with a very large or major scope of SOEs, the arbitrariness of the ownership policy is typical, while the policy itself is poorly codified and heavily subordinated to political objectives.

7 Our analysis of the state corporate control models in the sample of the world's largest economies leads us to the conclusion that in approximately 60% of the countries, the centralised - ministerial or agency - model is used, as recommended by the OECD. This model is used in the four economies with the highest shares of SOEs - China, Saudi Arabia, Russia and Indonesia.

Notes

1 In many countries private companies, formally independent, actually show a significant degree of dependence on the government. China's Huawei is an example here.

2 By the scope of SOEs we mean their share and importance in the economy, mostly in the group of the largest and most important national companies.

3 More on the so-called party patronage and informal mechanisms of corporate governance in SOEs see Postuła, Wąsowska, 2020.

Bibliography

Baltowski, M., & Mickiewicz, T. (2006). Politicians or Administrators? State Corporate Governance in Poland. In T. Mickiewicz (Ed.), *Corporate Governance and Finance in Poland & Russia*. Amsterdam; London: Palgrave Macmillan.

Bernier, L., Florio, M., & Bance, P. (Eds.). (2020). *The Routledge Handbook of State-Owned Enterprises*. London; New York: Routledge.

Bertay, A. C., Demirgüç-Kunt, A., & Huizinga, H. (2015). Bank Ownership and Credit Over the Business Cycle: is Lending by State Banks Less Procyclical? *Journal of Banking & Finance*, *50*, 326–339.

Böwer, U. (2017). State-Owned Enterprises in Emerging Europe: The Good, the Bad, and the Ugly. *IMF*, IMF Working Papers, *17*(221).

Christiansen, H. (2011). *The Size and Composition of the SOE Sector in OECD Countries*. OECD Corporate Governance Working Papers, No. 5. Paris: OECD Publishing.

Christiansen, H. (2013). *Balancing Commercial and Non-commercial Priorities of State-Owned Enterprise*. OECD Corporate Governance Working Papers, No. 5. Paris: OECD Publishing.

Floyd, M. R. H., Gray, M. C. S., & Short, R. P. (1984). *Public Enterprise in Mixed Economies: Some Macroeconomic Aspects*. Washington, DC: International Monetary Fund.

Gillis, M. (1980). The Role of State Enterprises in Economic Development. *Social Research*, *47*(2), 248–289.

Heath, J., & Norman, W. (2004). Stakeholder Theory, Corporate Governance and Public Management: What Can the History of State-Run Enterprises Teach Us in the Post-Enron Era? *Journal of Business Ethics*, *53*(3), 247–265.

Hooijmaaijers, B. (2019). Blackening skies for Chinese investment in the EU? *Journal of Chinese Political Science*, *24*(3), 451–470.

Kastner, S. L., & Pearson, M. M. (2021). Exploring the Parameters of China's Economic Influence. *Studies in Comparative International Development*, *56*(1), 18–44.

Kozarzewski, P. (2021). *State Corporate Control in Transition: Poland in a Comparative Perspective*. Cham: Palgrave Macmillan.

Levesque, G. (2017, April 12). China's Evolving Economic Statecraft. *The Diplomat*.

Matuszak, P., & Szarzec, K. (2019). The Scale and Financial Performance of State-Owned Enterprises in the CEE Region. *Acta Oeconomica*, *69*(4), 549–570.

Mühlenkamp, H. (2015). From State to Market Revisited: A Reassessment of the Empirical Evidence on the Efficiency of Public (and Privately-Owned) Enterprises. *Annals of Public and Cooperative Economics*, *86*(4), 23.

OECD. (2005). *Corporate Governance of State-Owned Enterprises: A Survey of OECD Countries*. Paris: OECD Publishing.

OECD. (2013). *State-Owned Enterprises in the Middle East and North Africa. Engines of Development and Competitiveness*. Paris: OECD Publishing.

OECD. (2015). *OECD Guidelines on Corporate Governance of State-Owned Enterprises, 2015 Edition*. Paris: OECD Publishing.

OECD. (2018). *Ownership and Governance of State-Owned Enterprises: A Compendium of National Practices*. Paris: OECD Publishing.

Pargendler, M. (2011). State Ownership and Corporate Governance. *Fordham L. Rev.*, *80*, 2917.

Pustuła, I., & Wąsowska, M. (2020). Corporate Governance in State-Owned Enterprises: The Role of Informal Institutions. In L. Bernier, M. Florio, & P. Bance (Eds.), *The Routledge Handbook of State-Owned Enterprises*. London; New York: Routledge.

Putniņš, T. J. (2020). State-Owned Enterprises and the Public Mission: A Multidimensional Lens. In L. Bernier, M. Florio, & P. Bance (Eds.), *The Routledge Handbook of State-Owned Enterprises*. London; New York: Routledge.

Qi, H., & Kotz, D. M. (2020). The Impact of State-Owned Enterprises on China's Economic Growth. *Review of Radical Political Economics*, *52*(1), 96–114.

Richmond, C., Benedek, D., Cegar, B., Dohlman, P., Hassine, M., Jajko, B., Kopyrski, P., et al. (2019). Reassessing the Role of State-Owned Enterprises in Central, Eastern and Southeastern Europe. *International Monetary Fund European Departmental Paper Series*, *19*(11), 127.

Sorrentino, M. (2020). State-Owned Enterprises and the Public Mission: A Multidimensional Lens. In L. Bernier, M. Florio, & P. Bance (Eds.), *The Routledge Handbook of State-Owned Enterprises*. London; New York: Routledge.

Szarzec, K., Dombi, Á., & Matuszak, P. (2021). State-Owned Enterprises and Economic Growth: Evidence from the Post-Lehman Period. *Economic Modelling, 99.*

The World Bank. (2014). *Corporate Governance of State-Owned Enterprises*. Washington, DC: The World Bank.

The World Bank. (2015). *Governance Reforms of State-Owned Enterprises: Lessons from Four Case Studies (Egypt, Iraq, Morocco, and Tunisia)*. Washington, DC: The World Bank.

3 Research objectives and assumptions

Methodological framework

This chapter presents methodological issues related to the empirical research and its results contained in this book. In Section 1, the research objectives are formulated and basic research assumptions are discussed. In Section 2, we present a procedure specially developed for the preparation of empirical data, the use of which is a prerequisite for obtaining methodologically correct research results. In Section 3, we introduce and justify four basic share ratios used in the aggregate data analyses and in the comparative analysis of the scope and significance of SOEs in 37 countries of the world and other indicators used in the analyses presented in Chapters 4-7. In Section 4, we outline the method and extent of presentation of the research results.

3.1 Research objectives and assumptions

3.1.1 Research objectives

This book has two major objectives. The first is to determine - based on original empirical research - the condition, share and significance of state-owned enterprises (SOEs) in the contemporary economy, and more specifically in the set of 32 of the world's largest economies (WLEs) (divided into groups of developed market economies (DMEs) and emerging market economies (EMEs)) and additionally in the 6 economies of post-communist countries, EU member states (PCEs). Given that one economy - that of Poland - is included in both sets, eventually, 37 economies are analysed. The second objective - closely related to the previous one - is to conduct an in-depth cross-country analysis concerning SOEs and, based on it, show diverse development trends and changes in the presence of SOEs in the various sets of economies after the financial crisis of 2008-2009. As part of the second objective, we also make a brief econometric analysis of the relationship between various characteristics of the economic system and SOE shares.

The first objective, seemingly fundamental for conducting research, has in fact never been given due consideration in the economic literature. The primary source of empirical knowledge on SOEs in the global economy are the analytical reports prepared by international organisations,

DOI: 10.4324/9781003244462-4

such as the World Bank (WB) (World Bank, 2014a; World Bank, 2014b), the Organisation for Economic Co-operation and Development (OECD) (Christiansen, 2011; Kowalski et al., 2013; OECD, 2014; OECD, 2017), the International Monetary Fund (IMF) (Böwer, 2017; Richmond et al., 2019; IMF, 2020) and the European Commission (2016). These reports, usually concerning either selected groups of countries or some regions of the world, differ - as their authors also note - in terms of definitions of SOEs adopted as well as the completeness of data. Therefore, the use of the information contained therein as the basis for in-depth scientific research, especially extensive comparative studies, is very limited. The OECD presents a database on SOEs on its website, which, however, contains information from different sources that is difficult to compare (mainly data provided by individual countries), while the most recent data is from 2014 (checked in mid-2021). For example, according to the data in the OECD report, there are 48 centrally controlled SOEs in France, while the 2020 report of the French government agency APE (*Agence des participations de l'État*) shows that the state has ownership stakes in 85 large entities, in 58 of which these shares exceed 25%. Similar discrepancies between data in the OECD database and the actual situation are seen also when it comes to the number of employees in SOEs in Poland.

Economists dealing with various aspects of the operation of SOEs are well aware of the shortcomings in the basic quantitative knowledge on this subject. The most recent important publication in this field states: "The empirical literature on SOEs is voluminous but disjointed, with hundreds of firm-level, industry-level and country-level case studies. Global analyses are uncommon" (Bernier et al., 2020, p. 6). And further: "[the] dataset is far from exhaustive, not just in terms of country coverage, but even for the countries considered". A similar view is expressed in the WB report: "a systematic inventory of SOEs worldwide by size, type, and economic weight is lacking" (2014a, p. 20).

The academic literature widely cites and uses rather general calculations concerning the scope of SOEs (often repeated in publications in subsequent years), based on outdated, partial empirical studies, which, for example, state that SOEs cover 10% of the global economy (Kowalski et al., 2013; Bruton et al., 2015; Bernier et al., 2020) or that SOEs account for some 20% of the global investments and 5% of employment (Robinett 2006; World Bank, 2014a). Our research, conducted based on the methodology that is comparable for many countries, shows a generally higher and highly variable share of SOEs in the global economy, at the same time very differentiated in various countries and country groups.

It should be made clear that empirical research on the scope of SOEs on a global scale, while undoubtedly important and necessary, is an unrewarding and difficult field of economic analysis. The set of economic entities generally referred to as "state-owned enterprises" is blurred and vague. In order to distinguish SOEs from all economic entities, the meticulous application of two methodologically complex procedures is necessary: one is to distinguish SOEs from private entities, and the other to distinguish SOEs from those state-owned entities that cannot be described as "enterprises" (or "companies"). Both of them must involve a degree of arbitrariness. However, the point is to limit this arbitrariness as much as possible and - most importantly - to systemise it, i.e. to make it apply equally to SOEs in a large group of surveyed countries so that the condition of comparability of the results obtained is met.

In the world statistics (and in the statistics of international organisations), as well as in the statistics of individual countries, it is possible to find a lot of information concerning "state-owned enterprises", but this term in different countries and different data sets covers various specific entities. Sometimes these are only 100% SOEs, and in other cases entities with majority state ownership and every so often with minority state ownership. A special and important group of SOEs, often ignored by public statistics and empirical studies, are entities with indirect state ownership - various types of first-tier subsidiaries or second-tier subsidiaries of state enterprises and/or other state entities or agencies.

The problem of distinguishing and defining SOEs, crucial for the reliability and quality of any empirical research concerning their condition, role and importance in the economy, is discussed in more detail in the following section. We are convinced that the approach we have adopted satisfactorily resolves the fundamental methodological difficulties the researchers of state ownership in the modern world are always faced with. Satisfactorily, meaning in a way that, with all natural deviations from the ideal, leads to reliable results allowing for comparative and synthetic analyses of a large group of countries.

It would be impossible to achieve the second objective concerning the various aspects of cross-country analysis of SOEs, presence of SOEs in various groups of countries and development trends in this area in recent years, without an adequate empirical database on the condition of SOEs in many countries over a longer time horizon. We have created such a database of an original nature in the research on SOEs to date and used it in the book for a wide range of analyses according to various criteria, such as size, industry, time, geography, political system, level of development, etc.

3.1.2 Basic research assumptions

The empirical research, the results of which are presented in this book, is based on two basic methodological assumptions. The first concerns the narrowing of the field of analysis to the collections of the largest SOEs in a given country. The second concerns the adoption of a definition of SOEs that is uniform for all countries, broad but possible to be operationalised, based on the category of actual corporate control and not on the category of formal state ownership. We discuss these in more detail below.

A. Focus on the set of the largest SOEs in each country

Researchers of SOEs, aiming for completeness of the results obtained, usually try to cover as many companies as possible. Consequently, as U. Böwer, the author of the IMF report referred to above, writes: "[the analysed] SOEs vary in size, from small local entities with only a few employees to large-scale companies, notably in the network industries" (Böwer, 2017, p. 5). While such an approach would make sense if an ideal database existed and in the absence of the problems with definitions of SOEs, which we discuss later in this chapter, in practice, in the global economy, this is impossible to achieve while maintaining methodological correctness. The inclusion of broad sets of SOEs in many countries comes at a price in the form of reducing the reliability and comparability of the data obtained. There are many differences - in the sense of the role and functions in the economy or the principles of management - between local SOEs of public utility and SOEs that compete in global markets with the major global industry players.

In our empirical research covering 37 countries, we focused on the collections of the largest SOEs in a given country. The largest, meaning those that are in the Top 100 of domestic non-financial companies, ranked by operating revenues (ORs). We do so for three reasons.

First, because the largest companies, both private and state-owned, are central to any modern economy. Their dynamics, innovativeness as well as sectoral and ownership structure determine the operation, capabilities and development directions of the economic system. This is particularly the case with so-called strategic industries - power sector, national transport, telecommunications or banking - which in most countries of the world are characterised by a high level of concentration.

Second, because when it comes to the scope and functions of the largest SOEs, differences between individual countries are substantial. These large SOEs - as we wrote in the previous chapter - are the tools used by the governments of many countries to fulfil various, not only economic, functions. In contrast, small SOEs, especially at the regional and local (municipal) levels, have a similar scope in most countries of the world. They usually fulfil public service functions. In this area, the differences between the countries are relatively small, and even if they do occur, they do not significantly affect the economy and the state.

Third, because financial data as well as ownership structure data related to the largest, relatively few SOEs - given all the reservations mentioned above as to the problems with data - are more easily available and verifiable, therefore being more reliable than the data related to a very large set of small SOEs. This reason is particularly important in our research methodology, presented below, which is based on an individual analysis of each (potential) SOE. Such an analysis is possible even for many countries of the world in the case of a dozen or a few dozen domestic enterprises (and thus in the case of the largest SOEs), but in practice, it is unrealistic in the case of many hundreds or thousands of small SOEs.

Finally, there are publications indicating the importance of large SOEs in the economy and using data on large SOEs in various analyses (e.g. Kowalski et al., 2013; Kwiatkowski & Augustynowicz, 2015; IMF, 2020). The authors of these publications usually use the lists of the world's largest companies (Fortune Global 500, Forbes Global 2000), distinguishing entities that meet the definition of SOEs. However, such an approach has fundamental methodological flaws. The Fortune Global 500 does recognise entities in which the state has 50% or more ownership shares, but in recent years there have only been around 120 of them, of which 70% are Chinese SOEs. Therefore, it is by no means a sample representative for the global economy, especially because the Fortune Global list is, for obvious reasons, very strongly dominated by the companies from the WLEs - American, Chinese and Japanese. In turn, the Forbes Global 2000 list contains four times more companies (and about two times more SOEs) than the Fortune 500, but it is limited to listed companies, thus also listed SOEs. Therefore, the list does not include a series of very large and important SOEs, from China and elsewhere, for example, Saudi Aramco (fully SOE by 2020), Petroleos Mexicanos (Pemex) and the American US Postal Service (USPS).

In our research, we focus not on the set of the world's largest SOEs, which is very strongly dominated by the SOEs from China (discussed in detail in Conclusions), but the set of the largest SOEs in each of the 32 WLEs. It seems that such a delimitation of the field of analysis is more conducive to recognising and understanding the phenomenon of SOEs in the contemporary global economy and forms a good basis for cross-country analysis.

B. Adoption of a detailed definition of an SOE uniform for all countries

While 100 or even 50 years ago, the distinction between "private companies" and "state companies" was not very problematic,[1] in the last 20–30 years, the situation has changed significantly. Mixed capital state-private companies emerged in many countries, which fundamentally distorted the old dichotomous "SOE vs. non-SOE" division. Since the last decade of the 20th century in most countries of the world, large-scale privatisation processes of SOEs were carried out, also using the capital market. In many cases, involving large entities, these were only partial privatisations, resulting in the creation of large, economically significant state-private companies, sometimes referred to as "hybrid organisations" (Bruton et al., 2015), such as Sinopec (China, 68% state shareholding), Indian Oil Corporation (India, 73%), Korea Electric Power Corporation (South Korea, 58%), Vale (Brazil, 31%), Deutsche Telekom (Germany, 32%), Orange (France, 29%) and Enel (Italy, 24%).

But these partial privatisation processes have sometimes led to a situation where the government - e.g. through certain provisions in the articles of association of the company - still retained actual corporate control over the formally private company with majority private capital. This kind of privatisation, as we mentioned in Chapter 1, has been given the name of "reluctant privatisation" in the literature. The creators of this term, based on the study of a large group of privatised companies in the OECD countries – find that "many cases of privatisation are characterized by the sale of equity without a proportional transfer of control" (Bortolotti & Faccio 2009, p. 2908). Similar conclusions emerge from detailed studies of many cases of privatisations in Poland (Baltowski, 2017). This means that the borderline between "private" and "state" becomes difficult to define clearly. The actual state governance over an enterprise may often be of a non-ownership type, so the definition of a "state-owned enterprise" cannot refer only to the formal ownership stake of the state in an enterprise.

Obviously, this is not a revealing observation. Many contemporary scholars rightly assume the actual corporate control (corporate control, similarly to property rights, is gradable) of the state over the enterprise as the feature that distinguishes the entities referred to in the literature as "state-owned enterprises" (or "state companies") from "private-owned enterprises" (or "private companies"). Here, reference can be made to the studies of Shapiro & Globerman (2012), Cuervo-Cazurra et al. (2014), Musacchio & Lazzarini (2014) and Baltowski & Kozarzewski (2016). In an important OECD document, creating a framework for the reform and practice of SOE control, this view is stated explicitly: "[The term SOEs refers] to enterprises where the state has significant control..." (OECD, 2005, p. 183). In another OECD document, its authors write explicitly that "the term 'ownership' is understood to imply control" (OECD, 2016, p. 18). We find a similar statement in the report of the WB: "The SOE sector [...] includes SOEs that are government-owned or controlled" (World Bank 2014a, p. 26).

However - so far - this kind of definitional approach has not been sufficiently translated into empirical studies of SOEs, especially into extensive comparative studies on a global scale, meaning comprising many countries. A fundamental and difficult methodological problem arises here - how to operationalise the expression "the state has significant control" in the study of relations between states (governments) and enterprises? How can this general statement defining SOEs by actual control of the government be used to distinguish them in the case of extensive sets of enterprises operating in various countries and under different legal and institutional systems? In the vast majority of empirical studies in the literature, including important and frequently cited ones, the authors adopt simple, but incomplete and misleading definitions of SOEs, reduced to the size of the formal ownership stake of the state capital. This is even done by the OECD in its empirical research, which does not apply its own definitions of SOEs cited above. For example, in the research of Kowalski et al. (2013), the issue of corporate control with lower ownership stakes is acknowledged, but the underlying definition of SOEs covers the entities with the threshold of 50% of government ownership exceeded.

The IMF research, carried out similarly to our research, based on the source data contained in the Orbis database provided by Bureau van Dijk, adopts a similar, very restrictive definition of SOEs: "state ownership is defined as a minimum stake of 50.1 percent" (Böwer, 2017, p. 5). The threshold of 50% of state ownership is also adopted in the research of Kwiatkowski and Augustynowicz (2015) and Kowalski et al. (2013). There are also studies in which this threshold is set - arbitrarily - at a lower level. The most common level is 25% (e.g. Szarzec & Nowara, 2017 for European countries or Baltowski & Kozarzewski, 2016 for Poland), and some researchers push this limit even to 10% - e.g. Christiansen & Kim (2014) and De Lange & Marlevede (2020). UNCTAD (United Nations Conference on Trade and Development) reports adopt a very capacious definition of SOEs, based on the threshold of state ownership of 10%: "a governmental entity [SOE] should either own at least 10 percent of the capital, be the largest shareholder, or hold a 'golden share'" (UNCTAD, 2019, p. 32). Bruton et al. (2015) distinguish three types of SOEs, based on the different scale of government ownership: "We defined 'high level of government ownership' as ownership greater than 50%, 'intermediate level' as 25% to 50%, and 'low level' as less than 25%". In the OECD report concerning the sizes of SOEs, minority-owned state enterprises are defined as the entities "in which the state holds between 10 and 50 percent ordinary share capital or voting rights" (OECD, 2014, p. 10), with the condition of state control met. However, neither clear criteria nor procedures are given to determine - especially in the case of large sets of enterprises - the circumstances under which the condition of state control is met.

In the case of listed companies, when there are many small shareholders, the shareholding of the government (or of any other shareholder) at the level of 25%-30% usually means actual corporate control, so qualifying such an entity as an SOE (listed SOE) is correct. Examples of such SOEs include the French Orange (29.5%), Italian Enel (23.6%) and Polish PKN Orlen (27.5%). However, this is not an absolute rule. For example, in the listed company Telekom Austria, the Austrian government holds (via state holding ÖBAG) 28.4% of the stocks. Yet, this company is not classified as an SOE in our analysis, as 51% of the stocks (so the stake guaranteeing actual corporate control) are held by the Mexican telecommunications giant - América Móvil.

Our solution to the problem of defining SOEs by determining the size of actual state control, and not only the formal ownership stake, is – drawing on researches like Faccio & Lang (2002) and Bortolotti & Faccio (2009) – based on the specific individualised research procedure outlined in the further part. The procedure is applied to those companies for which the ownership criterion does not provide a clear answer as to whether we are dealing with an entity controlled by the state (SOE) or a private entity. The procedure covers two main groups of entities: (a) companies with state-private capital with minority state shareholding of 15%-50% and (b) companies indirectly dependent on the state, i.e. subsidiaries and second-tier subsidiaries of various state entities.

The second, important problem with defining SOEs as commercial entities, operating on the market, is to distinguish them from other state-owned entities, often similar in organisational and legal terms, but of a non-commercial type. The difficulty stems from the fact that frequently the commercial activities of state-owned entities are combined with the activities that can be described as missionary, financed from state subsidies rather than from revenues obtained from the market. In many countries, this is the case for radio and television broadcasters, and in some countries for postal services and other groups of public services. A good example of this kind of problem is found in the IMF report:

> Hospitals and medical centres account for around half of SOEs in Bulgaria as they are set up as trade companies since a healthcare reform in 2000. In other countries, the healthcare sector plays a far smaller role or is completely absent from the SOE dataset.
>
> (Bӧwer, 2017, p. 6)

This problem, like many others in the case of research on SOEs, cannot be solved by making one generally valid assumption or one delimiting principle. There are so many specific cases arising from national law (and common law) that only a "case by case" analysis can lead to satisfactory results. It should be noted that these non-commercial state-owned entities, cultural or healthcare institutions, are generally not large enough to be included in the Top 100 largest domestic companies. Thus, if we limit the research and analysis to a group of the largest SOEs, as is done in this book, the problem of distinguishing state-owned commercial and non-commercial entities becomes marginal and may occur only occasionally.

3.2 Procedure for the preparation of empirical data

3.2.1 Sets of source data used and their general characteristics

The basic source of raw data for our research was the Orbis (Bureau van Dijk/Moody's) worldwide database of companies. In addition, we used other sources quite extensively - ranking lists such as the Fortune Global 500 and Forbes Global 2000, or regional and national lists of the largest companies, such as Coface Top 500 CEE, etc. We also used information from websites of individual companies and various studies and reports, for individual countries, regions, as well as industries (OECD, WB, IMF, etc.).

Most governments, especially of the countries with a centralised state ownership control model (except, for example, the US or Italy), publish annual reports showing the current condition of the SOE sector (usually of the largest, centrally overseen entities). We have, of course, used these documents in our research, although to a limited extent. These national official reports are divided into two groups. The first group of reports (e.g. Germany, Sweden, Norway and Turkey) contains relatively comprehensive individual information, including financial information, on a large set of SOEs (which - it should be highlighted - are defined differently), but often lacks the "operating revenues" category, fundamental to the data contained in the Orbis database, creating problems with data comparability. Naturally, the accuracy and completeness of the data contained in these reports vary from country to country. The second group (the best example of which is China, as we mentioned in Section 2.3.2) includes reports containing only aggregate data on the entire SOE sector, without data on individual companies. They are therefore completely useless for our research. It should be added that national reports usually do not include data on SOEs with indirect state ownership and rarely include data on companies with minority state ownership, controlled using non-ownership tools.

Using all possible available data and following a special procedure of cleaning the source data (as discussed below) for each of the 37 countries, ranking lists of the 100 largest (by ORs) non-financial companies for the years 2009, 2013, 2018 were compiled – in total 111 Top 100 lists. Additionally, Top 20 lists for all countries for 2011 and 2015 (74 Top 20 lists) were created. This meant that the research covered 12,580 statistical units (companies on 185 Top 100 and Top 20 lists), with most of the companies from a given country recurring on the lists for different years, although quite often their ownership characteristics (so the type of the owner or the size of ownership) changed.

Each statistical unit was assigned three economic parameters available in the Orbis database, also cross-checked against other sources:

a operating revenues (ORs),
b total assets (TAs),
c industry,

and one of the two ownership features: SOE or non-SOE. For the set of SOEs (so the entities actually controlled by the state), the level of state ownership (direct and indirect) was also determined for each entity, which enabled the identification of two groups of companies:

a with the majority ownership (more than 50%), including full ownership (100%),
b with the minority ownership (50% and less).

Semantic doubts may be raised by including SOEs with full state ownership in the "majority ownership" group. However, it is done by many authors dealing with SOE-related issues (Bernier et al., 2020, p. 311; Musacchio & Lazzarini, 2014, Figure 1.1).

Additionally, listed SOEs have been distinguished from the set of SOEs. From our database, we have also distinguished a category of companies that are directly or indirectly controlled by the governments of other countries. We refer to these companies as "foreign SOEs" (for more, see Section 7.2). In both cases, the distinction was made based on special, individual research procedures.

Finally, it is necessary to explain the principles of determining the set of countries for the empirical research. The basis was the List of Countries by GDP (nominal) for 2018, according to the IMF, on the one hand, and a set of data collected based on the Orbis database and other sources, on the other. The data collected enabled the compilation of the lists of the Top 100 non-financial companies for 2009, 2013, 2018 for the 27 WLEs (from the US to Austria), as well as for Norway (item 29) and Ireland (item 32). For three countries (Iran - item 28, United Arab Emirates - item 30, Nigeria - item 31) the data were exceptionally incomplete and did not meet the reliability condition. These countries were therefore replaced with three subsequent countries from close geographic surroundings, for which it was possible - with considerable effort and workload - to achieve complete lists of the Top 100 non-financial companies for the analysed years: Singapore, South Africa, Egypt. For the subsequent, smaller and smaller countries, obtaining reliable lists of the Top 100 companies for 2009, 2013, 2018 was impossible; therefore, we limited our analysis to 32 countries.

In the case of five post-communist countries, EU member states, not included in the group of the 32 WLEs, the data in the Orbis database were also incomplete. We supplemented them with various reliable data, mainly from the "COFACE CEE Top 500" rankings of companies in this group of countries available for all the analysed years. The sixth analysed post-communist economy, Poland, was among the 32 WLEs.

3.2.2 Processing, cleaning and enhancement of source data

Using the source data contained in the Orbis database and other data sets as the basis for the empirical research required two types of cleaning procedures that enabled us to

a avoid double counting of certain companies - due to the presence in the Orbis database of parent companies including consolidated data of subsidiaries, as well as subsidiaries with their own data,

b move from the information contained in the Orbis database on the basic ownership structure of a given company ("direct ownership of controlling shareholders") to the identification of SOEs, so the entities over which the state has "significant control".

Re (a)

The risk of the possibility of double counting some company data based on the Orbis database has been noticed in the past by researchers using this database (Gal & Hijzen, 2016; Freund & Sidhu, 2017). In our analysis, we applied the solutions presented by these authors, and, additionally, we verified the data relating to each specific (questionable) entity, using other sources of information.

When the ownership interest of a parent company having a consolidated financial account with the subsidiary was greater than 50%, the subsidiary was excluded. In the case of duplicate data for a holding company and a company belonging to the holding, as a rule, the holding was excluded while the holding companies were left. In some disputable cases, the final decision whether to retain or exclude a given company from the examined set was made based on the information from other sources than the Orbis database - we analysed financial statements of parent companies (holding companies) and the information from their websites.

Re (b)

The Orbis database contains information on the ownership structure of each company, which is not always complete and unambiguous. The data shows ownership interests - direct and indirect - of all main company's shareholders (usually holding at least 5% of the shares). They are also presented according to timelines although a full history of ownership changes is frequently not available.

Of the 12,580 statistical units (companies) considered, for the years 2009, 2011, 2013, 2015, 2018, in less than 85% of cases the readout of the ownership structure did not raise any doubts. Thus, about 8,800 statistical units were assigned the "non-SOE" feature and about 1,800 - the "SOE" feature (the latter as majority state-owned entities). For the remaining nearly 2,000 units, the ownership feature (SOE or non-SOE) was not clear, i.e. it was not directly apparent from the data contained in the Orbis database. These were statistical units comprising mixed ownership enterprises with minority state ownership (15%–50%), sometimes even split between different state entities and companies with indirect state ownership.

Each of these statistical units (a significant part of companies reappeared in successive years, although sometimes their ownership situation changed, so in fact, there were about 650 companies) was subjected to individual research conducted by a dedicated team of doctoral students (this work was carried out as part of a research project funded by the National Science Centre, project No. 2017/25/B/HS4/01103). The research aimed to determine whether "significant control" was exercised by the state in a specific case (of a given company in a particular year). The research procedure involved searching for and analysing a variety of information on these "debatable" companies. They analysed "annual reports" and other documents of individual companies, websites and press releases, and in some cases also minutes of general shareholder meetings and meetings of supervisory boards, where key corporate decisions determining the issues of "significant control" were made (appointing members of company bodies, distributing profits, determining company plans, etc.).

As a result of this painstaking analysis, it was found that in approximately 65% of the doubtful cases, the analysed entity could be classified as state-controlled (and thus meeting the definition of an SOE), while the remaining cases were classified as private companies. Consequently, ownership features, SOE or non-SOE, were assigned to each entity on each Top 100 list (and Top 20, respectively). The entities classified as "SOEs" were further divided into majority SOEs and minority SOEs.

The problem of a cascading ownership structure (indirect government ownership) has been addressed by analysing the ownership structure of the entities that control a given company, and sometimes also the entities that control these entities. The aim was to determine the influence of the government and/or the influence of government-controlled entities and whether this influence could be described as "significant". This was the basis for assigning a given company the "SOE" or "non-SOE" feature. When necessary, in order to determine the scope of the actual control of the government over a given enterprise, other information from outside the Orbis database was also used - company websites, industry reports, press releases, etc. - relating to company owners.

3.3 Share ratios of SOEs and other indicators used in the analysis

3.3.1 Share ratios of SOEs

The most important indicator used in the analysis to determine the share of SOEs in the economy is the **SS-100** index (share of SOEs in the Top 100), i.e. the arithmetic mean of the share of SOEs (as a percentage) in the Top 100 non-financial companies by ORs and by total assets, so two basic financial categories available in the Orbis database for each company:

$$\boldsymbol{SS-100} = \frac{1}{2}\left(\frac{ORS}{ORL} + \frac{TAS}{TAL}\right) x\ 100\%$$

where:

ORS - the sum of values of ORs of a group of SOEs from the Top 100 set in a given year,

TAS - the sum of values of TAs of a group of SOEs from the Top 100 set in a given year,

ORL - the sum of values of ORs of all enterprises from the Top 100 set in a given year,

TAL - the sum of values of TAs of all enterprises from the Top 100 set in a given year.

Throughout the book, when the general term "share of SOEs" is used, we mean precisely the share expressed by the SS-100 index.

We determine the **SS-20** index (share of SOEs in the Top 20) in the same way, taking into account the Top 20 set of non-financial companies. The SS-20 index is treated as the basis for determining the importance of SOEs in the economy.

The second share ratio of SOEs is **Rev-100/GDP** (and **Rev-20/GDP**, respectively). We define it as the percentage relation of the sum of values of ORs of all SOEs from the Top 100 (Top 20) set to the nominal GDP of a country in a given year.

$$\frac{\boldsymbol{Rev-100}}{\boldsymbol{GDP}} = \frac{ORS}{GDP} x\ 100\%$$

where:

GDP - the value of nominal GDP in a given year.

The miS-100 ratio defines the share of minority SOEs in the total group of SOEs in a given set. We define it as the arithmetic mean of the shares by ORs and total assets of minority SOEs from the Top 100 in the shares of all SOEs from the Top 100 in a given year:

$$\boldsymbol{miS-100} = \frac{1}{2}\left(\frac{ORmiS}{ORS} + \frac{TAmiS}{TAS}\right)$$

where:

ORmiS - the sum of values of ORs of a group of minority SOEs from the Top 100 set in a given year,

TAmiS - the sum of values of TAs of a group of minority SOEs from the Top 100 set in a given year.

The **CS-20** ratio shows the degree of concentration of SOEs in the Top 20 group. We define it as the ratio of the share of SOEs in the Top 20 to the share of SOEs in the Top 100:

$$\boldsymbol{CS-20} = \frac{SS-20}{SS-100}$$

The value of CS-20 greater than 1 means that the share of SOEs in the Top 20 is greater than the share in the Top 100.

3.3.2 Indicators for estimating the share of SOEs in strategic industries

In addition to identifying and analysing the detailed data on the largest SOEs in the Top 100 non-financial domestic companies, as part of the empirical research, we have estimated the presence of SOEs in six industries. These are industries in which SOEs have traditionally had and continue to have a strong presence and which can be described as strategic:

- railways,
- postal sector,
- telecommunications,
- energy,
- oil and gas,
- banking sector.

Our analysis generally covers non-financial companies. In the estimation of SOEs' shares in strategic industries, the banking sector is an exception.

The estimation followed the procedure presented below:

1 Determining the top five companies by revenue (and in the case of banks, by assets) in a given industry (Top 5), using data from the Orbis database as well as various industry reports. For some countries and highly concentrated oligopolistic industries, these were four or even three largest companies.
2 Identifying a group of SOEs among the Top 5, i.e. entities over which the government - directly or indirectly - exercises corporate control.
3 Determining the share of revenues of the SOE group in the revenues of the Top 5 (for banks - assets, respectively). The basis for the estimation was the ratio of the revenues of the SOEs in the Top 5 to the revenues of all companies making up the Top 5 of a given industry, determining the share of SOEs in each industry.

We have adopted the following scale of SOE shares in each industry:

- index "4" - monopolistic or near-monopolistic share of SOEs,
- index "3" - dominating share of SOEs, exceeding 50%,
- index "2" - significant share of SOEs, 15%-50%,
- index "1" - low share of SOEs, 5%-15%,
- index "0" - no or negligible share of SOEs.

In the case of industries strongly dominated by large players (oil and gas, telecommunications, energy), estimating the share of SOEs did not pose many problems, although it required an in-depth search for data, as quite often the companies from the Top 5 of a given industry were not in the Top 100 non-financial companies, for which we had precise, verified data. Similarly, the estimation in the case of the banking sector was fairly easy, as almost all examined countries publish reports covering the largest financial institutions. More difficult, although feasible at the estimation level, was the determination of the share of SOEs in the railway industry, typically more fragmented and consisting of two distinct sub-sectors - railway operating companies and railway infrastructure organisation companies.

The most problematic was the estimation of the share of SOEs in the industry traditionally defined as the postal sector. Nowadays, the postal sector consists of two quite distinct subindustries - traditional postal services and the so-called CEP (courier, express and parcel) industry. When it comes to traditional postal services, state-owned monopolists or quasi-monopolists still exist in many of the surveyed countries. By contrast, the CEP industry is dominated by private operators in every country, although very often the role of the traditional national postal service is also significant there. The problem also lies in the fact that the CEP industry tends to be highly fragmented, with many entities that are not in the Top 100 operating in it. Additionally, the fact that postal companies in many countries are also involved in financial activities (banking and insurance), often with higher revenues than from the traditional postal activity, must be taken into account. In such cases, we have only included the revenues from postal activities.

We also introduced a synthetic indicator **SS-I** (share of SOEs in strategic industries), which we define as the arithmetic mean of the previously estimated shares of SOEs in six strategic industries. The SS-I indicator can take a value between 0 and 4. We use it in the sectoral analysis (Section 6.2), as well as in econometric analysis (Section 7.3).

The choice of industries to be analysed, slightly different than the arrangement of industries used to characterise the largest domestic SOEs in Chapters 4 and 5, as well as the way SOE share ratios are defined are not coincidental. We refer to the analogous analysis contained in the book edited by P.A. Toninelli (2000, p. 275), which covers 18 countries (all of which are also analysed in our book) and presents the situation as of 1978.[2] A detailed comparison of the results of both analyses is presented in Section 6.2.

3.4 Presentation of research results

3.4.1 Data for individual countries

The presentation of the main research results for individual countries is divided into two chapters. In the very extensive Chapter 4, we present data for 2018, and some data also for earlier years, i.e. 2009, 2011, 2013, 2015, for the 32 WLEs, arranged alphabetically. In the next, much shorter chapter, we present analogous data for the five post-communist countries. The data for each country consists of the following elements:

1 The number and position of SOEs on the lists of the world's largest companies, i.e. Forbes Global and Fortune Global for 2018 and 2009 - based on our detailed analysis of these lists.
2 The list of the largest SOEs (from the Top 100 group of non-financial companies in the country) in 2018.

We present ten largest SOEs by ORs. For each SOE, we also provide the industry, value of total assets, employment size, position on the

Top 100 list and the size of state ownership (direct or indirect). If the number of SOEs in the Top 100 is less than ten, the table is limited to that number.

The reliability of data on the employment size, provided for all companies, can sometimes be questionable. Though the Orbis database contains information on employment in individual companies, it does not always seem to be fully reliable. The entities with consolidated financial data of subsidiaries are also problematic, as the data on "consolidated" employment is difficult to obtain. Yet, the data on the employment size is practically not taken into account in the further synthetic and comparative analyses.

3 Tables showing the position of SOEs in the sets of the largest non-financial companies in the country - Top 10, Top 20, Top 50 and Top 100 for 2009, 2013 and 2018 in three dimensions: number of SOEs, share in ORs, share in total assets. In each case, we also distinguish between "majority SOEs" and "minority SOEs".
4 Figures showing the changes over time of selected data concerning SOEs:

   a shares of SOEs in the Top 20 in 2009, 2011, 2013, 2015, 2018.
   b shares of SOEs in the Top 10, Top 20, Top 50, Top 100 in 2009, 2013, 2018.

5 Tables showing other characteristics of the set of SOEs of a given country:

   a the estimated share of SOEs in selected industries, according to the principles set out above in Section 3.3.2,
   b the number of listed SOEs in the Top 100 in 2009, 2013, 2018, including minority listed SOEs,
   c the number and basic characteristics of foreign SOEs in the Top 100 (which are not included in the set of SOEs of a given country analysed further).

6 The table with share ratios for a given economy calculated according to the formulae above.

3.4.2 Aggregated and comparative data

In Chapter 6, we present the most important aggregate research results referring mainly to the four identified groups of countries. The first, basic group consists of 32 WLEs by nominal GDP - see Section 3.2.1 above. We divide the WLE group into two smaller groups based on two criteria:

- the value of Human Development Index (HDI) 2018,
- the value of Democracy Index 2018.

On this basis (each of the above criteria forms an essentially analogous division) we distinguish:

- 19 developed market economies (DMEs) - Australia, Austria, Belgium, Canada, France, Germany, Ireland, Italy, Japan, Korea, the Netherlands, Norway, Singapore, Spain, Sweden, Switzerland, Taiwan, the UK, the US;
- 13 emerging market economies (EMEs) - Argentina, Brazil, China, Egypt, India, Indonesia, Mexico, Poland, Russia, Saudi Arabia, South Africa, Thailand, Turkey.

The DME group includes countries for which the HDI value in 2018 exceeds 0.87 and which are described as "full democracies" or "flawed democracies"; the EME group includes the remaining countries of the 32 WLEs. As is well known, the set of countries referred to as emerging market economies or emerging markets is inconsistently defined by various international agencies, organisations and funds. Our division is closest to the approach used by the BBVA Research Emerging and Growth-Leading Economies (EAGLEs) - https://www.bbvaresearch.com/wp-content/uploads/2016/05/BBVA-EAGLEs-20161.pdf.

The fourth group consists of six post-communist economies, EU member states - Bulgaria, the Czech Republic, Hungary, Poland, Romania, Slovakia. As we mentioned, the Polish economy appears twice - as the only one - in our lists: in the EME group as well as in the PCE group.

Chapter 6 consists of four parts, the first three of which contain data for 2018. In the first, we examine the condition, shares in the economy and types of SOEs. In the second, we show and analyse the sectoral distribution of the world's largest SOEs. In the third, we present and analyse the set of the largest SOEs on a global scale. In the fourth, we present the data in dynamic terms, showing the changes that SOEs underwent in the global economy after the financial crisis, between 2009 and 2018. The analysis is based on the share ratios of SOEs and other indicators defined above in Section 3.3.

In Chapter 7, we analyse two specific types of SOEs – listed SOEs and foreign SOEs – primarily using the results of our empirical research. In the last section, we perform a brief statistical and econometric analysis to determine the relationship between indicators describing the state's ownership stake in the economy (share ratios) and indicators characterising the "environment of SOEs", i.e. the socio-economic system and the institutional environment.

Notes

1 Bruton et al. (2015) note that a similar dichotomy was present in the research on SOEs: "The existing research on SOEs has tended to view state ownership in black-and-white terms – that is, a firm is either state owned or it is not".

2 The source of data contained in the study by L. Galambos listed in the book is identified as follows: *Harvard Business Review*, March–April 1979, p. 16.

Bibliography

Baltowski, M. (2017). Więcej władzy niż własności – Skarb Państwa jako szczególny inwestor na GPW w Warszawie [More Control Than Ownership: State as a Specific Investor on Warsaw Stock Exchange], *Studia Ekonomiczne*, *1*(92), 31.

Baltowski, M., & Kozarzewski, P. (2016). Formal and Real Ownership Structure of the Polish Economy: State-Owned Versus State-Controlled Enterprises. *Post-Communist Economies*, *28*(3), 405–413.

Bernier, L., Florio, M., & Bance, P. (Eds.). (2020). *The Routledge Handbook of State-Owned Enterprises*. London; New York: Routledge.

Bortolotti, B., & Faccio, M. (2009). Government Control of Privatized Firms. *The Review of Financial Studies*, *22*(8), 2907–2939.

Böwer, U. (2017). State-Owned Enterprises in Emerging Europe: The Good, the Bad, and the Ugly. *IMF Working Papers*, *17*(221), 27.

Bruton, G. D., Peng, M. W., Ahlstrom, D., Stan, C., & Xu, K. (2015). State-owned Enterprises Around the World as Hybrid Organizations. *Academy of Management Perspectives*, *29*(1), 92–114.

Christiansen, H. (2011). The Size and Composition of the SOE Sector in OECD Countries. *OECD Corporate Governance Working Papers*, No. 5. Paris: OECD Publishing.

Christiansen, H., & Kim, Y. (2014). State-Invested Enterprises in the Global Marketplace: Implications for a Level Playing Field (No. 14). *OECD Corporate Governance Working Papers*. Paris: OECD Publishing.

Cuervo-Cazurra, A., Inkpen, A., Musacchio, A., & Ramaswamy, K. (2014). Governments as Owners: State-Owned Multinational Companies. *Journal of International Business Studies*, *45*(8), 919–942.

De Lange, B., & Merlevede, B. (2020). State-Owned Enterprises across Europe: Stylized Facts from a Large Firm-level Dataset. *Working Papers of Faculty of Economics and Business Administration, Ghent University*, (20/1006).

European Commission. (2016). State-Owned Enterprises in the EU: Lessons Learnt and Ways Forward in a Post-Crisis Context (No. 031). *Institutional Paper*. Luxembourg.

Faccio, M., & Lang, L. H. (2002). The Ultimate Ownership of Western European Corporations. *Journal of Financial Economics*, *65*(3), 365–395.

Freund, C., & Sidhu, D. (2017). Global Competition and the Rise of China. *Peterson Institute for International Economics Working Paper*, (17–3).

Gal, P. N., & Hijzen, A. (2016). *The Short-Term Impact of Product Market Reforms: A Cross-Country Firm-Level Analysis*. Washington, DC: International Monetary Fund.

IMF. (2020). State-owned Enterprises: The Other Government. *IMF Fiscal Monitor*. Washington, D.C.: International Monetary Fund.

Kowalski, P., Büge, M., Sztajerowska, M., & Egeland, M. (2013). State-Owned Enterprises: Trade Effects and Policy Implications. *OECD Trade Policy Papers*. Paris: OECD.

Kwiatkowski, G., & Augustynowicz, P. (2015). *State-Owned Enterprises in the Global Economy – Analysis Based on Fortune Global 500 List* (Managing Intellectual Capital and Innovation for Sustainable and Inclusive Society: Managing Intellectual Capital and Innovation; Proceedings of the MakeLearn and TIIM Joint International Conference 2015).

Musacchio, A., & Lazzarini, S. G. (2014). *Reinventing State Capitalism: Leviathan in Business, Brazil and Beyond*. Cambridge, MA: Harvard University Press.

OECD. (2005). *Corporate Governance of State-Owned Enterprises A Survey of OECD Countries: A Survey of OECD Countries*. Paris: OECD Publishing.

OECD. (2014). *The Size and Sectoral Distribution of SOEs in OECD and Partner Countries*. Paris: OECD Publishing.

OECD. (2016). *State-Owned Enterprises as Global Competitors: A Challenge or an Opportunity?* Paris: OECD Publishing.

OECD. (2017). *The Size and Sectoral Distribution of State-Owned Enterprises*. Paris: OECD Publishing.

Richmond, C., Benedek, D., Cegar, B., Dohlman, P., Hassine, M., Jajko, B., Kopyrski, P., et al. (2019). Reassessing the Role of State-Owned Enterprises in Central, Eastern and Southeastern Europe. *International Monetary Fund European Departmental Paper Series, 19*(11), 127.

Robinett, D. (2006). *Held by the Visible Hand: The Challenge of SOE Corporate Governance for Emerging Markets*. Washington, DC: World Bank Group.

Shapiro, D. M., & Globerman, S. (2012). The International Activities and Impacts of State-Owned Enterprises. In K. P. Sauvant, L. E. Sachs, & W. P. F. S. Jongbloed (Eds.), *Sovereign Investment*. Oxford; New York: Oxford University Press.

Szarzec, K., & Nowara, W. (2017). The Economic Performance of State-Owned Enterprises in Central and Eastern Europe. *Post-Communist Economies, 29*(3), 375–391.

The World Bank. (2014a). *Corporate Governance of State-Owned Enterprises*. Washington, DC: The World Bank.

The World Bank. (2014b). *Corporate Governance of State-owned Enterprises in Latin America: Current Trends and Country Cases*. Washington, DC: The World Bank.

Toninelli, P. M. (Ed.). (2000). *The Rise and Fall of State-owned Enterprise in the Western World*. Cambridge: Cambridge University Press.

UNCTAD. (2019). *World Investment Report 2019*. United Nations Conference on Trade and Development (UNCTAD) World Investment Report (WIR).

4 State-owned enterprise sector in 32 largest economies in the world

4.1 State-owned enterprise sector in Argentina

4.1.1 The largest SOEs in Argentina and their characteristics

There were no Argentine companies on the Fortune Global 500 list from 2005 to 2019. In contrast, there were two Argentine companies on the Forbes Global 2000 list in 2019, one of which was state-owned - Yacimientos Petrolíferos Fiscales (YPF), at position 845.

The largest state-owned enterprise (SOE) in Argentina, and the largest Argentine company overall, is the listed company YPF. The company is operating a fully integrated oil and gas chain. YPF, founded by the state, has undergone very diverse ownership changes in its almost 100-year history. Since May 2012, the Argentine state holds a 51% stake in the company, with 26.01%

Table 4.1 The largest SOEs in Argentina and their positions in the Top 100, 2018

No.	*Name of the SOE*	*Industry*	*OR (bill. €)*	*TA (bill. €)*	*Empl. worldwide (thousand)*	*State shares[a] (%)*	*Position Top 100*
1	YPF	Oil & gas	10.5	23.1	21.3	51.0	1
2	Aerolineas Argentinas	Transport	2.0	2.1	10.6	100.0	18
3	Enarsa	Oil & gas	1.6	2.7	0.7	100.0	23
4	Correo Argentina	Post & telecomm.	0.5	0.2	15.5	100.0	49
5	AySA	Water & sewage	0.4	1.7	4.0	90.0	55
6	Ferrocarriles Argentinos	Transport	0.3[b]	0.4[b]	22.9	100.0	57
7	Nucleoeléctrica Argentina	Energy	0.3	5.7	3.6	100.0	61

Source: Own compilation based on the Orbis database and other data (including Fortune Global, Forbes Global lists, and companies' websites).

a Direct and indirect.

b Estimated.

DOI: 10.4324/9781003244462-5

distributed to the federal government and 24.99% to the provincial governors. Table 4.1 contains the characteristics of the largest Argentine SOEs and their positions in the Top 100 non-financial companies.

4.1.2 Shares of SOEs in the sets of the largest Argentine companies

Tables 4.2–4.4 contain data on the shares of SOEs in the various sets of the largest Argentine non-financial companies. In terms of the shares in operating revenues (ORs) and total assets (TAs), there were large increases between 2009 and 2013. This is the result of the nationalisation of YPF in 2012. In the second part of our analysis period, there were slight decreases in the shares, but the number increased again.

Table 4.2 SOEs in the sets of the largest Argentine companies – number

	Top 10			*Top 20*			*Top 50*			*Top 100*		
	2009	*2013*	*2018*	*2009*	*2013*	*2018*	*2009*	*2013*	*2018*	*2009*	*2013*	*2018*
maSOEs	1	1	1	1	2	2	3	4	4	5	6	7
miSOEs	0	0	0	0	0	0	0	0	0	0	0	0
SOEs	1	1	1	1	2	2	3	4	4	5	6	7

Source: As in Table 4.1.

Table 4.3 SOEs in the sets of the largest Argentine companies – share in ORs (%)

	Top 10			*Top 20*			*Top 50*			*Top 100*		
	2009	*2013*	*2018*	*2009*	*2013*	*2018*	*2009*	*2013*	*2018*	*2009*	*2013*	*2018*
maSOEs	6.58	31.58	26.48	4.31	24.05	20.63	5.41	19.05	16.25	5.43	17.97	15.57
miSOEs	0	0	0	0	0	0	0	0	0	0	0	0
SOEs	6.58	31.58	26.48	4.31	24.05	20.63	5.41	19.05	16.25	5.43	17.97	15.57

Source: As in Table 4.1.

Table 4.4 SOEs in the sets of the largest Argentine companies – share in TAs (%)

	Top 10			*Top 20*			*Top 50*			*Top 100*		
	2009	*2013*	*2018*	*2009*	*2013*	*2018*	*2009*	*2013*	*2018*	*2009*	*2013*	*2018*
maSOEs	7.43	47.92	29.83	4.46	32.23	25.52	5.10	24.23	21.59	8.16	25.87	22.82
miSOEs	0	0	0	0	0	0	0	0	0	0	0	0
SOEs	7.43	47.92	29.83	4.46	32.23	25.52	5.10	24.23	21.59	8.16	25.87	22.82

Source: As in Table 4.1.

Figure 4.1a shows the changes in the shares in ORs and TAs of SOEs in the Top 20 over the analysis period and Figure 4.1b shows the changes in the shares of SOEs in the various sets of the largest companies. A graphical representation of the data presented earlier shows a jump in the importance of SOEs in this economy in 2013.

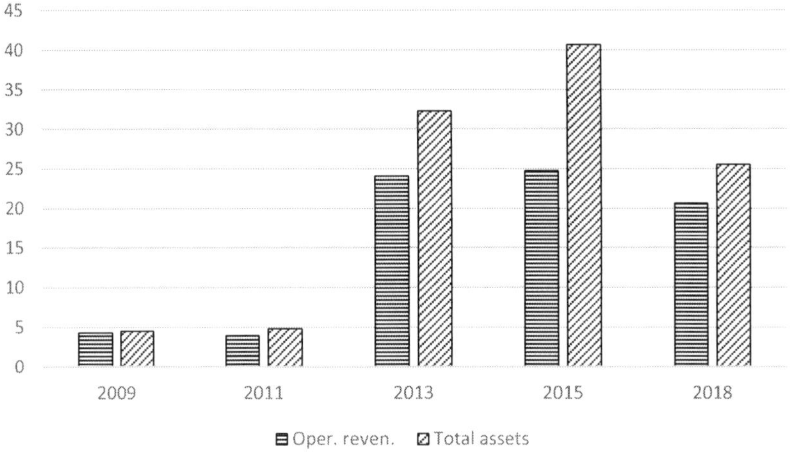

Figure 4.1a SOEs in the Top 20 of the Argentine non-financial companies – shares in ORs and TAs (%).

Source: As in Table 4.1.

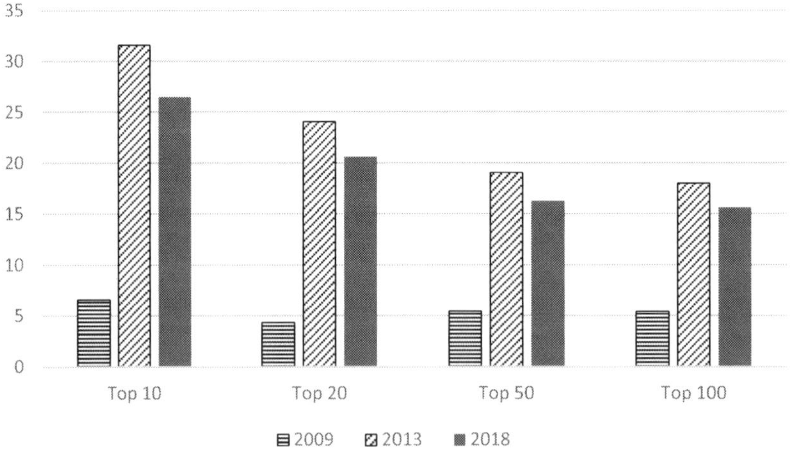

Figure 4.1b Changes in the shares of SOEs in the various sets of the largest Argentine companies (%).

Source: As in Table 4.1.

Table 4.5 Relationship of ORs of SOEs and nominal GDP (%)

	2009	*2013*	*2018*
Rev-100/GDP	1.4	3.6	3.5
Rev-20/GDP	0.8	3.0	2.8

Source: Own calculations.

Table 4.6 Estimated share of SOEs in selected industries of the Argentine economy, 2018

Oil and gas	*Energy*	*Railways*	*Postal sector*	*Telecomm.*	*Banking sector*	*SS-I*
3	1	3	3	0	3	2.17

Source: Own estimation according to the rules given in Section 3.3.2.

4.1.3 Other characteristics of the Argentine SOE sector

Revenues of the largest SOEs in relation to GDP

The acquisition of YPF also had a large impact on the relative value of ORs of SOEs to the GDP indicator. It should be stressed, however, that its value is very low in this economy when compared to other countries (Table 4.5).

SOEs in selected industries

SOEs are widely present in many parts of the Argentine economy. SOEs dominate in the following industries: oil and gas, railways, postal and banking sectors - Table 4.6.

Listed SOEs

In the period analysed there was only one listed SOE in the Top 100 non-financial companies (as mentioned – YPF since 2012 as an SOE).

4.1.4 Foreign SOEs in Argentina

The share of foreign SOEs (FSOEs) in the Argentine economy clearly decreased in 2009–2018. The largest FSOE in 2018 (and the only one in the Top 100) was Edesur SA, ranked 33rd on the list. This company operates in the energy sector and is controlled by the Italian conglomerate Enel. Data on FSOEs in the Argentine economy are presented in Table 4.7.

Table 4.7 FSOEs in the Top 100 of Argentine companies

	2009	*2013*	*2018*
Number	3	5	1
Share in ORs (%)	6.6	3.7	1.0
Share in TAs (%)	9.1	4.3	0.9

Source: As in Table 4.1.

Table 4.8 Share ratios for the Argentine economy

Share ratio	*2009*	*2013*	*2018*
SR-100 (%)	6.8	21.9	19.2
SR-20 (%)	4.4	28.1	23.1
CS-20	0.65	1.28	1.20
miS-100 (%)	0	0	0

Source: Own calculations.

4.1.5 Summary

The share of SOEs in the group of the largest Argentine companies is at a moderate level (around 20%). There was only one SOE in the Top 10. Of the seven SOEs in the Top 100, five are fully owned by the state. Minority SOEs are not present in this economy. There is no concentration of SOEs in the Top 20 group. YPF, the largest Argentine SOE, is responsible for a very large part of all revenues of SOEs in the Top 100 (67%). The indicators of shares of SOEs are mainly affected by the re-nationalisation of the petrochemical giant YPF, which was carried out in 2012. However, between 2013 and 2018, a slight decrease in the shares of SOEs is noticeable. An overview of key values on SOEs' share in the Argentine economy is in Table 4.8.

4.2 SOE sector in Australia

4.2.1 The largest SOEs in Australia and their characteristics

Australia is one of the countries with the smallest share of SOEs in the economy. Both the Fortune Global list and the Forbes Global list lacked Australian SOEs in 2010 and 2019. In 2018, among the Top 100 Australian non-financial companies, only three were state-owned. The largest Australian SOE is the postal operator Australia Post. Table 4.9 contains the characteristics of the largest Australian SOEs and their position in the Top 100 non-financial companies.

Table 4.9 The largest SOEs in Australia and their position in the Top 100, 2018

No.	*Name of the SOE*	*Industry*	*OR (bill. €)*	*TA (bill. €)*	*Empl. worldwide (thousand)*	*State shares[a] (%)*	*Position Top 100*
1	Australia Post	Post & telecomm.	4.3	3.5	80.0	100.0	36
2	Energy Queensland	Energy	3.0	16.3	7.0	100.0	57
3	Stanwell Corporation	Energy	2.0	2.5	0.8	100.0	95
4	Ergon Energy	Energy	1.9	0.8	4.5	100.0	100

a Direct and indirect.
Source: Own compilation based on the Orbis database and other data (including Fortune Global, Forbes Global lists and companies' websites).

4.2.2 Shares of SOEs in the sets of the largest Australian companies

Tables 4.10–4.12 contain data on the shares of SOEs in the various sets of the largest Australian non-financial companies. In no year examined did SOEs appear in either the Top 10 or the Top 20 of Australian companies. In the other sets, the share of SOEs decreased significantly.
Figure 4.2 shows the changes in the shares of SOEs in the various sets of the largest companies.

Table 4.10 SOEs in the sets of the largest Australian companies – number

	Top 50			*Top 100*		
	2009	*2013*	*2018*	*2009*	*2013*	*2018*
maSOEs	3	1	1	7	4	4
miSOEs	0	0	0	0	0	0
SOEs	3	1	1	7	4	4

Source: As in Table 4.9.

Table 4.11 SOEs in the sets of the largest Australian companies – share in ORs (%)

	Top 50			*Top 100*		
	2009	*2013*	*2018*	*2009*	*2013*	*2018*
maSOEs	1.96	0.92	0.87	3.02	1.79	1.81
miSOEs	0	0	0	0	0	0
SOEs	1.96	0.92	0.87	3.02	1.79	1.81

Source: As in Table 4.9.

Table 4.12 SOEs in the sets of the largest Australian companies – share in TAs (%)

	Top 50			*Top 100*		
	2009	*2013*	*2018*	*2009*	*2013*	*2018*
maSOEs	3.76	0.58	0.51	6.21	3.04	2.57
miSOEs	0	0	0	0	0	0
SOEs	3.76	0.58	0.51	6.21	3.04	2.57

Source: As in Table 4.9

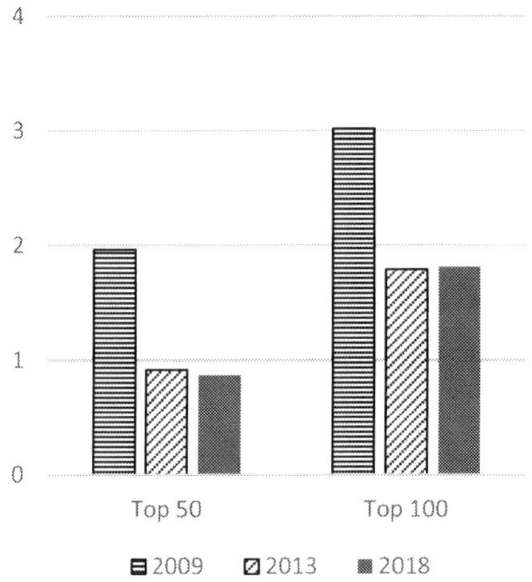

Figure 4.2 Changes in the shares of SOEs in the various sets of the largest Australian non-financial companies (%).

Source: As in Table 4.9.

4.2.3 Other characteristics of the Australian SOE sector

Revenues of the largest SOEs in relation to GDP

Table 4.13 provides data on the relationship of the values of OR of SOEs and the value of the nominal GDP of Australia in selected years. The importance of Australian SOEs, as measured by this indicator, is small and declining.

Table 4.13 Relationship of ORs of SOEs and nominal GDP (%)

	2009	*2013*	*2018*
Rev-100/GDP	1.9	0.9	0.7
Rev-20/GDP	0	0	0

Source: Own calculations.

Table 4.14 Estimated share of SOEs in selected industries of the Australian economy, 2018

Oil and gas	*Energy*	*Railways*	*Postal sector*	*Telecomm.*	*Banking sector*	*SS-I*
0	2	0	2	0	0	0.67

Source: Own estimation according to the rules given in Section 3.3.2.

Table 4.15 FSOEs in the Top 100 Australian companies

	2009	*2013*	*2018*
Number	5	7	10
Share in ORs (%)	3.0	3.7	5.6
Share in TAs (%)	2.8	2.1	6.9

Source: As in Table 4.9

SOEs in selected industries

The share of SOEs in strategic sectors is minor. In the postal sector, the state-owned Australia Post dominates, and SOEs have a significant share in the energy sector. In the remaining sectors, either there are no SOEs at all or their role is negligible. Our estimates are presented in Table 4.14.

Listed SOEs

There were no listed companies among the largest Australian SOEs during the years analysed.

4.2.4 FSOEs in Australia

In 2018, there were as many as 11 companies in the Australian Top 100 that can be classified as FSOEs. The largest FSOE is Singtel Optus Pty, ranked 28th in the Top 100. It is owned by Singapore's Temasek and operates in the telecommunications industry. The share of FSOEs in Australia was relatively high and increasing during the period considered (Table 4.15).

4.2.5 Summary

SOEs' share in the Top 100 non-financial companies in the Australian economy in 2018, at the level of 2.2%, is the second lowest share (after the US) among the 32 world's largest economies. There were no SOEs in the Top 10. All four SOEs from the Top 100 were fully owned by the state. The largest SOE – Australia Post – is responsible for 38.7% of the revenues of all SOEs in the Top 100. Between 2009 and 2018, the share of SOEs decreased significantly - Table 4.16.

Table 4.16 Share ratios for the Australian economy

Share ratio	*2009*	*2013*	*2018*
SR-100 (%)	4.6	2.4	2.2
SR-20 (%)	0	0	0
CS-20	0	0	0
miS-100 (%)	0	0	0

Source: Own calculations.

4.3 SOE sector in Austria

4.3.1 The largest SOEs in Austria and their characteristics

In the Fortune Global 500 list for 2010, there were three Austrian companies, of which one was an SOE – OMV, ranked 333rd. The same company was ranked 459th in 2019. On the Forbes Global 2000 list in 2010, there were 12 Austrian companies, of which five were state-owned. Nine years later these numbers were nine and three, respectively.

Austria's largest SOE (and also the largest Austrian company overall) is the petrochemical conglomerate OMV, listed on the Vienna Stock Exchange since 1987. As of 2018, OMV is the only Austrian company listed in the Dow Jones Sustainability Index. Table 4.17 contains the characteristics of the largest Austrian SOEs and their positions in the Top 100 non-financial companies.

Table 4.17 The largest SOEs in Austria and their position in the Top 100, 2018

No.	*Name of the SOE*	*Industry*	*OR (bill. €)*	*TA (bill. €)*	*Empl. worldwide (thousand)*	*State shares[a] (%)*	*Position Top 100*
1	OMV Group	Oil & gas	23.2	37.0	20.2	31.6	1
2	Östereich. Bundesbahnen	Transport	7.0	29.7	41.6	100.0	7
3	Verbund	Energy	2.9	11.7	2.8	81.6	25
4	ASFIN	Transport	2.7	17.1	2.8	100.0	31
5	EVN Group	Energy	2.1	7.8	6.8	51.0	43
6	Österreichische Post	Post & telecomm.	2.0	1.7	20.5	52.8	45
7	Energie AG Oberöster.	Energy	1.6	3.2	2.8	70.2	59
8	Salzburg	Energy	1.5	1.5	2.0	100.0	62
9	Wien Energie	Energy	1.5	2.4	2.3	100.0	63
10	Kärntner Energieholding	Energy	1.3	2.0	1.5	100.0	69

a Direct and indirect.

Source: Own compilation based on the Orbis database and other data (including Fortune Global, Forbes Global lists and companies' websites).

4.3.2 Shares of SOEs in the sets of the largest Austrian companies

Tables 4.18–4.20 contain data on the shares of SOEs in the various sets of the largest Austrian non-financial companies.

The SOE sector in Austria is quite large, especially for a Western country. At the same time the importance of SOEs among the largest Austrian companies is rather low and slightly decreasing.

Figure 4.3a shows the changes in the shares in ORs and TAs of SOEs in the Top 20 over the analysis period and Figure 4.3b shows the changes in the shares of SOEs in the various sets of the largest companies.

Table 4.18 SOEs in the sets of the largest Austrian companies – number

	Top 10			*Top 20*			*Top 50*			*Top 100*		
	2009	*2013*	*2018*	*2009*	*2013*	*2018*	*2009*	*2013*	*2018*	*2009*	*2013*	*2018*
maSOEs	1	1	1	4	2	1	9	7	5	12	13	14
miSOEs	2	1	1	2	2	1	2	2	1	4	3	2
SOEs	3	2	2	6	4	2	11	9	6	16	16	16

Source: As in Table 4.17.

Table 4.19 SOEs in the sets of the largest Austrian companies – share in ORs (%)

	Top 10			*Top 20*			*Top 50*			*Top 100*		
	2009	*2013*	*2018*	*2009*	*2013*	*2018*	*2009*	*2013*	*2018*	*2009*	*2013*	*2018*
maSOEs	7.60	4.91	6.88	13.55	5.61	4.78	14.16	8.41	7.64	13.21	9.19	10.11
miSOEs	30.29	33.70	22.91	21.46	27.45	15.93	15.01	19.81	10.60	13.45	16.36	8.62
SOEs	37.89	38.61	29.79	35.01	33.05	20.71	29.17	28.22	18.23	26.66	25.55	18.74

Source: As in Table 4.17.

Table 4.20 SOEs in the sets of the largest Austrian companies – share in TAs (%)

	Top 10			*Top 20*			*Top 50*			*Top 100*		
	2009	*2013*	*2018*	*2009*	*2013*	*2018*	*2009*	*2013*	*2018*	*2009*	*2013*	*2018*
maSOEs	31.96	26.72	18.93	35.67	31.58	28.00	35.99	32.94	32.62	31.96	26.72	18.93
miSOEs	24.94	28.34	23.55	17.75	18.81	15.22	15.97	14.35	11.36	24.94	28.34	23.55
SOEs	56.90	55.07	42.47	53.42	50.39	43.21	51.96	47.28	43.98	56.90	55.07	42.47

Source: As in Table 4.17.

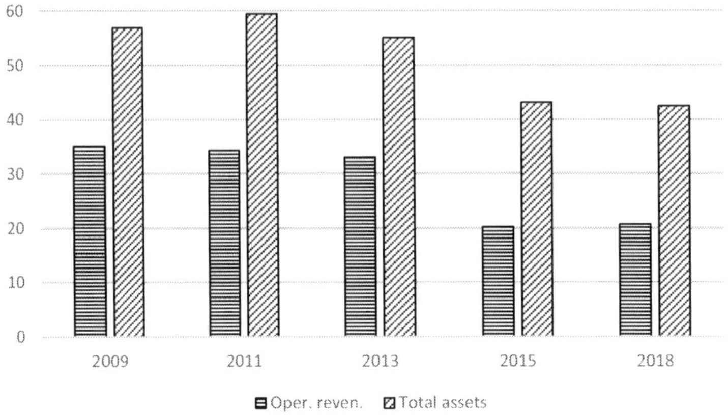

Figure 4.3a SOEs in the Top 20 of the Austrian non-financial companies – shares in ORs and TAs (%).

Source: As in Table 4.17.

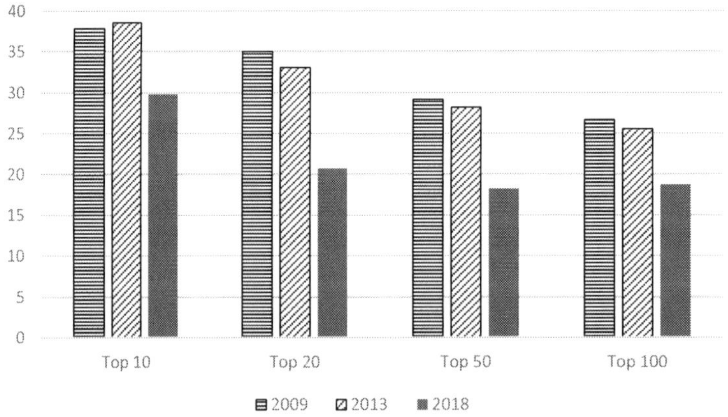

Figure 4.3b Changes in the shares of SOEs in the various sets of the largest Austrian non-financial companies (%).

Source: As in Table 4.17.

4.3.3 Other characteristics of the Austrian SOE sector

Revenues of the largest SOEs in relation to GDP

ORs of the largest SOEs in relation to GDP are on moderate levels. There were increases from 2009 to 2013, but later we see clear declines in the values of both analysed categories (Table 4.21).

Table 4.21 Relationship of ORs of SOEs and nominal GDP (%)

	2009	*2013*	*2018*
Rev-100/GDP	17.3	24.1	13.3
Rev-20/GDP	13.5	18.3	7.6

Source: Own calculations.

Table 4.22 Estimated share of SOEs in selected industries of the Austrian economy, 2018

Oil and gas	*Energy*	*Railways*	*Postal sector*	*Telecomm.*	*Banking sector*	*SS-I*
3	4	4	3	0	0	2.33

Source: Own estimation according to the rules given in Section 3.3.2.

Table 4.23 Number of listed SOEs in Austrian Top 100

	2009	*2013*	*2018*
Listed SOEs	6	5	4
including minority SOEs	3	2	1

Source: As in Table 4.17.

SOEs in selected industries

The share of SOEs in the strategic industries of the Austrian economy is varied. In four industries SOEs clearly dominate, while the "telecom" industry is fully private. The situation is similar in the banking sector, although it is important to note the specificity of this sector in Austria related to the strong position of cooperative and regional banks. Our estimates on this subject are presented in Table 4.22.

Listed SOEs

Of the 16 Austrian SOEs in 2018, only four – as mixed private-state companies – were listed on the Vienna Stock Exchange. More detailed data on this is provided in Table 4.23.

FSOEs in Austria

The number of FSOEs in the Top 100 Austrian non-financial companies increased significantly during the period under review. However, the importance of FSOEs in the Austrian economy is not very high. In 2018, largest of them was Borealis AG, controlled by the state fund Mubadala from the United Arab Emirates. Boralias, a producer of polyethylene and polypropylene, was ranked fourth in the Top 100 and was the only FSOEs in the Top 20 group. A summary presentation of the data described above is presented in Table 4.24.

Table 4.24 FSOEs in the Top 100 of the Austrian companies

	2009	*2013*	*2018*
Number	3	6	6
Share in ORs (%)	3.9	13.5	5.8
Share in TAs (%)	2.7	4.7	4.1

Source: As in Table 4.17.

Table 4.25 Share ratios for the Austrian economy

Share ratio	*2009*	*2013*	*2018*
SR-100 (%)	39.3	36.4	31.4
SR-20 (%)	45.9	44.1	31.6
CS-20	1.17	1.21	1.01
miS-100 (%)	36.9	42.6	31.2

Source: Own calculations.

4.3.4 Summary

The share of SOEs in the group of the largest Austrian enterprises is at a quite high level, exceeding 30%. There were two SOEs in the Top 10. Of the 16 SOEs in the Top 100, 8 are fully owned by the state. The concentration of SOEs in the Top 20 is low. The largest Austrian SOE (OMV) is responsible for a large part of all revenues of SOEs in the Top 100 (43.9%). The share of minority SOEs is significant and quite stable. There is a clear decline in the share of SOEs in the Top 100 and a larger decline in the Top 20 during the period under review. The data for the Austrian economy can be found in Table 4.25.

4.4 SOE sector in Belgium

4.4.1 The largest SOEs in Belgium and their characteristics

There was no Belgian SOE on the Fortune Global 500 list for both 2010 and 2019 (out of – respectively – six and one Belgian companies in general in those years). In turn, the Forbes 2000 list in 2010 included 12 Belgian companies, 2 of which were SOEs. In 2019, it was ten companies overall and one SOE (Proximus).

The largest Belgian SOE in 2018 was Proximus SA, a landline and mobile operator founded by the state in 1930. In 2004, the government partially privatised the company, listing its shares on the stock exchange while retaining a majority stake in the company. Table 4.26 contains the characteristics of the largest Belgian SOEs and their position in the Top 100 non-financial companies.

Table 4.26 The largest SOEs in Belgium and their position in the Top 100, 2018

No.	*Name of the SOE*	*Industry*	*OR (bill. €)*	*TA (bill. €)*	*Empl. worldwide (thousand)*	*State shares[a] (%)*	*Position Top 100*
1	Proximus	Post & telecomm.	5.8	8.7	13.4	56.3	15
2	Bpost	Post & telecomm.	3.8	3.3	34.1	51.0	29
3	NMBS/SNCB	Transport	3.0	11.7	18.3	100.0	35
4	Infrabel	Transport	2.3	22.1	11.6	100.0	54
5	Publi-T	Energy	2.0	13.8	1.4	100.0	58
6	HR Rail	Transport	2.0	0.4	30.1	100.0	62
7	Elia System Operator	Energy	1.9	13.8	2.4	56.1	67
8	Fluvius System Operator	Energy	1.7	4.7	4.3	100.0	76
9	Loterie Nationale	Other	1.5	0.5	0.4	100.0	82
10	Fluxys	Oil & gas	1.4	8.6	1.3	100.0	62

a Direct and indirect.
Source: Own compilation based on the Orbis database and other data (including Fortune Global, Forbes Global lists and companies' websites).

4.4.2 Shares of SOEs in the sets of the largest Belgian companies

Tables 4.27–4.29 contain data on the shares of SOEs in the various sets of the largest Belgian non-financial companies. The overall number of SOEs in the Belgian Top 100 is increasing but at the same time their shares in this group in revenues and assets are very stable. There are no SOEs in the Top 10 set.

Table 4.27 SOEs in the sets of the largest Belgian companies – number

	Top 20			*Top 50*			*Top 100*		
	2009	*2013*	*2018*	*2009*	*2013*	*2018*	*2009*	*2013*	*2018*
maSOEs	2	1	1	3	3	3	6	7	9
miSOEs	0	0	0	0	0	0	0	0	0
SOEs	2	1	1	3	3	3	6	7	9

Source: As in Table 4.26.

Table 4.28 SOEs in the sets of the largest Belgian companies – share in ORs (%)

	Top 20			*Top 50*			*Top 100*		
	2009	*2013*	*2018*	*2009*	*2013*	*2018*	*2009*	*2013*	*2018*
maSOEs	5.10	2.62	2.15	4.81	3.89	3.44	5.13	4.56	5.23
miSOEs	0	0	0	0	0	0	0	0	0
SOEs	5.10	2.62	2.15	4.81	3.89	3.44	5.13	4.56	5.23

Source: As in Table 4.26.

Table 4.29 SOEs in the sets of the largest Belgian companies – share in TAs (%)

	Top 20			*Top 50*			*Top 100*		
	2009	*2013*	*2018*	*2009*	*2013*	*2018*	*2009*	*2013*	*2018*
maSOEs	11.77	2.74	1.85	10.69	9.57	4.16	11.04	10.80	11.68
miSOEs	0	0	0	0	0	0	0	0	0
SOEs	11.77	2.74	1.85	10.69	9.57	4.16	11.04	10.80	11.68

Source: As in Table 4.26.

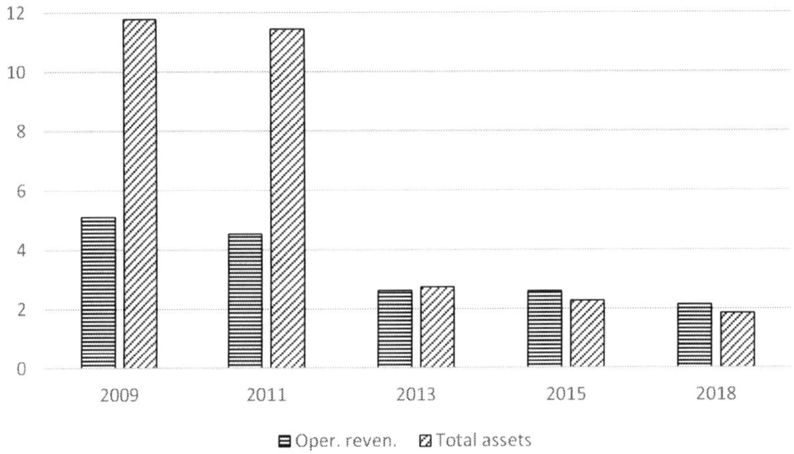

Figure 4.4a SOEs in the Top 20 of the Belgian non-financial companies – shares in ORs and TAs (%).

Source: As in Table 4.26.

Figure 4.4a shows the changes in the shares in ORs and TAs of SOEs in the Top 20 over the analysis period and Figure 4.4b shows the changes in the shares of SOEs in the various sets of the largest companies. We can see a very clear decrease in the share of SOEs in the Top 20 since 2013, while at the same time a slight increase in the share of SOEs in the Top 100 can be seen.

4.4.3 Other characteristics of the Belgian SOE sector

Revenues of the largest SOEs in relation to GDP

ORs of SOEs from Top 100 and Top 20 in relation to GDP are at low levels. There were increases from 2009 to 2013, but later we see clear declines in the values of both analysed categories. The relevant data are presented in Table 4.30.

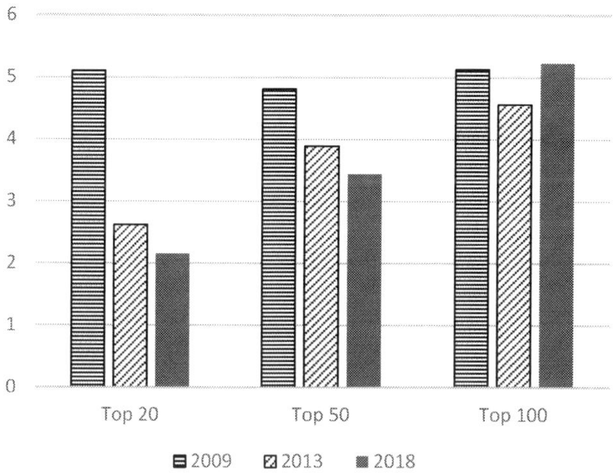

Figure 4.4b Changes in the shares of SOEs in the various sets of the largest Belgian non-financial companies (%).

Source: As in Table 4.26.

SOEs in selected industries

The share of SOEs in all strategic sectors of the Belgian economy is relatively high. Only the oil & gas sector lacks SOEs. Our estimates on this are presented in Table 4.31.

Table 4.30 Relationship of ORs of SOEs and nominal GDP (%)

	2009	*2013*	*2018*
Rev-100/GDP	4.5	4.6	4.9
Rev-20/GDP	2.9	1.7	1.2

Source: Own calculations.

Table 4.31 Estimated share of SOEs in the selected industries of the Belgian economy, 2018

Oil and gas	*Energy*	*Railways*	*Postal sector*	*Telecomm.*	*Banking sector*	*SS-I*
0	2	3	3	3	2	2.17

Source: Own estimation according to the rules given in Section 3.3.2.

Table 4.32 Number of listed SOEs in Belgian Top 100

	2009	*2013*	*2018*
Listed SOEs	2	2	3
including minority SOEs	0	0	0

Source: As in Table 4.26.

Table 4.33 FSOEs in the Top 100 of the Belgian companies

	2009	*2013*	*2018*
Number	6	6	4
Share in ORs (%)	7.7	6.5	3.8
Share in TAs (%)	12.6	15.2	6.9

Source: As in Table 4.26.

Listed SOEs

Of the ten Belgian SOEs from the Top 100 non-financial companies in 2018, only three - as companies with mixed capital - were present on the Brussels Stock Exchange. For data on this, see Table 4.32.

4.4.4 FSOEs in the Belgian economy

In 2018, there were five FSOEs (not included in the tables and charts discussed above) among the 100 largest Belgian companies. The largest of these was Electrabel occupying the tenth position. Electrabel SA is an energy corporation, a subsidiary of the French multinational company Engie. Of the five FSOEs, one made it to the Top 20. See Table 4.33 for details.

4.4.5 Summary

The share of SOEs in the Belgian economy is low in the Top 100 and very low in the Top 20. There is no SOE in the Top 10. Of the nine SOEs in the Top 100, seven are fully owned by the state. There are also

Table 4.34 Share ratios for the Belgian economy

Share ratio	*2009*	*2013*	*2018*
SR-100 (%)	8.1	7.7	8.5
SR-20 (%)	8.4	2.7	2.0
CS-20	1.0	0.3	0.2
miS-100 (%)	0	0	0

Source: Own calculations.

no minority SOEs in Belgium. The concentration of SOEs in the Top 20 is very low and decreasing. Proximus, the largest Belgian SOE, is responsible for moderate part of all ORs of SOEs in the Top 100 (22.8%). The share in Top 100 is fairly stable and the share in Top 20 decreased sharply between 2009 and 2018, mainly in the first part of the period under review – Table 4.34.

4.5 SOE sector in Brazil

4.5.1 The largest SOEs in Brazil and their characteristics

On the Fortune Global list in 2010, there were three Brazilian SOEs (out of seven) and in 2019 there were four (out of eight). The largest of them was Petrobras, ranked 74th in 2019. On the Forbes Global 2000 list in 2010, there were 33 Brazilian companies, including nine SOEs. In 2019, the number of Brazilian companies dropped to 20 and the number of SOEs to six.

The largest Brazilian SOE and also the largest Brazilian company as well is Petrobras, one of the world's leading petrochemical companies. It was founded by the state in 1953 and has been a listed company since 1995, with the majority ownership by the Brazilian government. Table 4.35 contains the characteristics of the largest Brazilian SOEs and their positions in the Top 100 non-financial companies.

Table 4.35 The largest SOEs in Brazil and their position in the Top 100, 2018

No.	*Name of the SOE*	*Industry*	*OR (bill. €)*	*TA (bill. €)*	*Empl. worldwide (thousand)*	*State shares[a] (%)*	*Position Top 100*
1	Petrobras	Oil & gas	83.5	193.9	46.4	50.3	1
2	Vale	Mining/ Metals	30.4	77.0	70.0	33.0	3
3	Eletrobras	Energy	8.3	40.9	25.1	70.9	13
4	Cemig	Energy	5.0	13.5	6.8	62.1	23
5	Correios	Post & telecomm.	4.1	3.0	115.0	100.0	27
6	Sabesp	Water & sewage	3.6	9.8	13.6	50.2	32
7	Copel	Energy	3.4	8.1	7.6	85.0	35
8	Light	Energy	2.7	4.1	3.7	46.9	44
9	Celesc	Energy	1.7	2.2	3.3	61.0	63
10	Cedae	Water & sewage	1.2	3.3	2.1	100.0	78

a Direct and indirect.

Source: Own compilation based on the Orbis database and other data (including Fortune Global, Forbes Global lists and companies' websites).

Table 4.36 SOEs in the sets of the largest Brazilian companies – number

	Top 10			*Top 20*			*Top 50*			*Top 100*		
	2009	*2013*	*2018*	*2009*	*2013*	*2018*	*2009*	*2013*	*2018*	*2009*	*2013*	*2018*
maSOEs	3	2	1	5	3	2	9	7	6	13	12	11
miSOEs	0	0	1	0	0	1	2	2	2	3	4	3
SOEs	3	2	2	5	3	3	11	9	8	16	16	14

Source: As in Table 4.35.

Table 4.37 SOEs in the sets of the largest Brazilian companies – share in ORs (%)

	Top 10			*Top 20*			*Top 50*			*Top 100*		
	2009	*2013*	*2018*	*2009*	*2013*	*2018*	*2009*	*2013*	*2018*	*2009*	*2013*	*2018*
maSOEs	61.44	52.22	32.88	51.75	43.29	27.90	42.29	37.35	24.76	38.51	34.00	22.55
miSOEs	0	0	11.98	0	0	9.24	2.11	1.59	7.60	2.20	1.95	6.76
SOEs	61.44	52.22	44.85	51.75	43.29	37.14	44.40	38.94	32.36	40.70	35.95	29.31

Source: As in Table 4.35.

Table 4.38 SOEs in the sets of the largest Brazilian companies – share in TAs (%)

	Top 10			*Top 20*			*Top 50*			*Top 100*		
	2009	*2013*	*2018*	*2009*	*2013*	*2018*	*2009*	*2013*	*2018*	*2009*	*2013*	*2018*
maSOEs	72.53	73.62	50.45	61.15	65.41	46.50	50.06	54.43	39.18	44.89	49.25	34.77
miSOEs	0	0	20.04	0	0	15.26	2.14	1.87	11.79	2.24	2.05	10.16
SOEs	72.53	73.62	70.48	61.15	65.41	61.76	52.20	56.21	50.97	47.13	51.30	44.93

Source: As in Table 4.35.

4.5.2 Shares of SOEs in the sets of the largest Brazilian companies

Tables 4.36–4.38 contain data on the shares of SOEs in the various sets of the largest Brazilian non-financial companies. The shares of SOEs in the Brazilian Top 100 are high, although generally declining over the years.

Figure 4.5a shows the changes in the shares in ORs and TAs of SOEs in the Top 20 over the analysis period and Figure 4.5b shows the changes in the shares of SOEs in the various sets of the largest companies.

4.5.3 Other characteristics of the Brazilian SOE sector

Revenues of the largest SOEs in relation to GDP

Table 4.39 provides data on the relationship of the value of ORs of SOEs from the Top 100 and Top 20 and the value of the nominal GDP of Brazil in a given year. Slight but steady declines in the values are evident.

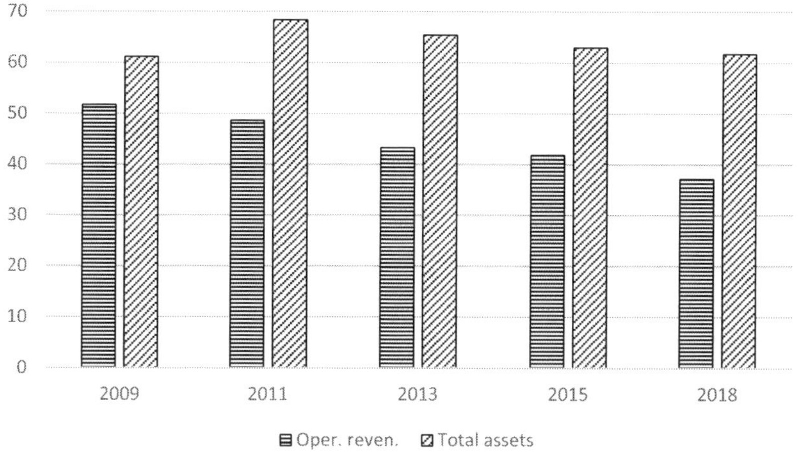

Figure 4.5a SOEs in the Top 20 of the Brazilian non-financial companies – shares in ORs and TAs (%).

Source: As in Table 4.35.

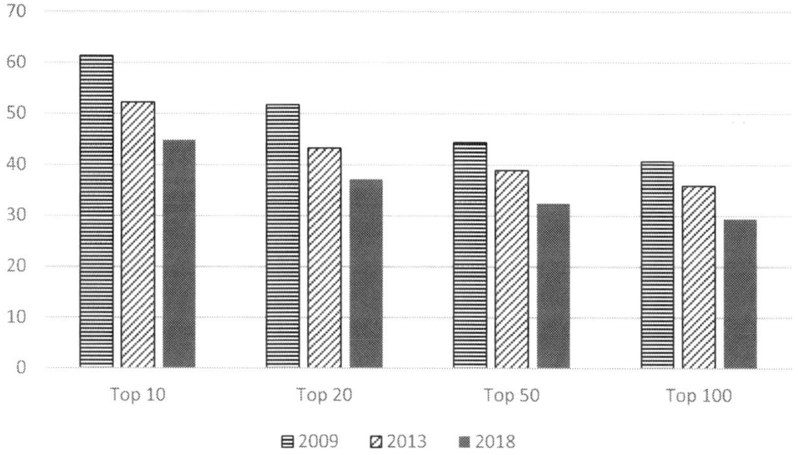

Figure 4.5b Changes in the shares of SOEs in the various sets of the largest Brazilian non-financial companies (%).

Source: As in Table 4.35.

Table 4.39 Relationship of ORs of SOEs and nominal GDP (%)

	2009	*2013*	*2018*
Rev-100/GDP	12.0	9.8	9.0
Rev-20/GDP	10.5	8.1	7.4

Source: Own calculations.

Table 4.40 Estimated share of SOEs in the selected industries of the Brazilian economy, 2018

Oil and gas	*Energy*	*Railways*	*Postal sector*	*Telecomm.*	*Banking sector*	*SS-I*
3	3	1	3	0	2	2.00

Source: Own estimation according to the rules given in Section 3.3.2.

Table 4.41 Number of listed SOEs in Brazilian Top 100

	2009	*2013*	*2018*
Listed SOEs	13	14	12
including minority SOEs	3	4	3

Source: As in Table 4.35.

SOEs in selected industries

SOEs are dominant in three strategic industries of the Brazilian economy - in the oil & gas, the energy and the postal industries. Our estimations for selected industries are presented in Table 4.40.

Listed SOEs

Out of 14 Brazilian SOEs from the Top 100 non-financial companies in 2018, as many as 12 were listed on the São Paulo Stock Exchange. For more detailed data see Table 4.41.

4.5.4 FSOEs in Brazil

In 2018, there were seven FSOEs in the Top 100 Brazilian companies. The largest of them, Cpfl Energia, which was controlled by the Chinese State Grid Corporation, was 18th in the Top 100. Among six other FSOEs, there are two more companies controlled – directly or indirectly – by the Chinese government, three by the Italian and one by the French. The relevant data are presented in Table 4.42.

Table 4.42 FSOEs in the Top 100 of the Brazilian companies

	2009	*2013*	*2018*
Number	3	3	7
Share in ORs (%)	1.2	0.8	3.6
Share in TAs (%)	2.0	0.8	3.7

Source: As in Table 4.35.

Table 4.43 Share ratios for the Brazilian economy

Share ratio	*2009*	*2013*	*2018*
SR-100 (%)	43.9	43.6	37.1
SR-20 (%)	56.5	54.3	49.5
CS-20	1.3	1.2	1.3
miS-100 (%)	5.0	4.4	22.7

Source: Own calculations.

4.5.5 Summary

The share of SOEs in the Brazilian economy is at a high level, almost 50% in the Top 20 and over 37% in the Top 100, with as many as 14 SOEs in the Top 100. There were two SOEs in the Top 10. Of the 14 SOEs in the Top 100, only two are 100% state-owned. The high share of minority SOEs in the whole group of SOEs is distinctive. The concentration of SOEs in the Top 20 has remained at a similar level. Petrobras, the largest Brazilian SOE, is responsible for a large part of all of ORs of SOEs in the Top 100 (56.3%). Between 2009 and 2018, there was a significant decline in the shares of SOEs in both the Top 100 and Top 20 – see Table 4.43.

4.6 SOE sector in Canada

4.6.1 The largest SOEs in Canada and their characteristics

There were no SOEs on the Fortune Global 500 list in the years examined (out of 13 Canadian companies in 2019 and 11 in 2010). On the Forbes Global list in 2019, among 56 Canadian companies, there was one SOE – Hydro One; there were no SOEs on this list in 2009.

Table 4.44 The largest SOEs in Canada and their position in the Top 100, 2018

No.	*Name of the SOE*	*Industry*	*OR (bill. €)*	*TA (bill. €)*	*Empl. worldwide (thousand)*	*State shares[a] (%)*	*Position Top 100*
1	Hydro-Québec	Energy	9.2	49.3	19.9	100.0	19
2	Canada Post	Post & telecomm.	5.7	5.9	64.0	100.0	31
3	Hydro One	Energy	3.9	16.3	8.6	47.4	47
4	Ontario Power Gen.	Energy	3.5	33.5	9.0	100.0	49
5	BC Hydro	Energy	3.3	21.6	5.4	100.0	55
6	Toronto Hydro	Energy	2.2	3.4	1.4	100.0	84
7	Quebec Alcohol	Trade	2.1	0.5	7.5	100.0	92

a Direct and indirect.

Source: Own compilation based on the Orbis database and other data (including Fortune Global, Forbes Global lists and companies' websites).

The largest state-owned company in Canada is Hydro-Québec, whose main activity is the generation, transmission and distribution of electricity in the province of Québec. Its sole owner is the Government of Québec. The set of the 100 largest non-financial companies in Canada in 2018 included seven SOEs – Table 4.44.

4.6.2 Shares of SOEs in the sets of the largest Canadian companies

Tables 4.45–4.47 contain data on the shares of SOEs in the various sets of the largest Canadian non-financial companies. The share of SOEs in Canada's economy is low, in addition with a slight decreasing trend. In the Top 20 group, there was only one state-owned entity in each of the years analysed – the energy company Hydro-Québec.

Table 4.45 SOEs in the sets of the largest Canadian companies – number

	Top 20			*Top 50*			*Top 100*		
	2009	*2013*	*2018*	*2009*	*2013*	*2018*	*2009*	*2013*	*2018*
maSOEs	1	1	1	4	5	3	7	7	6
miSOEs	0	0	0	0	0	1	0	0	1
SOEs	1	1	1	4	5	4	7	·7	7

Source: As in Table 4.44.

Table 4.46 SOEs in the sets of the largest Canadian companies – share in ORs (%)

	Top 20			*Top 50*			*Top 100*		
	2009	*2013*	*2018*	*2009*	*2013*	*2018*	*2009*	*2013*	*2018*
maSOEs	4.42	2.92	2.57	6.49	5.6	3.47	6.46	5.23	3.96
miSOEs	0	0	0	0	0	0.74	0	0	0.6
SOEs	4.42	2.92	2.57	6.49	5.60	4.21	6.46	5.23	4.55

Source: As in Table 4.44.

Table 4.47 SOEs in the sets of the largest Canadian companies – share in TAs (%)

	Top 20			*Top 50*			*Top 100*		
	2009	*2013*	*2018*	*2009*	*2013*	*2018*	*2009*	*2013*	*2018*
maSOEs	15.27	11.5	8.20	12.97	14.48	8.69	12.53	12.33	9.01
miSOEs	0	0	0	0	0	1.61	0	0	1.30
SOEs	15.27	11.5	8.20	12.97	14.48	10.30	12.53	12.33	10.31

Source: As in Table 4.44.

Figure 4.6a shows the changes in the shares in ORs and TAs of SOEs in the Top 20 over the analysis period and Figure 4.6b shows the changes in the shares of SOEs in the various sets of the largest companies.

Figure 4.6a SOEs in the Top 20 of the Canadian non-financial companies – shares in ORs and TAs (%).

Source: As in Table 4.44.

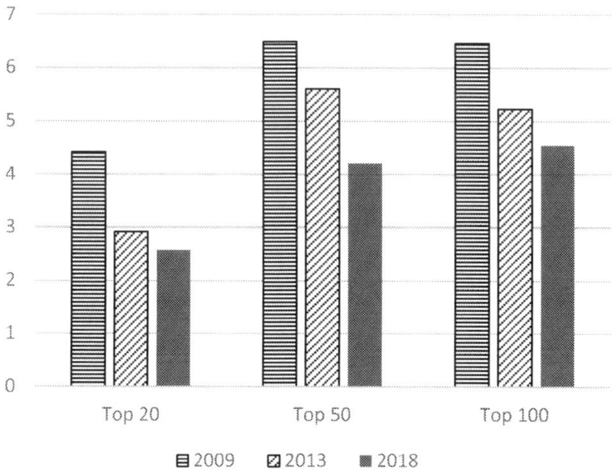

Figure 4.6b Changes in the shares of SOEs in the various sets of the largest Canadian non-financial companies (%).

Source: As in Table 4.44.

Table 4.48 Relationship of ORs of SOEs and nominal GDP (%)

	2009	*2013*	*2018*
Rev-100/GDP	2.6	2.1	2.0
Rev-20/GDP	1.0	0.7	0.6

Source: Own calculations.

4.6.3 Other characteristics of the Canadian SOE sector

Revenues of the largest SOEs in relation to GDP

The importance of SOEs in the Canadian economy as measured by this next indicator is low and declining over time – see Table 4.48.

SOEs in selected industries

The share of SOEs in the selected industries of the Canadian economy is low. In the postal services, the state-owned monopoly Canada Post Corporation is the main entity. In the energy sector the share of SOEs is significant and also several large regional SOEs were ranked close to the Top 5 of this industry. The rest of the industries are essentially private. Our estimates are presented in Table 4.49.

Listed SOEs

Hydro One in which Ontario Province holds around 47% of shares is the only listed SOE in the Top 100 non-financial companies in Canada.

4.6.4 FSOEs in the Canadian economy

The representation of FSOEs among Canada's Top 100 companies during the period under review was negligible - Table 4.50.

Table 4.49 Estimated share of SOEs in the selected industries of the Canadian economy, 2018

Oil and gas	*Energy*	*Railways*	*Postal sector*	*Telecomm.*	*Banking sector*	*SS-I*
0	3	1	3	0	0	1.17

Source: Own estimation according to the rules given in Section 3.3.2.

Table 4.50 FSOEs in the Top 100 of the Canadian companies

	2009	*2013*	*2018*
Number	2	1	0
Share in ORs (%)	1.3	0.7	0
Share in TAs (%)	0.9	0.4	0

Source: As in Table 4.44.

Table 4.51 Share ratios for the Canadian economy

Share ratio	*2009*	*2013*	*2018*
SR-100 (%)	9.5	8.8	7.4
SR-20 (%)	9.8	7.2	5.4
CS-20	1.0	0.8	0.7
miS-100 (%)	0.0	0.0	12.7

Source: Own calculations.

4.6.5 Summary

The share of SOEs in Canada in 2018 was rather small – below 8% in the Top 100 set and slightly over 5% in the Top 20 set. There were no SOEs in the Top 10, and only one SOE in the Top 20. Of the seven SOEs in the Top 100, six are fully owned by the state. The share of minority SOEs was small. Hydro-Québec, the largest Canadian SOE, is responsible for 30.63% of all ORs of SOEs in the Top 100. A decline in the shares of SOEs during the studied period is visible – see Table 4.51.

4.7 SOE sector in China

4.7.1 The largest SOEs in China and their characteristics

Among the five largest enterprises in the world on the Fortune Global 500 list in 2019, as many as three are Chinese SOEs. In total, of the 119 Chinese companies on this list, as many as 89 are SOEs. Back in 2009, there were only 37 Chinese companies on the list and 34 of them were state-owned. According to the Forbes Global 2000 list for 2019, among the ten largest Chinese enterprises, nine are SOEs. In total, there were 251 Chinese enterprises on the list in 2019 and 140 of them were SOEs. In 2010, those numbers were – respectively – 113 and 84.

The largest SOE (using the revenue criterion) in China in 2018 was the petrochemical conglomerate Sinopec. In China, the ten largest non-financial companies are by far dominated by SOEs, with only one enterprise classified as private (a major problem in researching China's SOEs are the large discrepancies in data even in reliable sources) – Table 4.52.

4.7.2 Shares of SOEs in the sets of the largest Chinese companies

Tables 4.53–4.55 contain data on the SOEs' shares in the various sets of the largest Chinese non-financial companies. In most of them the government is the sole owner or majority shareholder.

Figure 4.7a shows the changes in the shares in the operating revenues (ORs) and total assets (TAs) of SOEs in the Top 20 over the analysis period and Figure 4.7b shows the changes in the shares of SOEs in the various sets of the largest companies.

Table 4.52 The largest SOEs in China and their position in the Top 100, 2018

No.	*Name of the SOE*	*Industry*	*OR (bill. €)*	*TA (bill. €)*	*Empl. worldwide (thousand)*	*State shares[a] (%)*	*Position Top 100*
1	Sinopec	Oil & gas	369.4	202.9	423.5	68.3	1
2	State Grid Corporation	Energy	303.4	500.0	913.5	100.0	2
3	Petrochina Company	Oil & gas	299.9	310.0	476.2	80.9	3
4	China State Constr. Eng.	Construction	150.8	237.3	302.8	59.6	4
5	Saic Motor	Automotive	114.5	99.8	217.5	80.0	5
6	China Mobile Communic.	Post & telecomm.	97.9	223.0	459.2	72.5	6
7	China State Railway	Transport	97.6	1019.0	2000.0	100.0	7
8	China Railway Group (CREC)	Construction	94.6	120.1	282.3	50.7	9
9	China Railway Constr.	Construction	92.5	117.0	295.9	51.1	10
10	China National Offshore Oil	Oil & gas	87.7	155.0	98.8	100.0	11

[a] Direct and indirect.
Source: Own compilation based on the Orbis database and other data (including Fortune Global, Forbes Global lists and companies' websites).

Table 4.53 SOEs in the sets of the largest Chinese companies – number

	Top 10			*Top 20*			*Top 50*			*Top 100*		
	2009	*2013*	*2018*	*2009*	*2013*	*2018*	*2009*	*2013*	*2018*	*2009*	*2013*	*2018*
maSOEs	9	9	9	18	18	18	39	40	39	72	72	71
miSOEs	0	0	0	0	0	0	3	1	1	11	5	7
SOEs	9	9	9	18	18	18	42	41	40	83	77	78

Source: As in Table 4.52.

Table 4.54 SOEs in the sets of the largest Chinese companies – share in ORs (%)

	Top 10			*Top 20*			*Top 50*			*Top 100*		
	2009	*2013*	*2018*	*2009*	*2013*	*2018*	*2009*	*2013*	*2018*	*2009*	*2013*	*2018*
maSOEs	100.0	94.89	94.47	95.23	93.99	93.13	89.11	89.35	84.92	85.97	85.00	79.90
miSOEs	0	0	0	0	0	0	2.20	0.78	0.99	4.06	2.09	3.47
SOEs	100.0	94.89	94.47	95.23	93.99	93.13	91.31	90.13	85.90	90.03	87.10	83.37

Source: As in Table 4.52.

Table 4.55 SOEs in the sets of the largest Chinese companies – share in TAs (%)

	Top 10			*Top 20*			*Top 50*			*Top 100*		
	2009	*2013*	*2018*	*2009*	*2013*	*2018*	*2009*	*2013*	*2018*	*2009*	*2013*	*2018*
maSOEs	100.0	99.25	97.02	95.52	98.55	97.37	93.66	93.40	88.69	91.77	90.51	85.01
miSOEs	0	0	0	0	0	0	1.21	0.57	2.59	2.40	1.45	3.48
SOEs	100.0	99.25	97.02	95.52	98.55	97.37	94.86	93.98	91.28	94.17	91.97	88.49

Source: As in Table 4.52.

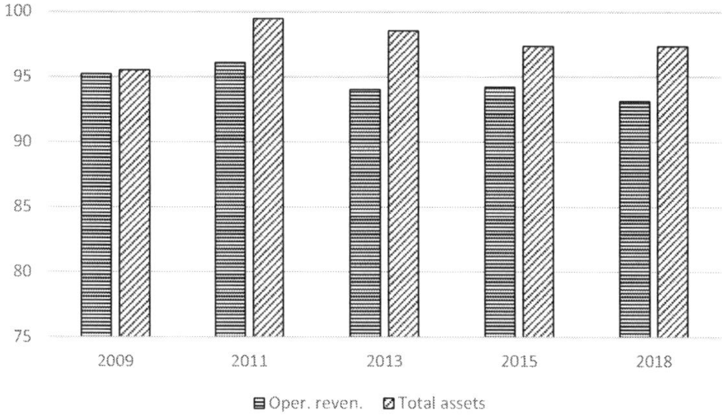

Figure 4.7a SOEs in the Top 20 of the Chinese non-financial companies – shares in ORs and TAs (%).

Source: As in Table 4.52.

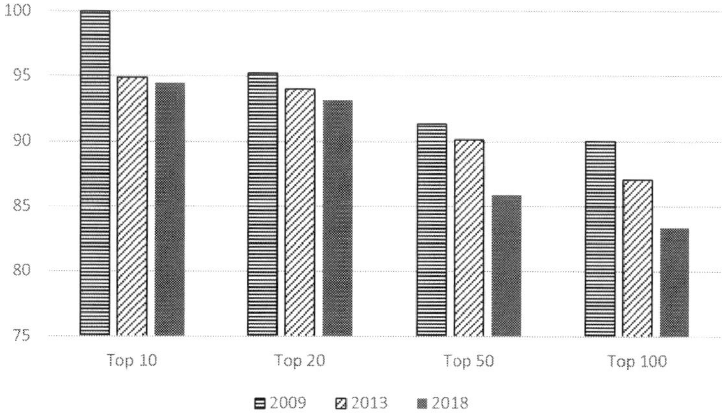

Figure 4.7b Changes in the shares of SOEs in the various sets of the largest Chinese non-financial companies (%).

Source: As in Table 4.52.

Table 4.56 Relationship of ORs of SOEs and nominal GDP (%)

	2009	*2013*	*2018*
Rev-100/GDP	35.0	39.9	34.9
Rev-20/GDP	22.3	25.2	18.9

Source: Own calculations.

Table 4.57 Estimated share of SOEs in the selected industries of the Chinese economy, 2018

Oil and gas	*Energy*	*Railways*	*Postal sector*	*Telecomm.*	*Banking sector*	*SS-I*
4	4	4	3	4	4	3.83

Source: Own estimation according to the rules given in Section 3.3.2.

Table 4.58 Number of listed SOEs in Chinese Top 100

	2009	*2013*	*2018*
Listed SOEs	59	54	45
including minority SOEs	11	5	7

Source: As in Table 4.52.

4.7.3 Other characteristics of the Chinese SOE sector

Revenues of the largest SOEs in relation to GDP

The values of the next indicator analysed confirm that the importance of SOEs in the Chinese economy is very high - Table 4.56.

SOEs in selected industries

The share of SOEs in strategic sectors in China is extremely high. In all six sectors analysed, this share is monopolistic or near monopolistic. Our estimations for selected industries are presented in Table 4.57.

Listed SOEs

There were 78 SOEs in Chinese Top 100 of non-financial companies in 2018 and 45 of them were listed companies (see Table 4.58).

4.7.4 FSOEs in China

There are no FSOEs among China's Top 100 companies.

Table 4.59 Share ratios for the Chinese economy

Share ratio	*2009*	*2013*	*2018*
SR-100 (%)	92.1	89.5	85.9
SR-20 (%)	95.4	96.3	95.3
CS-20	1.0	1.1	1.1
miS-100 (%)	3.2	1.9	4.0

Source: Own calculations.

4.7.5 Summary

The share of SOEs in the Chinese economy is the highest among the studied countries – almost 95% in the Top 20 and over 85% in the Top 100. There were nine SOEs in the Top 10. Of the 78 SOEs in the Top 100, 33 are fully owned by the state. Revenues of minority SOEs represent a negligible percentege of the revenues of all SOEs in the Top 100. In the Top 100 the share of SOEs between 2009 and 2013 decreased slightly and in the Top 20 the share of SOEs has remained at a similar level – see Table 4.59.

4.8 SOE sector in Egypt

4.8.1 The largest SOEs in Egypt and their characteristics

There were no Egyptian enterprises on the Fortune Global 500 list, both in 2010 and in 2019. In contrast, on the Forbes Global 2000 list, there were five Egyptian companies in 2010, one of which was an SOE. Nine years later, there was only one (private) Egyptian company on this list.

The largest SOE of Egypt and also the country's largest non-financial company is the Egyptian General Petroleum Company (EGPC). It is active in the exploration, storage and refining of crude oil. Table 4.60 contains the characteristics of the largest Egyptian SOEs and their positions in the Top 100 non-financial companies. These companies operate in various industries.

4.8.2 Shares of SOEs in the sets of the largest Egyptian companies

Tables 4.61–4.63 contain data on the shares of SOEs in the various sets of the largest Egyptian non-financial companies. The tables show that in addition to the increase in the number of SOEs, their share in revenues and assets has also increased.

Figure 4.8a shows the changes in the shares in ORs and TAs of SOEs in the Top 20 over the analysis period and Figure 4.8b shows the changes in the shares of SOEs in the various sets of the largest companies.

Table 4.60 The largest SOEs in Egypt and their position in the Top 100, 2018

No.	*Name of the SOE*	*Industry*	*OR (bill. €)*	*TA (bill. €)*	*Empl. worldwide (thousand)*	*State shares[a] (%)*	*Position Top 100*
1	Egyptian General Petroleum	Oil & gas	17.0[b]	18.8[b]	2.0	100.0	1
2	Egypt Air Airlines	Transport	1.4	1.2	9.0	100.0	7
3	Arab Contractors	Construction	1.3	3.1	77.0	100.0	8
4	National Post Authority	Post & telecomm.	1.2	2.5[b]	55.0	100.0	10
5	Telecom Egypt	Post & telecomm.	1.1	3.1	53.3	80.0	12
6	Middle East Oil Refining	Chemicals	0.8	0.9	0.5	100.0	14
7	Alexandria Mineral Oils	Oil & gas	0.5	0.2	1.4	90.8	17
8	Egypt Aluminium	Metals	0.5	0.5	6.0	90.0	18
9	Eastern Company	Agribusiness	0.5	0.8	13.9	55.0	20
10	Cairo Electricity Production	Energy	0.4	1.5[b]	5.5	100.0	24

a Direct and indirect.
b Estimated.
Source: Own compilation based on the Orbis database and other data (including Fortune Global, Forbes Global lists and companies' websites).

Table 4.61 SOEs in the sets of the largest Egyptian companies – number

	Top 10			*Top 20*			*Top 50*			*Top 100*		
	2009	*2013*	*2018*	*2009*	*2013*	*2018*	*2009*	*2013*	*2018*	*2009*	*2013*	*2018*
maSOEs	4	4	4	8	10	9	16	16	17	32	32	34
miSOEs	0	0	0	0	0	0	0	1	1	1	4	4
SOEs	4	5	4	8	10	9	16	17	18	33	36	37

Source: As in Table 4.60.

Table 4.62 SOEs in the sets of the largest Egyptian companies – share in ORs (%)

	Top 10			*Top 20*			*Top 50*			*Top 100*		
	2009	*2013*	*2018*	*2009*	*2013*	*2018*	*2009*	*2013*	*2018*	*2009*	*2013*	*2018*
maSOEs	49.69	55.57	58.98	46.77	53.75	57.24	44.37	49.75	51.39	43.71	48.58	49.56
miSOEs	0	0	0	0	0	0	0	0.34	0.82	0.23	1.05	1.39
SOEs	49.69	55.57	58.98	46.77	53.75	57.24	44.37	50.09	52.21	43.93	49.57	50.75

Source: As in Table 4.60.

Table 4.63 SOEs in the sets of the largest Egyptian companies – share in TAs (%)

	Top 10			*Top 20*			*Top 50*			*Top 100*		
	2009	*2013*	*2018*	*2009*	*2013*	*2018*	*2009*	*2013*	*2018*	*2009*	*2013*	*2018*
maSOEs	46.68	55.81	61.19	43.60	54.02	57.87	42.07	50.24	51.39	41.32	45.80	47.91
miSOEs	0	0	0	0	0	0	0	2.54	0.82	0.41	0.77	2.58
SOEs	46.68	55.81	61.19	43.60	54.02	57.87	42.07	52.78	52.21	41.73	46.58	50.49

Source: As in Table 4.60.

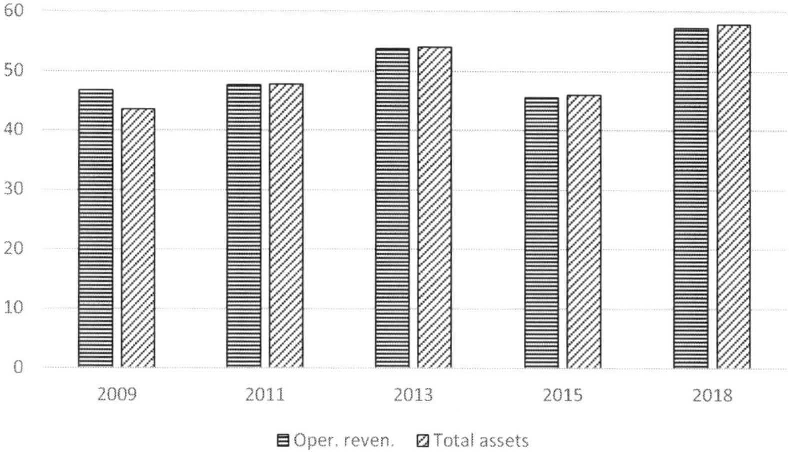

Figure 4.8a SOEs in the Top 20 of the Egyptian non-financial companies – shares in ORs and TAs (%).

Source: As in Table 4.60.

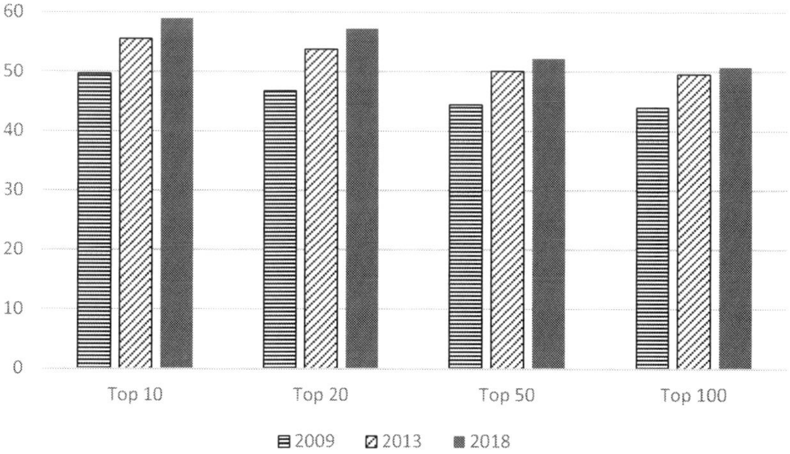

Figure 4.8b Changes in the shares of SOEs in the various sets of the largest Egyptian non-financial companies (%).

Source: As in Table 4.60.

Table 4.64 Relationship of ORs of SOEs and nominal GDP (%)

	2009	*2013*	*2018*
Rev-100/GDP	15.6	12.6	13.2
Rev-20/GDP	13.3	10.6	11.1

Source: Own calculations.

Table 4.65 Estimated share of SOEs in the selected industries of the Egyptian economy, 2018

Oil and gas	*Energy*	*Railways*	*Postal sector*	*Telecomm.*	*Banking sector*	*SS-I*
3	2	4	3	2	3	2.83

Source: Own estimation according to the rules given in Section 3.3.2.

Table 4.66 Number of listed SOEs in Egyptian Top 100

	2009	*2013*	*2018*
Listed SOEs	20	23	16
including minority SOEs	1	4	3

Source: As in Table 4.60.

4.8.3 Other characteristics of the Egyptian SOE sector

Revenues of the largest SOEs in relation to GDP

The importance of SOEs in the Egyptian economy as measured by the next indicator – ORs of the largest SOEs in relation to GDP – is high although there were significant decreases in values of this indicator in the first part of the period considered (Table 4.64).

SOEs in selected industries

The share of SOEs in all of the selected industries of the Egyptian economy is significant. In four industries SOEs have a dominant position. Our estimates are presented in Table 4.65.

Listed SOEs

While the number of listed SOEs in Top 100 non-financial companies decreased between 2013 and 2018, it is still large – see Table 4.66.

Table 4.67 FSOEs in the Top 100 of the Egyptian companies

	2009	*2013*	*2018*
Number	5	5	3
Share in ORs (%)	6.5	4.8	6.2
Share in TAs (%)	5.5	4.0	4.6

Source: As in Table 4.60.

Table 4.68 Share ratios for the Egyptian economy

Share ratio	*2009*	*2013*	*2018*
SR-100 (%)	42.8	49.6	50.6
SR-20 (%)	45.2	53.9	57.6
CS-20	1.07	1.16	1.18
miS-100 (%)	0.8	1.8	4.1

Source: Own calculations.

4.8.4 FSOEs in the Egyptian economy

In 2018, there were three FSOEs in the Top 100 Egyptian non-financial companies. In the Top 20, there was one FSOE – Orange Egypt for Telecommunications. It was ranked ninth in 2018 and was controlled by the French parent company. Data on FSOEs in the Egyptian economy are presented in Table 4.67.

4.8.5 Summary

The share of SOEs in the group of the largest Egyptian companies is at a very high level (over 50%). There were four SOEs in the Top 10. Of the 38 SOEs in the Top 100, 15 are fully owned by the state. Minority SOEs are of negligible importance. The concentration of SOEs in the Top 20 group is low and stable. The EGPC, the largest Egyptian SOE, is responsible for a very large part of all revenues of SOEs in the Top 100 (59.2%). The shares of SOEs increased significantly in the analysed period, both in the Top 100 and in the Top 20 set. A summary presentation of the data described above is presented in Table 4.68.

4.9 SOE sector in France

4.9.1 The largest SOEs in France and their characteristics

There were 9 French SOEs on the 2019 Fortune Global 500 list (out of 31 in total), and in 2009, there were 11 (out of 39 in total). The largest SOE was Électricité de France (EDF) (ranked 110th), followed by Engie (ranked 126th) and Renault (143rd). Additionally, in 123rd place, there was Airbus Group (formely European Aeronautic Defence and Space Company – EADS), which is a company controlled jointly by the governments of Germany, France and Spain, and in which France is the largest shareholder (although only 0.1 percentage point larger than the German government). Out of 64 companies on the Forbes Global list in 2010, 11 were SOEs. After nine years, the number of companies dropped to 57 and the number of SOEs to 9.

The largest French SOE is the energy conglomerate – EDF, one of the world's largest producers of electricity. EDF was created in April 1946 through the nationalisation of some 1,700 smaller energy producers, transmitters and distributors. Since November 2005, it has been listed on the Paris Stock Exchange and the French government holds a majority stake. The EDF Group has subsidiaries in most European countries, as well as in the US, Brazil and China, among others. Table 4.69 contains the characteristics of the largest French SOEs and their position in the Top 100 non-financial companies.

Table 4.69 The largest SOEs in France and their position in the Top 100, 2018

No.	*Name of the SOE*	*Industry*	*OR (bill. €)*	*TA (bill. €)*	*Empl. worldwide (thousand)*	*State shares[a] (%)*	*Position Top 100*
1	Électricité de France	Energy	76.0	283.3	162.2	83.8	3
2	Engie	Energy/Oil & gas	65.6	153.7	160.3	34.9	5
3	Airbus	Aerospace	60.1	66.3	133.0	10.9[b]	6
4	Renault	Automotive	57.4	115.0	183.0	15.0[c]	7
5	Orange	Post & telecomm.	42.0	96.6	150.7	29.5	14
6	SNCF Mobilités	Transport	31.7	42.4	272.7	100.0	18
7	Air France-KLM	Transport	26.5	29.1	84.7	14.3[c]	21
8	Safran	Aerospace	22.1	40.6	92.6	32.9	27
9	La Poste	Post & telecomm.	19.2	261.5	251.2	100.0	31
10	Suez	Water & sewage/ energy	17.6	33.6	88.7	34.6	33

a Direct and indirect.
b The German and Spanish governments also own shares in Airbus.
c Shares of less than 25% but giving substantial corporate control over the company.
Source: Own compilation based on the Orbis database and other data (including Fortune Global, Forbes Global lists and companies' websites).

4.9.2 Shares of SOEs in the sets of the largest French companies

Tables 4.70–4.72 contain data on the shares of SOEs in the various sets of the largest French non-financial companies. The shares are quite high as for the Western European country, but – as presented in the tables – they are generally declining over time.

Figure 4.9a shows the changes in the shares in Ors and Tas of SOEs in the Top 20 over the analysis period and Figure 4.9b shows the changes in the shares of SOEs in the various sets of the largest companies.

Table 4.70 SOEs in the sets of the largest French companies – number

	Top 10			*Top 20*			*Top 50*			*Top 100*		
	2009	*2013*	*2018*	*2009*	*2013*	*2018*	*2009*	*2013*	*2018*	*2009*	*2013*	*2018*
maSOEs	1	1	1	2	2	2	4	4	3	7	7	6
miSOEs	3	2	3	5	5	4	8	8	8	8	8	8
SOEs	4	3	4	7	7	6	12	12	11	15	15	14

Source: As in Table 4.69.

Table 4.71 SOEs in the sets of the largest French companies – share in ORs (%)

	Top 10			*Top 20*			*Top 50*			*Top 100*		
	2009	*2013*	*2018*	*2009*	*2013*	*2018*	*2009*	*2013*	*2018*	*2009*	*2013*	*2018*
maSOEs	10.69	10.97	10.60	10.26	10.54	9.81	9.78	9.21	7.90	9.18	8.82	7.62
miSOEs	27.47	20.75	25.54	24.38	24.48	20.52	20.39	20.18	19.12	17.73	17.25	16.22
SOEs	38.11	31.72	36.14	34.64	35.02	30.33	30.18	29.38	27.02	26.91	26.07	23.84

Source: As in Table 4.69.

Table 4.72 SOEs in the sets of the largest French companies – share in TAs (%)

	Top 10			*Top 20*			*Top 50*			*Top 100*		
	2009	*2013*	*2018*	*2009*	*2013*	*2018*	*2009*	*2013*	*2018*	*2009*	*2013*	*2018*
maSOEs	27.68	28.38	24.86	21.60	20.48	19.43	25.80	24.78	22.23	24.27	22.72	20.45
miSOEs	37.62	21.93	29.41	29.95	26.78	25.76	22.96	20.71	21.22	21.05	18.13	18.72
SOEs	65.30	50.31	54.26	51.55	47.26	45.19	48.77	45.49	43.45	45.32	40.85	39.17

Source: As in Table 4.69.

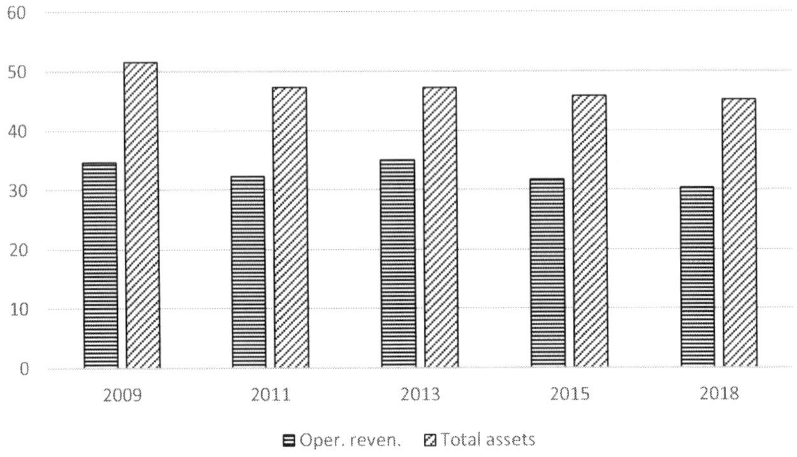

Figure 4.9a SOEs in the Top 20 of the French non-financial companies – shares in ORs and TAs (%).

Source: As in Table 4.69.

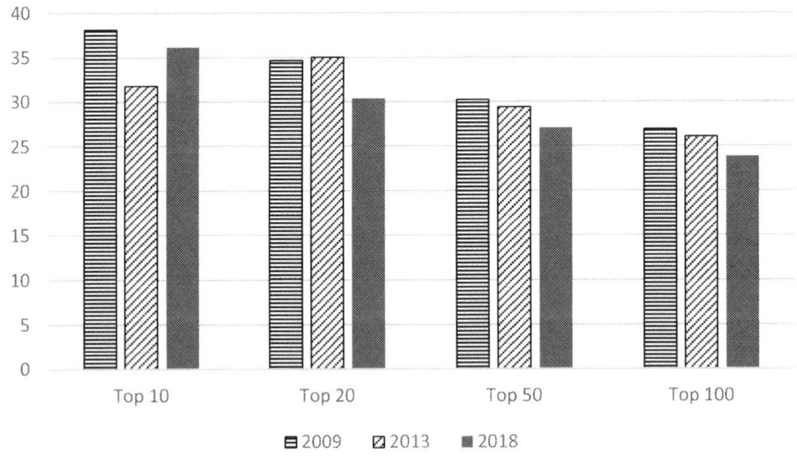

Figure 4.9b Changes in the shares of SOEs in the various sets of the largest French non-financial companies (%).

Source: As in Table 4.69.

4.9.3 Other characteristics of the French SOE sector

Revenues of the largest SOEs in relation to GDP

Values of ORs of SOEs from the Top 100 and Top 20 compared to the value of the nominal GDP of France are presented in Table 4.73. These values are rather high compared to other similar countries.

Table 4.73 Relationship of ORs of SOEs and nominal GDP (%)

	2009	*2013*	*2018*
Rev-100/GDP	19.9	22.1	18.5
Rev-20/GDP	15.9	18.0	13.7

Source: Own calculations.

Table 4.74 Estimated share of SOEs in the selected industries of the French economy, 2018

Oil and gas	*Energy*	*Railways*	*Postal sector*	*Telecomm.*	*Banking sector*	*SS-I*
0	3	3	3	3	1	2.17

Source: Own estimation according to the rules given in Section 3.3.2.

Table 4.75 Number of listed SOEs in French Top 100

	2009	*2013*	*2018*
Listed SOEs	11	10	10
including minority SOEs	8	8	8

Source: As in Table 4.69.

SOEs in selected industries

SOEs' share in strategic industries is relatively high. In energy, the French state controls two of the world's leading companies in this sector EDF Engie (which was created in 2008 by the merger of Gas de France and Suez). The French postal service (La Poste) and French railways (SNCF Mobilités) are 100% state-owned. Orange, one of the largest European companies in telecom sector, is still under state control. In the banking sector, an important role is played by the credit institution Dexia, jointly owned by the Belgian and French governments. Our estimations for selected industries are presented in Table 4.74.

Listed SOEs

Out of 14 French SOEs from the Top 100 non-financial companies in 2018, ten - as mixed capital companies - were listed on the Paris Stock Exchange. For more detailed data on this, see Table 4.75.

4.9.4 FSOEs in France

The share of FSOEs in the Top 100 of the French economy is very low. In the 2018 Top 100, there was only one FSOE (ranked 89th) – 75% indirectly

Table 4.76 FSOEs in the Top 100 of the French companies

	2009	*2013*	*2018*
Number	0	1	1
Share in ORs (%)	0	0.2	0.3
Share in TAs (%)	0	0.1	0.1

Source: As in Table 4.69.

Table 4.77 Share ratios for the French economy

Share ratio	*2009*	*2013*	*2018*
SR-100 (%)	36.1	33.5	31.5
SR-20 (%)	43.1	41.1	37.8
CS-20	1.2	1.2	1.2
miS-100 (%)	51.9	51.1	53.4

Source: Own calculations.

owned by the Russian Federation Gefco. Data on FSOEs in the French economy are presented in Table 4.76.

4.9.5 Summary

The shares of SOEs in France in 2018 were high – over 30% in the Top 100 set and over 35% in the Top 20 set. There were four SOEs in the Top 10. Of the 14 SOEs in the Top 100, 2 are fully owned by the state. The concentration of SOEs in the Top 20 did not change substantially throughout the period studied, nor did the share of minority SOEs. EDF, the largest French SOE, is responsible for a relatively small part of all revenues of SOEs in the Top 100 (16.8%). A slight decrease in the share of SOEs, both in the Top 100 and in the Top 20, is evident during the period studied. An overview of key values on SOEs' share in the French economy is presented in Table 4.77.

4.10 SOE sector in Germany

4.10.1 The largest SOEs in Germany and their characteristics

In 2010, there were 9 SOEs among 37 German companies on the Fortune Global 500 list; in 2019, there were only 3 SOEs among 29 companies. The largest ones were Deutsche Telekom (ranked 90th) and Deutsche Post (124th). On the Forbes Global 2000 list in 2010, there were 7 SOEs among 57 German entities, while nine years later there were 5 SOEs among 53 companies.

The two largest German companies under state control (although this control is only partial due to gradual privatisation) are Deutsche Telekom and Deutsche Post, both listed on the Frankfurt Stock Exchange. Both companies

Table 4.78 The largest SOEs in Germany and their position in the Top 100, 2018

No.	*Name of the SOE*	*Industry*	*OR (bill. €)*	*TA (bill. €)*	*Empl. worldwide (thousand)*	*State shares[a] (%)*	*Position Top 100*
1	Deutsche Telekom	Post & telecomm.	76.9	145.4	215.7	31.9	7
2	Deutsche Post	Post & telecomm.	62.9	50.5	547.5	21.0	9
3	Deutsche Bahn	Transport	46.4	58.5	318.5	100.0	12
4	EnBW Energie	Energy	21.1	39.6	21.5	99.6	32
5	Salzgitter	Metal	9.5	8.8	25.4	26.5	57
6	EWE	Energy	6.1	9.3	8.5	100.0	75
7	Stadtwerke Koeln	Energy	5.8	5.5	12.2	100.0	77
8	Thuega Holding	Energy	5.5	3.8	0.8	100.0	78

a Direct and indirect.
Source: Own compilation based on the Orbis database and other data (including Fortune Global, Forbes Global lists and companies' websites).

are in the Top 10 of the largest German non-financial companies. Table 4.78 contains the characteristics of the largest German SOEs and their positions in the Top 100 non-financial companies.

The German state has direct or indirect minority shareholdings in important and significant companies such as Airbus/EADS (12% shareholding of the state) or Volkswagen (20% shareholding of the state of Lower Saxony). However, an analysis of the shareholding structure indicates that these shares do not provide such a degree of control to classify these entities as SOEs.

4.10.2 Shares of SOEs in the sets of the largest German companies

Tables 4.79–4.81 contain data on the shares of SOEs in the various sets of the largest German non-financial companies. In terms of the number, the share of SOEs in German Top 100 is very stable. In relation to assets, however, we see a decline in the share of such entities, while in relation to revenues we first see a decline and then a slight rebound (between 2013 and 2018).

Table 4.79 SOEs in the sets of the largest German companies – number

	Top 10			*Top 20*			*Top 50*			*Top 100*		
	2009	*2013*	*2018*	*2009*	*2013*	*2018*	*2009*	*2013*	*2018*	*2009*	*2013*	*2018*
maSOEs	0	0	0	1	1	1	2	2	2	5	5	5
miSOEs	2	2	2	2	2	2	3	2	2	3	3	3
SOEs	2	2	2	3	3	3	5	4	4	8	8	8

Source: As in Table 4.78.

Figure 4.10a shows the changes in the shares in Ors and Tas of SOEs in the Top 20 over the analysis period and Figure 4.10b shows the changes in the shares of SOEs in the various sets of the largest companies.

Table 4.80 SOEs in the sets of the largest German companies – share in ORs (%)

	Top 10			*Top 20*			*Top 50*			*Top 100*		
	2009	*2013*	*2018*	*2009*	*2013*	*2018*	*2009*	*2013*	*2018*	*2009*	*2013*	*2018*
maSOEs	0	0	0	3.07	3.15	3.2	3.34	3.31	3.28	3.84	3.74	3.56
miSOEs	16.03	12.98	13.62	11.04	8.97	9.64	8.5	6.26	6.78	7.22	5.52	6.26
SOEs	16.03	12.98	13.62	14.1	12.11	12.85	11.84	9.57	10.06	11.06	9.26	9.82

Source: As in Table 4.78.

Table 4.81 SOEs in the sets of the largest German companies – share in TAs (%)

	Top 10			*Top 20*			*Top 50*			*Top 100*		
	2009	*2013*	*2018*	*2009*	*2013*	*2018*	*2009*	*2013*	*2018*	*2009*	*2013*	*2018*
maSOEs	0	0	0	3.68	3.38	2.87	4.98	4.59	3.82	5.71	5.03	3.99
miSOEs	17.36	12.83	12.58	12.66	9.81	9.59	10.37	7.95	7.62	9.33	7.05	7.00
SOEs	17.36	12.83	12.58	16.34	13.19	12.46	15.35	12.54	11.43	15.05	12.08	10.99

Source: As in Table 4.78.

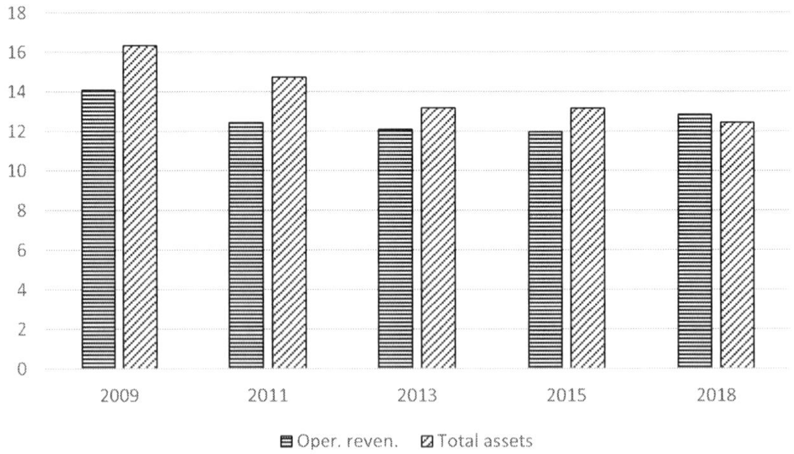

Figure 4.10a SOEs in the Top 20 of the German non-financial companies – shares in ORs and TAs (%).

Source: As in Table 4.78.

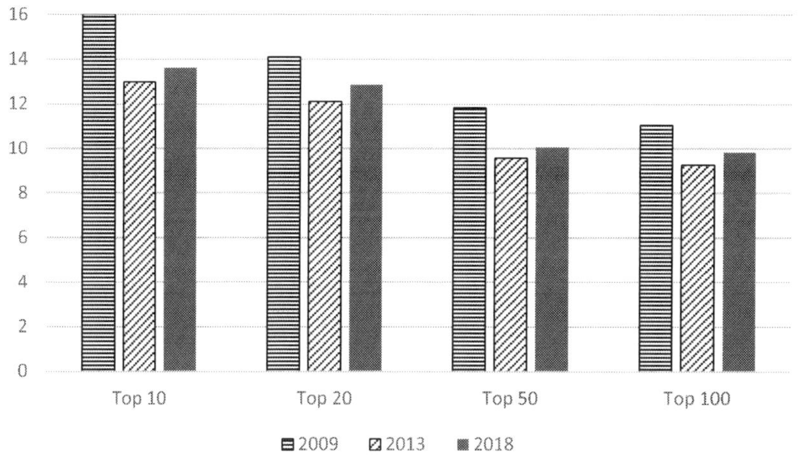

Figure 4.10b Changes in the shares of SOEs in the various sets of the largest German non-financial companies (%).

Source: As in Table 4.78.

Table 4.82 Relationship of ORs of SOEs and nominal GDP (%)

	2009	*2013*	*2018*
Rev-100/GDP	7.9	7.9	6.8
Rev-20/GDP	6.2	7.0	5.9

Source: Own calculations.

4.10.3 Other characteristics of the German SOE sector

Revenues of the largest SOEs in relation to GDP

Table 4.82 provides data on the relationship of the value of Ors of SOEs from the Top 100 and Top 20 compared to the value of the nominal GDP of Germany in selected years. Values of these indicators were at moderate levels and declined from 2009 to 2018.

SOEs in selected industries

German SOEs play an important role in the network sectors: railways, postal and telecommunication. They are also present in energy and banking (Table 4.83).

Table 4.83 Estimated share of SOEs in the selected industries of the German economy, 2018

Oil and gas	*Energy*	*Railways*	*Postal sector*	*Telecomm.*	*Banking sector*	*SS-I*
0	1	3	3	3	1	1.83

Source: Own estimation according to the rules given in Section 3.3.2.

Table 4.84 Number of listed SOEs in German Top 100

	2009	*2013*	*2018*
Listed SOEs	4	4	4
including minority SOEs	3	3	3

Source: As in Table 4.78.

Listed SOEs

Out of eight German SOEs from the Top 100 non-financial companies in 2018, four were listed on the stock exchange. Three of them was controlled with minority shares. The relevant data are presented in Table 4.84.

It is worth noting here that the German state has direct or indirect minority shareholdings in important and significant companies such as Airbus/EADS (12% shareholding of the state) or Volkswagen (20% shareholding of the state of Lower Saxony). However, an analysis of the shareholding structure indicates that these shares do not provide such a degree of control that these entities can be described as German SOEs.

4.10.4 FSOEs in Germany

In 2018, there were six FSOEs (not included in the tables and charts above) in the Top 100 German non-financial companies. In Top 20 there were two FSOEs. The largest of them was the energy company Uniper, which ranked fourth on the list in 2018 and is controlled by the Finnish SOE Fortum. Although the number of FSOEs has decreased during the period considered, their shares have increased (Table 4.85).

Table 4.85 FSOEs in the Top 100 of the German companies

	2009	*2013*	*2018*
Number	7	7	6
Share in ORs (%)	3.6	4.8	8.2
Share in TAs (%)	1.0	1.2	2.5

Source: As in Table 4.78.

Table 4.86 Share ratios for the German economy

Share ratio	*2009*	*2013*	*2018*
SR-100 (%)	13.1	10.7	10.4
SR-20 (%)	15.2	12.4	12.7
CS-20	1.2	1.2	1.2
miS-100 (%)	63.3	58.9	63.7

Source: Own calculations.

4.10.5 Summary

The share of SOEs in Germany in 2018 was rather low – slightly over 10% in the Top 100 set and 12% in the Top 20 set. There were two SOEs in the Top 10. Of the eight SOEs in the Top 100, four are fully owned by the state. The concentration of SOEs in the Top 20 was stable over the period under review. The share of minority SOEs in the total set of SOEs is high, exceeding 50%. Deutsche Telekom, the largest German SOE, is responsible for 32.8% of all revenues of SOEs in the Top 100. The shares of SOEs declined moderately over the period considered, in both the Top 100 and the Top 20. A summary presentation of the data described above is presented in Table 4.86.

4.11 SOE sector in India

4.11.1 The largest SOEs in India and their characteristics

The 2010 Fortune Global 500 list included eight Indian companies, out of which five should be considered SOEs. In the 2019 list (2018 data), there were seven Indian companies, including four SOEs. These were Indian Oil (ranked 117th), Oil & Natural Gas (160th), State Bank of India (236th) and Bharat Petroleum (275th). In the Forbes Global 2000 list in 2010, there were 56 Indian companies, of which 25 can be classified as state-owned. Nine years later these numbers were almost identical (57 Indian companies including 25 SOEs).

The largest Indian state-owned company in 2018 was Indian Oil Corporation, which operates in the petrochemical industry. Indian Oil's equity shares are listed on the Bombay Stock Exchange. Table 4.87 contains the characteristics of the largest Indian SOEs and their positions in the Top 100 non-financial companies.

4.11.2 Shares of SOEs in the sets of the largest Indian companies

Tables 4.88–4.90 contain data on the SOEs' shares in the various sets of the largest Indian non-financial companies. From the data presented below, it can be concluded that the share of SOEs in revenues and assets is high, especially among the group of the largest companies. Comparing 2009 and 2018, we see that the number of companies controlled by the Indian government has declined slightly, and it is similar with the shares in revenues and assets.

Table 4.87 The largest SOEs in India and their position in the Top 100, 2018

No.	Name of the SOE	Industry	OR (bill. €)	TA (bill. €)	Empl. worldwide (thousand)	State shares[a] (%)	Position Top 100
1	Indian Oil	Oil & gas	67.8	43.1	33.5	72.9	2
2	Oil and Natural Gas	Oil & gas	54.3	63.8	31.1	85.6	3
3	Bharat Petroleum	Oil & gas	38.5	17.6	11.9	56.3	5
4	Indian Railways	Transport	22.3	67.1	1 308.0	100.0	7
5	Coal India	Mining	13.0	17.1	272.4	86.1	11
6	National Thermal Power	Energy	12.3	40.8	20.2	74.4	12
7	Gail	Oil & gas	9.8	8.8	4.5	63.9	20
8	Steel Authority of India	Metals	8.6	15.2	72.3	86.9	21
9	MSEDCL	Energy	8.3	14.5	66.5	100.0	23
10	Hpcl-Mittal Energy	Oil & gas	8.1	5.4	2.1	50.6	25

[a]Direct and indirect.
Source: Own compilation based on the Orbis database and other data (including Fortune Global, Forbes Global lists and companies' websites).

Table 4.88 SOEs in the sets of the largest Indian companies – number

	Top 10			Top 20			Top 50			Top 100		
	2009	2013	2018	2009	2013	2018	2009	2013	2018	2009	2013	2018
maSOEs	6	5	4	11	8	7	17	18	16	32	26	31
miSOEs	0	0	0	0	0	0	0	0	0	1	1	1
SOEs	6	5	4	11	8	7	17	18	16	33	27	32

Source: As in Table 4.87.

Table 4.89 SOEs in the sets of the largest Indian companies – share in ORs (%)

	Top 10			Top 20			Top 50			Top 100		
	2009	2013	2018	2009	2013	2018	2009	2013	2018	2009	2013	2018
maSOEs	60.67	56.44	48.96	58.65	50.54	44.66	49.61	47.11	41.50	46.89	42.13	39.67
miSOEs	0	0	0	0	0	0	0	0	0	0.31	0.25	0.30
SOEs	60.67	56.44	48.96	58.65	50.54	44.66	49.61	47.11	41.50	47.20	42.38	39.97

Source: As in Table 4.87.

Table 4.90 SOEs in the sets of the largest Indian companies – share in TAs (%)

	Top 10			*Top 20*			*Top 50*			*Top 100*		
	2009	*2013*	*2018*	*2009*	*2013*	*2018*	*2009*	*2013*	*2018*	*2009*	*2013*	*2018*
maSOEs	59.02	52.77	43.21	58.62	44.78	40.68	46.92	44.79	38.77	44.85	41.12	41.24
miSOEs	0	0	0	0	0	0	0	0	0	0.09	0.15	0.23
SOEs	59.02	52.77	43.21	58.62	44.78	40.68	46.92	44.79	38.77	44.94	41.37	41.47

Source: As in Table 4.87.

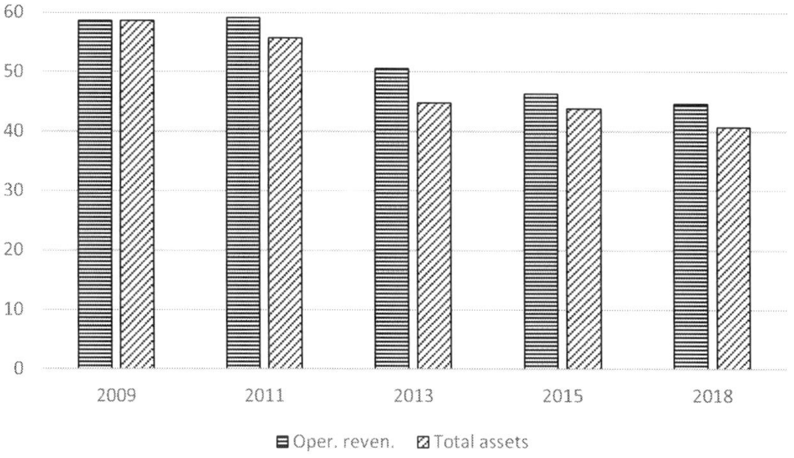

Figure 4.11a SOEs in the Top 20 of the Indian non-financial companies – shares in ORs and TAs (%).

Source: As in Table 4.87.

Figure 4.11a shows the changes in the shares in ORs and TAs of SOEs in the Top 20 over the analysis period and Figure 4.11b shows the changes in the shares of SOEs in the various sets of the largest companies.

4.11.3 Other characteristics of the Indian SOE sector

Revenues of the largest SOEs in relation to GDP

Table 4.91 provides data on the relationship of the value of ORs of SOEs from the Top 100 and Top 20 compared to the value of the nominal GDP of India in selected years. Values of these indicators were at moderate levels and clearly declined in the period analysed.

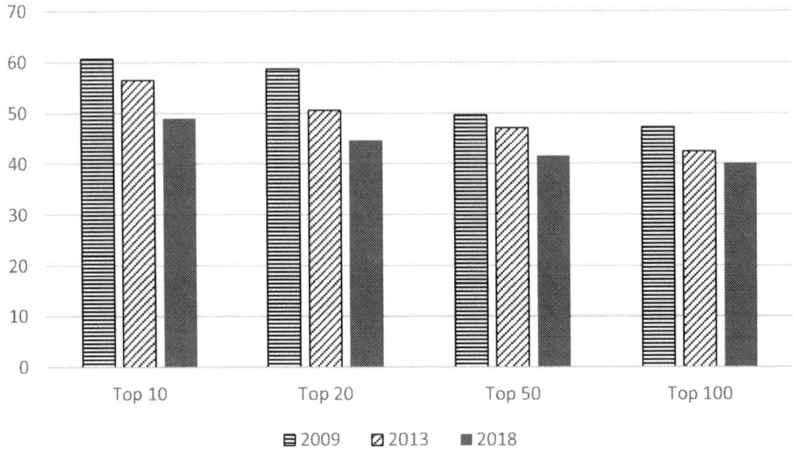

Figure 4.11b Changes in the shares of SOEs in the various sets of the largest Indian non-financial companies (%).

Source: As in Table 4.87.

Table 4.91 Relationship of ORs of SOEs and nominal GDP (%)

	2009	*2013*	*2018*
Rev-100/GDP	20.5	18.0	12.6
Rev-20/GDP	16.5	13.6	9.2

Source: Own calculations.

Table 4.92 Estimated share of SOEs in the selected industries of the Indian economy, 2018

Oil and gas	*Energy*	*Railways*	*Postal sector*	*Telecomm.*	*Banking sector*	*SS-I*
4	3	4	3	1	3	3.00

Source: Own estimation according to the rules given in Section 3.3.2.

SOEs in selected industries

SOEs are widespread in strategic sectors of the Indian economy. Of the selected sectors, only in telecommunications their share cannot be described as monopolistic or dominant. Our estimates are presented in Table 4.92.

Listed SOEs

More than half of India's SOEs from Top 100 are listed companies. However, there was only one entity with minority shares among them – see Table 4.93.

Table 4.93 Number of listed SOEs in Indian Top 100

	2009	*2013*	*2018*
Listed SOEs	18	16	18
including minority SOEs	1	1	1

Source: As in Table 4.78.

Table 4.94 Share ratios for the Indian economy

Share ratio	*2009*	*2013*	*2018*
SR-100 (%)	46.9	41.8	40.7
SR-20 (%)	58.6	47.7	42.7
CS-20	1.2	1.1	1.0
miS-100 (%)	0.4	0.5	0.6

Source: Own calculations.

4.11.4 FSOEs in India

No foreign SOE was in the lists of the 100 largest Indian enterprises in the years under review.

4.11.5 Summary

The share of SOEs in India in 2018 was high – over 40%. There were four SOEs in the Top 10. Of the 31 SOEs in the Top 100, 12 are fully owned by the state. There is a complete lack of minority SOEs. The concentration of SOEs in the Top 20 is decreasing. Indian Oil, the largest Indian SOE, is responsible for 22.8% of all revenues of SOEs in the Top 100. The share of SOEs decreased in the years studied, which is much more pronounced in the Top 20 group. An overview of key values on SOEs' share in the Indian economy is in Table 4.94.

4.12 SOE sector in Indonesia

4.12.1 The largest SOEs in Indonesia and their characteristics

There were no Indonesian companies on the Fortune Global 500 list in 2010, and there was one in 2019 (Petramina at the 175th position). On the Forbes Global 2000 list in 2009, there were ten Indonesian companies, including seven SOEs. In 2019, the number of Indonesian companies dropped to six and SOEs to four.

The largest Indonesian SOE, and the largest company in the country, is the petrochemical conglomerate Petramina. The company was established in 1968, after the merger of two former SOEs, then operating on the

Table 4.95 The largest SOEs in Indonesia and their position in the Top 100, 2018

No.	*Name of the SOE*	*Industry*	*OR (bill. €)*	*TA (bill. €)*	*Empl. worldwide (thousand)*	*State shares*[a] *(%)*	*Position Top 100*
1	Pertamina	Oil & gas	50.6	56.6	13.7	100.0	1
2	Listrik Negara	Energy	15.9	89.5	45.5	100.0	2
3	Telekomunikasi Indonesia	Post & telecomm.	8.0	12.4	24.1	52.1	3
4	Inalum	Metals	3.9	5.6	2.1	100.0	7
5	Garuda Indonesia	Transport	3.8	3.6	16.3	60.5	8
6	Waskita Karya	Construction	3.1	7.5	2.4	66.0	12
7	Jasa Marga	Transport	2.2	5.0	7.0	70.0	18
8	Wijaya Karya	Construction	1.9	3.6	2.6	65.1	22
9	Semen Indonesia	Chemicals	1.9	3.1	9.6	51.0	23
10	Kereta Api	Transport	1.6	2.3	27.4	100.0	26

a Direct and indirect.
Source: Own compilation based on the Orbis database and other data (including Fortune Global, Forbes Global lists and companies' websites).

nationalised Dutch oil assets. Activities of Petramina – carried out by more than 20 subsidiaries – include oil and gas production, processing and retailing, as well as a wide range of other petrochemical production processes. Table 4.95 contains the characteristics of the largest Indonesian SOEs and their positions in the Top 100 non-financial companies.

4.12.2 Shares of SOEs in the sets of the largest Indonesian companies

Tables 4.96–4.98 contain data on the shares of SOEs in the various sets of the largest Indonesian non-financial companies. Two things are noteworthy here: the high and minority SOEs.

Table 4.96 SOEs in the sets of the largest Indonesian companies – number

	Top 10			*Top 20*			*Top 50*			*Top 100*		
	2009	*2013*	*2018*	*2009*	*2013*	*2018*	*2009*	*2013*	*2018*	*2009*	*2013*	*2018*
maSOEs	5	5	6	8	8	7	15	13	13	22	21	19
miSOEs	0	0	0	0	0	0	0	0	0	1	0	0
SOEs	5	5	6	8	8	7	15	13	13	23	21	19

Source: As in Table 4.95.

Figure 4.12a shows the changes in the shares in ORs and TAs of SOEs in the Top 20 over the analysis period and Figure 4.12b shows the changes in the shares of SOEs in the various sets of the largest companies.

Table 4.97 SOEs in the sets of the largest Indonesian companies – share in ORs (%)

	Top 10			*Top 20*			*Top 50*			*Top 100*		
	2009	*2013*	*2018*	*2009*	*2013*	*2018*	*2009*	*2013*	*2018*	*2009*	*2013*	*2018*
maSOEs	80.48	83.23	80.31	71.83	73.97	68.22	60.70	61.23	57.93	55.03	54.73	51.35
miSOEs	0	0	0	0	0	0	0	0	0	0.31	0	0
SOEs	80.48	83.23	80.31	71.83	73.97	68.22	60.70	61.23	57.93	55.33	54.73	51.35

Source: As in Table 4.95.

Table 4.98 SOEs in the sets of the largest Indonesian companies – share in TAs (%)

	Top 10			*Top 20*			*Top 50*			*Top 100*		
	2009	*2013*	*2018*	*2009*	*2013*	*2018*	*2009*	*2013*	*2018*	*2009*	*2013*	*2018*
maSOEs	81.57	80.36	90	72.39	72.39	78.39	60.36	59.16	68.12	55.41	53.00	62.75
miSOEs	0	0	0	0	0	0	0	0	0	0.23	0	0
SOEs	81.57	80.36	90.00	72.39	72.39	78.39	60.36	59.16	68.12	55.65	53.00	62.75

Source: As in Table 4.95.

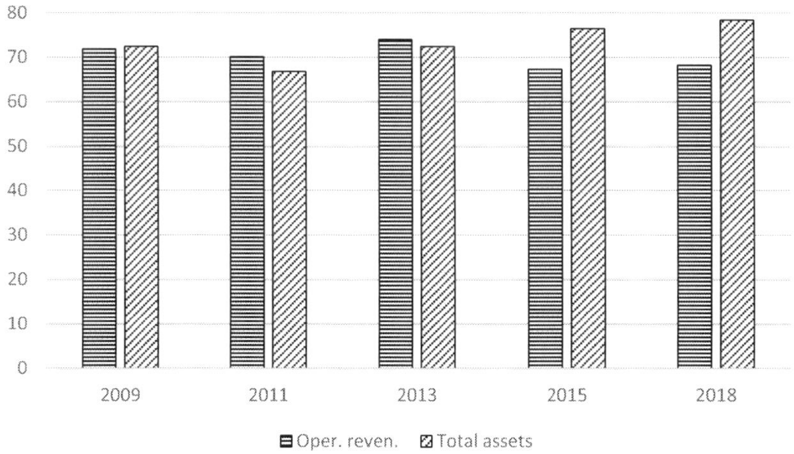

Figure 4.12a SOEs in the Top 20 of the Indonesian non-financial companies – shares in ORs and TAs (%).

Source: As in Table 4.95.

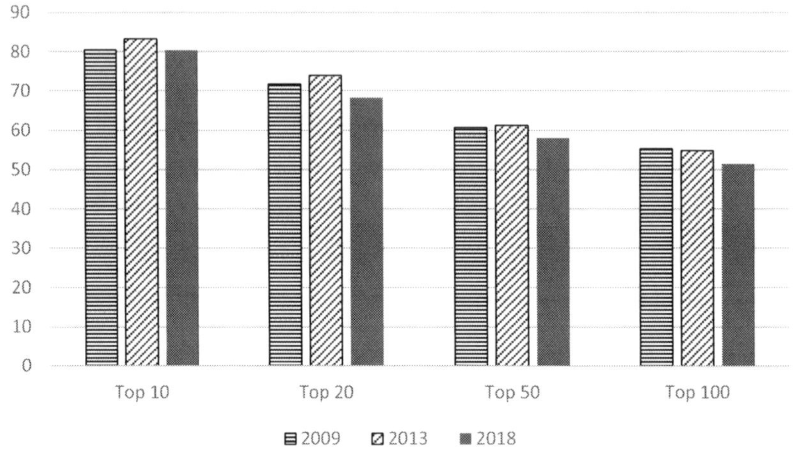

Figure 4.12b Changes in the shares of SOEs in the various sets of the largest Indonesian non-financial companies (%).

Source: As in Table 4.95.

Table 4.99 Relationship of ORs of SOEs and nominal GDP (%)

	2009	*2013*	*2018*
Rev-100/GDP	14.7	12.5	11.0
Rev-20/GDP	13.1	11.4	9.6

Source: Own calculations.

4.12.3 Other characteristics of the Indonesian SOE sector

Revenues of the largest SOEs in relation to GDP

Table 4.99 provides data on the relationship of the value of ORs of the Indonesian SOEs from the Top 100 and Top 20 compared to the value of the nominal GDP in selected years. Values of these indicators were at moderate levels and declined from 2009 to 2018.

SOEs in selected industries

Indonesian SOEs play a very important role in the strategic sectors. They dominate in the following industries: oil and gas, energy, railways, telecommunications and banking. Our estimations for selected industries are presented in Table 4.100.

Table 4.100 Estimated share of SOEs in the selected industries of the Indonesian economy, 2018

Oil and gas	*Energy*	*Railways*	*Postal sector*	*Telecomm.*	*Banking sector*	*SS-I*
3	3	4	2	3	3	3.00

Source: Own estimation according to the rules given in Section 3.3.2.

Table 4.101 Number of listed SOEs in Indonesian Top 100

	2009	*2013*	*2018*
Listed SOEs	12	14	11
including minority SOEs	1	0	0

Source: As in Table 4.95.

Table 4.102 FSOEs in the Top 100 of the Indonesian companies

	2009	*2013*	*2018*
Number	2	2	3
Share in ORs (%)	2.4	1.8	1.8
Share in TAs (%)	4.5	3.1	2.1

Source: As in Table 4.95.

Listed SOEs

Out of 19 Indonesian SOEs from the Top 100 non-financial companies in 2018, 11 were listed on the stock exchange. In 2018 all of them were companies with majority state ownership (Table 4.101).

4.12.4 FSOEs in Indonesia

In 2018, there were three FSOEs in the Top 100 Indonesian non-financial companies. In the Top 20, there were no FSOEs. The largest FSOE was Xl Axiata TBK, which ranked 33rd and is controlled by the Malaysian Axiata Group Berhad. The relevant data are presented in Table 4.102.

4.12.5 Summary

The share of SOEs in Indonesia in 2018 was very high – over 55% in the Top 100 set and over 70% in the Top 20 set. There were five SOEs in the Top 10. Of the 19 SOEs in the Top 100, 8 are fully owned by the state. There is a complete lack of minority SOEs. The concentration of SOEs in the Top 20 is visible. Petramina, the largest Indonesian SOE, is responsible for a very large part of all revenues of SOEs in the Top 100 (50.5%). The shares of SOEs are stable over time (Table 4.103).

Table 4.103 Share ratios for the Indonesian economy

Share ratio	*2009*	*2013*	*2018*
SR-100 (%)	55.5	53.9	57.0
SR-20 (%)	72.2	73.2	73.3
CS-20	1.30	1.36	1.29
miS-100 (%)	47.4	0	0

Source: Own calculations.

4.13 SOE sector in Ireland

4.13.1 The largest SOEs in Ireland and their characteristics

There were four Irish companies in the Fortune Global 500 list in 2019 and two in 2010, but not one of them was state-owned. On the Forbes Global 2000 as many as 18 companies were classified as Irish and one of them was state-owned – financial AIB (Allied Irish Banks) Group.

In 2018, Ireland's largest SOE was a corporation Electricity Supply Board, once a state monopoly (established in 1927) and currently operating in a liberalised and competitive market. Information on largest non-financial SOEs in Ireland, their financial results and positions in the Top 100 of Irish companies is provided in Table 4.104.

Table 4.104 The largest SOEs in Ireland and their position in the Top 100, 2018

No.	*Name of the SOE*	*Industry*	*OR (bill. €)*	*TA (bill. €)*	*Empl. worldwide (thousand)*	*State shares[a] (%)*	*Position Top 100*
1	Electricity Supply Board	Energy	3.4	13.3	7.9	95.0	35
2	Córas Iompair Éireann	Transport	1.3	2.8	10.0	100.0	72
3	Irish Water	Water & sewage	1.0	3.0	0.8	100.0	86
4	An Post	Post & telecomm.	0.9	1.1	7.6	100.0	89
5	Dublin Airport Authority	Transport	0.9	2.8	3.0	100.0	90
6	EirGrid	Energy	0.8	1.1	1.0	100.0	97

[a] Direct and indirect.
Source: Own compilation based on the Orbis database and other data (including Fortune Global, Forbes Global lists and companies' websites).

4.13.2 Shares of SOEs in the sets of the largest Irish companies

Tables 4.105–4.107 contain data on the shares of SOEs in the various sets of the largest Irish non-financial companies. Ireland's largest SOEs are small relative to the country's largest companies overall. SOEs are not included in the Top 10.

Figure 4.13a shows the changes in the shares in ORs and TAs of SOEs in the Top 20 and Figure 4.13.b shows the changes in the shares of SOEs in the various sets of the largest Irish companies.

Table 4.105 SOEs in the sets of the largest Irish companies – number

	Top 20			*Top 50*			*Top 100*		
	2009	*2013*	*2018*	*2009*	*2013*	*2018*	*2009*	*2013*	*2018*
maSOEs	1	0	0	2	1	1	7	3	6
miSOEs	0	0	0	0	0	0	0	0	0
SOEs	1	0	0	2	1	1	7	3	6

Source: As in Table 4.104.

Table 4.106 SOEs in the sets of the largest Irish companies – share in ORs (%)

	Top 20			*Top 50*			*Top 100*		
	2009	*2013*	*2018*	*2009*	*2013*	*2018*	*2009*	*2013*	*2018*
maSOEs	2.05	0	0	2.26	0.72	0.74	3.33	0.96	1.57
miSOEs	0	0	0	0	0	0	0	0	0
SOEs	2.05	0	0	2.26	0.72	0.74	3.33	0.96	1.57

Source: As in Table 4.104.

Table 4.107 SOEs in the sets of the largest Irish companies – share in TAs (%)

	Top 20			*Top 50*			*Top 100*		
	2009	*2013*	*2018*	*2009*	*2013*	*2018*	*2009*	*2013*	*2018*
maSOEs	5.82	0	0	6.53	2.43	1.84	8.25	2.42	2.99
miSOEs	0	0	0	0	0	0	0	0	0
SOEs	5.82	0	0	6.53	2.43	1.84	8.25	2.42	2.99

Source: As in Table 4.104.

Figure 4.13a SOEs in the Top 20 of the Irish non-financial companies – shares in ORs and TAs (%).

Source: As in Table 4.104.

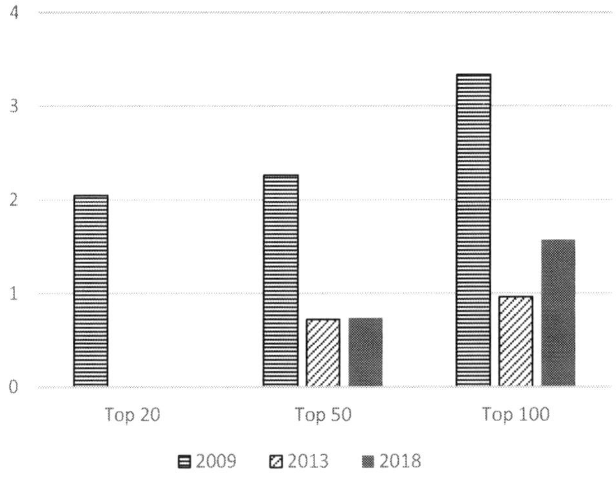

Figure 4.13b Changes in the shares of SOEs in the various sets of the largest Irish non-financial companies (%).

Source: As in Table 4.104.

4.13.3 Other characteristics of the Irish SOE sector

Revenues of the largest SOEs in relation to GDP

Table 4.108 provides data on the relationship of the value of ORs of SOEs from the Top 100 and Top 20 compared to the value of the nominal GDP in

Table 4.108 Relationship of ORs of SOEs and nominal GDP (%)

	2009	*2013*	*2018*
Rev-100/GDP	4.5	3.0	2.5
Rev-20/GDP	1.9	0	0

Source: Own calculations.

Table 4.109 Estimated share of SOEs in the selected industries of the Irish economy, 2018

Oil and gas	*Energy*	*Railways*	*Postal sector*	*Telecomm.*	*Banking sector*	*SS-I*
0	3	3	2	0	2	1.67

Source: Own estimation according to the rules given in Section 3.3.2.

selected years. The importance of Irish SOEs as measured by this indicator is at a low level and it is declining over time.

SOEs in selected industries

Largest Irish SOEs are present in the following industries: energy, railways, postal and banking. There are no big SOEs in oil and gas and telecommunication. The relevant data are presented in Table 4.109.

Listed SOEs

Between 2009 and 2018 there were no listed SOEs in the Top 100 of the non-financial companies.

4.13.4 FSOEs in Ireland

In 2018, there were five FSOEs in the Top 100 Irish non-financial companies. In Top 20 there were two FSOEs. The largest of them was Societe Air France, controlled by the French government. The company was ranked tenth in the Top 100 set. Data on FSOEs in the Irish economy are presented in Table 4.110.

Table 4.110 FSOEs in the Top 100 of the Irish companies

	2009	*2013*	*2018*
Number	4	2	5
Share in ORs (%)	1.9	2.8	5.9
Share in TAs (%)	1.1	1.6	5.1

Source: As in Table 4.104.

Table 4.111 Share ratios for the Irish economy

Share ratio	*2009*	*2013*	*2018*
SR-100 (%)	5.8	1.7	2.3
SR-20 (%)	4.0	0	0
CS-20	0.68	0	0
miS-100 (%)	0	0	0

Source: Own calculations.

4.13.5 Summary

The share of SOEs in the group of the largest Irish companies is very low. There were no SOEs either in the Top 10 or in the Top 20 in 2018, and only one in the Top 50. Of the six SOEs in the Top 100, five are fully owned by the state. There are no minority SOEs in the Top 100. The Electricity Supply Board, the largest Irish SOE, was responsible for quite a large part of all revenues of SOEs in the Top 100 (41.4%). A summary presentation of the data described above is presented in Table 4.111.

4.14 SOE sector in Italy

4.14.1 The largest SOEs in Italy and their characteristics

There were 11 Italian companies on the Fortune Global 500 list in 2010, including four SOEs. In 2019, there were six Italian companies including three SOEs. These were Eni (ranked 83rd), Enel (89th) and Poste Italiane (355th). The Forbes Global 2000 list in 2010 (data for 2009) included 38 Italian companies, six of which were identified as state-owned. Nine years later there were 27 Italian companies on the list, 7 of which can be identified as state-owned.

The list of Italy's largest non-financial companies is led by two similarly sized state-controlled companies: the multinational oil and gas company Eni Group and the multinational energy company Enel Group. Eni was created in 1953 on the basis of the pre-existing state-controlled petrochemical company Agip. Since 1995, it has been listed on the Milan Stock Exchange in Italy and on the NYSE in New York. Enel was created in 1962 following the nationalisation of the Italian electricity system. Since 1999, after partial privatisation, Enel has been a listed company. It is one of Europe's largest energy companies. Table 4.112 contains the characteristics of the largest Italian SOEs and their position in the Top 100 non-financial companies.

4.14.2 Shares of SOEs in the sets of the largest Italian companies

Tables 4.113–4.115 contain data on the shares of SOEs in the various sets of the largest Italian non-financial companies. The data presented below show a

Table 4.112 The largest SOEs in Italy and their position in the Top 100, 2018

No.	*Name of the SOE*	*Industry*	*OR (bill. €)*	*TA (bill. €)*	*Empl. worldwide (thousand)*	*State shares*[a] *(%)*	*Position Top 100*
1	Eni	Oil & gas	76.9	118.4	31.7	30.1	1
2	Enel	Energy	75.3	165.4	69.3	23.6	2
3	GSE	Energy	32.5	8.8	1.3	100.0	3
4	Ferrovie D. Stato Ital.	Transport	13.8	72.5	81.7	100.0	7
5	Leonardo	Defence	12.4	25.5	46.5	32.5	8
6	Saipem	Technology	8.5	11.7	31.7	42.5	16
7	Poste Italiane	Post & telecomm.	8.2	72.5	134.4	64.3	17
8	Hera	Water & sewage	6.6	9.1	8.6	46.1	21
9	A2A	Energy/water	6.5	10.3	12.1	50.0	22
10	Fincantieri	Shipbuilding	5.5	7.3	19.3	72.5	28

[a] Direct and indirect.
Source: Own compilation based on the Orbis database and other data (including Fortune Global, Forbes Global lists and companies' websites).

Table 4.113 SOEs in the sets of the largest Italian companies – number

	Top 10			*Top 20*			*Top 50*			*Top 100*		
	2009	*2013*	*2018*	*2009*	*2013*	*2018*	*2009*	*2013*	*2018*	*2009*	*2013*	*2018*
maSOEs	2	1	2	3	2	3	6	6	5	8	6	7
miSOEs	4	4	3	4	4	4	5	8	6	5	9	9
SOEs	6	5	5	7	6	7	11	14	11	13	15	16

Source: As in Table 4.112.

Table 4.114 SOEs in the sets of the largest Italian companies – share in ORs (%)

	Top 10			*Top 20*			*Top 50*			*Top 100*		
	2009	*2013*	*2018*	*2009*	*2013*	*2018*	*2009*	*2013*	*2018*	*2009*	*2013*	*2018*
maSOEs	10.77	8.38	15.67	10.32	8.80	14.30	10.25	9.72	12.33	9.20	8.08	10.72
miSOEs	55.52	53.54	55.76	45.42	44.25	45.47	36.06	37.58	35.9	29.71	31.50	30.16
SOEs	66.29	61.92	71.43	55.74	53.04	59.77	46.31	47.3	48.24	38.91	39.58	40.88

Source: As in Table 4.112.

small increase in the importance of SOEs in the Italian economy during the period under study.

Figure 4.14a shows the changes in the shares in ORs and TAs of SOEs in the Top 20 over the analysis period and Figure 4.14b shows the changes in the shares of SOEs in the various sets of the largest Italian companies.

Table 4.115 SOEs in the sets of the largest Italian companies – share in TAs (%)

	Top 10			*Top 20*			*Top 50*			*Top 100*		
	2009	*2013*	*2018*	*2009*	*2013*	*2018*	*2009*	*2013*	*2018*	*2009*	*2013*	*2018*
maSOEs	15.65	1.29	16.76	15.66	10.85	22.15	14.57	16.46	19.18	15.00	14.24	17.32
miSOEs	55.39	63.69	63.76	48.9	53.44	46.24	41.03	43.50	38.51	35.19	39.06	36.55
SOEs	71.04	64.98	80.52	64.56	64.28	68.39	55.61	59.96	57.7	50.0	53.30	53.87

Source: As in Table 4.112.

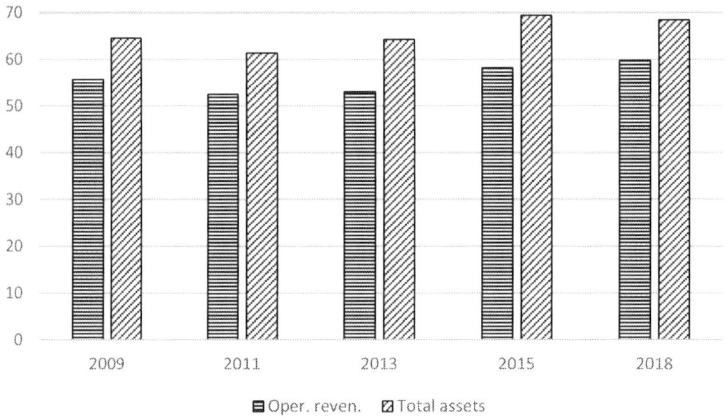

Figure 4.14a SOEs in the Top 20 of the Italian non-financial companies – shares in ORs and TAs (%).

Source: As in Table 4.112.

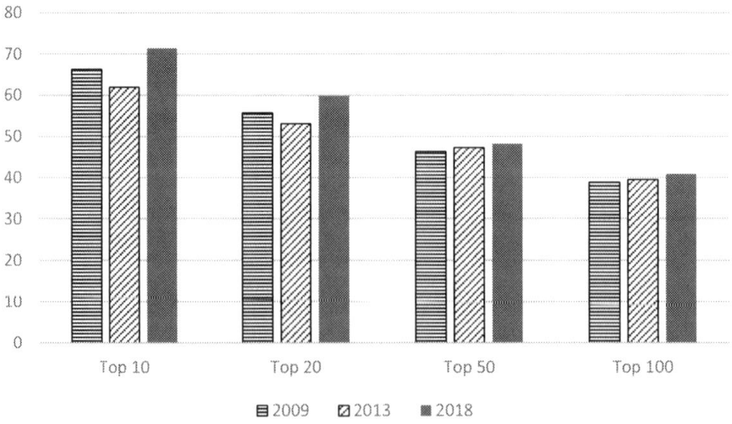

Figure 4.14b Changes in the shares of SOEs in the various sets of the largest Italian non-financial companies (%).

Source: As in Table 4.112.

Table 4.116 Relationship of ORs of SOEs and nominal GDP (%)

	2009	*2013*	*2018*
Rev-100/GDP	15.8	19.4	14.4
Rev-20/GDP	14.4	17.1	12.5

Source: Own calculations.

Table 4.117 Estimated share of SOEs in the selected industries of the Italian economy, 2018

Oil and gas	*Energy*	*Railways*	*Postal sector*	*Telecomm.*	*Banking sector*	*SS-I*
3	3	3	3	0	1	2.17

Source: Own estimation according to the rules given in Section 3.3.2.

Table 4.118 Number of listed SOEs in Italian Top 100

	2009	*2013*	*2018*
Listed SOEs	9	10	12
including minority SOEs	5	8	8

Source: As in Table 4.112.

4.14.3 Other characteristics of the Italian SOE sector

Revenues of the largest SOEs in relation to GDP

Table 4.116 provides data on the relationship of the value of ORs of SOEs from the Top 100 and Top 20 compared to the value of the nominal GDP in selected years. The importance of Italian SOEs as measured by this indicator is at a quite high level.

SOEs in selected industries

SOEs are widespread in four strategic industries of the Italian economy. Only in telecommunications and banking their share cannot be classified as monopolistic or dominant (see Table 4.117).

Listed SOEs

The number of listed SOEs in the Italian Top 100 increased during the period under review, with 12 such entities in 2018. The relevant data are presented in Table 4.118.

Table 4.119 FSOEs in the Top 100 of the Italian companies

	2009	*2013*	*2018*
Number	3	5	7
Share in ORs (%)	3.3	4.8	5.8
Share in TAs (%)	2.4	2.0	3.2

Source: As in Table 4.112.

Table 4.120 Share ratios for the Italian economy

Share ratio	*2009*	*2013*	*2018*
SR-100 (%)	44.6	46.4	47.4
SR-20 (%)	60.2	58.7	64.1
CS-20	1.35	1.27	1.41
miS-100 (%)	72.2	75.5	69.7

Source: Own calculations.

4.14.4 FSOEs in Italy

In 2018, there were seven FSOEs in the Top 100 Italian non-financial companies. In Top 20 there were two FSOEs. The largest of them was Kuwait Petroleum Italia, which ranked ninth on the list in 2018 and is controlled by Kuwait Petroleum Corporation. Data on FSOEs in the Italian economy are presented in Table 4.119.

4.14.5 Summary

The share of SOEs in Italy in 2018 was very high – over 45% in the Top 100 set and almost 65% in the Top 20 set and slightly increasing in the analysed period. There were five SOEs in the Top 10. Italy is one of five large countries in the world (along with China, Indonesia, Norway and Saudi Arabia) where all three largest non-financial enterprises are under state control. Of the 16 SOEs in the Top 100, three are fully owned by the state. The share of SOEs with minority state holdings is very significant. The concentration of SOEs in the Top 20 has increased in recent years. Eni, the largest Italian SOE, is responsible for 29.2% of all revenues of SOEs in the Top 100 – see Table 4.120.

4.15 SOE sector in Japan

4.15.1 The largest SOEs in Japan and their characteristics

The 2019 Fortune Global 500 list included three Japanese SOEs, which were also the three in 2010: Japan Post Holdings (ranked 52nd), Nippon Telegraph & Telephone (NTT) (64th) and Tokyo Electric Power (178th). In the 2010 the

Table 4.121 The largest SOEs in Japan and their position in the Top 100, 2018

No.	*Name of the SOE*	*Industry*	*OR (bill. €)*	*TA (bill. €)*	*Empl. worldwide (thousand)*	*State shares[a] (%)*	*Position Top 100*
1	Nippon Telegr. & Teleph.	Post & telecomm.	95.3	178.9	303.4	42.4	4
2	Tokyo Electric Power	Energy	50.9	102.4	41.1	54.7	17
3	Japan Post Holding	Post & telecomm.	31.8[b]	41.6	195.2	71.4	28
4	Japan Tobacco	Agribusiness	17.5	43.0	64.0	33.4	57
5	East Nippon Expressway	Transport	15.6	10.0	15.0	100.0	74

[a] Direct and indirect.
[b] Without the revenues from financial services.
Source: Own compilation based on the Orbis database and other data (including Fortune Global, Forbes Global lists and companies' websites).

same three companies were on the Fortune list. On the Forbes Global 2000 list in 2019 there were as many as 233 Japanese companies, including five SOEs. These were NTT (ranked 51st), Japan Post Holdings (66th), Japan Tobacco (286th), Tokyo Electric Power (414th) and Inpex (892nd).

The largest Japanese non-financial SOE is NTT, which is also the largest Japanese SOE in terms of employment and market value. Japan Post Holdings has the highest revenues among Japanese SOEs. However, the majority of its revenues come not from postal services but from the provision of financial services (Japan Post Bank, Japan Post Insurance).

Table 4.121 contains the characteristics of the largest Japanese SOEs and their position in the Top 100 non-financial companies.

4.15.2 Shares of SOEs in the sets of the largest Japanese companies

Tables 4.122–4.124 contain data on the shares of SOEs in the various sets of the largest Japanese non-financial companies. The share of SOEs in the overall Top 100 group is increasing by number, although it is steady in the OR category.

Table 4.122 SOEs in the sets of the largest Japanese companies – number

	Top 10			*Top 20*			*Top 50*			*Top 100*		
	2009	*2013*	*2018*	*2009*	*2013*	*2018*	*2009*	*2013*	*2018*	*2009*	*2013*	*2018*
maSOEs	1	0	0	1	1	1	1	2	2	2	2	3
miSOEs	1	1	1	1	1	1	1	2	1	1	3	2
SOEs	2	1	1	2	2	2	2	4	3	3	5	5

Source: As in Table 4.121.

Figure 4.15a shows the changes in the shares in ORs and TAs of SOEs in the Top 20 over the analysis period and Figure 4.15b shows the changes in the shares of SOEs in the various sets of the largest companies.

Table 4.123 SOEs in the sets of the largest Japanese companies – share in ORs (%)

	Top 10			*Top 20*			*Top 50*			*Top 100*		
	2009	*2013*	*2018*	*2009*	*2013*	*2018*	*2009*	*2013*	*2018*	*2009*	*2013*	*2018*
maSOEs	7.10	0	0	4.70	3.79	3.09	2.95	3.47	3.31	2.83	2.64	3.02
miSOEs	11.78	9.71	8.69	7.80	6.25	5.79	4.90	4.92	3.82	3.68	4.12	3.47
SOEs	18.88	9.71	8.69	12.50	10.04	8.88	7.85	8.39	7.13	6.51	6.76	6.49

Source: As in Table 4.121.

Table 4.124 SOEs in the sets of the largest Japanese companies – share in TAs (%)

	Top 10			*Top 20*			*Top 50*			*Top 100*		
	2009	*2013*	*2018*	*2009*	*2013*	*2018*	*2009*	*2013*	*2018*	*2009*	*2013*	*2018*
maSOEs	3.38	0	0	2.27	6.25	4.42	1.45	5.70	4.38	1.61	4.38	3.52
miSOEs	16.55	13.36	10.34	11.12	8.57	7.72	7.09	7.19	5.45	5.32	6.42	5.08
SOEs	19.93	13.36	10.34	13.39	14.82	12.14	8.54	12.89	9.83	6.93	10.80	8.60

Source: As in Table 4.121.

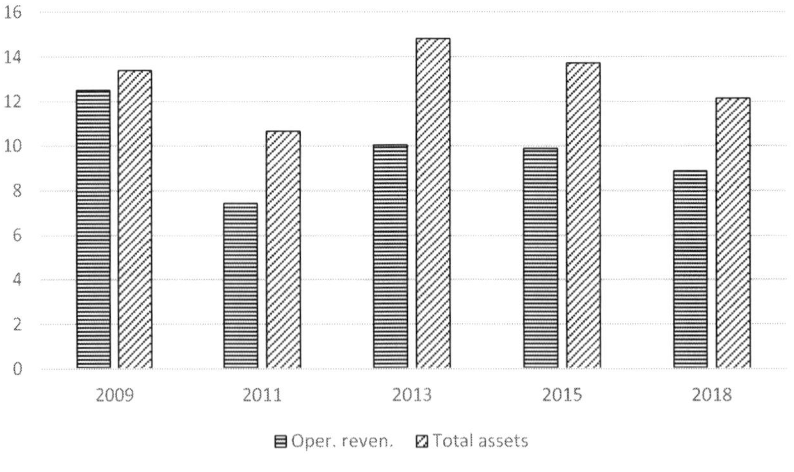

Figure 4.15a SOEs in the Top 20 of the Japanese non-financial companies – shares in ORs and TAs (%).

Source: As in Table 4.121.

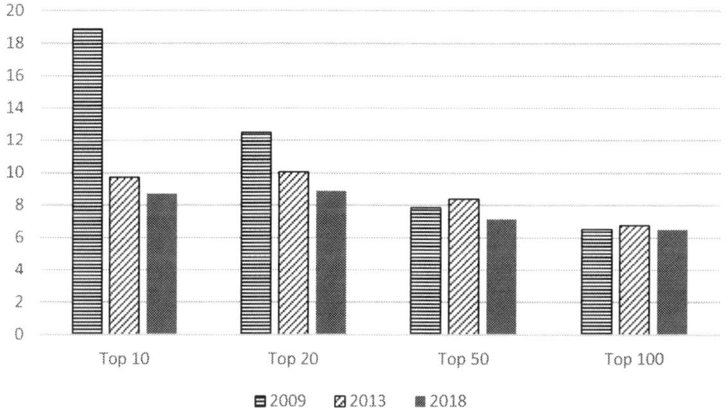

Figure 4.15b Changes in the shares of SOEs in the various sets of the largest Japanese non-financial companies (%).

Source: As in Table 4.121.

4.15.3 Other characteristics of the Japanese SOE sector

Revenues of the largest SOEs in relation to GDP

Table 4.125 provides data on the relationship of the value of ORs of SOEs from the Top 100 and Top 20 compared to the value of the nominal GDP in selected years.

SOEs in selected industries

Japan's SOEs are present in five strategic sectors (excluding oil and gas) and have a very significant presence in the postal and telecommunications industries. Our estimations for selected industries are presented in Table 4.126.

Table 4.125 Relationship of ORs of SOEs and nominal GDP (%)

	2009	*2013*	*2018*
Rev-100/GDP	4.0	4.5	4.9
Rev-20/GDP	3.6	3.3	3.4

Source: Own calculations.

Table 4.126 Estimated share of SOEs in the selected industries of the Japanese economy, 2018

Oil and gas	*Energy*	*Railways*	*Postal sector*	*Telecomm.*	*Banking sector*	*SS-I*
0	2	1	3	3	2	1.83

Source: Own estimation according to the rules given in Section 3.3.2.

Table 4.127 Number of listed SOEs in Japanese Top 100

	2009	*2013*	*2018*
Listed SOEs	2	4	4
including minority SOEs	1	3	2

Source: As in Table 4.121.

Table 4.128 FSOEs in the Top 100 of the Japanese companies

	2009	*2013*	*2018*
Number	1	1	1
Share in ORs (%)	2.7	2.9	2.9
Share in TAs (%)	2.9	3.4	3.7

Source: As in Table 4.121.

Listed SOEs

Of the Japanese Top 100 non-financial companies in 2018, four are listed and two are controlled with minority government shares. Data on listed SOEs in Japanese Top 100 are presented in Table 4.127.

4.15.4 FSOEs in Japan

In 2018, there was only one FSOE in the Top 100 Japanese non-financial companies. It was Nissan, which ranked sixth on the list in 2018 and is controlled by Renault so indirectly by the French government. The relevant data are presented in Table 4.128.

4.15.5 Summary

The share of SOEs in Japan in 2018 was low – below 10% in the Top 100 set and slightly over this level in the Top 20 set. There was only one SOE in the Top 10. Of the five SOEs in the Top 100, one is fully owned by the state. The share of minority SOEs is decreasing. The concentration of SOEs in the Top 20 is noticeable but decreasing. NTT, the largest Japanese SOE, is responsible for a large part of all revenues of SOEs in the Top 100 (45.2%). The shares of

Table 4.129 Share ratios for the Japanese economy

Share ratio	*2009*	*2013*	*2018*
SR-100 (%)	6.7	8.8	7.9
SR-20 (%)	12.9	12.4	11.3
CS-20	1.9	1.4	1.4
miS-100 (%)	68.2	59.9	57.0

Source: Own calculations.

SOEs were increasing in the Japanese economy, but only in the first part of the period under review. An overview of key values on SOEs' share in the Japanese economy is in Table 4.129.

4.16 SOE sector in Korea (South Korea)

4.16.1 The largest SOEs in Korea and their characteristics

On the Fortune Global list in 2010, there was one Korean SOE (Korea Electric Power Corporation (KEPCO) ranked 306th – out of 10 Korean companies overall), and also one in 2019 (KEPCO, ranked 193rd – out of 16 Korean companies overall). On the Forbes Global 2000 list in 2009 there were 51 Korean companies, including 5 SOEs. In 2019, the number of SOEs dropped to four – Woori Financial Group, KEPCO, Industrial Bank of Korea and Korea Gas – and the total number of Korean companies increased to 62.

Korea's largest SOE is the KEPCO, a power utility, founded in 1898 as the Seoul Electric Company. The current entity was formed by the merger of Korea Electric Power Company and Gyeongsung Electric Company and South Korea Electric Company in 1961. Since 1989 KEPCO has been listed on the Seoul Stock Exchange. Table 4.130 contains the characteristics of the largest South Korean SOEs and their position in the Top 100 non-financial companies.

4.16.2 Shares of SOEs in the sets of the largest Korean companies

Tables 4.131–4.133 contain data on the shares of SOEs in the various sets of the largest Korean non-financial companies. The importance of SOEs in the Korean economy have remained at a stable, moderate level.

Table 4.130 The largest SOEs in Korea and their position in the Top 100, 2018

No.	*Name of the SOE*	*Industry*	*OR (bill. €)*	*TA (bill. €)*	*Empl. worldwide (thousand)*	*State shares[a] (%)*	*Position Top 100*
1	KEPCO	Energy	47.3	144.7	47.5	58.3	6
2	Korea Gas	Oil & gas	20.5	31.0	4.0	54.5	16
3	Daewoo Engineer. & Constr.	Construction	8.3	6.8	5.4	51.3	36
4	Daewoo Shipbuild. & Marine Eng.	Shipbuilding	7.5	9.3	9.9	55.7	40
5	Korail	Transport	3.5	16.2	27.9	100.0	77
6	Korea Post	Post & telecomm.	3.1	5.2	50.0	100.0	84
7	Korea National Oil	Oil & gas	2.5	14.2	1.3	100.0	100

a Direct and indirect.

Source: Own compilation based on the Orbis database and other data (including Fortune Global, Forbes Global lists and companies' websites).

Table 4.131 SOEs in the sets of the largest Korean companies – number

	Top 10			*Top 20*			*Top 50*			*Top 100*		
	2009	*2013*	*2018*	*2009*	*2013*	*2018*	*2009*	*2013*	*2018*	*2009*	*2013*	*2018*
maSOEs	1	1	1	2	2	2	3	3	4	5	8	7
miSOEs	0	0	0	0	0	0	1	1	0	2	1	0
SOEs	1	1	1	2	2	2	4	4	4	7	9	7

Source: As in Table 4.130.

Table 4.132 SOEs in the sets of the largest Korean companies – share in ORs (%)

	Top 10			*Top 20*			*Top 50*			*Top 100*		
	2009	*2013*	*2018*	*2009*	*2013*	*2018*	*2009*	*2013*	*2018*	*2009*	*2013*	*2018*
maSOEs	5.26	6.79	7.50	6.21	8.49	8.04	5.16	7.09	7.45	5.09	7.38	7.08
miSOEs	0	0	0	0	0	0	1.16	1.03	0	1.19	0.91	0
SOEs	5.26	6.79	7.50	6.21	8.49	8.04	6.32	8.13	7.45	6.28	8.29	7.08

Source: As in Table 4.130.

Table 4.133 SOEs in the sets of the largest Korean companies – share in TAs (%)

	Top 10			*Top 20*			*Top 50*			*Top 100*		
	2009	*2013*	*2018*	*2009*	*2013*	*2018*	*2009*	*2013*	*2018*	*2009*	*2013*	*2018*
maSOEs	13.66	17.68	14.8	12.59	16.12	14.28	11.53	13.16	12.2	11.76	15.27	13.49
miSOEs	0	0	0	0	0	0	1.28	1.1	0	1.31	0.93	0
SOEs	13.66	17.68	14.8	12.59	16.12	14.28	12.79	14.26	12.2	13.06	16.2	13.49

Source: As in Table 4.130.

Figure 4.16a shows the changes in the shares in Ors and Tas of SOEs in the Top 20 over the analysis period and Figure 4.16b shows the changes in the shares of SOEs in the various sets of the largest companies.

4.16.3 Other characteristics of the Korean SOE sector

Revenues of the largest SOEs in relation to GDP

Table 4.134 provides data on the relationship of the value of ORs of SOEs from the Top 100 and Top 20 and the value of the nominal GDP of Korea in a given year. Sharp declines in the values are visible in the second part of the period under study.

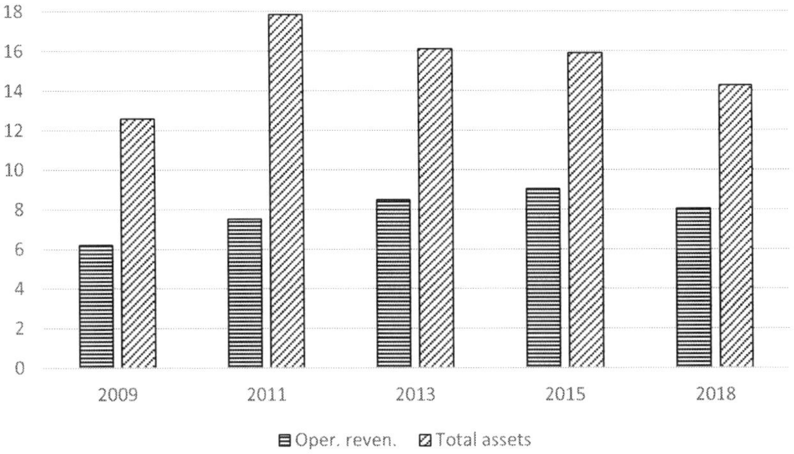

Figure 4.16a SOEs in the Top 20 of the Korean non-financial companies – shares in ORs and TAs (%).

Source: As in Table 4.130.

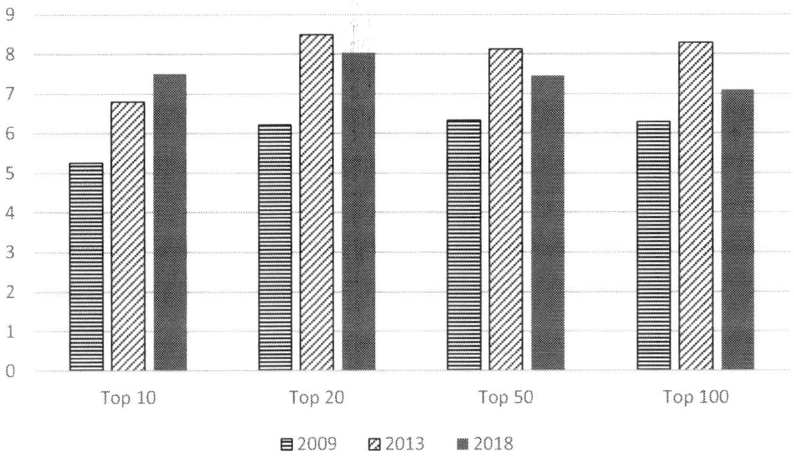

Figure 4.16b Changes in the shares of SOEs in the various sets of the largest Korean non-financial companies (%).

Source: As in Table 4.130.

Table 4.134 Relationship of ORs of SOEs and nominal GDP (%)

	2009	*2013*	*2018*
Rev-100/GDP	7.5	9.3	6.2
Rev-20/GDP	4.9	6.4	4.5

Source: Own calculations.

Table 4.135 Estimated share of SOEs in the selected industries of the South Korean economy, 2018

Oil and gas	*Energy*	*Railways*	*Postal sector*	*Telecomm.*	*Banking sector*	*SS-I*
2	4	3	3	0	1	2.17

Source: Own estimation according to the rules given in Section 3.3.2.

Table 4.136 Number of listed SOEs in Korean Top 100

	2009	*2013*	*2018*
Listed SOEs	5	7	4
including minority SOEs	2	1	0

Source: As in Table 4.130.

SOEs in selected industries

The share of SOEs in the selected strategic industries is relatively high. Only telecommunication is dominated by the private (including privatised) companies – see Table 4.135.

Listed SOEs

Out of seven Korean SOEs from the Top 100 non-financial companies in 2018, four - as mixed capital companies - were listed on the Seoul Stock Exchange. The largest one was KEPCO. For more detailed data on this, see Table 4.136.

4.16.4 FSOEs in Korea

In 2018, there were two FSOEs in the Top 100 South Korean non-financial companies. The largest of them was S-Oil, which ranked fifth on the list in 2018 and is controlled by Saudi Aramco. The second one was Renault Samsung Motors (ranked 67th), indirectly controlled by the French government. The relevant data are presented in Table 4.137.

Table 4.137 FSOEs in the Top 100 of the South Korean companies

	2009	*2013*	*2018*
Number	3	2	2
Share in ORs (%)	2.5	2.1	1.8
Share in TAs (%)	1.1	0.7	0.8

Source: As in Table 4.130.

Table 4.138 Share ratios for the Korean economy

Share ratio	*2009*	*2013*	*2018*
SR-100 (%)	9.7	12.3	10.3
SR-20 (%)	9.4	12.3	11.2
CS-20	97.2	100.5	108.4
miS-100 (%)	12.7	7.3	0

Source: Own calculations.

4.16.5 Summary

The share of SOEs in Korea in 2018 was quite low – around 10% in the Top 100 set and over 10% in the Top 20 set. There were one SOE in the Top 10. Of the seven SOEs in the Top 100, three are fully owned by the state. Minority SOEs in the past had a negligible importance and in 2018 all SOEs were majority or fully owned. The concentration of SOEs in the Top 20 is moderate but increasing slightly during the period under review. KEPCO, the largest South Korean SOE, is responsible for a very large part of all revenues of SOEs in the Top 100 (51.09%). A summary presentation of the data described above is presented in Table 4.138.

4.17 SOE sector in Mexico

4.17.1 The largest SOEs in Mexico and their characteristics

The 2019 Fortune Global 500 list included four Mexican companies and two of them were state-owned. Petroleos Mexicanos (Pemex) was on 95th place and Comision Federal De Electricidad (CFE) on 443rd. Nine years earlier Pemex was on this list as Mexican SOE (as one of the two Mexican companies). The Forbes Global 2000 list, which includes only publicly traded companies, did not include Mexican SOEs in either 2010 or 2019.

Table 4.139 The largest SOEs in Mexico and their position in the Top 100, 2018

No.	*Name of the SOE*	*Industry*	*OR (bill. €)*	*TA (bill. €)*	*Empl. worldwide (thousand)*	*State shares[a] (%)*	*Position Top 100*
1	Petroleos Mexicanos	Oil & gas	76.4	92.1	124.8	100.0	1
2	CFE	Energy	24.3	73.6	91.4	100.0	4
3	Diconsa	Trade	0.5	0.4	0.4	100.0	81

a Direct and indirect.
Source: Own compilation based on the Orbis database and other data (including Fortune Global, Forbes Global lists and companies' websites).

In 2018, the largest Mexican SOE, and also the largest company in Mexico, was the petrochemical giant Petroleos Mexicanos, which explores, produces, processes and distributes crude oil. Also in the Top 10 was the second big SOE, i.e. CFE, which operates in the energy sector. However, what is interesting is that despite the two SOEs in the entire list of Top 100 Mexican companies, there were only three SOEs. The relevant data can be found in Table 4.139.

4.17.2 Shares of SOEs in the sets of the largest Mexican companies

Tables 4.140–4.142 contain data on the shares of SOEs in the various sets of the largest Mexican non-financial companies. The share of SOEs in Top 100 revenue and assets is relatively stable with a slight downward trend.

Figure 4.17a shows the changes in the shares in ORs and TAs of SOEs in the Top 20 over the analysis period and Figure 4.17b shows the changes in the shares of SOEs in the various sets of the largest companies.

Table 4.140 SOEs in the sets of the largest Mexican companies – number

	Top 10			*Top 20*			*Top 50*			*Top 100*		
	2009	*2013*	*2018*	*2009*	*2013*	*2018*	*2009*	*2013*	*2018*	*2009*	*2013*	*2018*
maSOEs	2	2	2	2	2	2	2	2	2	2	3	3
miSOEs	0	0	0	0	0	0	0	0	0	0	0	0
SOEs	2	2	2	2	2	2	2	2	2	2	3	3

Source: As in Table 4.139.

Table 4.141 SOEs in the sets of the largest Mexican companies – share in ORs (%)

	Top 10			*Top 20*			*Top 50*			*Top 100*		
	2009	*2013*	*2018*	*2009*	*2013*	*2018*	*2009*	*2013*	*2018*	*2009*	*2013*	*2018*
maSOEs	44.42	44.91	37.02	37.05	37.09	29.04	31.06	29.48	24.05	29.63	26.89	22.57
miSOEs	0	0	0	0	0	0	0	0	0	0	0	0
SOEs	44.42	44.91	37.02	37.05	37.09	29.04	31.06	29.48	24.05	29.63	26.89	22.57

Source: As in Table 4.139.

Table 4.142 SOEs in the sets of the largest Mexican companies – share in TAs (%)

	Top 10			*Top 20*			*Top 50*			*Top 100*		
	2009	*2013*	*2018*	*2009*	*2013*	*2018*	*2009*	*2013*	*2018*	*2009*	*2013*	*2018*
maSOEs	50.58	52.73	46.29	43.13	43.68	34.78	36.62	35.25	28.76	34.03	30.73	25.80
miSOEs	0	0	0	0	0	0	0	0	0	0	0	0
SOEs	50.58	52.73	46.29	43.13	43.68	34.78	36.62	35.25	28.76	34.03	30.73	25.80

Source: As in Table 4.139.

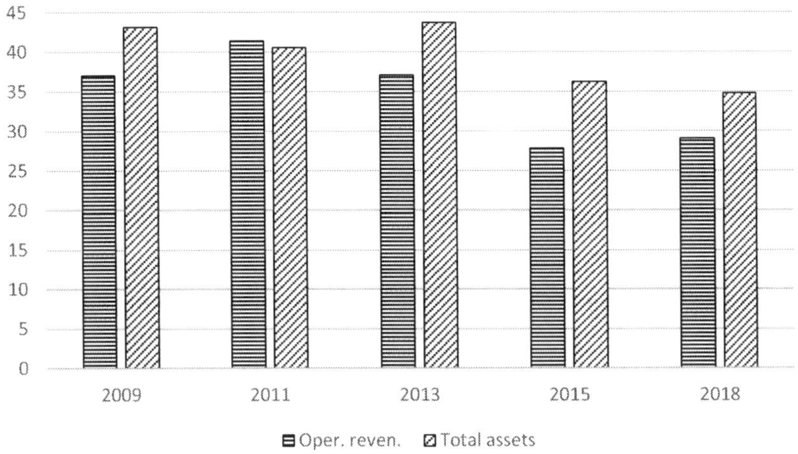

Figure 4.17a SOEs in the Top 20 of the Mexican non-financial companies – shares in ORs and TAs (%).

Source: As in Table 4.139.

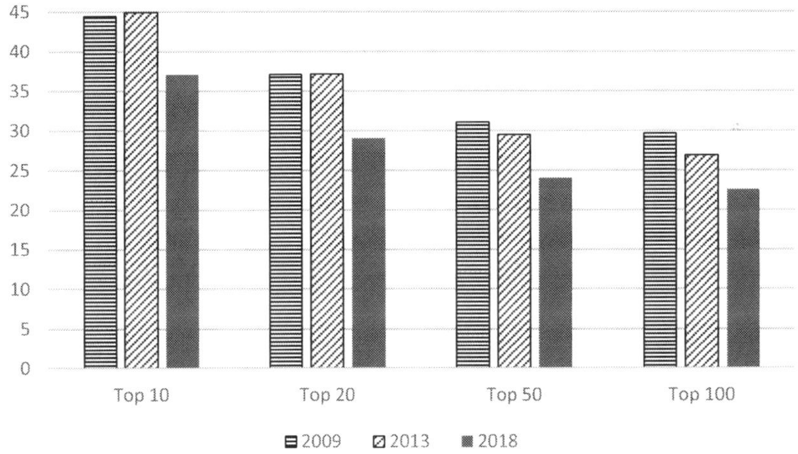

Figure 4.17b Changes in the shares of SOEs in the various sets of the largest Mexican non-financial companies (%).

Source: As in Table 4.139.

4.17.3 Other characteristics of the Mexican SOE sector

Revenues of the largest SOEs in relation to GDP

Table 4.143 provides data on the relationship of the value of ORs of SOEs from the Top 100 and Top 20 and the value of the nominal GDP in a given year. Slight but steady declines in the values are evident.

Table 4.143 Relationship of ORs of SOEs and nominal GDP (%)

	2009	*2013*	*2018*
Rev-100/GDP	11.6	12.0	9.5
Rev-20/GDP	11.6	11.9	9.4

Source: Own calculations.

Table 4.144 Estimated share of SOEs in the selected industries of the Mexican economy, 2018

Oil and gas	*Energy*	*Railways*	*Postal sector*	*Telecomm.*	*Banking sector*	*SS-I*
3	4	0	2	0	0	1.50

Source: Own estimation according to the rules given in Section 3.3.2.

SOEs in selected industries

Due to their small number, SOEs are not widely present in the different industries of the Mexican economy, while they dominate the oil & gas and energy industries. Our estimates are presented in Table 4.144.

Listed SOEs

Between 2009 and 2018 there were no listed Mexican SOEs in the Top 100 of the non-financial companies.

4.17.4 FSOEs in Mexico

Between 2009 and 2018 there were no FSOEs in the Top 100 Mexican non-financial companies.

4.17.5 Summary

In the Top 100 of the Mexican economy there are only three SOEs; the petrochemical giant Petroleos Mexicanos, which is responsible for 75.5% of all SOEs' ORs, is among them. Consequently, the share of SOEs in the Top 100 Mexican companies is at a high level, almost 25%, and in the Top 20 set, more than 30%. There were two SOEs in the Top 10. Three SOEs from the Top 100 set are fully owned by the state. The concentration of SOEs in the Top 20 group is clear. The importance of SOEs in the Mexican economy is declining over time. For the summary of the data described above, see Table 4.145.

Table 4.145 Share ratios for the Mexican economy

Share ratio	*2009*	*2013*	*2018*
SR-100 (%)	31.8	28.8	23.7
SR-20 (%)	40.1	40.4	31.9
CS-20	1.26	1.40	1.35
miS-100 (%)	0	0	0

Source: Own calculations.

4.18 SOE sector in the Netherlands

4.18.1 The largest SOEs in the Netherlands and their characteristics

In 2019, there were 11 Dutch companies on the Fortune Global list, of which one is an SOE. Nine years earlier there were 2 SOEs out of 13 companies. Similarly, on the Forbes Global list, in both years analysed there was only one Dutch SOEs out of – respectively – 22 and 25 Dutch companies overall.

The largest SOE in the Netherlands is GasTerra B.V. Its main business is trading and supplying natural gas. It is 50% owned by the Dutch government and 50% by Royal Dutch Shell and ExxonMobil. Table 4.146 contains the characteristics of the largest Dutch SOEs and their position in the Top 100 non-financial companies. SOEs play a minor role among the largest Dutch companies.

4.18.2 Shares of SOEs in the sets of the largest Dutch companies

Tables 4.147–4.149 contain data on the shares of SOEs in the various sets of the largest Dutch non-financial companies. SOEs in this economy are few in number and, in addition, their numbers and shares of revenues and assets are declining over time.

Table 4.146 The largest SOEs in the Netherlands and their position in the Top 100, 2018

No.	*Name of the SOE*	*Industry*	*OR (bill. €)*	*TA (bill. €)*	*Empl. worldwide (thousand)*	*State shares[a] (%)*	*Position Top 100*
1	GasTerra	Oil & gas	11.1	2.0	0.2	50.0	31
2	Nederlandse Spoorwegen	Transport	6.1	7.0	33.3	100.0	56
3	TenneT	Energy	4.2	20.7	3.4	100.0	73
4	EBN B.V.	Oil & gas	2.7	5.9	0.2	100.0	92

a Direct and indirect.
Source: Own compilation based on the Orbis database and other data (including Fortune Global, Forbes Global lists and companies' websites).

Table 4.147 SOEs in the sets of the largest Dutch companies – number

	Top 20			*Top 50*			*Top 100*		
	2009	*2013*	*2018*	*2009*	*2013*	*2018*	*2009*	*2013*	*2018*
maSOEs	0	0	0	3	1	0	6	3	3
miSOEs	1	1	0	1	1	1	1	1	1
SOEs	1	1	0	4	2	1	7	4	4

Source: As in Table 4.146.

Table 4.148 SOEs in the sets of the largest Dutch companies – share in ORs (%)

	Top 20			*Top 50*			*Top 100*		
	2009	*2013*	*2018*	*2009*	*2013*	*2018*	*2009*	*2013*	*2018*
maSOEs	0	0	0	2.12	0.73	0	2.43	1.33	0.94
miSOEs	3.28	2.69	0	2.40	2.02	0.95	2.05	1.74	0.81
SOEs	3.28	2.69	0	4.52	2.75	0.95	4.47	3.08	1.74

Source: As in Table 4.146.

Table 4.149 SOEs in the sets of the largest Dutch companies – share in TAs (%)

	Top 20			*Top 50*			*Top 100*		
	2009	*2013*	*2018*	*2009*	*2013*	*2018*	*2009*	*2013*	*2018*
maSOEs	0	0	0	3.27	0.77	0	5.62	2.36	2.73
miSOEs	0.85	0.77	0	0.61	0.55	0.21	0.49	0.44	0.16
SOEs	0.85	0.77	0	3.88	1.32	0.21	6.10	2.80	2.88

Source: As in Table 4.146.

Figure 4.18a shows the changes in the shares in ORs and TAs of SOEs in the Top 20 over the analysis period and Figure 4.18b shows the changes in the shares of SOEs in the various sets of the largest companies.

4.18.3 Other characteristics of the Dutch SOE sector

Revenues of the largest SOEs in relation to GDP

Table 4.150 provides data on the relationship of the value of ORs of SOEs from the Top 100 and Top 20 and the value of the nominal GDP in selected years. In the first part of the period under review, those values were stable, and in the second part they decreased sharply.

Figure 4.18a SOEs in the Top 20 of the Dutch non-financial companies – shares in ORs and TAs (%).

Source: As in Table 4.146.

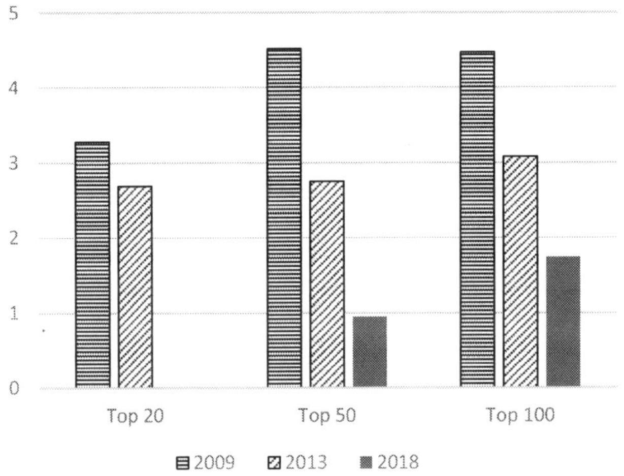

Figure 4.18b Changes in the shares of SOEs in the various sets of the largest Dutch non-financial companies (%).

Source: As in Table 4.146.

Table 4.150 Relationship of ORs of SOEs and nominal GDP (%)

	2009	*2013*	*2018*
Rev-100/GDP	6.7	6.7	3.0
Rev-20/GDP	3.1	3.8	0

Source: Own calculation.

Table 4.151 Estimated share of SOEs in the selected industries of the Dutch economy, 2018

Oil and gas	*Energy*	*Railways*	*Postal sector*	*Telecomm.*	*Banking sector*	*SS-I*
1	2	3	0	0	1	1.17

Source: Own estimation according to the rules given in Section 3.3.2.

Table 4.152 FSOEs in the Top 100 of the Dutch companies

	2009	*2013*	*2018*
Number	10	12	11
Share in ORs (%)	6.3	8.5	7.7
Share in TAs (%)	8.5	10.3	11.9

Source: As in Table 4.151.

SOEs in selected industries

Dutch SOEs dominate in railways and are present in energy, oil and gas and banking sectors. Our estimations for selected industries are presented in Table 4.151.

Listed SOEs

Between 2009 and 2018 there were no listed SOEs controlled by the Dutch government in Top 100 non-financial companies.

4.18.4 FSOEs in Netherlands

In 2018, there were as many as 11 FSOEs in the Top 100 Dutch non-financial companies and this was a high number relative to other countries. In Top 20 there were two FSOEs. The largest of them was Aramco Overseas Company B.V., ranked 12th, which is indirectly owned by the government of Saudi Arabia. The revelant data are presented in Table 4.152.

4.18.5 Summary

The share of SOEs in the group of the largest Dutch companies is very small. There is not a single SOE in the Top 10. Of the four SOEs in the Top 100, three are fully owned by the state. Minority SOEs are not present. The largest Dutch SOE (GasTerra) is responsible for a large part of all revenues of SOEs in the Top 100 (46.3%). The shares of state-owned entities have clearly declined during the period under review – Table 4.153.

Table 4.153 Share ratios for the Dutch economy

Share ratio	*2009*	*2013*	*2018*
SR-100 (%)	5.3	2.9	2.3
SR-20 (%)	2.1	1.7	0
CS-20	0.39	0.57	0
miS-100 (%)	26.6	41.5	22.0

Source: Own calculations.

4.19 SOE sector in Norway

4.19.1 The largest SOEs in Norway and their characteristics

There was only one Norwegian company on the Fortune Global 500 list both in 2010 and in 2019 - state-controlled Equinor, which ranked 113th in 2019. Eight Norwegian companies were included in the 2019 Forbes Global 2000 list, including five SOEs: Equinor (82nd), Den Norske Bank (337th), Telenor (555th), Norsk Hydro (932nd) and Yara International (1184th). Three private companies were ranked further down.

Norway's largest SOE is the oil & gas company Equinor ASA, known as Statoil until 2018. The company was established in 1972 in order for the state to develop the significant oil fields discovered earlier. It is one of the world's largest petrochemical companies, and in recent years has invested heavily in

Table 4.154 The largest SOEs in Norway and their position in the Top 100, 2018

No.	*Name of the SOE*	*Industry*	*OR (bill. €)*	*TA (bill. €)*	*Empl. worldwide (thousand)*	*State shares[a] (%)*	*Position Top 100*
1	Equinor	Oil & gas	69.5	98.3	20.7	67.0	1
2	Norsk Hydro	Metals/ Energy	16.1	16.3	36.2	34.3	2
3	Telenor	Post & telecomm.	12.0	19.2	21.0	54.0	3
4	Yara International	Chemicals	11.4	14.5	16.6	42.2	4
5	Norsk Tipping	Other (gambling)	3.9	0.6	0.4	100.0	12
6	Statkraft	Energy	2.8	18.1	3.6	100.0	21
7	Posten Norge	Post & telecomm.	2.4	1.6	15.0	100.0	27
8	Vygruppen	Transport	1.6	1.8	11.0	100.0	43
9	Bane NOR	Construction	1.5	17.9	4.5	100.0	44
10	Kongsberg Gr.	Technology	1.5	2.8	6.8	57.5	47

a Direct and indirect.
Source: Own compilation based on the Orbis database and other data (including Fortune Global, Forbes Global lists and companies' websites).

renewable energy (one reason for the name change). Since 2001, the company has been partially privatised, and its shares are listed on the Oslo and New York stock exchanges.

Table 4.154 shows the characteristics of the largest Norwegian SOEs and their position in the Top 100 non-financial companies. It is worth noting that as many as four leading companies in the Top 100 are state-controlled. Among the analysed 32 largest economies in the world, such a situation exists in only two more - in China and in Saudi Arabia.

4.19.2 Shares of SOEs in the sets of the largest Norwegian companies

Tables 4.155–4.157 contain data on the shares of SOEs in the various sets of the largest Norwegian non-financial companies.

Table 4.155 SOEs in the sets of the largest Norwegian companies – number

	Top 10			*Top 20*			*Top 50*			*Top 100*		
	2009	*2013*	*2018*	*2009*	*2013*	*2018*	*2009*	*2013*	*2018*	*2009*	*2013*	*2018*
maSOEs	2	2	2	4	4	3	9	9	8	21	15	16
miSOEs	2	2	2	2	2	2	2	3	2	3	3	2
SOEs	4	4	4	6	6	5	11	12	10	24	18	18

Source: As in Table 4.154.

Table 4.156 SOEs in the sets of the largest Norwegian companies – share in ORs (%)

	Top 10			*Top 20*			*Top 50*			*Top 100*		
	2009	*2013*	*2018*	*2009*	*2013*	*2018*	*2009*	*2013*	*2018*	*2009*	*2013*	*2018*
maSOEs	57.92	59.29	57.20	50.96	50.66	48.06	43.89	43.04	40.15	40.60	37.66	35.62
miSOEs	13.26	13.03	19.29	10.66	10.13	15.48	8.35	8.47	11.61	7.46	7.03	9.43
SOEs	71.18	72.32	76.50	61.62	60.79	63.54	52.24	51.51	51.76	48.06	44.69	45.05

Source: As in Table 4.154.

Table 4.157 SOEs in the sets of the largest Norwegian companies – share in TAs (%)

	Top 10			*Top 20*			*Top 50*			*Top 100*		
	2009	*2013*	*2018*	*2009*	*2013*	*2018*	*2009*	*2013*	*2018*	*2009*	*2013*	*2018*
maSOEs	63.40	68.12	65.66	60.85	60.47	54.32	51.90	53.18	48.32	46.88	45.12	44.09
miSOEs	12.11	13.02	17.22	9.5	9.99	14.18	7.70	8.76	9.29	6.64	6.99	7.67
SOEs	75.52	81.14	82.88	70.34	70.47	68.50	59.6	61.94	57.61	53.52	52.11	51.76

Source: As in Table 4.154.

Figure 4.19a shows the changes in the shares in ORs and TAs of SOEs in the Top 20 over the analysis period. The value of both indicators is very high and stable. Figure 4.19b shows the changes in the shares of SOEs in the various sets of the largest companies.

Figure 4.19b shows an exceptionally high - and increasing over the period under study - share of SOEs in the Top 10 set of Norwegian non-financial companies and a comparable share in the Top 20, Top 50 and Top 100.

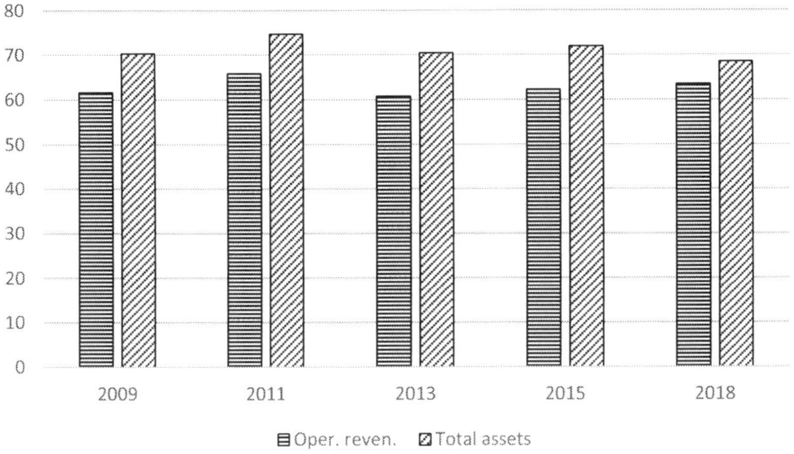

Figure 4.19a SOEs in the Top 20 of the Norwegian non-financial companies – shares in ORs and TAs (%).

Source: As in Table 4.154.

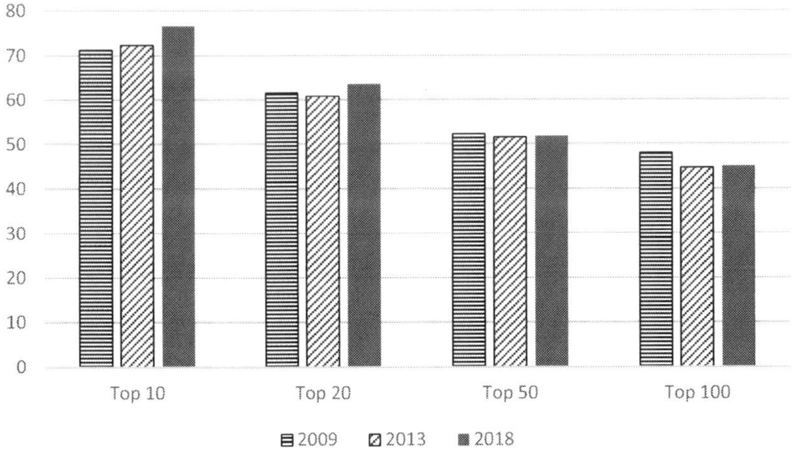

Figure 4.19b Changes in the shares of SOEs in the various sets of the largest Norwegian non-financial companies (%).

Source: As in Table 4.154.

4.19.3 Other characteristics of the Norwegian SOE sector

Revenues of the largest SOEs in relation to GDP

Table 4.158 provides data on the relationship of the value of ORs of SOEs from the Top 100 and Top 20 and the value of the nominal GDP in selected years. These indicators are at very high levels compared to other similar countries.

SOEs in selected industries

The share of SOEs in all strategic sectors of the Norwegian economy is very large, by far the largest of all developed country economies. Our estimations for selected industries are presented in Table 4.159.

Listed SOEs

Out of 18 Norwegian SOEs from the Top 100 non-financial companies in 2018, five - as mixed capital companies - were listed on the Oslo Stock Exchange. Two of them were controlled with minority shares. For more detailed data on this, see Table 4.160.

Table 4.158 Relationship of ORs of SOEs and nominal GDP (%)

	2009	*2013*	*2018*
Rev-100/GDP	39.6	35.0	34.6
Rev-20/GDP	33.6	30.6	29.8

Source: Own calculations.

Table 4.159 Estimated share of SOEs in the selected industries of the Norwegian economy, 2018

Oil and gas	*Energy*	*Railways*	*Postal sector*	*Telecomm.*	*Banking sector*	*SS-I*
3	4	3	3	3	3	3.17

Source: Own estimation according to the rules given in Section 3.3.2.

Table 4.160 Number of listed SOEs in Norwegian Top 100

	2009	*2013*	*2018*
Listed SOEs	6	7	5
including minority SOEs	3	3	2

Source: As in Table 4.154.

Table 4.161 FSOEs in the Top 100 of the Norwegian companies

	2009	*2013*	*2018*
Number	1	3	6
Share in ORs (%)	0.3	1.3	3.3
Share in TAs (%)	0.7	1.7	4.6

Source: As in Table 4.154.

Table 4.162 Share ratios for the Norwegian economy

Share ratio	*2009*	*2013*	*2018*
SR-100 (%)	50.8	48.4	48.4
SR-20 (%)	66.0	65.6	66.0
CS-20	1.30	1.36	1.36
miS-100 (%)	13.7	14.4	17.2

Source: Own calculations.

4.19.4 FSOEs in Norway

The number of FSOEs in the Top 100 Norwegian non-financial companies increased significantly during the analysed period. In 2018, the largest FSOE is the 28th ranked chemical group Elkem ASA, controlled by Chinese SOE National Bluestar Group. However, the importance of FSOEs in the Norwegian economy is not high. Detailed data on this is provided in Table 4.161.

4.19.5 Summary

The share of SOEs in Norway in 2018 was exceptionally high for a Western economy – it reached nearly 50% in the Top 100 set and exceeded 65% in the Top 20 set. It is the highest value among all highly developed countries. There were four SOEs in the Top 10. Of the 18 SOEs in the Top 100, 13 are fully owned by the state. Minority SOEs are present in this economy; however, their share is not very high and stable. The concentration of SOEs in the Top 20 is clear. Equinor, the largest Norwegian SOE, was responsible for majority of all revenues of SOEs in the Top 100 (52.9%). The shares of SOEs in the Norwegian economy are stable over time. A summary presentation of the data described above is presented in Table 4.162.

4.20 SOE sector in Poland

4.20.1 The largest SOEs in Poland and their characteristics

On the Fortune Global list, both in 2009 and in 2018, there was one Polish SOE PKN Orlen. As for the Forbes Global 2000 list in both analysed years

Table 4.163 The largest SOEs in Poland and their position in the Top 100, 2018

No.	*Name of the SOE*	*Industry*	*OR (bill. €)*	*TA (bill. €)*	*Empl. worldwide (thousand)*	*State shares[a] (%)*	*Position Top 100*
1	PKN Orlen	Oil & gas	25.9	14.9	21.3	27.5	1
2	PGNiG	Oil & gas	9.6	12.4	24.8	71.9	3
3	Lotos	Oil & gas	7.1	5.2	5.1	53.2	4
4	PGE	Energy	6.1	17.6	41.4	57.4	5
5	KGHM PM	Mining/ Metals	4.8	8.7	33.6	31.8	7
6	Tauron	Energy	4.3	8.6	25.6	30.1	8
7	Enea	Energy	3.0	7.0	16.5	51.5	13
8	JSW	Mining	2.7	3.2	28.3	50.1	15
9	Energa	Energy	2.4	5.0	9.5	51.5	20
10	PSE	Energy	2.4	4.7	2.3	100.0	21

a Direct and indirect.
Source: Own compilation based on the Orbis database and other data (including Fortune Global, Forbes Global lists and companies' websites).

all Polish companies on the list were state-owned. In 2010, there were six of them, and nine years later the number increased to seven.

The largest SOE of Poland and at the same time the largest company in the Polish economy in 2018 was the petrochemical concern PKN Orlen. The company was established in 1999 through a merger of two SOEs from the socialist era – a petrochemical plant (refinery) in Plock and a petroleum products distribution and trading company. Subsequently, in the same year, a part of the PKN Orlen shares were floated on the Warsaw Stock Exchange. Table 4.163 presents the characteristics of the largest Polish SOEs and their position in the Top 100 non-financial companies.

4.20.2 Shares of SOEs in the sets of the largest Polish companies

Tables 4.164–4.166 contain data on the shares of SOEs in the various sets of the largest Polish non-financial companies.

Table 4.164 SOEs in the sets of the largest Polish companies – number

	Top 10			*Top 20*			*Top 50*			*Top 100*		
	2009	*2013*	*2018*	*2009*	*2013*	*2018*	*2009*	*2013*	*2018*	*2009*	*2013*	*2018*
maSOEs	3	3	3	8	6	6	11	10	12	16	14	15
miSOEs	2	3	3	2	4	3	5	4	4	6	4	5
SOEs	5	6	6	10	10	9	16	14	16	22	18	20

Source: As in Table 4.163.

The number and the share of SOEs among the largest Polish non-financial companies are high and quite stable. Those categories have especially large value in the Top 10 and Top 20 sets.

Figure 4.20a shows the changes in the shares of SOEs in the Top 20 over the analysis period, and Figure 4.20b shows the changes in the shares of SOEs in the various sets of the largest companies. Those values are among the largest of the studied countries.

Table 4.165 SOEs in the sets of the largest Polish companies – share in ORs (%)

	Top 10			*Top 20*			*Top 50*			*Top 100*		
	2009	*2013*	*2018*	*2009*	*2013*	*2018*	*2009*	*2013*	*2018*	*2009*	*2013*	*2018*
maSOEs	26.93	28.15	27.34	32.59	28.42	27.89	24.89	24.48	25.79	21.63	21.04	21.20
miSOEs	38.62	48.58	42.05	28.32	39.86	31.66	22.59	28.56	22.68	17.78	22.32	17.69
SOEs	65.55	76.72	69.39	60.91	68.27	59.55	47.48	53.04	48.47	39.41	43.35	38.89

Source: As in Table 4.163.

Table 4.166 SOEs in the sets of the largest Polish companies – share in TAs (%)

	Top 10			*Top 20*			*Top 50*			*Top 100*		
	2009	*2013*	*2018*	*2009*	*2013*	*2018*	*2009*	*2013*	*2018*	*2009*	*2013*	*2018*
maSOEs	43.45	44.22	45.52	47.97	47.28	45.82	42.76	43.02	47.85	36.01	37.00	41.98
miSOEs	27.64	40.86	41.63	21.22	34.60	29.28	19.25	25.37	21.01	15.52	20.95	18.27
SOEs	71.08	85.08	87.15	69.19	81.88	75.10	62.01	68.39	68.85	51.53	57.95	60.25

Source: As in Table 4.163.

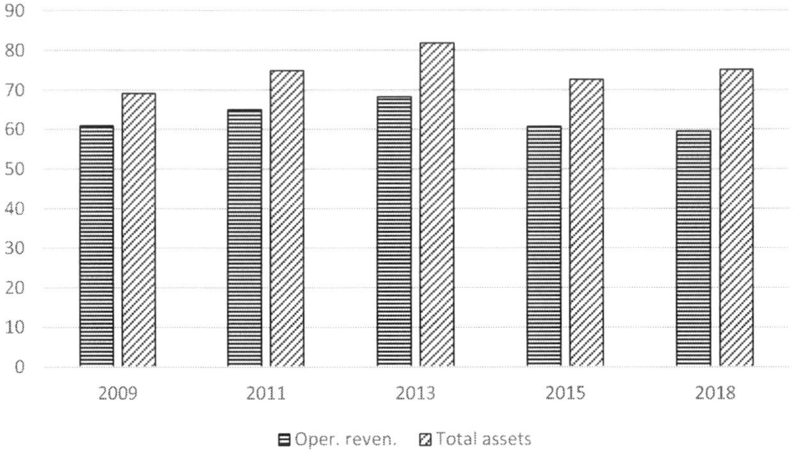

Figure 4.20a SOEs in the Top 20 of the Polish non-financial companies – shares in ORs and TAs (%).

Source: As in Table 4.163.

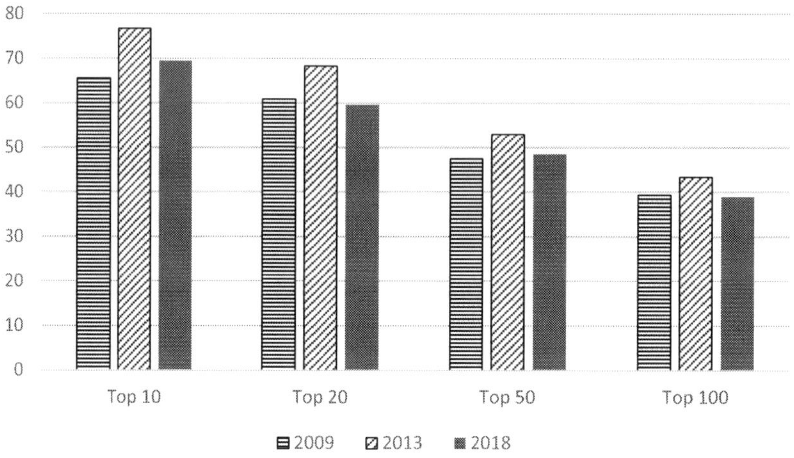

Figure 4.20b Changes in the shares of SOEs in the various sets of the largest Polish non-financial companies (%).

Source: As in Table 4.163.

Table 4.167 Relationship of ORs of SOEs and nominal GDP (%)

	2009	*2013*	*2018*
Rev-100/GDP	17.8	20.9	16.5
Rev-20/GDP	14.1	18.5	12.8

Source: Own calculations.

4.20.3 Other characteristics of the Polish SOE sector

Revenues of the largest SOEs in relation to GDP

Table 4.167 provides data on the relationship of the value of ORs of SOEs from the Top 100 and Top 20 and the value of the nominal GDP of Poland in a given year. The importance of Polish SOEs measured by these indicators is at a high level; there were increases of values in both groups between 2009 and 2013, but later these indicators decreased.

SOEs in selected industries

The share of SOEs in the selected industries in Poland is quite large. SOEs dominate in oil and gas, energy and railways industries. They also have a large share in the postal and banking sectors. There are no SOEs among the largest telecoms. Our estimates are presented in Table 4.168.

Table 4.168 Estimated share of SOEs in the selected industries of the Polish economy, 2018

Oil and gas	*Energy*	*Railways*	*Postal sector*	*Telecomm.*	*Banking sector*	*SS-I*
4	3	3	2	0	2	2.33

Source: Own estimation according to the rules given in Section 3.3.2.

Table 4.169 Number of listed SOEs in Polish Top 100

	2009	*2013*	*2018*
Listed SOEs	8	11	11
including minority SOEs	3	4	5

Source: As in Table 4.163.

Table 4.170 FSOEs in the Top 100 of the Polish companies

	2009	*2013*	*2018*
Number	3	3	5
Share in ORs (%)	4.9	3.2	3.4
Share in TAs (%)	9.0	4.9	4.6

Source: As in Table 4.163.

Listed SOEs

As many as 11 of 20 Polish SOEs from Top 100 included in our study are listed companies. This number increased from 8 in 2009 to 11 in 2013 and was the same in 2018 (Table 4.169).

4.20.4 FSOEs in Poland

The number of FSOEs (not included in the tables and charts above) increased in the recent years from three in 2013 to five in 2008. In Top 20 there were one FSOE – Orange Polska which ranked 16th on the list in 2018 and is controlled by the French parent company. The relevant data are presented in Table 4.170.

4.20.5 Summary

The share of SOEs in Poland in 2018 was very high – in the Top 100 set this value is nearly 50%, and in the Top 20 group over 65%. There were as many as six SOEs in the Top 10 in 2018. Of the 20 SOEs in the Top 100, nine are fully owned by the state. PKN Orlen, the largest Polish SOE, was responsible for 30.6% revenues of SOEs in the Top 100. The share of minority SOEs in the total set of SOEs is high but a dominating form of control is a majority share.

Table 4.171 Share ratios for the Polish economy

Share ratio	*2009*	*2013*	*2018*
SR-100 (%)	45.5	50.7	49.6
SR-20 (%)	65.0	75.1	67.3
CS-20	1.41	1.51	1.36
miS-100 (%)	38.3	44.9	40.1

Source: Own calculations.

The concentration of SOEs in the Top 20 is evident. A summary presentation of the data described above is presented in Table 4.171.

4.21 SOE sector in Russia

4.21.1 The largest SOEs in Russia and their characteristics

There were four Russian companies on the 2019 Fortune Global 500 list, three of which were state-owned: Gazprom (ranked 42nd), Rosneft (86th) and Sberbank (255th). In 2010, there were six Russian companies on this list, four of which were state-owned. The Forbes Global 2000 list for 2019 includes 13 Russian SOEs (out of 28 in total). In 2010, there were 10 companies on this list (out of 29 total).

The largest SOE and also the largest Russian company is petrochemical giant Gazprom, which is also the world's largest natural gas producer. The second largest SOE in 2018 was Rosneft, also operating in the petrochemical sector. Table 4.172 contains the characteristics of the largest Russian SOEs and their position in the Top 100 non-financial companies.

Table 4.172 The largest SOEs in Russia and their position in the Top 100, 2018

No.	*Name of the SOE*	*Industry*	*OR (bill. €)*	*TA (bill. €)*	*Empl. worldwide (thousand)*	*State shares[a] (%)*	*Position Top 100*
1	Gazprom	Oil & gas	104.9	262.0	462.0	51.1	1
2	Rosneft	Oil & gas	103.6	165.5	315.0	51.1	2
3	Russian Railways	Transport	22.6	60.1	741.0	100.0	4
4	Magnit	Trade	15.6	7.7	300.0	30.0	7
5	Rosatom	Energy	13.0	43.2	260.0	100.0	8
6	Rosseti	Energy	12.8	31.7	217.5	89.3	9
7	Transneft	Oil & gas	12.3	40.1	116.0	100.0	10
8	Inter RAO	Energy	12.2	9.1	58.5	65.8	11
9	Tatneft	Oil & gas	11.7	15.1	60.0	29.6	12
10	Aeroflot Russian Airlines	Transport	7.8	4.0	30.3	51.2	19

a Direct and indirect.
Source: Own compilation based on the Orbis database and other data (including Fortune Global, Forbes Global lists and companies' websites).

4.21.2 Shares of SOEs in the sets of the largest Russian companies

Tables 4.173–4.175 contain data on the shares of SOEs in the various sets of the largest Russian non-financial companies. As the data show, the share of SOEs in the Russian economy is high and remains stable.

Figure 4.21a shows the changes in the shares in ORs and TAs of SOEs in the Top 20 over the analysis period and Figure 4.21b shows the changes in the shares of SOEs in the various sets of the largest companies.

4.21.3 Other characteristics of the Russian SOE sector

Revenues of the largest SOEs in relation to GDP

Table 4.176 provides data on the relationship of the value of ORs of SOEs from the Top 100 and Top 20 and the value of the nominal GDP of Russia in a given year.

Table 4.173 SOEs in the sets of the largest Russian companies – number

	Top 10			*Top 20*			*Top 50*			*Top 100*		
	2009	*2013*	*2018*	*2009*	*2013*	*2018*	*2009*	*2013*	*2018*	*2009*	*2013*	*2018*
maSOEs	5	5	6	6	6	8	16	16	16	34	30	29
miSOEs	1	1	1	1	2	2	1	3	3	3	4	4
SOEs	6	6	7	7	8	10	17	19	19	37	34	33

Source: As in Table 4.172.

Table 4.174 SOEs in the sets of the largest Russian companies – share in ORs (%)

	Top 10			*Top 20*			*Top 50*			*Top 100*		
	2009	*2013*	*2018*	*2009*	*2013*	*2018*	*2009*	*2013*	*2018*	*2009*	*2013*	*2018*
maSOEs	58.63	64.05	63.34	50.08	54.73	55.13	46.72	49.96	49.26	44.96	46.78	45.65
miSOEs	3.42	3.24	3.67	2.77	4.48	5.21	2.20	4.57	4.79	2.53	4.16	4.39
SOEs	62.04	67.29	67.01	52.85	59.21	60.34	48.93	54.53	54.05	47.49	50.94	50.04

Source: As in Table 4.172.

Table 4.175 SOEs in the sets of the largest Russian companies – share in TAs (%)

	Top 10			*Top 20*			*Top 50*			*Top 100*		
	2009	*2013*	*2018*	*2009*	*2013*	*2018*	*2009*	*2013*	*2018*	*2009*	*2013*	*2018*
maSOEs	71.64	79.49	79.84	63.11	71.85	72.56	62.90	67.35	67.84	61.88	65.24	66.32
miSOEs	2.26	1.45	1.02	1.82	2.97	2.69	1.49	3.46	2.98	1.83	3.29	2.81
SOEs	73.90	80.95	80.86	64.93	74.82	75.25	64.38	70.81	70.82	63.71	68.54	69.13

Source: As in Table 4.172.

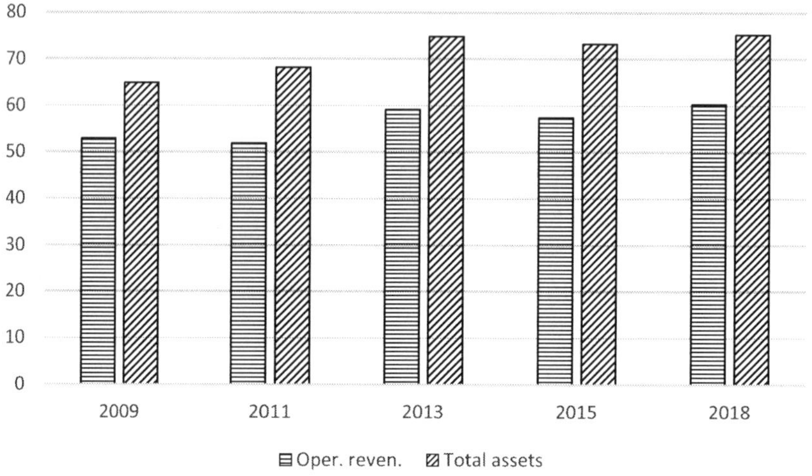

Figure 4.21a SOEs in the Top 20 of the Russian non-financial companies – shares in ORs and TAs (%).

Source: As in Table 4.172.

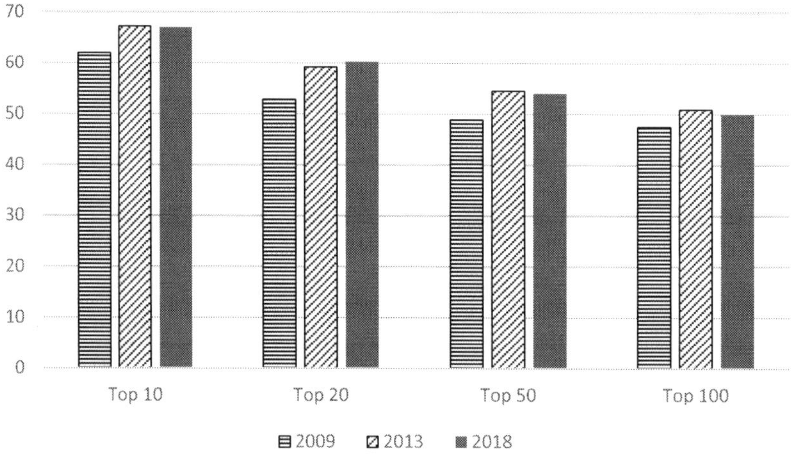

Figure 4.21b Changes in the shares of SOEs in the various sets of the largest Russian non-financial companies (%).

Source: As in Table 4.172.

Table 4.176 Relationship of ORs of SOEs and nominal GDP (%)

	2009	*2013*	*2018*
Rev-100/GDP	26.2	25.8	26.5
Rev-20/GDP	19.9	19.8	21.7

Source: Own calculations.

Table 4.177 Estimated share of SOEs in the selected industries of the Russian economy, 2018

Oil and gas	*Energy*	*Railways*	*Postal sector*	*Telecomm.*	*Banking sector*	*SS-I*
3	4	4	3	2	3	3.17

Source: Own estimation according to the rules given in Section 3.3.2.

Table 4.178 Number of listed SOEs in Russian Top 100

	2009	*2013*	*2018*
Listed SOEs	19	17	17
including minority SOEs	3	4	4

Source: As in Table 4.177.

SOEs in selected industries

Russian SOEs play a significant role in the selected strategic sectors. Only in telecommunications do they not have a monopolistic or dominant position. Our estimations for selected industries in the Russian economy are presented in Table 4.177.

Listed SOEs

Listed companies account for a significant part of Russian SOEs, most of which are majority-owned. The relevant data are presented in Table 4.178.

4.21.4 FSOEs in Russia

Among the largest Russian companies in 2018, only three can qualify as FSOEs, and their importance in the Russian economy is negligible. There were no FSOEs in Top 20. The largest SOE was JTI Russia LLC, which is indirectly owned by Japan Tobacco. This company ranked 34th on the 2018 Top 100 list. Data on FSOEs are presented in Table 4.179.

Table 4.179 FSOEs in the Top 100 of the Russian companies

	2009	*2013*	*2018*
Number	3	4	3
Share in ORs (%)	1.2	1.6	1.5
Share in TAs (%)	0.6	0.5	0.3

Source: As in Table 4.177.

Table 4.180 Share ratios for the Russian economy

Share ratio	*2009*	*2013*	*2018*
SR-100 (%)	55.6	59.7	59.6
SR-20 (%)	58.9	67.0	67.8
CS-20	1.05	1.12	1.14
miS-100 (%)	3.6	6.0	5.6

Source: Own calculations.

4.21.5 Summary

The share of SOEs in Russia in 2018 was very high – almost 60% in the Top 100 set and over 65% in the Top 20 set - and has increased in the given period. The Top 10 Russian non-financial companies include as many as seven SOEs. Of the 33 SOEs in the Top 100, 15 are fully owned by the state. SOEs with minority state holdings have a minor importance. The concentration of SOEs in the Top 20 has increased in recent years, although it is not particularly high. Gazprom, the largest Russian SOE, is responsible for 27% of all revenues of SOEs in the Top 100. An overview of key values on SOEs' share in the Russian economy is in Table 4.180.

4.22 SOE sector in Saudi Arabia

4.22.1 The largest SOEs in Saudi Arabia and their characteristics

The Fortune Global 500 list for 2019 included two companies from Saudi Arabia and both of them were state-owned. Saudi Aramco ranked 6th on the list and Sabic ranked 252nd. Nine years earlier Sabic was the only Saudi company on the list as Saudi Aramco wasn't included. The latter company has only recently started to publish its financial data in preparation for listing, which made it possible to include it in the list. Regarding the Forbes Global 2000 list there were 17 Saudi companies in 2010 and 7 of them were state-owned and nine years later this number was – respectively – 15 and 8.

The largest Saudi SOE is oil giant Saudi Aramco, which is one of the largest companies in the world. In November 2019, there was an initial public offering of Saudi Aramco shares. Currently (in mid-2021), about 1.5% of the shares are in private hands. Table 4.181 contains the characteristics of the largest Saudi Arabian SOEs and their position in the Top 100 non-financial companies.

4.22.2 Shares of SOEs in the sets of the largest Saudi Arabian companies

Tables 4.182-4.184 contain data on the shares of SOEs in the various sets of the largest Saudi Arabian non-financial companies. The number of SOEs in

Table 4.181 The largest SOEs in Saudi Arabia and their position in the Top 100, 2018

No.	*Name of the SOE*	*Industry*	*OR (bill. €)*	*TA (bill. €)*	*Empl. worldwide (thousand)*	*State shares*[a] *(%)*	*Position Top 100*
1	Saudi Aramco	Oil & gas	309.6	346.6	96.0	100.0	1
2	Saudi Basic Industries	Chemicals	39.7	74.5	32.7	70.0	2
3	Saudi Electricity	Energy	15.2	108.2	37.8	81.2	3
4	Saudi Telecom	Post & telecomm.	12.2	26.1	17.0	83.7	4
5	Rabigh Refining & Petrochem.	Chemicals	9.6	14.9	2.8	37.5	5
6	Saudi Arabian Airlines	Transport	3.5	3.0	25.0	100.0	7
7	Saudi Arabian Mining	Mining	3.4	7.5	7.0	49.9	9
8	Saudi Kayan Petrochemical	Chemicals	2.9	9.5	0.1	35.0	11
9	National Shipping	Others	1.5	4.9	0.3	53.5	21
10	Saudi Arabian Fertilizer	Chemicals	1.1	2.2	1.3	100.0	68

a Direct and indirect.
Source: Own compilation based on the Orbis database and other data (including Fortune Global, Forbes Global lists and companies' websites).

the Arab economy is high and growing in almost each of the groups analysed, and the shares of SOEs are very high due to the size of oil giant Saudi Aramco. While these shares are stable in the Top 10 group, small declines can be observed in other sets.

Figure 4.22a shows the changes in the shares in Ors and Tas of SOEs in the Top 20 over the analysis period and Figure 4.22b shows the changes in the shares of SOEs in the various sets of the largest companies.

Table 4.182 SOEs in the sets of the largest Saudi Arabian companies – number

	Top 10			*Top 20*			*Top 50*			*Top 100*		
	2009	*2013*	*2018*	*2009*	*2013*	*2018*	*2009*	*2013*	*2018*	*2009*	*2013*	*2018*
maSOEs	5	5	5	5	6	5	8	10	11	12	11	13
miSOEs	1	1	2	1	2	3	6	5	6	11	12	9
SOEs	6	6	7	6	8	8	14	15	17	23	23	22

Source: As in Table 4.181.

Table 4.183 SOEs in the sets of the largest Saudi Arabian companies – share in ORs (%)

	Top 10			*Top 20*			*Top 50*			*Top 100*		
	2009	*2013*	*2018*	*2009*	*2013*	*2018*	*2009*	*2013*	*2018*	*2009*	*2013*	*2018*
maSOEs	92.88	93.51	93.97	89.56	90.61	89.28	86.63	87.65	85.16	84.73	85.36	82.09
miSOEs	2.47	2.57	3.2	2.38	2.99	3.71	2.84	3.19	4.05	3.11	3.52	4.08
SOEs	95.35	96.09	97.17	91.94	93.60	92.99	89.47	90.83	89.21	87.84	88.87	86.17

Source: As in Table 4.181.

Table 4.184 SOEs in the sets of the largest Saudi Arabian companies – share in TAs (%)

	Top 10			*Top 20*			*Top 50*			*Top 100*		
	2009	*2013*	*2018*	*2009*	*2013*	*2018*	*2009*	*2013*	*2018*	*2009*	*2013*	*2018*
maSOEs	91.64	93.32	90.38	86.72	89.19	85.05	82.30	84.78	80.40	79.93	81.92	76.88
miSOEs	2.98	1.71	6.11	2.82	3.22	7.19	5.46	3.58	7.59	5.75	4.15	7.58
SOEs	94.61	95.03	96.49	89.54	92.41	92.24	87.76	88.36	87.99	85.68	86.07	84.46

Source: As in Table 4.181.

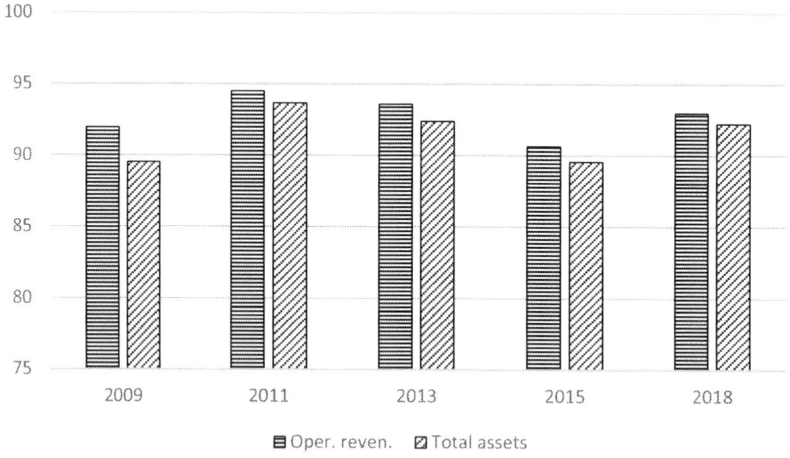

Figure 4.22a SOEs in the Top 20 of the Saudi Arabian non-financial companies – shares in ORs and TAs (%).

Source: As in Table 4.181.

4.22.3 Other characteristics of the Saudi Arabian SOE sector

Revenues of the largest SOEs in relation to GDP

Table 4.185 provides data on the relationship of the value of Ors of SOEs from the Top 100 and Top 20 and the value of the nominal GDP of Saudi

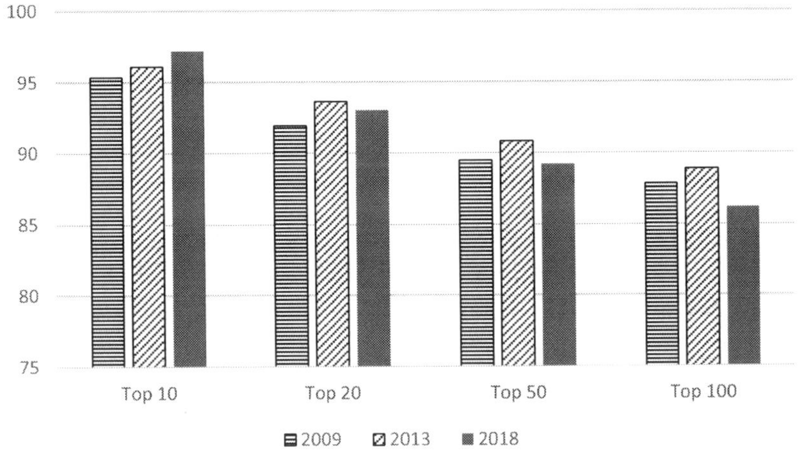

Figure 4.22b Changes in the shares of SOEs in the various sets of the largest Saudi Arabian non-financial companies (%).

Source: As in Table 4.181.

Table 4.185 Relationship of ORs of SOEs and nominal GDP (%)

	2009	*2013*	*2018*
Rev-100/GDP	72.4	70.2	58.9
Rev-20/GDP	71.1	69.2	57.7

Source: Own calculations.

Arabia in selected years. Very sharp declines in the values are evident (Table 4.185).

SOEs in selected industries

SOEs are present and dominating in all selected industries in the Saudi economy. Our estimations for selected industries are presented in Table 4.186.

Listed SOEs

In 2018, there were 16 listed companies controlled by the Saudi Arabian government in the Top 100 non-financial companies and 9 of them were controlled with minority shares. The relevant data are presented in Table 4.187.

Table 4.186 Estimated share of SOEs in the selected industries of the Saudi Arabian economy, 2018

Oil and gas	*Energy*	*Railways*	*Postal sector*	*Telecomm.*	*Banking sector*	*SS-I*
3	4	4	3	3	3	3.33

Source: Own estimation according to the rules given in Section 3.3.2.

Table 4.187 Number of listed SOEs in Saudi Arabian Top 100

	2009	*2013*	*2018*
Listed SOEs	18	19	16
including minority SOEs	11	12	9

Source: As in Table 4.181.

Table 4.188 FSOEs in the Top 100 of the Saudi Arabian companies

	2009	*2013*	*2018*
Number	3	5	4
Share in ORs (%)	2.2	1.9	1.6
Share in TAs (%)	3.5	3.3	3.0

Source: As in Table 4.181.

4.22.4 FSOEs in Saudi Arabia

The largest foreign state-owned company in Saudi Arabia was the tenth ranked Etihad Etisalat Company, which is owned by the government of the United Arab Emirates and operates in the telecommunications industry. Another such large company is Saudi Arabian Saipem Company, which is directly controlled by Italian state-owned ENI. For more detailed data, see Table 4.188.

4.22.5 Summary

The share of SOEs among the largest Saudi companies is at a very high level (around 90%). However, this is mainly due to the existence of giant state-owned oil company Saudi Aramco. It accounts for 76.5% of the revenue of the entire SOEs from Top 100 group. There are also six other SOEs in the Top 10 group. There were a total of 22 SOEs in the Top 100 in 2018, of which only 3 were fully owned by the state. The share of minority SOEs in the total set of SOEs is low (Saudi Aramco also influenced the outcome). The concentration of SOEs in the Top 20 is clear. The shares of SOEs in the Saudi economy are stable over time (Table 4.189).

Table 4.189 Share ratios for the Saudi Arabian economy

Share ratio	*2009*	*2013*	*2018*
SR-100 (%)	90.5	87.5	85.3
SR-20 (%)	90.7	93.0	92.6
CS-20	1.05	1.06	1.09
miS-100 (%)	5.5	4.5	7.3

Source: Own calculations.

4.23 SOE sector in Singapore

4.23.1 The largest SOEs in Singapore and their characteristics

There were no SOEs on the Fortune Global 500 list in both 2009 and 2018. By contrast, for the Forbes list in 2019, of the 13, 6 were state-owned and nine years earlier, of the 18, 7 were state-owned.

Singapore's largest SOE is Olam International LTD, a conglomerate operating in the food and agriculture industry. In 2005 the company was listed on the main board of the Singapore Exchange. The company's majority shareholder is state-owned Temasek Holdings. Table 4.190 contains the characteristics of the largest Singaporean SOEs and their position in the Top 100 non-financial companies.

Table 4.190 The largest SOEs in Singapore and their position in the Top 100, 2018

No.	*Name of the SOE*	*Industry*	*OR (bill. €)*	*TA (bill. €)*	*Empl. worldwide (thousand)*	*State shares[a] (%)*	*Position Top 100*
1	Olam International	Food	19.6	15.0	74.5	53.8	16
2	Singtel	Post & telecomm.	11.5	32.1	24.1	49.8	28
3	Singapore Airlines	Transport	10.7	20.0	27.1	100.0	32
4	Sembcorp Industries	Energy	7.5	14.9	7.0	49.0	41
5	Singapore Pools	Other (gambling)	5.2	13.3	0.8	100.0	59
6	Singapore Technologies Eng.	Technology	4.3	4.8	22.0	51.0	68
7	Singapore Power	Energy	2.7	12.9	6.4	100.0	82

a Direct and indirect.

Source: Own compilation based on the Orbis database and other data (including Fortune Global, Forbes Global lists and companies' websites).

4.23.2 Shares of SOEs in the sets of the largest Singaporean companies

Tables 4.191–4.193 contain data on the shares of SOEs in the various sets of the largest Singaporean non-financial companies. It should be noted, however, that a significant proportion of Singapore's SOEs are – excluded from our analysis – financial entities.

Figure 4.23a shows the changes in the shares in ORs and TAs of SOEs in the Top 20 over the analysis period and Figure 4.23b shows the changes in the shares of SOEs in the various sets of the largest companies.

Table 4.191 SOEs in the sets of the largest Singaporean companies – number

	Top 10			*Top 20*			*Top 50*			*Top 100*		
	2009	*2013*	*2018*	*2009*	*2013*	*2018*	*2009*	*2013*	*2018*	*2009*	*2013*	*2018*
maSOEs	1	0	0	2	0	1	5	4	2	9	8	5
miSOEs	0	0	0	0	0	0	1	1	2	2	1	2
SOEs	1	0	0	2	0	1	6	5	4	11	9	7

Source: As in Table 4.190.

Table 4.192 SOEs in the sets of the largest Singaporean companies – share in ORs (%)

	Top 10			*Top 20*			*Top 50*			*Top 100*		
	2009	*2013*	*2018*	*2009*	*2013*	*2018*	*2009*	*2013*	*2018*	*2009*	*2013*	*2018*
maSOEs	5.51	0	0	6.77	0	2.45	8.13	3.55	2.76	8.20	4.28	3.31
miSOEs	0	0	0	0	0	0	1.44	0.74	1.74	1.42	0.61	1.48
SOEs	5.51	0	0	6.77	0	2.45	9.57	4.29	4.50	9.62	4.89	4.80

Source: As in Table 4.190.

Table 4.193 SOEs in the sets of the largest Singaporean companies – share in TAs (%)

	Top 10			*Top 20*			*Top 50*			*Top 100*		
	2009	*2013*	*2018*	*2009*	*2013*	*2018*	*2009*	*2013*	*2018*	*2009*	*2013*	*2018*
maSOEs	28.80	0	0	28.08	0	5.59	23.59	16.07	8.38	18.98	18.78	11.03
miSOEs	0	0	0	0	0	0	2.67	2.84	11.25	3.33	2.05	7.86
SOEs	28.80	0	0	28.08	0	5.59	26.06	18.91	19.63	22.31	20.84	18.89

Source: As in Table 4.190.

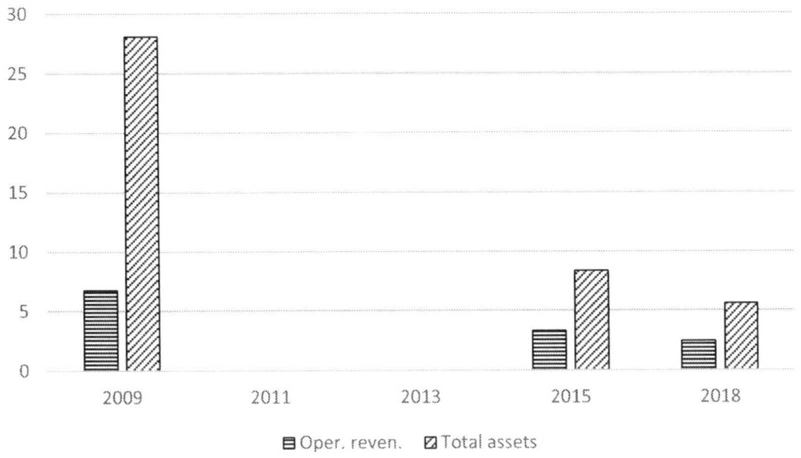

Figure 4.23a SOEs in the Top 20 of the Singaporean non-financial companies – shares in ORs and TAs (%).

Source: As in Table 4.190.

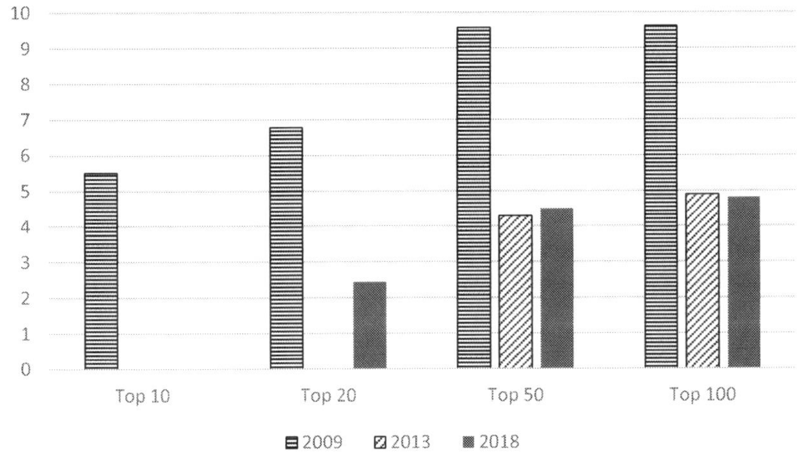

Figure 4.23b Changes in the shares of SOEs in the various sets of the largest Singaporean non-financial companies (%).

Source: As in Table 4.190.

4.23.3 Other characteristics of the Singaporean SOE sector

Revenues of the largest SOEs in relation to GDP

Table 4.194 provides data on the relationship of the value of ORs of SOEs from the Top 100 and Top 20 and the value of the nominal GDP in a given year.

Table 4.194 Relationship of ORs of SOEs and nominal GDP (%)

	2009	*2013*	*2018*
Rev-100/GDP	28.4	22.5	18.9
Rev-20/GDP	11.7	0.0	6.0

Source: Own calculation.

Table 4.195 Estimated share of SOEs in the selected industries of the Singaporean economy, 2018

Oil and gas	*Energy*	*Railways*	*Postal sector*	*Telecomm.*	*Banking sector*	*SS-I*
0	1	3	3	3	2	2.00

Source: Own estimation according to the rules given in Section 3.3.2.

Table 4.196 Number of listed SOEs in Singaporean Top 100

	2009	*2013*	*2018*
Listed SOEs	7	5	5
including minority SOEs	2	1	2

Source: As in Table 4.190.

SOEs in selected industries

Singaporean SOEs shares in four of the six featured industries are significant. Our estimates are presented in Table 4.195.

Listed SOEs

The number of listed Top 100 SOEs declined slightly during the period under review. In 2018, it was five companies, two of which were controlled with minority shares. Data on listed SOEs in the Singaporean Top 100 are presented in Table 4.196.

4.23.4 FSOEs in Singapore

The number of FSOEs in the Top 100 Singaporean non-financial companies is very high throughout the period under review. In 2018, there were 15 FSOEs (the most of all 37 countries analysed) and in Top 20 there were four FSOEs. The largest of them was CNOOC Trading (Singapore), which ranked seventh and is controlled by the Chinese parent company. The relevant data are presented in Table 4.197.

Table 4.197 FSOEs in the Top 100 of the Singaporean companies

	2009	*2013*	*2018*
Number	18	16	15
Share in ORs (%)	13.3	16.0	15.1
Share in TAs (%)	7.4	6.6	5.9

Source: As in Table 4.190.

Table 4.198 Share ratios for the Singaporean economy

Share ratio	*2009*	*2013*	*2018*
SR-100 (%)	16.0	12.9	11.9
SR-20 (%)	17.4	0	4.0
CS-20	1.09	0	0.37
miS-100 (%)	12.4	10.9	37.9

Source: Own calculations.

4.23.5 Summary

The share of SOEs in Singapore in 2018 was at a low level (around 10%). There were no SOEs in the Top 10 and only one in the Top 20. Of the seven SOEs in the Top 100, two were fully owned by the state. The share of minority SOEs in the total set of SOEs is significant. The concentration of SOEs in the Top 20 is low and increased slightly during the period under review. Olam International, the largest Singaporean SOE, was responsible for 31.7% of all ORs of SOEs in the Top 100. There is a clear decline in the share of SOEs in the Top 100 and a larger decline in the Top 20 during the period under review. A summary presentation of the data described above is presented in Table 4.198.

4.24 SOE sector in South Africa

4.24.1 The largest SOEs in South Africa and their characteristics

There were no South African companies on the Fortune Global 500 list, either in 2010 or in 2019. On the Forbes list in 2010 there were as many as 23 South African companies, of which three were state-owned, while nine years later it was – respectively – 12 and 1.

The largest SOE in South Africa and also the country's largest non-financial company is energy and chemical corporation Sasol, which operates in around 30 countries. Sasol is the world's leading company using the Fischer-Tropsch process for converting coal into liquid fuel. Sasol lists on the New York Stock Exchange. A slightly smaller entity is Eskom, which is in the energy business and accounts for 90% of South Africa's energy supply. Table 4.199 contains the characteristics of the largest South African SOEs and their position in the Top 100 non-financial companies.

Table 4.199 The largest SOEs in South Africa and their position in the Top 100, 2018

No.	*Name of the SOE*	*Industry*	*OR (bill. €)*	*TA (bill. €)*	*Empl. worldwide (thousand)*	*State shares[a] (%)*	*Position Top 100*
1	Sasol	Chemicals	11.4	27.3	31.2	27.0	1
2	Eskom	Energy	11.2	45.8	46.0	100.0	2
3	Bidvest	Trade	4.8	3.6	130.8	17.0	18
4	Transnet	Transport	4.5	23.0	2.6	100.0	20
5	Telkom	Post & telecomm.	2.6	3.2	15.2	51.9	32
6	South African Airways	Transport	1.9	0.9	11.0	100.0	39
7	Passenger Rail Agency	Transport	0.8	4.8	16.0	100.0	62
8	Rand Water	Water & sewage	0.8	1.6	0.4	100.0	64
9	Hulamin	Metals	0.7	0.3	2.0	29.6	66
10	PetroSa	Oil & gas	0.6	1.0	1.6	100.0	69

[a] Direct and indirect.
Source: Own compilation based on the Orbis database and other data (including Fortune Global, Forbes Global lists and companies' websites).

Table 4.200 SOEs in the sets of the largest South African companies – number

	Top 10			*Top 20*			*Top 50*			*Top 100*		
	2009	*2013*	*2018*	*2009*	*2013*	*2018*	*2009*	*2013*	*2018*	*2009*	*2013*	*2018*
maSOEs	0	1	1	2	1	2	2	3	4	5	5	7
miSOEs	2	2	1	2	2	2	2	2	2	3	2	3
SOEs	2	3	2	4	3	4	4	5	6	8	7	10

Source: As in Table 4.199.

4.24.2 *Shares of SOEs in the sets of the largest South African companies*

Tables 4.200–4.202 contain data on SOEs in the various sets of South Africa's largest enterprises. The data show increases in SOEs' shares during the period under review.

Figure 4.24a shows the changes in the shares in ORs and TAs of SOEs in the Top 20 over the analysis period and Figure 4.24b shows the changes in the shares of SOEs in the various sets of the largest companies.

Table 4.201 SOEs in the sets of the largest South African companies – share in ORs (%)

	Top 10			*Top 20*			*Top 50*			*Top 100*		
	2009	*2013*	*2018*	*2009*	*2013*	*2018*	*2009*	*2013*	*2018*	*2009*	*2013*	*2018*
maSOEs	0	9.30	12.98	8.27	5.92	11.44	5.13	6.11	9.62	5.85	6.25	9.27
miSOEs	22.09	20.98	13.12	13.84	13.37	11.73	8.58	8.64	7.68	7.42	7.36	6.93
SOEs	22.09	30.28	26.10	22.11	19.29	23.17	13.71	14.75	17.30	13.27	13.62	16.20

Source: As in Table 4.199.

Table 4.202 SOEs in the sets of the largest South African companies – share in TAs (%)

	Top 10			*Top 20*			*Top 50*			*Top 100*		
	2009	*2013*	*2018*	*2009*	*2013*	*2018*	*2009*	*2013*	*2018*	*2009*	*2013*	*2018*
maSOEs	0	22.03	38.03	18.53	17.67	33.55	11.78	18.72	18.03	11.54	15.11	23.77
miSOEs	18.82	14.20	22.69	12.68	11.39	15.09	8.06	7.81	7.53	6.45	5.92	9.27
SOEs	18.82	36.23	60.27	31.21	29.07	48.64	19.84	26.53	25.56	17.99	21.02	33.04

Source: As in Table 4.199.

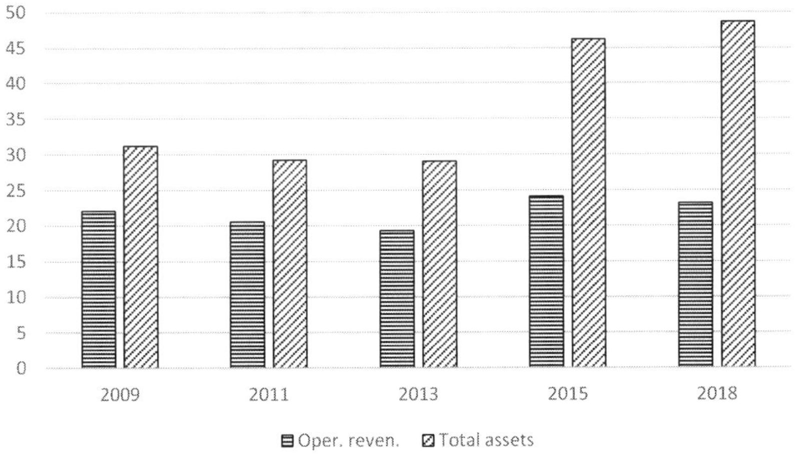

Figure 4.24a SOEs in the Top 20 of the South African non-financial companies – shares in ORs and TAs (%).

Source: As in Table 4.199.

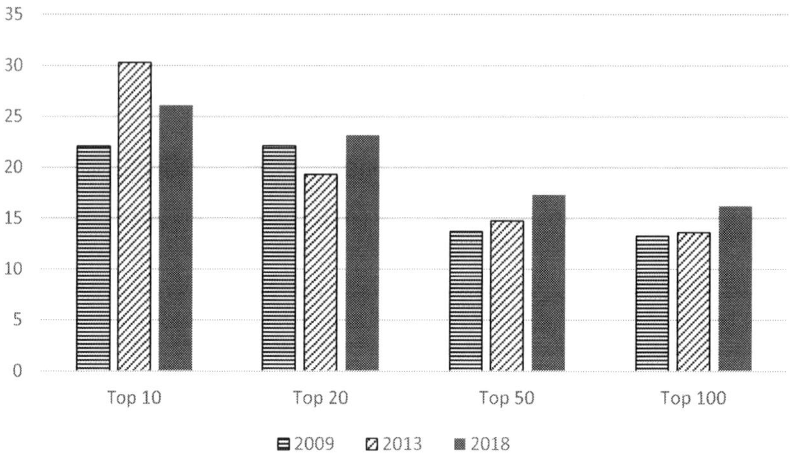

Figure 4.24b Changes in the shares of SOEs in the various sets of the largest South African non-financial companies (%).

Source: As in Table 4.199.

Table 4.203 Relationship of ORs of SOEs and nominal GDP (%)

	2009	*2013*	*2018*
Rev-100/GDP	20.3	17.2	12.3
Rev-20/GDP	17.8	13.4	10.0

Source: Own calculations.

4.24.3 Other characteristics of the South African SOE sector

Revenues of the largest SOEs in relation to GDP

Table 4.203 provides data on the relationship of the value of ORs of SOEs from the Top 100 and Top 20 and the value of the nominal GDP of South Africa in a given year. These values indicate the significant importance, decreasing in the analysed period, of SOEs in this economy.

SOEs in selected industries

SOEs in South Africa dominate in three industries: energy, railways and postal sectors. Our estimations for selected industries are presented in Table 4.204.

Table 4.204 Estimated share of SOEs in the selected industries of the South African economy, 2018

Oil and gas	*Energy*	*Railways*	*Postal sector*	*Telecomm.*	*Banking sector*	*SS-I*
1	4	4	3	1	1	2.33

Source: Own estimation according to the rules given in Section 3.3.2.

Table 4.205 Number of listed SOEs in South African Top 100

	2009	*2013*	*2018*
Listed SOEs	4	3	4
including minority SOEs	3	2	3

Source: As in Table 4.199.

Table 4.206 FSOEs in the Top 100 of the South African companies

	2009	*2013*	*2018*
Number	2	1	1
Share in ORs (%)	2.6	2.4	2.1
Share in TAs (%)	0.9	0.7	1.8

Source: As in Table 4.199.

Listed SOEs

In 2018, there were four listed SOEs controlled by the South African government in Top 100 non-financial companies (see Table 4.205).

4.24.4 FSOEs in South Africa

In 2018, there was one FSOE in Top 100 South African non-financial companies. It was Engen, which ranked 15th on the list in 2018 and is controlled by the Malaysian SOE Petronas. The relevant data are presented in Table 4.206.

4.24.5 Summary

The share of SOEs in South Africa, growing in the analysed period, in 2018 was at a significant level (around 30%). There were two SOEs in the Top 10. Of the ten SOEs in the Top 100, six are fully owned by the state. The share of minority SOEs in the total set of SOEs is significant. The concentration of SOEs in the Top 20 is visible but generally decreased during the period under review. Sasol, the largest South African SOE, is responsible for 28.8% of all revenues of SOEs in the Top 100. South Africa is one of the few economies in which SOEs are more important over time – Table 4.207.

Table 4.207 Share ratios for the South African economy

Share ratio	*2009*	*2013*	*2018*
SR-100 (%)	15.5	17.3	24.6
SR-20 (%)	26.7	24.2	35.9
CS-20	1.72	1.41	1.46
miS-100 (%)	45.3	37.2	31.9

Source: Own calculations.

4.25 SOE sector in Spain

4.25.1 The largest SOEs in Spain and their characteristics

The 2010 Fortune Global list included ten Spanish companies, of which one was state-owned. In contrast, the 2019 Fortune Global 500 list lacked Spanish SOEs. On the Forbes Global 2000 list for 2010 there were 29 Spanish companies, including one SOE. In 2019, there were three SOEs.

The largest Spanish SOE is Loterías y Apuestas del Estado, an operator of all types of lotteries and games. Table 4.208 contains the characteristics of the largest Spanish SOEs and their position in the Top 100 non-financial companies.

4.25.2 Shares of SOEs in the sets of the largest Spanish companies

Tables 4.209–4.211 contain data on the shares of SOEs in the various sets of the largest Spanish non-financial companies. Spanish SOEs are relatively small – the largest SOE is only ranked 19th in the Top 100.

Table 4.208 The largest SOEs in Spain and their position in the Top 100, 2018

No.	*Name of the SOE*	*Industry*	*OR (bill. €)*	*TA (bill. €)*	*Empl. worldwide (thousand)*	*State shares[a] (%)*	*Position Top 100*
1	Loterías y Apuestas del Estado	Other	9.1	23.0	0.6	100.0	19
2	Aena	Transport	4.3	14.9	8.4	51.0	40
3	Renfe Operadora	Transport	3.5	7.0	9.4	100.0	46
4	Indra Sistemas	Information technology	3.2	4.0	43.7	20.0	52
5	Correos	Post & telecomm.	2.1	2.1	78.0	100.0	69
6	Red Electrica	Energy	2.0	11.2	1.8	20.0	71

a Direct and indirect.
Source: Own compilation based on the Orbis database and other data (including Fortune Global, Forbes Global lists and companies' websites).

Table 4.209 SOEs in the sets of the largest Spanish companies – number

	Top 20			*Top 50*			*Top 100*		
	2009	*2013*	*2018*	*2009*	*2013*	*2018*	*2009*	*2013*	*2018*
maSOEs	0	1	1	1	2	3	4	4	4
miSOEs	0	0	0	1	1	0	1	2	2
SOEs	0	1	1	2	3	3	5	6	6

Source: As in Table 4.208.

Table 4.210 SOEs in the sets of the largest Spanish companies – share in ORs (%)

	Top 20			*Top 50*			*Top 100*		
	2009	*2013*	*2018*	*2009*	*2013*	*2018*	*2009*	*2013*	*2018*
maSOEs	0	3.52	3.74	4.31	4.65	5.65	4.83	4.72	5.00
miSOEs	0	0	0	0.31	0.47	0	0.28	1.32	1.63
SOEs	0	3.52	3.74	4.62	5.13	5.65	5.11	6.04	6.62

Source: As in Table 4.208.

Table 4.211 SOEs in the sets of the largest Spanish companies – share in TAs (%)

	Top 20			*Top 50*			*Top 100*		
	2009	*2013*	*2018*	*2009*	*2013*	*2018*	*2009*	*2013*	*2018*
maSOEs	0	3.52	3.83	4.31	4.65	5.65	4.83	4.72	5.00
miSOEs	0	0	0	0.31	0.47	0	0.28	1.32	1.63
SOEs	0	3.52	3.83	4.62	5.13	5.65	5.11	6.04	6.62

Source: As in Table 4.208.

Figure 4.25a shows the changes in the shares in Ors and Tas of SOEs in the Top 20 over the analysis period and Figure 4.25b shows the changes in the shares of SOEs in the various sets of the largest companies.

4.25.3 Other characteristics of the Spanish SOE sector

Revenues of the largest SOEs in relation to GDP

Table 4.212 provides data on the relationship of the value of Ors of SOEs from the Top 100 and Top 20 and the value of the nominal GDP of Spain in selected years. The values are larger than in 2009 but this indicator in the Spanish economy is low.

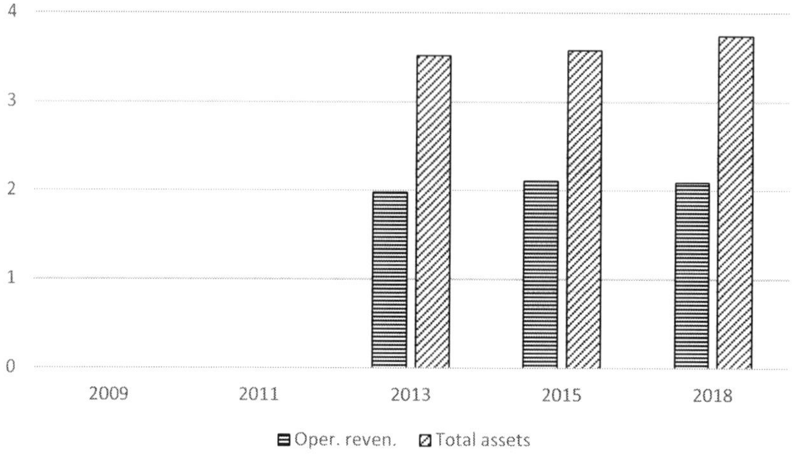

Figure 4.25a SOEs in the Top 20 of the Spanish non-financial companies – shares in ORs and TAs (%).

Source: As in Table 4.208.

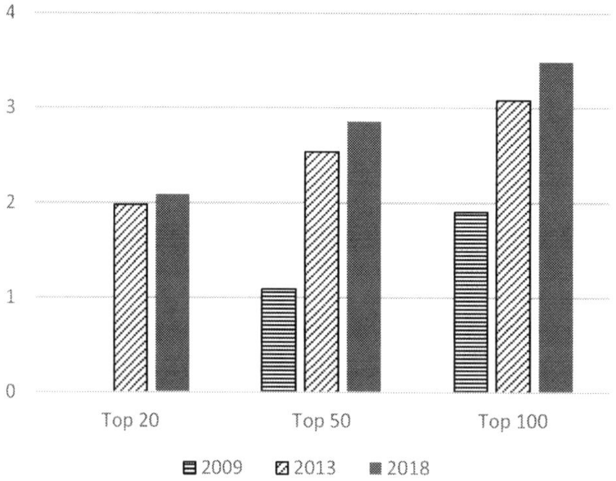

Figure 4.25b Changes in the shares of SOEs in the various sets of the Spanish non-financial companies (%).

Source: As in Table 4.208.

Table 4.212 Relationship of ORs of SOEs and nominal GDP (%)

	2009	*2013*	*2018*
Rev-100/GDP	1.0	2.1	1.9
Rev-20/GDP	0	0.9	0.7

Source: Own calculations.

Table 4.213 Estimated share of SOEs in the selected industries of the Spanish economy, 2018

Oil and gas	*Energy*	*Railways*	*Postal sector*	*Telecomm.*	*Banking sector*	*SS-I*
0	0	3	3	0	1	1.17

Source: Own estimation according to the rules given in Section 3.3.2.

SOEs in selected industries

SOEs are not widespread in strategic sectors in the Spanish economy. Only in the postal sector and in railways the dominant position is still held by SOEs. The state as an owner is almost absent – as a result of privatisations carried out – in the sectors of energy, telecommunications, oil & gas and banking (Table 4.213).

Listed SOEs

Out of six Spanish SOEs from the Top 100 non-financial companies in 2018, three - as mixed capital companies - were listed on the Madrid Stock Exchange. For more detailed data on this, see Table 4.214.

4.25.4 FSOEs in Spain

In 2018, there were seven FSOEs in the Top 100 Spanish companies. The largest of them was Compania Espanola de Petroleos SAU, ranked sixth on the list, owned indirectly by the government of the United Arab Emirates. The other large FSOE is Endesa, ranked 11th on the list, owned by Italy's Enel. The relevant data are presented in Table 4.215.

Table 4.214 Number of listed SOEs in Spanish Top 100

	2009	*2013*	*2018*
Listed SOEs	1	2	3
including minority SOEs	1	2	2

Source: As in Table 4.208.

Table 4.215 FSOEs in the Top 100 of the Spanish companies

	2009	*2013*	*2018*
Number	10	11	7
Share in ORs (%)	14.6	13.0	9.1
Share in TAs (%)	13.8	15.4	9.1

Source: As in Table 4.208.

Table 4.216 Share ratios for the Spanish economy

Share ratio	*2009*	*2013*	*2018*
SR-100 (%)	3.5	4.6	5.1
SR-20 (%)	0	2.7	2.9
CS-20	0	0.6	0.6
miS-100 (%)	9.0	22.1	23.6

Source: Own calculations.

4.25.5 Summary

The share of SOEs in Spain in 2018 was very low – around 5% in the Top 100 set and 3% in the Top 20 set. The economic importance of large SOEs is low. The largest SOE is ranked 19th in the Top 100 largest non-financial companies. Of the six SOEs in the Top 100, three are fully owned by the state. Minority SOEs are of negligible importance. Loterías y Apuestas del Estado, the largest Spanish SOE, is responsible for a third of all revenues of SOEs in the Top 100. An overview of key values on SOEs' share in the Spanish economy is in Table 4.216.

4.26 SOE sector in Sweden

4.26.1 The largest SOEs in Sweden and their characteristics

There were five Swedish companies on the Fortune Global 500 list in 2010, and two of them were state-owned. Nine years later there was only one (private) company from Sweden on that list. On the Forbes Global 2000 list in 2010 there were 27 Swedish companies, of which one was state-owned, and nine years later these values were almost identical - 26 and 1.

Sweden's largest SOE in 2018 was the energy company Vattenfall, whose subsidiaries operate in many European countries, including Denmark, Finland and Germany. The corporation owns coal-fired, nuclear, gas, hydroelectric, wind and solar power plants. Table 4.217 contains the characteristics of the largest Swedish SOEs and their position in the Top 100 non-financial companies.

4.26.2 Shares of SOEs in the sets of the largest Swedish companies

Tables 4.218–4.220 contain data on the shares of SOEs in the various sets of the largest Swedish non-financial companies. The number of SOEs in Sweden decreased slightly between 2009 and 2018. This was not a result of privatisation, but only a declining ranking of these enterprises.

Despite only a slight decrease in numbers, the share in revenue and assets fell sharply in all groups of companies analysed. The main reason for this phenomenon was the relative faster development of private enterprises in Sweden.

Table 4.217 The largest SOEs in Sweden and their position in the Top 100, 2018

No.	*Name of the SOE*	*Industry*	*OR (bill. €)*	*TA (bill. €)*	*Empl. worldwide (thousand)*	*State shares[a] (%)*	*Position Top 100*
1	Vattenfall	Energy	15.3	45.1	20.0	100.0	6
2	Telia Company	Post & telecomm.	8.9	24.2	20.8	37.3	15
3	SAS[b]	Transport	4.3	3.3	10.1	14.8	29
4	Postnord	Post & telecomm.	3.9	2.3	30.0	60.0	33
5	Systembolaget	Trade	3.0	0.6	3.5	100.0	43
6	LKAB	Mining	2.5	6.7	4.5	100.0	54
7	Storstockholms Lokaltrafik	Transport	2.0	5.9	5.5	100.0	63
8	Apoteket	Trade	2.0	0.8	3.2	100.0	66
9	Goteborgs Stadshus	Other	1.9	6.6	6.5	100.0	70
10	Stockholms Stadshus	Other	1.6	13.0	3.0	100.0	85

a Direct and indirect.
b Although the Swedish government owns only 14.8% of the shares, SAS should be regarded as an SOE, albeit of a special type. The second largest shareholder, Denmark, has a similar, although slightly smaller, shares.
Source: Own compilation based on the Orbis database and other data (including Fortune Global, Forbes Global lists and companies' websites).

Table 4.218 SOEs in the sets of the largest Swedish companies – number

	Top 10			*Top 20*			*Top 50*			*Top 100*		
	2009	*2013*	*2018*	*2009*	*2013*	*2018*	*2009*	*2013*	*2018*	*2009*	*2013*	*2018*
maSOEs	1	1	1	1	1	1	5	4	3	11	9	9
miSOEs	1	1	0	1	1	1	2	2	2	2	2	2
SOEs	2	2	1	2	2	2	7	6	5	13	11	11

Source: As in Table 4.217.

Table 4.219 SOEs in the sets of the largest Swedish companies – share in ORs (%)

	Top 10			*Top 20*			*Top 50*			*Top 100*		
	2009	*2013*	*2018*	*2009*	*2013*	*2018*	*2009*	*2013*	*2018*	*2009*	*2013*	*2018*
maSOEs	16.95	11.85	8.29	11.82	7.90	5.60	12.15	8.22	5.65	12.01	8.61	6.95
miSOEs	7.64	7.04	0	5.54	4.69	3.24	5.46	4.55	3.35	4.52	3.75	2.72
SOEs	24.89	18.89	8.29	17.36	12.59	8.84	17.61	12.77	9.00	16.53	12.37	9.68

Source: As in Table 4.217.

Table 4.220 SOEs in the sets of the largest Swedish companies – share in TAs (%)

	Top 10			*Top 20*			*Top 50*			*Top 100*		
	2009	*2013*	*2018*	*2009*	*2013*	*2018*	*2009*	*2013*	*2018*	*2009*	*2013*	*2018*
maSOEs	33.36	25.17	21.15	25.46	19.96	15.24	22.32	15.20	10.97	21.52	17.32	14.57
miSOEs	13.07	13.11	0	9.98	10.39	8.19	8.67	7.64	6.30	7.35	6.40	4.90
SOEs	46.43	38.27	21.15	35.43	30.35	23.42	30.99	22.84	17.27	28.87	23.73	19.47

Source: As in Table 4.217.

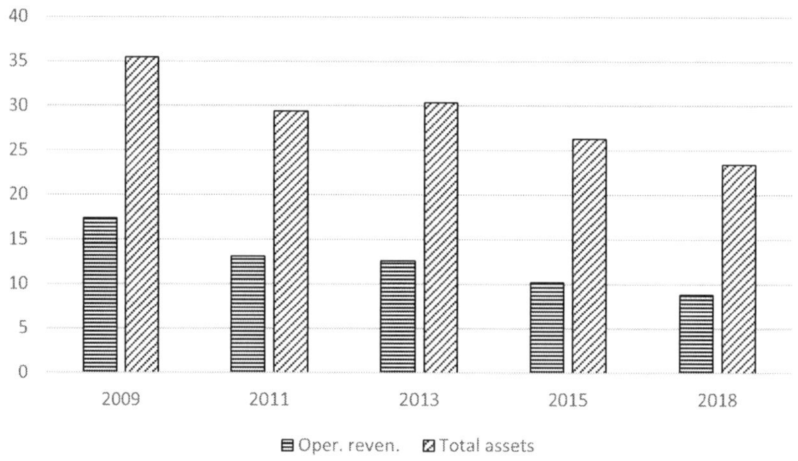

Figure 4.26a SOEs in the Top 20 of the Swedish non-financial companies – shares in ORs and TAs (%).

Source: As in Table 4.217.

Figure 4.26a shows the changes in the shares in ORs and TAs of SOEs in the Top 20 over the analysis period and Figure 4.26.b shows the changes in the shares of SOEs in the various sets of the largest companies.

4.26.3 Other characteristics of the Swedish SOE sector

Revenues of the largest SOEs in relation to GDP

Table 4.221 provides data on the relationship of the value of ORs of SOEs from the Top 100 and Top 20 and the value of the nominal GDP of Sweden in a given year. Sharp decreases in the values are evident.

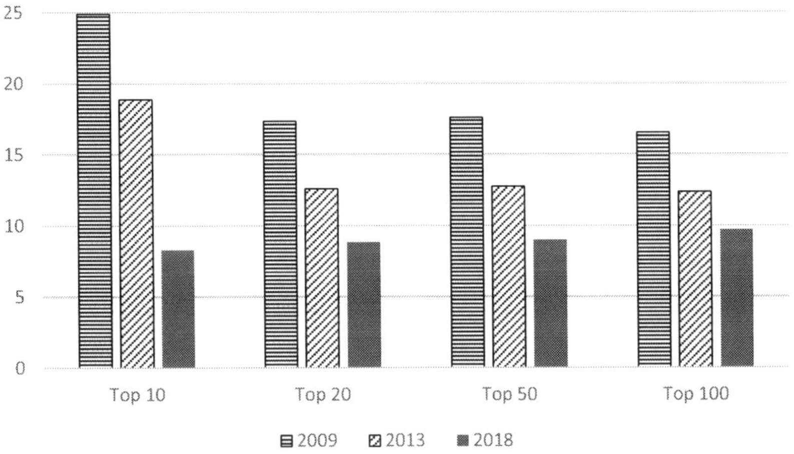

Figure 4.26b Changes in the shares of SOEs in the various sets of the largest Swedish non-financial companies (%).

Source: As in Table 4.217.

Table 4.221 Relationship of ORs of SOEs and nominal GDP (%)

	2009	*2013*	*2018*
Rev-100/GDP	18.4	12.7	9.6
Rev-20/GDP	11.2	7.3	5.0

Source: Own calculations.

Table 4.222 Estimated share of SOEs in the selected industries of the Swedish economy, 2018

Oil and gas	*Energy*	*Railways*	*Postal sector*	*Telecomm.*	*Banking sector*	*SS-I*
0	3	3	3	3	0	2.00

Source: Own estimation according to the rules given in Section 3.3.2.

SOEs in selected industries

Swedish SOEs dominate in energy, railways, postal and telecommunications industries. They are not present – according to the methodology used – in the oil and gas and banking sectors. Our estimates are presented in Table 4.222.

Listed SOEs

Between 2009 and 2018 in Top 100 non-financial companies there were two listed SOEs controlled by the Swedish government. Both were minority-owned. The relevant data are presented in Table 4.223.

Table 4.223 Number of listed SOEs in Swedish Top 100

	2009	*2013*	*2018*
Listed SOEs	2	2	2
including minority SOEs	2	2	2

Source: As in Table 4.217.

Table 4.224 FSOEs in the Top 100 of the Swedish companies

	2009	*2013*	*2018*
Number	7	5	5
Share in ORs (%)	2.5	2.3	1.7
Share in TAs (%)	2.2	0.9	1.0

Source: As in Table 4.217.

4.26.4 FSOEs in Sweden

In 2018, there were five FSOEs in the Top 100 Swedish non-financial companies and this was a moderate number relative to other countries. The largest FSOE in Sweden was petrochemical OK-Q8 AB, ranked 57th on the list and owned indirectly by the Kuwait government. Data on FSOEs in the Swedish Top 100 are presented in Table 4.224.

4.26.5 Summary

The share of SOEs in Sweden in 2018 was at an average level – around 15%. There was only one SOE in the Top 10. Of the 11 SOEs in the Top 100, 8 are fully owned by the state. The share of minority SOEs in the total set of SOEs is significant and fairly stable. The concentration of SOEs in the Top 20 group is low. Vattenfall, the largest Swedish SOE, is responsible for 32.7% of all revenues of SOEs in the Top 100. The shares of SOEs in the Swedish economy are very clearly decreasing over time. A summary presentation of the data described above is presented in Table 4.225.

Table 4.225 Share ratios for the Swedish economy

Share ratio	*2009*	*2013*	*2018*
SR-100 (%)	22.7	18.0	14.6
SR-20 (%)	26.4	21.5	16.1
CS-20	1.16	1.19	1.14
miS-100 (%)	26.1	28.0	26.1

Source: Own calculations.

4.27 SOE sector in Switzerland

4.27.1 The largest SOEs in Switzerland and their characteristics

There were 15 Swiss companies on the Fortune Global 500 list in 2010, but none of them were SOEs. Nine years later there were 14 Swiss companies on that list, but again none of them were state-owned. On the Forbes list in 2010 there were 48 Swiss companies, of which 7 were state-owned, while in 2019 these numbers dropped to – respectively – 41 and 3.

The largest Swiss SOE in 2018 was Swisscom AG, which operates in the telecommunications industry. The company has been listed on the Zurich Stock Exchange since 1998. The second largest SOE was SSS-CFF-FFS, the national railway operator in Switzerland. Table 4.226 contains the characteristics of the largest Swiss SOEs and their position in the Top 100 non-financial companies.

4.27.2 Shares of SOEs in the sets of the largest Swiss companies

Tables 4.227–4.229 contain data on the shares of SOEs in the various sets of the largest Swiss non-financial companies. It is distinctive that there is a lack of SOEs among the largest (Top 20), while there are relatively many SOEs in the second half of the ranking.

Table 4.226 The largest SOEs in Switzerland and their position in the Top 100, 2018

No.	*Name of the SOE*	*Industry*	*OR (bill. €)*	*TA (bill. €)*	*Empl. worldwide (thousand)*	*State shares[a] (%)*	*Position Top 100*
1	Swisscom	Post & telecomm.	10.5	20.0	19.8	51.0	12
2	SBB-CFF-FFS	Transport	8.6	41.2	33.1	100.0	16
3	Swiss Post	Post & telecomm.	5.2	7.1	62.3	100.0	29
4	Axpo	Energy	4.3	19.6	4.4	100.0	33
5	BKW	Energy	2.3	8.0	6.7	64.5	57
6	Repower	Energy	1.9	1.7	3.5	100.0	62
7	RUAG	Machinery	1.8	1.8	9.0	100.0	63
8	Flughafen Zűrich	Transport	1.0	3.9	1.8	38.4	82
9	BLS	Transport	1.0	4.7	2.8	77.5	84
10	Swissgrid	Energy	0.8	2.7	0.5	100.0	92

a Direct and indirect.

Source: Own compilation based on the Orbis database and other data (including Fortune Global, Forbes Global lists and companies' websites).

Table 4.227 SOEs in the sets of the largest Swiss companies – number

	Top 20			*Top 50*			*Top 100*		
	2009	*2013*	*2018*	*2009*	*2013*	*2018*	*2009*	*2013*	*2018*
maSOEs	3	2	2	5	5	4	15	13	10
miSOEs	0	0	0	0	0	0	1	1	1
SOEs	3	2	2	5	5	4	16	14	11

Source: As in Table 4.226.

Table 4.228 SOEs in the sets of the largest Swiss companies – share in ORs (%)

	Top 20			*Top 50*			*Top 100*		
	2009	*2013*	*2018*	*2009*	*2013*	*2018*	*2009*	*2013*	*2018*
maSOEs	5.81	4.44	4.59	6.40	6.39	5.27	7.56	7.27	6.06
miSOEs	0	0	0	0	0	0	0.13	0.15	0.17
SOEs	5.81	4.44	4.59	6.40	6.39	5.27	7.69	7.43	6.23

Source: As in Table 4.226.

Table 4.229 SOEs in the sets of the largest Swiss companies – share in TAs (%)

	Top 20			*Top 50*			*Top 100*		
	2009	*2013*	*2018*	*2009*	*2013*	*2018*	*2009*	*2013*	*2018*
maSOEs	11.02	9.04	10.07	11.06	11.97	11.23	12.88	13.18	12.08
miSOEs	0	0	0	0	0	0	0.42	0.49	0.43
SOEs	11.02	9.04	10.07	11.06	11.97	11.23	13.31	13.67	12.51

Source: As in Table 4.226.

Figure 4.27.a shows the changes in the shares in ORs and TAs of SOEs in the Top 20 over the analysis period and Figure 4.27.b shows the changes in the shares of SOEs in the various sets of the largest companies.

4.27.3 Other characteristics of the Swiss SOE sector

Revenues of the largest SOEs in relation to GDP

Table 4.230 provides data on the relationship of the value of ORs of SOEs from the Top 100 and Top 20 and the value of the nominal GDP of Switzerland in a given year. There were moderate decreases over time.

Figure 4.27a SOEs in the Top 20 of the Swiss non-financial companies – shares in ORs and TAs (%).

Source: As in Table 4.226.

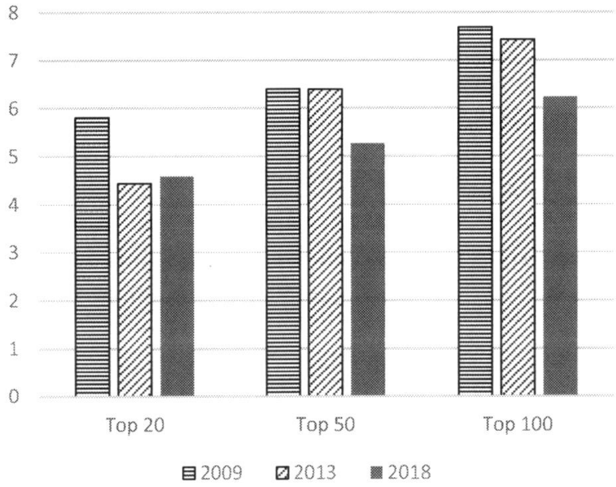

Figure 4.27b Changes in the shares of SOEs in the various sets of the largest Swiss non-financial companies (%).

Source: As in Table 4.226.

Table 4.230 Relationship of ORs of SOEs and nominal GDP (%)

	2009	*2013*	*2018*
Rev-100/GDP	8.8	7.7	6.2
Rev-20/GDP	4.8	3.2	3.1

Source: Own calculations.

Table 4.231 Estimated share of SOEs in the selected industries of the Swiss economy, 2018

Oil and gas	*Energy*	*Railways*	*Postal sector*	*Telecomm.*	*Banking sector*	*SS-I*
1	3	4	3	3	0	2.33

Source: Own estimation according to the rules given in Section 3.3.2.

SOEs in selected industries

SOEs are widely present in various sectors of the Swiss economy. They dominate in energy, railways, postal and telecommunication industries. It is worth mentioning that, in line with the methodology used, there was no state-owned bank among the five largest banks, but a state-controlled bank was ranked sixth. Our estimations for selected industries are presented in 4.231.

Listed SOEs

In 2018, there were four listed SOEs controlled by the Swiss government in Top 100 non-financial companies. Most of them were majority-owned. The relevant data are presented in Table 4.232.

4.27.4 FSOEs in Switzerland

In 2018, there were four FSOEs in the Top 100 Swiss non-financial companies and this was a moderate number relative to other countries. In Top 20 there was one FSOEs. The largest FSOE was chemical company Syngenta AG, ranked eighth on the Top 100 list, which has been (since 2015) owned by China National Chemical Corporation. The relevant data are presented in Table 4.233.

Table 4.232 Number of listed SOEs in Swiss Top 100

	2009	*2013*	*2018*
Listed SOEs	5	4	4
including minority SOEs	1	1	1

Source: As in Table 4.226.

Table 4.233 FSOEs in the Top 100 of the Swiss companies

	2009	*2013*	*2018*
Number	2	2	4
Share in ORs (%)	2.6	1.7	4.0
Share in TAs (%)	2.7	2.0	3.9

Source: As in Table 4.226.

Table 4.234 Share ratios for the Swiss economy

Share ratio	*2009*	*2013*	*2018*
SR-100 (%)	10.5	10.5	9.4
SR-20 (%)	8.4	6.7	7.3
CS-20	0.81	0.64	0.78
miS-100 (%)	2.7	3.1	3.2

Source: Own calculations.

4.27.5 Summary

The share of SOEs in Switzerland in 2018 was at a low level, i.e. below 10%. There were no SOEs in the Top 10. Of the 11 SOEs in the Top 100, 5 are fully owned by the state. The share of minority SOEs in the total set of SOEs is negligible. There is no concentration of SOEs in the Top 20. Swisscom, the largest Swiss SOE, is responsible for 27.6% of all revenues of SOEs in the Top 100. The share of SOEs in both analysed groups of companies decreased over time. An overview of key values on SOEs' share in the Swiss economy is in Table 4.234.

4.28 SOE sector in Taiwan

4.28.1 The largest SOEs in Taiwan and their characteristics

There were eight Taiwanese companies on the Fortune Global 500 list in 2010, and one of them was state-owned. Nine years later there were ten companies from Taiwan and again one was state-owned. It was CPC, which ranked 394th. On the Forbes Global 2000 list in 2010 there were 39 Taiwanese companies, of which 6 were state-owned, and nine years later these values were – respectively – 47 and 6.

The largest SOE in Taiwan in 2018 was the CPC Corporation, which is fully owned by the state. It was founded in 1946 and operates in the oil and gas industry (from extraction through refining to selling oil and gas and products derived from petroleum). Table 4.235 contains the characteristics of the largest Taiwanese SOEs and their position in the Top 100 non-financial companies.

4.28.2 Shares of SOEs in the sets of the largest Taiwanese companies

Tables 4.236–4.238 contain data on the shares of SOEs in the various sets of the largest Taiwanese non-financial companies. SOEs' importance in Taiwan's economy has been stable over the years in terms of numbers and declining in terms of revenues (slightly) and assets (significantly).

Figure 4.28a shows the changes in the shares in ORs and TAs of SOEs in the Top 20 over the analysis period and Figure 4.28b shows the changes in the shares of SOEs in the various sets of the largest companies.

Table 4.235 The largest SOEs in Taiwan and their position in the Top 100, 2018

No.	*Name of the SOE*	*Industry*	*OR (bill. €)*	*TA (bill. €)*	*Empl. worldwide (thousand)*	*State shares*[a] *(%)*	*Position Top 100*
1	CPC Corporation	Oil & gas	29.6	21.9	15.7	100.0	3
2	Taiwan Power Company	Energy	16.7	57.6	26.9	100.0	9
3	China Steel	Metals	11.4	19.2	28.6	20.0	14
4	Chunghwa Telecom	Post & telecomm.	6.1	13.3	32.6	35.3	29
5	China Airlines	Transport	4.9	6.5	11.4	49.1	35
6	Yang Ming Marine Transport	Transport	4.0	4.0	5.8	42.8	42
7	Taiwan Tobacco & Liquor	Agribusiness	2.0	3.3	4.0	100.0	66
8	Chung Hung Steel	Metals	1.4	1.0	1.2	40.6	95
9	Taiwan High Speed Rail	Transport	1.3	12.3	4.5	55.7	99

[a] Direct and indirect.
Source: Own compilation based on the Orbis database and other data (including Fortune Global, Forbes Global lists and companies' websites).

Table 4.236 SOEs in the sets of the largest Taiwanese companies – number

	Top 10			*Top 20*			*Top 50*			*Top 100*		
	2009	*2013*	*2018*	*2009*	*2013*	*2018*	*2009*	*2013*	*2018*	*2009*	*2013*	*2018*
maSOEs	2	2	2	2	2	2	4	3	3	6	4	5
miSOEs	0	0	0	1	1	1	2	3	3	3	5	4
SOEs	2	2	2	3	3	3	6	6	6	9	9	9

Source: As in Table 4.235.

Table 4.237 SOEs in the sets of the largest Taiwanese companies – share in ORs (%)

	Top 10			*Top 20*			*Top 50*			*Top 100*		
	2009	*2013*	*2018*	*2009*	*2013*	*2018*	*2009*	*2013*	*2018*	*2009*	*2013*	*2018*
maSOEs	15.98	16.37	12.07	11.43	12.03	9.42	10.70	10.34	8.15	9.85	9.38	7.60
miSOEs	0	0	0	2.39	2.35	2.32	2.41	3.14	3.15	2.31	3.11	2.95
SOEs	15.98	16.37	12.07	13.81	14.37	11.74	13.10	13.48	11.31	12.16	12.50	10.55

Source: As in Table 4.235.

Table 4.238 SOEs in the sets of the largest Taiwanese companies – share in TAs (%)

	Top 10			*Top 20*			*Top 50*			*Top 100*		
	2009	*2013*	*2018*	*2009*	*2013*	*2018*	*2009*	*2013*	*2018*	*2009*	*2013*	*2018*
maSOEs	40.75	31.84	25.78	23.90	22.23	18.62	20.77	17.16	15.12	21.20	14.76	14.63
miSOEs	0	0	0	5.03	5.47	4.49	4.17	5.58	4.84	3.56	4.86	4.13
SOEs	40.75	31.84	25.78	28.93	27.70	23.10	24.95	22.74	19.96	24.76	19.62	18.76

Source: As in Table 4.235.

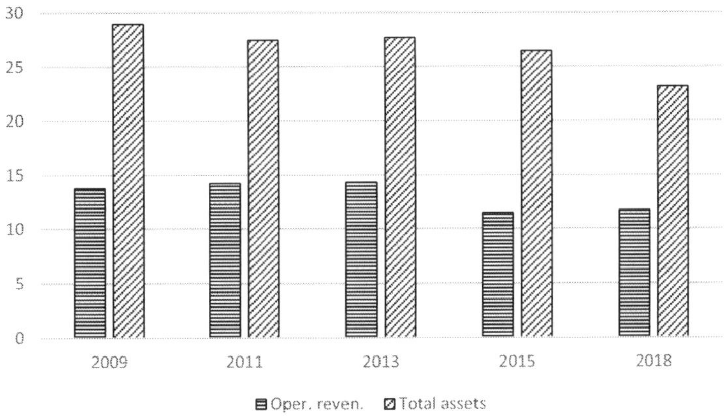

Figure 4.28a SOEs in the Top 20 of the Taiwanese non-financial companies – shares in ORs and TAs (%).

Source: As in Table 4.235.

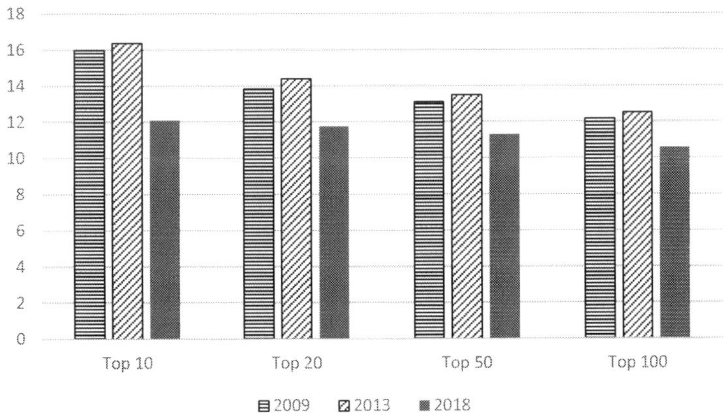

Figure 4.28b Changes in the shares of SOEs in the various sets of the largest Taiwanese non-financial companies (%).

Source: As in Table 4.235.

Table 4.239 Relationship of ORs of SOEs and nominal GDP (%)

	2009	*2013*	*2018*
Rev-100/GDP	16.2	18.1	14.0
Rev-20/GDP	11.9	13.9	10.4

Source: Own calculations.

Table 4.240 Estimated share of SOEs in the selected industries of the Taiwanese economy, 2018

Oil and gas	*Energy*	*Railways*	*Postal sector*	*Telecomm.*	*Banking sector*	*SS-I*
3	3	4	3	3	2	3.00

Source: Own estimation according to the rules given in Section 3.3.2.

Table 4.241 Number of listed SOEs in Taiwanese Top 100

	2009	2013	2018
Listed SOEs	5	6	6
including minority SOEs	3	5	4

Source: As in Table 4.235.

4.28.3 Other characteristics of the Taiwanese SOE sector

Revenues of the largest SOEs in relation to GDP

Table 4.239 provides data on the relationship of the value of ORs of SOEs from the Top 100 and Top 20 compared to the value of the nominal GDP of Taiwan in selected years. The importance of Taiwanese SOEs as measured by this indicator is at a rather high level; there were slight increases between 2009 and 2013, but later these indicators decreased.

SOEs in selected industries

SOEs play an important role in all strategic industries in Taiwan. Our estimations for selected industries are presented in Table 4.240.

Listed SOEs

In 2018, there were six listed SOEs in Top 100 non-financial companies, and four of them were controlled with minority shares. Data on listed SOEs in Taiwanese Top 100 are presented in Table 4.241.

4.28.4 FSOEs in Taiwan

There are no SOEs among the Top 100 largest Taiwanese non-financial companies.

Table 4.242 Share ratios for the Taiwanese economy

Share ratio	*2009*	*2013*	*2018*
SR-100 (%)	18.5	16.1	14.7
SR-20 (%)	21.4	21.0	17.4
CS-20	1.16	1.30	1.18
miS-100 (%)	15.9	24.8	24.2

Source: Own calculations.

4.28.5 Summary

The share of SOEs in Taiwan in 2018 was at a moderate level – around 15%. The share decreased markedly over the period considered. There were two SOEs in the Top 10. Of the nine SOEs in the Top 100, three are fully owned by the state. The proportion of minority SOEs in the total set of SOEs is significant and quite stable. The concentration of SOEs in the Top 20 is high. CPC, the largest Taiwanese SOE, is responsible for 38.2% ORs of SOEs in the Top 100. A summary of the data described above is presented in Table 4.242.

4.29 SOE sector in Thailand

4.29.1 The largest SOEs in Thailand and their characteristics

There was one Thai company on the Fortune Global 500 list in 2010. It was state-owned PTT. The same was the case in 2019. It ranked 130th. On the Forbes Global 2000 list in 2010 there were 14 Thai companies, of which 6 were state-owned, and nine years later these values were – respectively – 15 and 9.

The largest SOE in Thailand in 2018 was the PTT. It is a listed company and was founded in 1978 by the merger of Thai Fuel Organization and Thai Natural Gas Organization. Table 4.243 contains the characteristics of the largest Thai SOEs and their position is in the Top 100 non-financial companies.

4.29.2 Shares of SOEs in the sets of the largest Thai companies

Tables 4.244–4.246 contain data on the shares of SOEs in the various sets of the largest Thai non-financial companies. The overall number of SOEs in the Top 100 has significantly increased in the analysed period.

Figure 4.29a shows the changes in the shares in ORs and TAs of SOEs in the Top 20 over the analysis period and Figure 4.29b shows the changes in the shares of SOEs in the various sets of the largest companies.

Table 4.243 The largest SOEs in Thailand and their position in the Top 100, 2018

No.	*Name of the SOE*	*Industry*	*OR (bill. €)*	*TA (bill. €)*	*Empl. worldwide (thousand)*	*State shares[a] (%)*	*Position Top 100*
1	PTT	Oil & gas	63.1	63.4	24.7	58.9	1
2	Electricity Generating Authority	Energy	14.1	27.5	22.4	100.0	4
3	Provincial Electricity Authority	Energy	13.4	11.2	35.5	100.0	5
4	Siam Cement	Chemicals	13.2	15.9	54.0	41.9	6
5	Thai Oil	Oil & gas	10.5	7.2	2.3	65.1	8
6	IRPC	Chemicals	7.6	4.9	5.0	65.9	11
7	Thai Airways International	Transport	5.3	7.2	22.0	81.3	16
8	Metropolitan Electricity Authority	Energy	5.3	5.8	10.6	100.0	17
9	Bangchak Corporation	Oil & gas	5.2	3.2	3.2	49.8	18
10	Thai Polyethylene	Chemicals	2.3	2.0	0.9	100.0	39

a Direct and indirect.
Source: Own compilation based on the Orbis database and other data (including Fortune Global, Forbes Global lists and companies' websites).

Table 4.244 SOEs in the sets of the largest Thai companies – number

	Top 10			*Top 20*			*Top 50*			*Top 100*		
	2009	*2013*	*2018*	*2009*	*2013*	*2018*	*2009*	*2013*	*2018*	*2009*	*2013*	*2018*
maSOEs	5	4	4	6	6	7	10	10	9	11	13	16
miSOEs	2	2	1	3	3	2	3	3	2	4	5	5
SOEs	7	6	5	9	9	9	13	13	11	15	18	21

Source: As in Table 4.243.

Table 4.245 SOEs in the sets of the largest Thai companies – share in ORs (%)

	Top 10			*Top 20*			*Top 50*			*Top 100*		
	2009	*2013*	*2018*	*2009*	*2013*	*2018*	*2009*	*2013*	*2018*	*2009*	*2013*	*2018*
maSOEs	71.66	59.91	58.02	57.34	50.97	51.64	44.88	40.68	38.72	38.33	36.33	35.39
miSOEs	14.60	12.44	7.57	13.35	11.76	7.96	9.85	8.82	5.86	8.61	8.01	5.62
SOEs	86.27	72.35	65.59	70.69	62.74	59.60	54.72	49.50	44.48	46.95	44.34	41.02

Source: As in Table 4.243.

Table 4.246 SOEs in the sets of the largest Thai companies – share in TAs (%)

	Top 10			*Top 20*			*Top 50*			*Top 100*		
	2009	*2013*	*2018*	*2009*	*2013*	*2018*	*2009*	*2013*	*2018*	*2009*	*2013*	*2018*
maSOEs	77.91	74.53	71.65	66.23	65.03	66.36	56.94	51.80	48.58	49.64	48.33	44.37
miSOEs	15.87	16.09	10.41	14.24	13.51	9.93	10.37	9.78	6.97	9.86	8.64	7.62
SOEs	93.77	90.62	82.06	80.47	78.54	76.29	67.31	61.58	55.56	59.50	56.98	51.99

Source: As in Table 4.243.

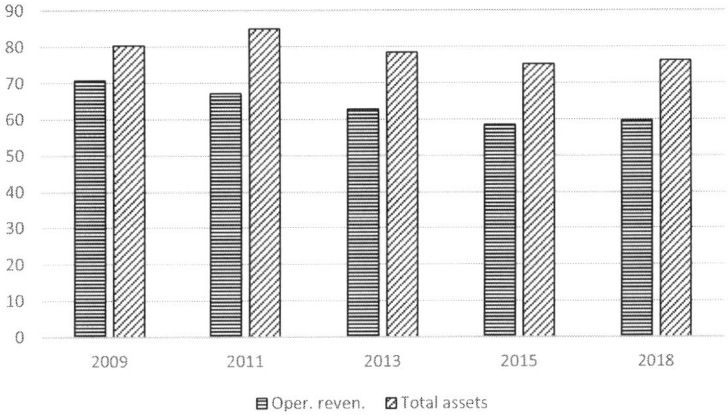

Figure 4.29a SOEs in the Top 20 of the Thai non-financial companies – shares in ORs and TAs (%).

Source: As in Table 4.243.

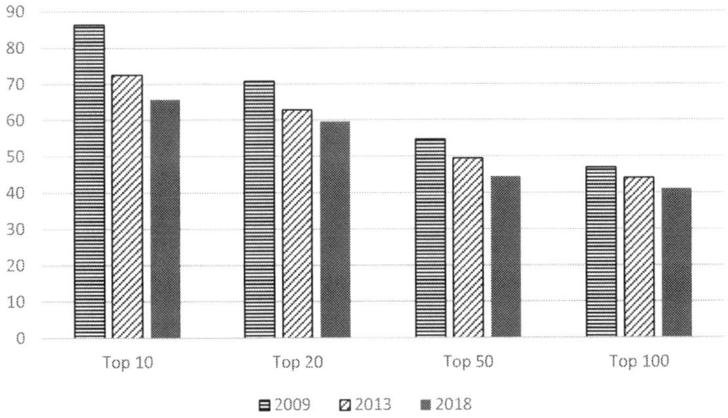

Figure 4.29b Changes in the shares of SOEs in the various sets of the largest Thai non-financial companies (%).

Source: As in Table 4.243.

4.29.3 Other characteristics of the Thai SOE sector

Revenues of the largest SOEs in relation to GDP

Table 4.247 provides data on the relationship of the value of ORs of SOEs from the Top 100 and Top 20 and the value of the nominal GDP of Thailand in a given year; there were slight increases between 2009 and 2013, but later these indicators decreased.

SOEs in selected industries

SOEs in Thailand play a significant role in all analysed industries, except for telecommunications. Our estimates are presented in Table 4.248.

Listed SOEs

In 2018, there were ten listed SOEs controlled by the Thai government in Top 100 non-financial companies. This number increased over time, from seven in 2009. The relevant data are presented in Table 4.249.

Table 4.247 Relationship of ORs of SOEs and nominal GDP (%)

	2009	*2013*	*2018*
Rev-100/GDP	38.4	44.0	35.0
Rev-20/GDP	36.2	40.4	31.1

Source: Own calculations.

Table 4.248 Estimated share of SOEs in the selected industries of the Thai economy, 2018

Oil and gas	*Energy*	*Railways*	*Postal sector*	*Telecomm.*	*Banking sector*	*SS-I*
3	4	4	3	1	2	2.83

Source: Own estimation according to the rules given in Section 3.3.2.

Table 4.249 Number of listed SOEs in Thai Top 100

	2009	*2013*	*2018*
Listed SOEs	7	8	10
including minority SOEs	3	3	3

Source: As in Table 4.243.

Table 4.250 FSOEs in the Top 100 of the Thai companies

	2009	*2013*	*2018*
Number	4	5	2
Share in ORs (%)	3.6	3.6	1.7
Share in TAs (%)	5.0	3.7	3.5

Source: As in Table 4.243.

Table 4.251 Share ratios for the Thai economy

Share ratio	*2009*	*2013*	*2018*
SR-100 (%)	53.2	50.6	46.5
SR-20 (%)	76.6	70.6	67.9
CS-20	1.42	1.38	1.46
miS-100 (%)	17.5	16.8	14.2

Source: Own calculations.

4.29.4 FSOEs in Thailand

In 2018, there were two FSOEs in the Top 100 Thai non-financial companies. The largest of FSOEs was Advanced Info Service, which ranked 23rd on the list in 2018 and is controlled by the Singaporean SOE Singtel. Data on FSOEs in the Thai economy are presented in Table 4.250.

4.29.5 Summary

The share of SOEs in Thailand in 2018 was very high – over 45% in the Top 100 set and over 65% in the Top 20 set. There were five SOEs in the Top 10. Of the 21 SOEs in the Top 100, only six are fully owned by the state. Minority SOEs are of negligible importance. The concentration of SOEs in the Top 20 is visible and stable during the period under review. PTT, the largest Thai SOE, is responsible for a large part of all revenues of SOEs in the Top 100 (47.2%). An overview of key values on SOEs' share in the Thai economy is in Table 4.251.

4.30 SOE sector in Turkey

4.30.1 The largest SOEs in Turkey and their characteristics

On the Fortune Global list there was only one private enterprise and no SOEs in both 2010 and 2019. There were two Turkish SOEs on the Forbes list in 2010, out of 12 total companies, and in 2019 the number of SOEs had increased to four (out of nine total).

Table 4.252 The largest SOEs in Turkey and their position in the Top 100, 2018

No.	*Name of the SOE*	*Industry*	*OR (bill. €)*	*TA (bill. €)*	*Empl. worldwide (thousand)*	*State shares[a] (%)*	*Position Top 100*
1	Türk Hava Yollari	Transport	10.5	18.1	35.2	49.1	2
2	BOTAŞ	Oil & gas	8.5	7.4	2.8	100.0	4
3	Erdemir	Metals	4.5	6.9	11.6	49.3	9
4	Elektrik Uretim	Energy	2.4	4.3	6.1	100.0	21
5	Aselsan	Defence	1.5	3.2	5.7	74.2	33
6	Turkiye Elektrik Iletim	Energy	1.5	3.4	8.1	100.0	35
7	TUSAŞ	Aerospace	1.3	7.6	8.5	100.0	38
8	Igdas Istanbul Gaz	Oil & gas	1.2	1.4	2.0	100.0	39
9	State Airports (DHMI)	Transport	1.1	2.0	10.3	100.0	44
10	T.C. Istanbul Buyuksehir	Water & sewage	0.9	4.9	6.2	100.0	51

a Direct and indirect.
Source: Own compilation based on the Orbis database and other data (including Fortune Global, Forbes Global lists and companies' websites).

The largest Turkish SOE is Türk Hava Yolları (Turkish Airlines), a state-owned company established in 1933 and listed on the Istanbul Stock Exchange since 1990. Turkey Assets Fund, which holds a minority stake, also has certain special privileges, which give it effective corporate control over the company, guaranteed by provisions in its articles of association. Table 4.252 contains the characteristics of the largest Turkish SOEs and their position in the Top 100 non-financial companies.

4.30.2 Shares of SOEs in the sets of the largest Turkish companies

Tables 4.253–4.255 contain data on the shares of SOEs in the various sets of the largest Turkish non-financial companies. The share of SOEs in the Turkish economy has remained stable.

Table 4.253 SOEs in the sets of the largest Turkish companies – number

	Top 10			*Top 20*			*Top 50*			*Top 100*		
	2009	*2013*	*2018*	*2009*	*2013*	*2018*	*2009*	*2013*	*2018*	*2009*	*2013*	*2018*
maSOEs	3	2	1	3	3	1	8	7	8	14	17	16
miSOEs	0	1	2	2	2	2	2	2	2	2	2	2
SOEs	3	3	3	5	5	3	10	9	10	16	19	18

Source: As in Table 4.252.

Figure 4.30a shows the changes in the shares in ORs and TAs of SOEs in the Top 20 over the analysis period and Figure 4.30b shows the changes in the shares of SOEs in the various sets of the largest companies.

Table 4.254 SOEs in the sets of the largest Turkish companies – share in ORs (%)

	Top 10			*Top 20*			*Top 50*			*Top 100*		
	2009	*2013*	*2018*	*2009*	*2013*	*2018*	*2009*	*2013*	*2018*	*2009*	*2013*	*2018*
maSOEs	30.00	23.63	11.47	20.54	20.04	7.96	19.76	17.64	12.03	18.66	18.24	12.86
miSOEs	0	9.28	20.35	7.15	9.76	14.12	5.34	7.00	9.87	4.57	5.67	8.15
SOEs	30.00	32.91	31.82	27.70	29.79	22.08	25.10	24.64	21.90	23.23	23.92	21.01

Source: As in Table 4.252.

Table 4.255 SOEs in the sets of the largest Turkish companies – share in TAs (%)

	Top 10			*Top 20*			*Top 50*			*Top 100*		
	2009	*2013*	*2018*	*2009*	*2013*	*2018*	*2009*	*2013*	*2018*	*2009*	*2013*	*2018*
maSOEs	46.76	19.78	13.57	33.88	21.89	7.07	32.25	20.81	20.61	29.50	27.06	21.56
miSOEs	0	17.36	45.92	11.05	16.02	23.02	7.64	10.27	15.05	6.28	7.74	12.25
SOEs	46.76	37.14	49.49	44.93	37.91	30.99	39.89	31.07	35.66	35.78	34.79	33.81

Source: As in Table 4.252.

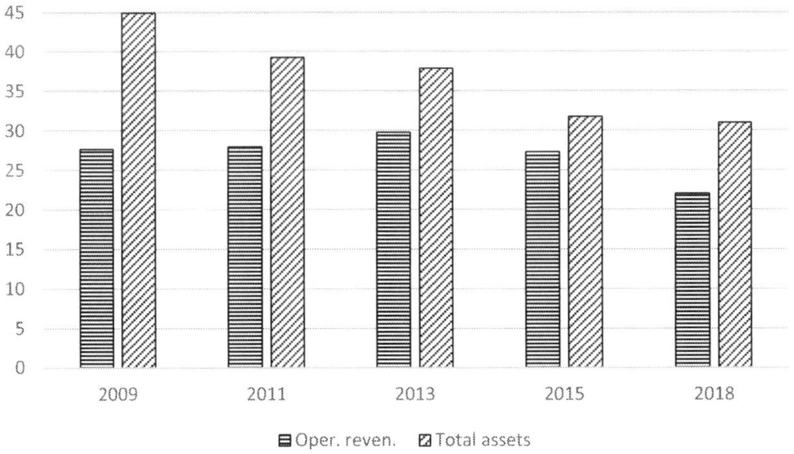

Figure 4.30a SOEs in the Top 20 of the Turkish non-financial companies – shares in ORs and TAs (%).

Source: As in Table 4.252.

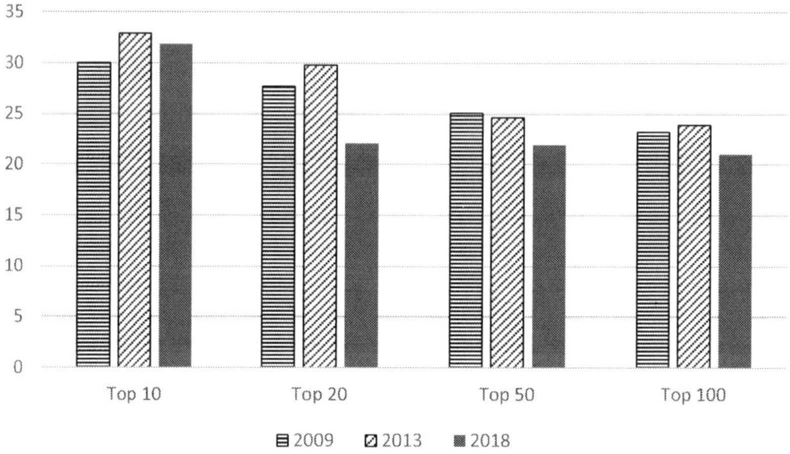

Figure 4.30b Changes in the shares of SOEs in the various sets of the largest Turkish non-financial companies (%).

Source: As in Table 4.252.

Table 4.256 Relationship of ORs of SOEs and nominal GDP (%)

	2009	*2013*	*2018*
Rev-100/GDP	6.5	5.9	5.7
Rev-20/GDP	5.0	4.3	3.5

Source: Own calculations.

4.30.3 Other characteristics of the Turkish SOE sector

Revenues of the largest SOEs in relation to GDP

Table 4.256 provides data on the relationship of the value of ORs of SOEs from the Top 100 and Top 20 and the value of the nominal GDP of Turkey in a given year. Slight but steady declines in the values are evident.

SOEs in selected industries

The presence of SOEs in strategic industries in Turkey is significant. Apart from the telecommunications industry, SOEs play an important or important role in the other five selected industries (Table 4.257).

Listed SOEs

Of the 18 Turkish SOEs in the Top 100 non-financial companies in 2018, only three – as companies with mixed capital – were listed on the Istanbul Stock Exchange. The relevant data are presented in Table 4.258.

Table 4.257 Estimated share of SOEs in the selected industries of the Turkish economy, 2018

Oil and gas	*Energy*	*Railways*	*Postal sector*	*Telecomm.*	*Banking sector*	*SS-I*
2	2	3	3	0	2	2.00

Source: Own estimation according to the rules given in Section 3.3.2.

Table 4.258 Number of listed SOEs in Turkish Top 100

	2009	*2013*	*2018*
Listed SOEs	3	3	3
including minority SOEs	2	2	2

Source: As in Table 4.252.

Table 4.259 FSOEs in the Top 100 of the Turkish companies

	2009	*2013*	*2018*
Number	1	4	3
Share in ORs (%)	0.8	8.1	2.5
Share in TAs (%)	0.7	3.3	2.9

Source: As in Table 4.252.

4.30.4 FSOEs in Turkey

In 2018, there were three FSOEs in the Top 100 Turkish non-financial companies and this was a small number relative to other countries. The largest FSOEs in Turkey was JTI Tutun Urunleri, ranked 27th in the Top 100 non-financial enterprises and controlled by Japan Tobacco. The relevant data are presented in Table 4.259.

4.30.5 Summary

The share of SOEs in Turkey in 2018 was quite high – over 25%. The share decreased during the period considered. There were three SOEs in the Top 10. Of the 18 SOEs in the Top 100, 15 are fully owned by the state. There are only three minority SOEs; however, they are among the largest Turkish SOEs and hence their share in revenues is quite high. The concentration of SOEs in the Top 20 is low and increased slightly during the period under review. Turkish Airlines, the largest Turkish SOE, is responsible for 27.2% of all revenues of SOEs in the Top 100 – Table 4.260.

Table 4.260 Share ratios for the Turkish economy

Share ratio	*2009*	*2013*	*2018*
SR-100 (%)	29.5	29.4	27.4
SR-20 (%)	36.3	33.9	26.5
CS-20	1.23	1.15	0.97
miS-100 (%)	18.3	22.8	37.2

Source: Own calculations.

4.31 SOE sector in the UK

4.31.1 The largest SOEs in the UK and their characteristics

There were 17 British companies on the 2019 Fortune Global 500 list, including no SOEs. Until recently, the UK SOEs on the list were Royal Mail (finally privatised in 2015), the Lloyds Banking Group (the government sold its last stake in 2017), the Royal Bank of Scotland (RBoS) (still state-owned, fell off the list in 2016). State ownership of Lloyds, like RBoS, was the result of nationalisation under the bailout. Among the 29 UK companies in 2010 were two SOEs. In the Forbes Global list in 2019, among 82 British companies there was one SOE – RBoS (ranked 185th). In 2010, there were two SOEs on the list out of 86 companies – beside RBoS (385th) it was then the newly nationalised Lloyds Banking Group (29th).

For many years the largest SOE in the UK was the Royal Mail (post office). In 2009, it was ranked as the 43rd largest British SOE in the Top 100 non-financial companies and in 2013 it was ranked 45th. Currently the largest UK SOE is the railway infrastructure construction and operation company Network Rail Infrastructure Limited. Table 4.261 contains the characteristics of the three largest British SOEs and their position in the Top 100 non-financial companies.

Table 4.261 The largest SOEs in the UK and their position in the Top 100, 2018

No.	*Name of the SOE*	*Industry*	*OR (bill. €)*	*TA (bill. €)*	*Empl. worldwide (thousand)*	*State shares[a] (%)*	*Position Top 100*
1	Network Rail Infrastruct.	Transport	7.7	63.3	35.1	100.0	80
2	Transport Trading	Transport	6.7	42.2	21.2	100.0	90
3	Urenco	Energy	2.2	1.5	7.5	33.3	-

a Direct and indirect.
Source: Own compilation based on the Orbis database and other data (including Fortune Global, Forbes Global lists and companies' websites).

Table 4.262 SOEs in the sets of the largest British companies – number

	Top 50			*Top 100*		
	2009	*2013*	*2018*	*2009*	*2013*	*2018*
maSOEs	1	0	0	2	2	2
miSOEs	0	1	0	0	1	0
SOEs	1	1	0	2	3	2

Source: As in Table 4.261.

Table 4.263 SOEs in the sets of the largest British companies – share in ORs (%)

	Top 50			*Top 100*		
	2009	*2013*	*2018*	*2009*	*2013*	*2018*
maSOEs	0.62	0	0	0.83	0.58	0.61
miSOEs	0	0.69	0	0	0.57	0
SOEs	0.62	0.69	0	0.83	1.15	0.61

Source: As in Table 4.261.

Table 4.264 SOEs in the sets of the largest British companies – share in TAs (%)

	Top 50			*Top 100*		
	2009	*2013*	*2018*	*2009*	*2013*	*2018*
maSOEs	0.26	0	0	1.42	3.80	3.98
miSOEs	0	0.34	0	0	0.26	0
SOEs	0.26	0.34	0	1.42	4.06	3.98

Source: As in Table 4.261.

4.31.2 Shares of SOEs in the sets of the largest British companies

Tables 4.262-4.264 contain data on the shares of SOEs in the various sets of the largest British non-financial companies. The data show the minimal scope and importance of SOEs in the UK economy.

Figure 4.31a shows the changes in the shares of SOEs in the various sets of the largest companies.

4.31.3 Other characteristics of the British SOE sector

Revenues of the largest SOEs in relation to GDP

The importance of British SOEs as measured by the next indicator is at a very low level. Our estimates are presented in Table 4.265.

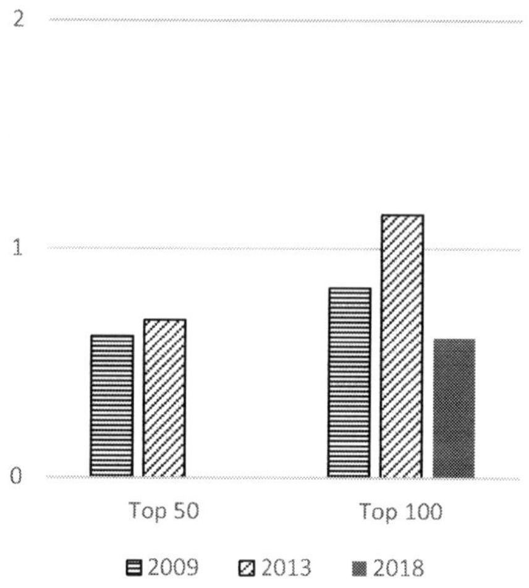

Figure 4.31a Changes in the shares of SOEs in the various sets of the largest British non-financial companies (%).

Source: As in Table 4.261.

Table 4.265 Relationship of ORs of SOEs and nominal GDP (%)

	2009	*2013*	*2018*
Rev-100/GDP	0.8	1.3	0.6
Rev-20/GDP	0	0	0

Source: Own calculations.

Table 4.266 Estimated share of SOEs in the selected industries of the British economy, 2018

Oil and gas	*Energy*	*Railways*	*Postal sector*	*Telecommunications*	*Banking sector*	*SS-I*
0	0	2	0	0	1	0.50

Source: Own estimation according to the rules given in Section 3.3.2.

SOEs in selected industries

The share of SOEs in the selected strategic industries is very low (see Table 4.266). In the financial sector, the only but significant state-owned entity is the RBoS taken over by the state as part of the rescue privatisation during the crisis of 2008–2009. It is the fourth largest British bank by TAs. Rail infrastructure is managed predominantly by state-owned Network Rail.

Listed SOEs

Between 2009 and 2018 there was only one listed SOEs controlled by the British government in Top 100 non-financial companies. It was (in 2013) Royal Mail.

4.31.4 FSOEs in the UK

In 2018, there were eight FSOEs in the Top 100 British non-financial companies, and this was a large number relative to other countries. In the Top 20 there were two FSOEs. The largest of them was Sinochem International Oil controlled by the Chinese government (ranked 14th), followed by Unipec UK (21st), controlled by Chinese state-owned Sinopec. The relevant data are presented in Table 4.267.

4.31.5 Summary

Because of the extremely small share of SOEs in the UK economy, the table containing "share ratios" is largely filled with zero or near-zero values (Table 4.268). There were only two SOEs in Top 100. Although their share has increased compared to 2009, these values – at such low levels – cannot be interpreted as a significant increase in the importance of SOEs. Key values on SOEs' share in the British economy are presented in Table 4.268.

Table 4.267 FSOEs in the Top 100 of the British companies

	2009	*2013*	*2018*
Number	5	9	8
Share in ORs (%)	3.6	5.3	5.4
Share in TAs (%)	1.4	5.7	2.6

Source: As in Table 4.261.

Table 4.268 Share ratios for the British economy

Share ratio	*2009*	*2013*	*2018*
SR-100 (%)	1.1	2.6	2.3
SR-20 (%)	0	0	0
CS-20	0	0	0
miS-100 (%)	0	15.2	0

Source: Own calculations.

4.32 SOE sector in the US

4.32.1 The largest SOEs in the US and their characteristics

There were 139 US companies on the Fortune Global 500 list in 2010, of which 5 were SOEs, while in 2019, out of 121 US companies, 3 were classified as SOEs. These companies were the US Postal Service (USPS) (136th) and two financial government-sponsored enterprises (GSEs) – Fannie Mae (49th) and Freddie Mac (128th). For the Forbes list, these figures were – respectively – 536 and 3 in 2010 and 575 and 2 in 2019.

Currently, the only large non-financial SOE at the federal level is the USPS, which has been in operation since 1829 (since 1971 as an enterprise, previously as a government department named United States Post Office Department). The USPS has almost 580,000 workers, being (after Wal-Mart) the second largest employer in the US among businesses. Other noteworthy SOEs (placing outside the Top 100) are the energy conglomerate Tennessee Valley Authority (TVA) and rail transport company Amtrak.

Two relatively large and significant US companies, although outside the area of interest of this book due to operating in financial sector activities, are so-called government-sponsored enterprises, i.e. Fannie Mae and Freddie Mac. The former's OR in 2018 was around $120 billion, and for the second it was around $74 billion. Table 4.169 contains the characteristics of the three largest US SOEs and their position in the Top 100 non-financial companies.

4.32.2 Shares of SOEs in the sets of the largest US companies

Tables 4.270–4.272 contain data on the shares of SOEs in the various sets of the largest US non-financial companies. The share of SOEs in the Top 100 of the American economy is limited to the abovementioned USPS. In addition, in 2009, General Motors (GM), which was rescued by nationalisation, appeared in the Top 100 (in 12th position). GM since 2013 is no longer classified as an SOE due to the divestment of shares by the state.

Table 4.269 The three largest SOEs in the US and their position in the Top 100, 2018

No.	*Name of the SOE*	*Industry*	*OR (bill. €)*	*TA (bill. €)*	*Empl. worldwide (thousand)*	*State shares (%)*[a]	*Position Top 100*
1	USPS	Post & telecomm.	61.7	23.2	565.0	100.0	36
2	TVA	Energy	9.6	43.9	10.0	100.0	-
3	Amtrak	Transport	3.0	2.1	20.0	100.0	-

a Direct and indirect.

Source: Own compilation based on the Orbis database and other data (including Fortune Global, Forbes Global lists and companies' websites).

Table 4.270 SOEs in the sets of the largest US companies – number

	Top 20			*Top 50*			*Top 100*		
	2009	*2013*	*2018*	*2009*	*2013*	*2018*	*2009*	*2013*	*2018*
maSOEs	2	0	0	2	1	1	2	1	1
miSOEs	0	0	0	0	0	0	0	0	0
SOEs	2	0	0	2	1	1	2	1	1

Source: As in Table 4.269.

Table 4.271 SOEs in the sets of the largest US companies – share in ORs (%)

	Top 20			*Top 50*			*Top 100*		
	2009	*2013*	*2018*	*2009*	*2013*	*2018*	*2009*	*2013*	*2018*
maSOEs	6.69	0	0	4.44	1.29	1.19	3.52	0.99	0.93
miSOEs	0	0	0	0	0	0	0	0	0
SOEs	6.69	0	0	4.44	1.29	1.19	3.52	0.99	0.93

Source: As in Table 4.269.

Table 4.272 SOEs in the sets of the largest US companies – share in TAs (%)

	Top 20			*Top 50*			*Top 100*		
	2009	*2013*	*2018*	*2009*	*2013*	*2018*	*2009*	*2013*	*2018*
maSOEs	5.76	0	0	3.82	0.39	0.40	2.97	0.31	0.29
miSOEs	0	0	0	0	0	0	0	0	0
SOEs	5.76	0	0	3.82	0.39	0.40	2.97	0.31	0.29

Source: As in Table 4.269.

Figure 4.32a shows the changes in the shares of SOEs in the various sets of the largest companies.

4.32.3 Other characteristics of the US SOE sector

Revenues of the largest SOEs in relation to GDP

Table 4.273 provides data on the relationship of the value of ORs of SOEs from the Top 100 and Top 20 and the value of the nominal GDP of US in a given year. The importance of American SOEs as measured by this indicator is at a very low level.

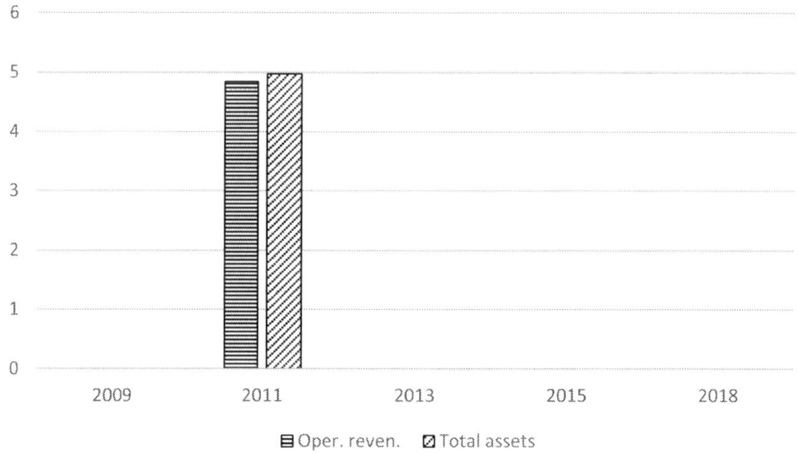

Figure 4.32a Changes in the shares of SOEs in the various sets of the largest US non-financial companies (%).

Source: As in Table 4.269.

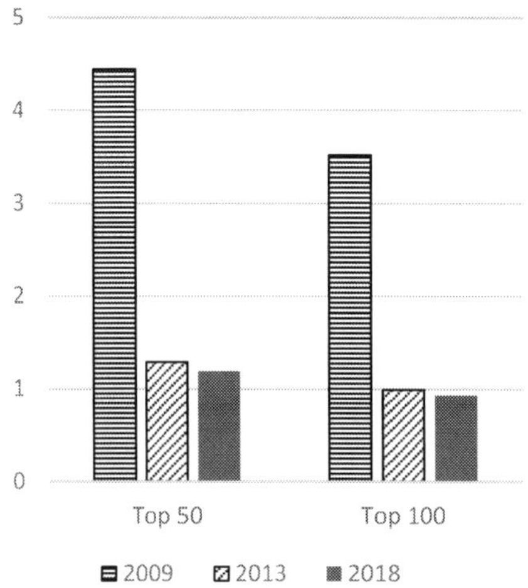

Figure 4.32b Changes in the shares of SOEs in the various sets of the largest US non-financial companies (%).

Table 4.273 Relationship of ORs of SOEs and nominal GDP (%)

	2009	*2013*	*2018*
Rev-100/GDP	1.2	0.4	0.3
Rev-20/GDP	1.2	0	0

Source: Own calculations.

Table 4.274 Estimated share of SOEs in the selected industries of the US economy, 2018

Oil and gas	*Energy*	*Railways*	*Postal sector*	*Telecomm.*	*Banking sector*	*SS-I*
0	1	0	2	0	1	0.67

Source: Own estimation according to the rules given in Section 3.3.2.

Table 4.275 FSOEs in the Top 100 of the US companies

	2009	*2013*	*2018*
Number	0	1	1
Share in ORs (%)	0	0.4	0.7
Share in TAs (%)	0	0.7	1.1

Source: As in Table 4.269.

SOEs in selected industries

The share of SOEs in strategic industries is very low. They have a significant presence only in the postal sector. Our estimations for selected industries are presented in Table 4.274.

Listed SOEs

The US government has no ownership stake in listed companies from Top 100 of non-financial companies. Between 2009 and 2013, the US government temporarily – as a result of a bailout nationalisation – was the largest owner in GM.

4.32.4 FSOEs in the US

On the list of the 100 largest companies in the US in recent years, there has been only one foreign state-owned company – T-Mobile US (ranked 60th). It belongs to Deutsche Telecom. The relevant data are presented in Table 4.275.

4.32.5 Summary

The share of SOEs in the US in 2018 was exceptionally low – below 1% in the Top 100 set of non-financial companies (Table 4.276). There was only one SOE in Top 100 – fully government-owned USPS, which was ranked 36th.

Table 4.276 Share ratios for the US economy

Share ratio	*2009*	*2013*	*2018*
SR-100 (%)	3.2	0.6	0.6
SR-20 (%)	6.2	0	0
CS-20	1.9	0	0
miS-100 (%)	0	0	0

Source: Own calculations.

5 State-owned enterprise sector in selected post-communist economies

5.1 SOE sector in Bulgaria

5.1.1 The largest SOEs in Bulgaria and their characteristics

There was no Bulgarian company either on the Fortune Global 500 or on the Forbes Global 2000 lists in the analysed years. The largest state-owned enterprise (SOE) in Bulgaria is the energy company NEK (National Electricity Company), whose activities include both electricity generation and trading. The state is the sole owner of this company through Bulgarian Energy Holding. Full state ownership is a noticeable peculiarity of the Bulgarian ownership policy - all other large SOEs have an identical ownership structure. Table 5.1 shows the characteristics of the largest Bulgarian SOEs and their position in the set of the Top 100 non-financial companies.

Table 5.1 The largest SOEs in Bulgaria and their position in the Top 100, 2018

No.	*Name of the SOE*	*Industry*	*OR (bill. €)*	*TA (bill. €)*	*Empl. worldwide (thousand)*	*State shares[a] (%)*	*Position Top 100*
1	NEK	Energy	1.6	2.7	5.1	100.0	4
2	Bulgargaz	Oil & gas	0.7	0.2	3.1	100.0	7
3	NPP Kozloduy	Energy	0.6	1.7	3.8	100.0	11
4	ESO	Energy	0.4	1.4	4.3	100.0	27
5	TPP Maritsa East 2	Energy	0.3	0.8	2.4	100.0	29
6	Mini Maritsa Iztok	Mining	0.3	0.6	7.4	100.0	32
7	Toplofikaciya Sofia	Energy	0.2	0.6	2.3	100.0	58
8	NRIC	Transport	0.2	2.2	11.8	100.0	64
9	Bulgartransgaz	Oil & gas	0.2	1.4	1.2	100.0	72

[a]Direct and indirect.

Source: Own compilation based on the Orbis database and other data (including Fortune Global, Forbes Global lists and companies' websites).

DOI: 10.4324/9781003244462-6

5.1.2 Shares of SOEs in the sets of the largest Bulgarian companies

Tables 5.2–5.4 contain data on the shares of SOEs in the various sets of the largest Bulgarian non-financial companies. There is a noticeable decrease in the number of SOEs among the largest companies in the Bulgarian economy, which can be interpreted as a continuation of economic transformation. A similar trend occurs in revenues, and there is a slight reverse trend in assets.

Figure 5.1a shows the changes in the shares s of SOEs in the Top 20 over the analysis period, and Figure 5.1b shows the changes in the shares s of SOEs in the various sets of the largest companies.

Table 5.2 SOEs in the sets of the largest Bulgarian companies – number

	Top 10			*Top 20*			*Top 50*			*Top 100*		
	2009	*2013*	*2018*	*2009*	*2013*	*2018*	*2009*	*2013*	*2018*	*2009*	*2013*	*2018*
maSOEs	2	2	2	4	3	3	9	8	6	14	11	9
miSOEs	0	0	0	0	0	0	0	0	0	0	0	0
SOEs	2	2	2	4	3	3	9	8	6	14	11	9

Source: As in Table 5.1.

Table 5.3 SOEs in the sets of the largest Bulgarian companies – share in ORs (%)

	Top 10			*Top 20*			*Top 50*			*Top 100*		
	2009	*2013*	*2018*	*2009*	*2013*	*2018*	*2009*	*2013*	*2018*	*2009*	*2013*	*2018*
maSOEs	20.89	17.12	17.41	21.13	15.56	16.05	20.63	16.07	14.25	18.76	13.81	12.30
miSOEs	0	0	0	0	0	0	0	0	0	0	0	0
SOEs	20.89	17.12	17.41	21.13	15.56	16.05	20.63	16.07	14.25	18.76	13.81	12.30

Source: As in Table 5.1.

Table 5.4 SOEs in the sets of the largest Bulgarian companies – share in TAs (%)

	Top 10			*Top 20*			*Top 50*			*Top 100*		
	2009	*2013*	*2018*	*2009*	*2013*	*2018*	*2009*	*2013*	*2018*	*2009*	*2013*	*2018*
maSOEs	35.65	45.41	37.30	38.91	38.37	36.59	38.44	36.8	35.96	33.7	34.39	36.19
miSOEs	0	0	0	0	0	0	0	0	0	0	0	0
SOEs	35.65	45.41	37.30	38.91	38.37	36.59	38.44	36.8	35.96	33.7	34.39	36.19

Source: As in Table 5.1.

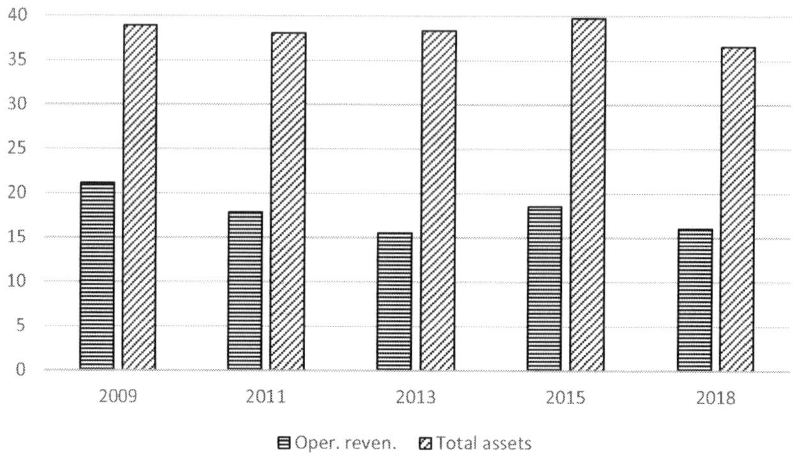

Figure 5.1a SOEs in the Top 20 of the Bulgarian non-financial companies – shares in ORs and TAs (%).

Source: As in Table 5.1.

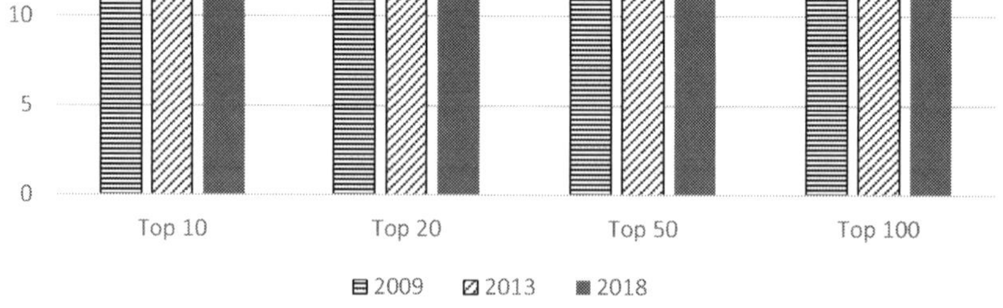

Figure 5.1b Changes in the shares of SOEs in the various sets of the largest Bulgarian non-financial companies (%).

Source: As in Table 5.1.

Table 5.5 Relationship of ORs of SOEs and nominal GDP (%)

	2009	*2013*	*2018*
Rev-100/GDP	11.3	10.5	7.7
Rev-20/GDP	7.7	6.6	5.0

Source: Own calculations.

Table 5.6 Estimated share of SOEs in selected industries of the Bulgarian economy, 2018

Oil and gas	*Energy*	*Railways*	*Postal sector*	*Telecomm.*	*Banking sector*	*SS-I*
1	3	4	2	0	0	1.67

Source: Own estimation according to the rules given in Section 3.3.2.

5.1.3 Other characteristics of the Bulgarian SOE sector

Revenues of the largest SOEs in relation to GDP

Table 5.5 provides data on the relationship of the value of operating revenues (ORs) of the SOEs from the Top 100 and Top 20 compared to the value of the nominal GDP of Bulgaria in selected years. The importance of Bulgarian SOEs as measured by these indicators is at a moderate level and it has declined over time.

SOEs in selected industries

The share of SOEs in the selected industries of the economy (Table 5.6) is typical for a Central European country, with the notable exception of the lack of a postal service operator in the Top 100.

Listed SOEs

Out of nine Bulgarian SOEs from the Top 100 non-financial companies in 2018, none was a listed company.

5.1.4 Foreign SOEs in Bulgaria

In 2018, there were seven foreign SOEs (FSOEs) in the Top 100 non-financial companies in Bulgaria. The largest of these was OMV Bulgaria (ranked 26th), controlled by the Austrian oil & gas company OMV. The number of FSOEs in the Bulgarian economy has been increasing in recent years; the share in assets has also been increasing, although, at the same time, their share in revenues has decreased from 2013 to 2018. The relevant data are presented in Table 5.7.

Table 5.7 FSOEs in the Top 100 of the Bulgarian companies

	2009	*2013*	*2018*
Number	4	5	7
Share in ORs (%)	6.1	7.5	4.8
Share in TAs (%)	3.0	3.8	4.9

Source: As in Table 5.1.

Table 5.8 Share ratios for the Bulgarian economy

Share ratio	*2009*	*2013*	*2018*
SS-100 (%)	26.2	24.1	24.2
SS-20 (%)	30.0	27.0	26.3
CS-20	1.14	1.11	1.08
miS-100 (%)	0	0	0

Source: Own calculations.

5.1.5 Summary

The share of SOEs in the group of the largest Bulgarian non-financial companies is quite high (about 25%). There are two SOEs in the Bulgarian Top 10. All SOEs in the Top 100 are fully owned by the government. The concentration of SOEs in the Top 20 is quite low. The largest SOE is responsible for 36.5% of all ORs of the SOEs in the Top 100 companies. There is a decline in the shares of SOEs in the Top 20 noticeable during the period under review and in the Top 100 group the shares have stabilised after a decline that happened in the first part of the period analysed. A summary of these data is given in Table 5.8.

5.2 SOE sector in the Czech Republic

5.2.1 The largest SOEs in the Czech Republic and their characteristics

There were no Czech companies on the Fortune Global 500 list in both years analysed. České Energetické Závody (ČEZ) is the only Czech company that was present on the Forbes Global 2000 list, both in 2008 and in 2018.

The largest SOE in the Czech Republic in 2018 was the energy company ČEZ, ranking second among the largest Czech non-financial companies behind automotive company Skoda Auto. As a joint-stock company, ČEZ is listed both on the Prague Stock Exchange and on the Warsaw Stock Exchange. Table 5.9 contains the characteristics of the largest Czech SOEs and their position in the Top 100 non-financial companies.

5.2.2 Shares of SOEs in the sets of the largest Czech companies

Tables 5.10–5.12 contain data on the shares of SOEs in the various sets of the largest Czech non-financial companies.

Table 5.9 The largest SOEs in the Czech Republic and their position in the Top 100, 2018

No.	*Name of the SOE*	*Industry*	*OR (bill. €)*	*TA (bill. €)*	*Empl. worldwide (thousand)*	*State shares[a] (%)*	*Position Top 100*
1	ČEZ	Energy	7.2	27.5	30.5	70.2	2
2	Čepro	Oil & gas	2.3	0.8	0.9	100.0	11
3	České dráhy	Transport	1.6	3.3	23.4	100.0	18
4	Správa železnic	Transport	1.3	2.6	17.2	100.0	26
5	Dopravní podnik Prahy	Transport	0.8	3.2	11.0	100.0	44
6	Česká pošta	Post & telecomm.	0.7	0.8	30.0	100.0	50
7	Pražská energetika	Energy	0.6	0.8	11.9	58.0	59
8	Čeps	Energy	0.6	1.6	0.8	100.0	69
9	Pražská plynárenská	Energy	0.5	0.5	1.5	100.0	78

Direct and indirect.
Source: Own compilation based on the Orbis database and other data (including Fortune Global, Forbes Global lists and companies' websites).

Table 5.10 SOEs in the sets of the largest Czech companies – number

	Top 10			*Top 20*			*Top 50*			*Top 100*		
	2009	*2013*	*2018*	*2009*	*2013*	*2018*	*2009*	*2013*	*2018*	*2009*	*2013*	*2018*
maSOEs	2	2	1	3	3	3	6	6	6	9	9	9
miSOEs	0	0	0	0	0	0	0	0	0	0	0	0
SOEs	2	2	1	3	3	3	7	7	6	9	9	9

Source: As in Table 5.9.

Table 5.11 SOEs in the sets of the largest Czech companies – share in ORs (%)

	Top 10			*Top 20*			*Top 50*			*Top 100*		
	2009	*2013*	*2018*	*2009*	*2013*	*2018*	*2009*	*2013*	*2018*	*2009*	*2013*	*2018*
maSOEs	28.15	24.02	13.09	22.78	20.23	15.03	20.28	18.50	13.21	17.19	15.94	11.83
miSOEs	0	0	0	0	0	0	0	0	0	0	0	0
SOEs	28.15	24.02	13.09	22.78	20.23	15.03	20.28	18.50	13.21	17.19	15.94	11.83

Source: As in Table 5.9.

Table 5.12 SOEs in the sets of the largest Czech companies – share in TAs (%)

	Top 10			*Top 20*			*Top 50*			*Top 100*		
	2009	*2013*	*2018*	*2009*	*2013*	*2018*	*2009*	*2013*	*2018*	*2009*	*2013*	*2018*
maSOEs	54.15	58.52	56.00	48.77	49.73	51.56	46.22	48.68	47.94	42.88	44.13	41.95
miSOEs	0	0	0	0	0	0	0	0	0	0	0	0
SOEs	54.15	58.52	56.00	48.77	49.73	51.56	46.22	48.68	47.94	42.88	44.13	41.95

Source: As in Table 5.9.

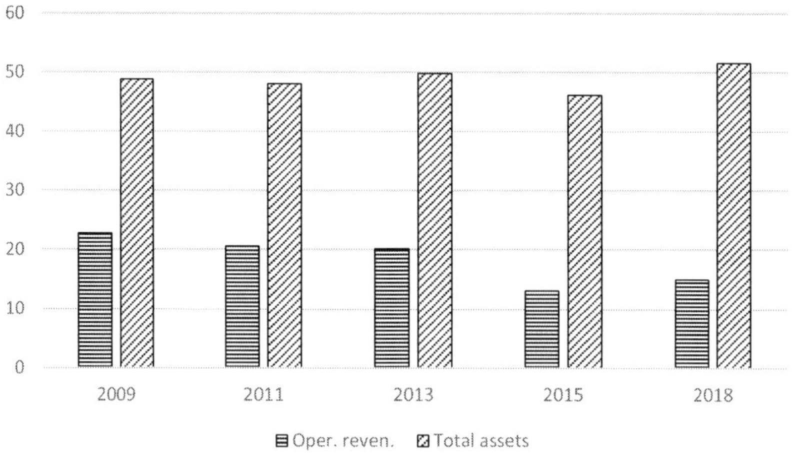

Figure 5.2a SOEs in the Top 20 of Czech non-financial companies – shares in ORs and TAs (%).

Source: As in Table 5.9.

The picture is slightly different in the next category (assets), where the share of SOEs is even slightly increasing. This is due to the growing assets of the ČEZ company.

Figure 5.2a shows the changes in the shares s in ORs and total assets (TAs) of the SOEs in the Top 20 over the analysis period and Figure 5.2b shows the changes in the shares of SOEs in the various sets of the largest companies.

5.2.3 Other characteristics of the Czech SOE sector

Revenues of the largest SOEs in relation to GDP

Table 5.13 provides data on the relationship of the value of OR of SOEs from the Top 100 and Top 20 compared to the value of the nominal GDP of the Czech Republic in selected years. The importance of Czech SOEs as

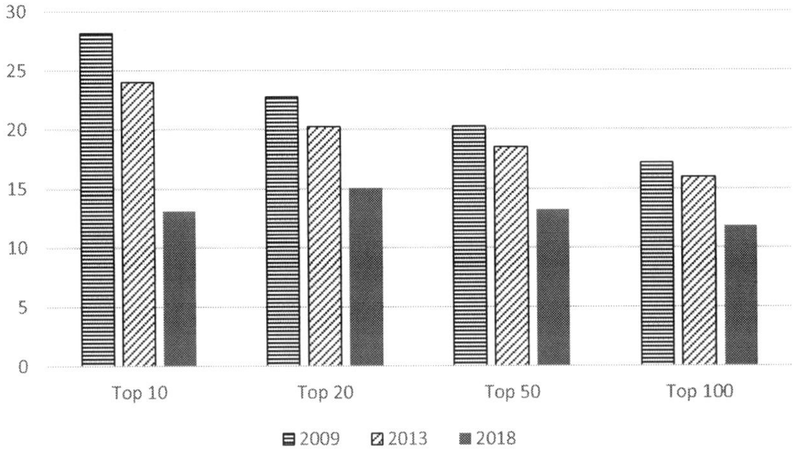

Figure 5.2b Changes in the shares of SOEs in the various sets of the largest Czech non-financial companies.

Source: As in Table 5.9

Table 5.13 Relationship of ORs of SOEs and nominal GDP (%)

	2009	*2013*	*2018*
Rev-100/GDP	10.1	10.6	7.2
Rev-20/GDP	7.4	8.2	5.1

Source: Own calculations.

Table 5.14 Estimated share of SOEs in selected branches of the Czech economy, 2018

Oil and gas	*Energy*	*Railways*	*Postal sector*	*Telecomm.*	*Banking sector*	*SS-I*
0	2	3	3	0	1	1.50

Source: Own estimation according to the rules given in Section 3.3.2.

measured by this indicator is at a moderate level; there were slight increases between 2009 and 2013, but later these indicators decreased.

SOEs in selected industries

The share of SOEs in selected industries in the Czech Republic is slightly lower than in other post-communist countries. SOEs dominate only in two industries: railway and postal sectors. Our estimations for selected industries are presented in Table 5.14.

Table 5.15 FSOEs in the Top 100 of the Czech companies

	2009	*2013*	*2018*
Number	3	6	5
Share in ORs (%)	5.9	6.9	7.0
Share in TAs (%)	4.6	4.1	5.7

Source: As in Table 5.9.

Table 5.16 Share ratios for the Czech economy

Share ratio	*2009*	*2013*	*2018*
SS-100 (%)	30.0	30.0	26.9
SS-20 (%)	35.8	35.0	33.3
CS-20	1.19	1.16	1.24
miS-100 (%)	0	0	0

Source: Own calculations.

Listed SOEs

From 2009 to 2018 there was only one listed SOE controlled by the Czech government (as mentioned – ČEZ) in the Top 100 non-financial companies.

5.2.4 FSOEs in the Czech Republic

In 2018, there were five FSOEs in the Top 100 Czech non-financial companies. In the Top 20, there were two FSOEs. The largest of them was Unipetrol, which ranked fifth on the list in 2018 and is controlled by the Polish oil & gas conglomerate PKN Orlen. The relevant data are presented in Table 5.15.

5.2.5 Summary

The share of SOEs in the Czech economy in 2018 was at a quite high level – over 25% in the Top 100 set and over 30% in the Top 20 set. There was only one SOE in the Top 10. Of the nine SOEs in the Top 100, seven are fully owned by the state. Minority SOEs are of negligible importance. The concentration of SOEs in the Top 20 is low and increased slightly during the period under review. ČEZ, the largest SOE of the Czech Republic, is responsible for a very large part of all revenues of the SOEs in the Top 100 (46.3%) – see Table 5.16.

5.3 SOE sector in Hungary

5.3.1 The largest SOEs in Hungary and their characteristics

No Hungarian company was on the Fortune Global 500 list in the years under review; however, MOL has been on the Fortune list in some years (2009,

Table 5.17 The largest SOEs in Hungary and their position in the Top 100, 2018

No.	*Name of the SOE*	*Industry*	*OR (bill. €)*	*TA (bill. €)*	*Empl. worldwide (thousand)*	*State shares[a] (%)*	*Position Top 100*
1	MOL Group	Oil & gas	16.2	14.3	26.0	25.2	1
2	MVM Group	Energy	5.7	5.7	10.9	100.0	3
3	MÁV Magyar Államvasutak	Transport	1.6	4.6	37.4	100.0	16
4	Szerencsejáték	Other	1.5	0.2	1.7	100.0	17
5	Richter Gedeon	Chemicals	1.4	2.5	12.7	25.3	19
6	Hungaropharma	Trade	1.0	0.2	0.7	30.7	28
7	NÚSZ	Transport	0.8	0.2	0.7	100.0	36
8	MAVIR	Energy	0.7	1.6	0.6	100.0	49
9	Magyar Posta	Post & telecomm.	0.7	0.7	31.2	100.0	50
10	BKK	Transport	0.6	0.6	1.8	100.0	59

[a] Direct and indirect.

Source: Own compilation based on the Orbis database and other data (including Fortune Global, Forbes Global lists and companies' websites).

2011, 2012, and 2013) first as a private company and then as a state-controlled company. On the Forbes Global 2000 list in 2019, there were two Hungarian companies – the private OTP Bank and – again – MOL.

Hungary's largest SOE, and also the largest non-financial enterprise overall, is the petrochemical company MOL, which was established in 1991 by the merger of nine separate state-owned companies of a socialist origin. In the early 2000s, MOL was privatised by selling a part of its shares to Austria's OMV and floatation of more than 30%. Several years later, the Russian company Surgutneftegas bought a stake in MOL from OMV for €1.4 billion. In May 2011, the Hungarian state purchased a large block of shares from a private owner, which de facto meant the nationalisation of the company. Table 5.17 shows the characteristics of the largest Hungarian SOEs and their position in the set of the Top 100 non-financial companies.

5.3.2 Shares of SOEs in the sets of the largest Hungarian companies

Tables 5.18–5.20 contain data on the shares of SOEs in the various sets of the largest Hungarian non-financial companies. In terms of the number of companies, only a slight rise is noticeable but in other categories the increases from 2009 to 2013 are significant. The main reason for that was the aforementioned acquisition of MOL.

Figure 5.3a shows the changes in the shares s in ORs and TAs of the SOEs in the Top 20 over the analysis period and Figure 5.3b shows the changes in the shares of SOEs in the various sets of the largest companies.

Table 5.18 SOEs in the sets of the largest Hungarian companies – number

	Top 10			*Top 20*			*Top 50*			*Top 100*		
	2009	*2013*	*2018*	*2009*	*2013*	*2018*	*2009*	*2013*	*2018*	*2009*	*2013*	*2018*
maSOEs	1	1	1	2	2	3	6	4	6	8	8	10
miSOEs	0	1	1	2	2	2	2	3	3	2	3	3
SOEs	1	2	2	4	4	5	8	7	9	10	11	13

Source: As in Table 5.17.

Table 5.19 SOEs in the sets of the largest Hungarian companies – share in ORs (%)

	Top 10			*Top 20*			*Top 50*			*Top 100*		
	2009	*2013*	*2018*	*2009*	*2013*	*2018*	*2009*	*2013*	*2018*	*2009*	*2013*	*2018*
maSOEs	7.42	8.32	12.09	8.73	8.96	13.86	9.88	8.33	12.31	8.68	8.80	11.31
miSOEs	0	46.07	34.35	4.53	37.60	27.66	3.21	27.50	20.53	2.64	22.26	16.28
SOEs	7.42	54.39	46.44	13.25	46.56	41.51	13.09	35.83	32.83	11.32	31.05	27.59

Source: As in Table 5.17.

Table 5.20 SOEs in the sets of the largest Hungarian companies – share in TAs (%)

	Top 10			*Top 20*			*Top 50*			*Top 100*		
	2009	*2013*	*2018*	*2009*	*2013*	*2018*	*2009*	*2013*	*2018*	*2009*	*2013*	*2018*
maSOEs	9.87	14.26	13.55	15.47	13.52	19.48	18.35	12.04	13.81	15.37	14.56	14.58
miSOEs	0	46.64	34.03	4.45	30.04	31.19	3.30	24.95	18.19	2.60	20.20	14.76
SOEs	9.87	60.90	47.58	19.92	43.56	50.67	21.65	36.99	32.00	17.97	34.75	29.34

Source: As in Table 5.17.

5.3.3 Other characteristics of the Hungarian SOE sector

Revenues of the largest SOEs in relation to GDP

Table 5.21 provides data on the relationship of the value of OR of the SOEs from the Top 100 and Top 20 compared to the value of the nominal GDP of Hungary in selected years. The importance of Hungarian SOEs as measured by this indicator increased strongly in the first part of the period analysed, and later there were slight decreases.

SOEs in selected industries

Hungarian SOEs dominate in four analysed industries: oil and gas, energy, railway and postal - Table 5.3.6.

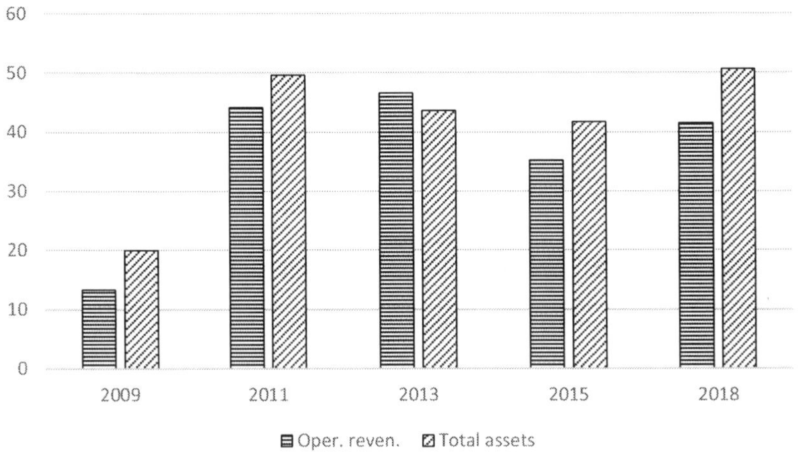

Figure 5.3a SOEs in the Top 20 of the Hungarian non-financial companies – shares in ORs and TAs (%).

Source: As in Table 5.17.

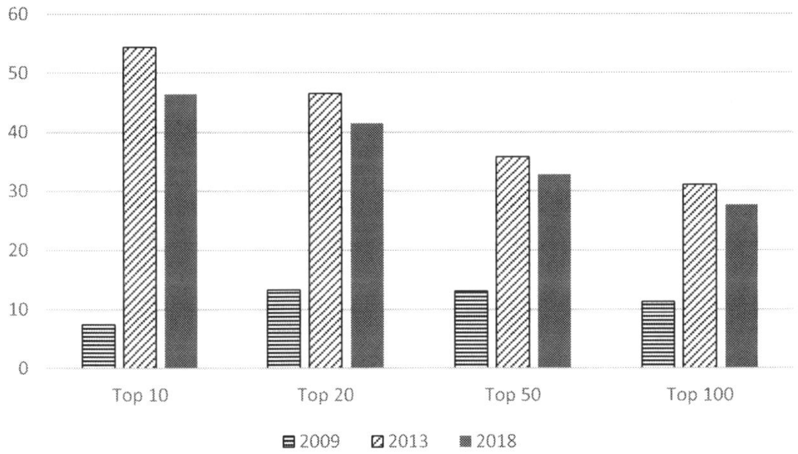

Figure 5.3b Changes in the shares of SOEs in the various sets of the largest Hungarian non-financial companies (%).

Source: As in Table 5.17.

Listed SOEs

From 2009 to 2018, there were only two listed SOEs controlled by the Hungarian government in the Top 100 non-financial companies. Both were minority-owned by the state. The relevant data are presented in Table 5.23.

Table 5.21 Relationship of ORs of SOEs and nominal GDP (%)

	2009	*2013*	*2018*
Rev-100/GDP	9.1	29.0	22.5
Rev-20/GDP	6.2	24.7	18.8

Source: Own calculations.

Table 5.22 Estimated share of SOEs in selected industries of the Hungarian economy, 2018

Oil and gas	*Energy*	*Railways*	*Postal sector*	*Telecomm.*	*Banking sector*	*SS-I*
3	3	3	3	0	1	2.17

Source: Own estimation according to the rules given in Section 3.3.2.

Table 5.23 Listed SOEs in the Top 100 of the Hungarian companies

	2009	*2013*	*2018*
Listed SOEs	1	2	2
including minority SOEs	1	2	2

Source: As in Table 5.17.

Table 5.24 FSOEs in the Top 100 of the Hungarian companies

	2009	*2013*	*2018*
Number	5	5	4
Share in ORs (%)	6.8	4.8	3.6
Share in TAs (%)	8.1	5.5	3.5

Source: As in Table 5.17.

5.3.4 FSOEs in Hungary

In 2018, there were four FSOEs in the Top 100 Hungarian non-financial companies and this was a moderate number relative to other countries. In the Top 20, there was only one FSOE – Magyar Telekom Tavkozlesi, which ranked tenth on the list in 2018 and is controlled by Deutsche Telekom. Data on FSOEs in the Hungarian economy are presented in Table 5.24.

5.3.5 Summary

The share of SOEs in the group of the largest Hungarian enterprises is relatively high compared to other post-communist countries, especially in the Top 20 group – more than 45%. A significant increase occurred after

Table 5.25 Share ratios for the Hungarian economy

Share ratio	*2009*	*2013*	*2018*
SS-100 (%)	14.6	32.9	28.5
SS-20 (%)	16.6	45.1	46.1
CS-20	1.13	1.37	1.62
miS-100 (%)	17.9	63.2	53.0

Source: Own calculations.

the nationalisation of MOL in 2011. There were two SOEs in the Top 10. Of the 13 SOEs in 2018 ten are fully owned by the state. But the share of minority SOEs in the total set of SOEs is high, exceeding 50%, which is, once again, due to the great importance of MOL. MOL, the largest SOE in Hungary, is responsible for a very large part of all ORs of the SOEs in the Top 100 (51.4%). The concentration of SOEs in the Top 20 is high – see Table 5.25.

5.4 SOE sector in Romania

5.4.1 The largest SOEs in Romania and their characteristics

No Romanian company was either on the Fortune Global 500 or on the Forbes Global 2000 lists in the years under review. Romania's largest SOE is Electrica, an electricity distributor. Until 2014, the Romanian state,

Table 5.26 The largest SOEs in Romania and their position in the Top 100, 2018

No.	*Name of the SOE*	*Industry*	*OR (bill. €)*	*TA (bill. €)*	*Empl. worldwide (thousand)*	*State shares[a] (%)*	*Position Top 100*
1	Electrica	Energy	1.2	1.6	8.0	48.8	16
2	Romgaz	Oil & gas	1.1	2.0	6.1	70.0	21
3	Hidroelectrica	Energy	0.9	4.0	3.3	80.1	23
4	CNAIR	Transport	0.8	3.2	6.5	100.0	33
5	CFR Infrastructură	Transport	0.7	3.0	22.6	100.0	41
6	Complexul Energ. Oltenia	Energy	0.6	1.4	13.1	77.1	48
7	Transelectrica	Energy	0.6	1.0	2.1	58.7	50
8	Nuclearelectrica	Energy	0.5	1.9	2.1	82.5	66
9	CFR Călători	Transport	0.5	0.7	12.8	100.0	67
10	Electrocentrale Bucuresti	Energy	0.4	1.2	1.8	97.5	84

a Direct and indirect.
Source: Own compilation based on the Orbis database and other data (including Fortune Global, Forbes Global lists and companies' websites).

through the Ministry of Energy, was its sole shareholder. It was then decided to sell a part of its shares and list them on the Bucharest and London Stock Exchanges.

Table 5.26 contains the characteristics of the largest Romanian SOEs and their position in the Top 100 non-financial companies.

5.4.2 Shares of SOEs in the sets of the largest Romanian companies

Tables 5.27–5.29 contain data on the shares of SOEs in the various sets of the largest Romanian non-financial companies. Although Romanian SOEs are quite numerous in the Top 100 set, they are mainly entities of relatively minor importance.

Table 5.27 SOEs in the sets of the largest Romanian companies – number

	Top 10			*Top 20*			*Top 50*			*Top 100*		
	2009	*2013*	*2018*	*2009*	*2013*	*2018*	*2009*	*2013*	*2018*	*2009*	*2013*	*2018*
maSOEs	1	1	0	5	3	0	11	9	6	15	17	11
miSOEs	0	0	0	0	0	1	0	0	1	0	0	1
SOEs	1	1	0	5	3	1	11	9	7	15	17	12

Source: As in Table 5.26.

Table 5.28 SOEs in the sets of the largest Romanian companies – share in ORs (%)

	Top 10			*Top 20*			*Top 50*			*Top 100*		
	2009	*2013*	*2018*	*2009*	*2013*	*2018*	*2009*	*2013*	*2018*	*2009*	*2013*	*2018*
maSOEs	5.61	5.67	0	14.23	10.01	0	15.87	13.98	7.44	14.45	14.06	7.92
miSOEs	0	0	0	0	0	3.11	0	0	1.96	0	0	1.48
SOEs	5.61	5.67	0	14.23	10.01	3.11	15.87	16.61	9.40	14.45	14.06	9.40

Source: As in Table 5.26.

Table 5.29 SOEs in the sets of the largest Romanian companies – share in TAs (%)

	Top 10			*Top 20*			*Top 50*			*Top 100*		
	2009	*2013*	*2018*	*2009*	*2013*	*2018*	*2009*	*2013*	*2018*	*2009*	*2013*	*2018*
maSOEs	14.22	10.71	0	38.51	23.41	0	47.93	43.09	28.42	41.87	39.13	29.37
miSOEs	0	0	0	0	0	6.05	0	0	3.15	0	0	2.41
SOEs	14.22	10.71	0	38.51	23.41	6.05	47.93	43.09	31.57	41.87	39.13	31.78

Source: As in Table 5.26.

Figure 5.4a shows the changes in the shares s in ORs and TAs of the SOEs in the Top 20 over the analysis period and Figure 5.4b shows the changes in the shares of SOEs in the various sets of the largest companies.

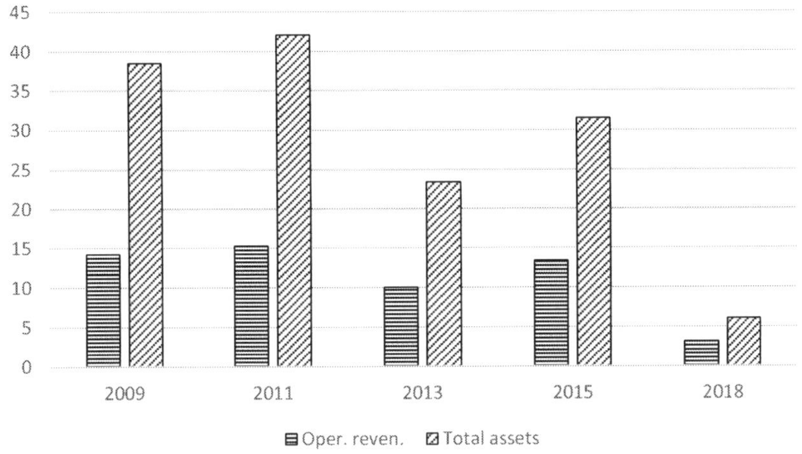

Figure 5.4a SOEs in the Top 20 of the Romanian non-financial companies – shares in ORs and TAs (%).

Source: As in Table 5.26.

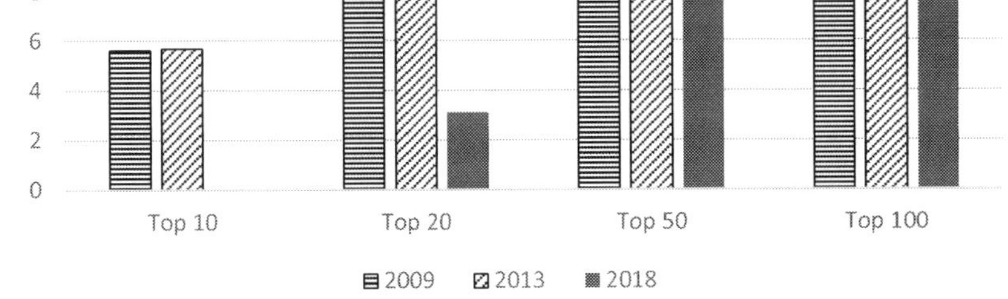

Figure 5.4b Changes in the shares of SOEs in the various sets of the largest Romanian non-financial companies (%).

Source: As in Table 5.26.

5.4.3 Other characteristics of the Romanian SOE sector

Revenues of the largest SOEs in relation to GDP

Table 5.30 provides data on the relationship of the value of ORs of the SOEs from the Top 100 and Top 20 compared to the value of the nominal GDP of Romania in selected years. The importance of Romanian SOEs as measured by this indicator is at a low (as for a post-communist economy) level. There were slight increases in these values between 2009 and 2013, but later these indicators sharply decreased.

SOEs in selected industries

SOEs dominate in energy and railway industries and there are no SOEs in other industries selected to this analysis. The Romanian postal operator is an SOE, although its revenue was too low to get to the Top 100. Nevertheless, its share in the market is significant. Our estimates are presented in Table 5.31.

Listed SOEs

In 2018, there were five listed SOEs in the Top 100 non-financial companies and this number increased over the years, from three in 2009. In most of the listed SOEs, the state owns majority shares, and in the only minority state-owned company (Electrica) in this set the government share is as high as 48.8%. The relevant data are presented in Table 5.32.

Table 5.30 Relationship of ORs of SOEs and nominal GDP (%)

	2009	*2013*	*2018*
Rev-100/GDP	5.2	5.9	3.7
Rev-20/GDP	2.6	4.4	0.6

Source: Own calculations.

Table 5.31 Estimated share of SOEs in selected industries of the Romanian economy, 2018

Oil and gas	*Energy*	*Railways*	*Postal sector*	*Telecomm.*	*Banking sector*	*SS-I*
0	3	4	3	0	0	1.67

Source: Own estimation according to the rules given in Section 3.3.2.

Table 5.32 Number of listed SOEs in the Romanian Top 100

	2009	*2013*	*2018*
Listed SOEs	3	4	5
including minority SOEs	0	0	1

Source: As in Table 5.26.

Table 5.33 FSOEs in the Top 100 of the Romanian companies

	2009	*2013*	*2018*
Number	9	8	9
Share in ORs (%)	24.6	26.5	22.9
Share in TAs (%)	22.1	23.3	23.7

Source: As in Table 5.26.

Table 5.34 Share ratios for the Romanian economy

Share ratio	*2009*	*2013*	*2018*
SS-100 (%)	28.2	26.2	20.6
SS-20 (%)	26.4	16.7	4.6
CS-20	0.94	0.63	0.22
miS-100 (%)	0	0	1.9

Source: Own calculations.

5.4.4 FSOEs in Romania

In 2018, there were nine FSOEs in the Top 100 non-financial companies and that was a relatively large number. In the Top 20, there were five FSOEs. The largest of them was Automobile-Dacia, which ranked first on the list in 2018 and is controlled by the French Renault. Data on FSOEs in the Romanian economy are presented in Table 5.33.

5.4.5 Summary

The share of SOEs in the Top 100 largest Romanian companies is at a quite high level (more than 20%). The share of SOEs in the Top 20 has significantly decreased in recent years. Interestingly, there are no SOEs in the Top 10 group and there is only one in the Top 20 group. Of the 12 SOEs in the Top 100, 3 are fully owned by the state. The share of minority SOEs in the total set of SOEs is negligible. The share of the largest SOE in the sum of ORs of all SOEs from the Top 100 is 15.8%. The concentration of SOEs in the Top 20 set is low and decreasing. The shares of SOEs have declined significantly in recent years. A summary presentation of the data described above is presented in Table 5.34.

5.5 SOE sector in Slovakia

5.5.1 The largest SOEs in Slovakia and their characteristics

No company from Slovakia was either on the Fortune Global 500 or on the Forbes Global 2000 lists in the years under review. The largest

Table 5.35 The largest SOEs in Slovakia and their position in the Top 100, 2018

No.	*Name of the SOE*	*Industry*	*OR (bill. €)*	*TA (bill. €)*	*Empl. worldwide (thousand)*	*State shares[a] (%)*	*Position Top 100*
1	SPP	Energy	1.5	3.0	0.7	100.0	8
2	Stredoslovenská energetika	Energy	1.0	0.9	1.5	51.0	15
3	ZSE Energia	Energy	0.8	0.2	1.3	51.0	19
4	Východoslovenská energetika	Energy	0.8	0.7	1.7	51.0	20
5	SEPS	Energy	0.5	1.0	0.8	100.0	30
6	Západoslovenská distribučná	Energy	0.5	1.1	1.5	51.0	32
7	ŽSR	Transport	0.5	3.6	15.0	100.0	34
8	TIPOS	Other	0.5	0.1	0.1	100.0	37
9	ŽSSK	Transport	0.4	1.3	7.5	100.0	39
10	Národná diaľničná spoločnosť	Transport	0.4	9.9	1.5	100.0	45

a Direct and indirect.
Source: Own compilation based on the Orbis database and other data (including Fortune Global, Forbes Global lists and companies' websites).

Slovak state-owned company by ORs in 2018 was an energy (gas and electricity) supplier Slovenský plynárenský priemysel (SPP), fully owned by the Slovak government. Table 5.35 contains the characteristics of the largest Slovak SOEs and their position in the Top 100 non-financial companies.

5.5.2 Shares of SOEs in the sets of the largest Slovak companies

Tables 5.36-5.38 contain data on the shares of SOEs in the various sets of the largest Slovak non-financial companies. The overall number of SOEs in Slovakia is quite high and stable in time with the lowest value in 2013.

Table 5.36 SOEs in the sets of the largest Slovak companies – number

	Top 10			*Top 20*			*Top 50*			*Top 100*		
	2009	*2013*	*2018*	*2009*	*2013*	*2018*	*2009*	*2013*	*2018*	*2009*	*2013*	*2018*
maSOEs	2	1	1	4	2	4	8	9	10	13	10	13
miSOEs	0	0	0	0	0	0	0	0	0	0	0	0
SOEs	2	1	1	4	2	4	8	9	10	13	10	13

Source: As in Table 5.35.

Table 5.37 SOEs in the sets of the largest Slovak companies – share in ORs (%)

	Top 10			*Top 20*			*Top 50*			*Top 100*		
	2009	*2013*	*2018*	*2009*	*2013*	*2018*	*2009*	*2013*	*2018*	*2009*	*2013*	*2018*
maSOEs	18.05	6.13	4.54	17.46	7.35	9.58	17.13	11.68	11.97	16.12	10.30	11.22
miSOEs	0	0	0	0	0	0	0	0	0	0	0	0
SOEs	18.05	6.13	4.54	17.46	7.35	9.58	17.13	11.68	11.97	16.12	10.30	11.22

Source: As in Table 5.35.

Table 5.38 SOEs in the sets of the largest Slovak companies – share in TAs (%)

	Top 10			*Top 20*			*Top 50*			*Top 100*		
	2009	*2013*	*2018*	*2009*	*2013*	*2018*	*2009*	*2013*	*2018*	*2009*	*2013*	*2018*
maSOEs	33.00	28.68	11.41	36.54	24.01	15.02	38.06	44.44	39.46	48.78	41.99	36.89
miSOEs	0	0	0	0	0	0	0	0	0	0	0	0
SOEs	33.00	28.68	11.41	36.54	24.01	15.02	38.06	44.44	39.46	48.78	41.99	36.89

Source: As in Table 5.35.

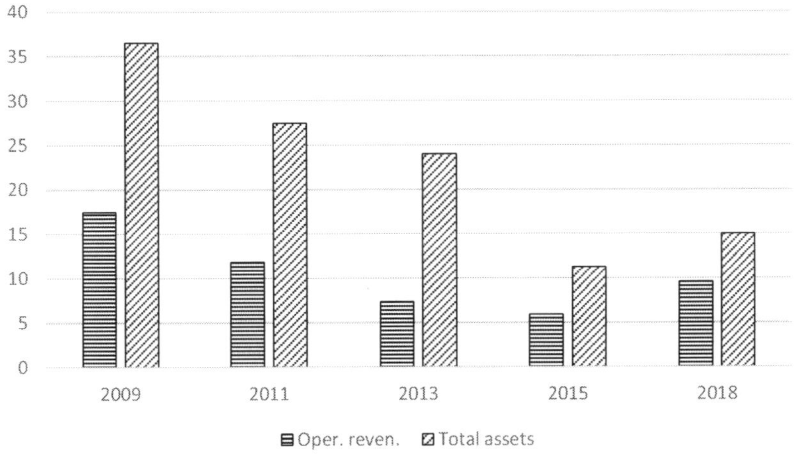

Figure 5.5a SOEs in the Top 20 of the Slovak non-financial companies – shares in ORs and TAs (%).
Source: As in Table 5.35.

Figure 5.5a shows the changes in the shares s in ORs and TAs of the SOEs in the Top 20 over the analysis period and Figure 5.5b shows the changes in the shares of SOEs in the various sets of the largest companies.

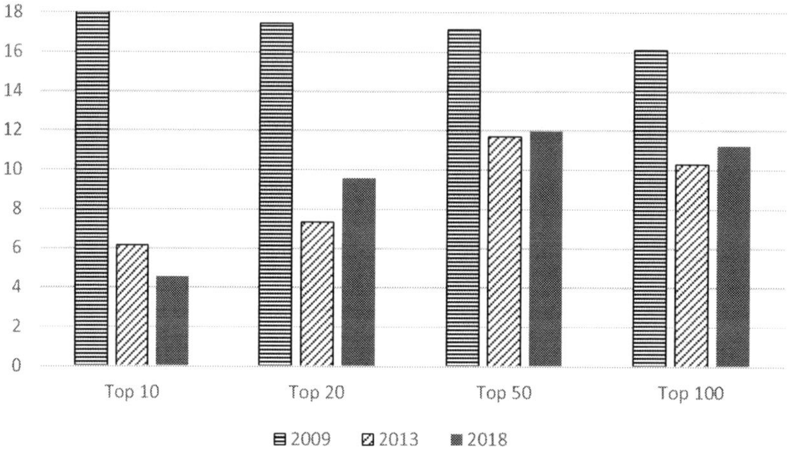

Figure 5.5b Changes in the shares of SOEs in the various sets of the largest Slovak non-financial companies (%).

Source: As in Table 5.35.

Table 5.39 Relationship of ORs of SOEs and nominal GDP (%)

	2009	*2013*	*2018*
Rev-100/GDP	10.0	8.0	8.6
Rev-20/GDP	7.4	3.7	4.6

Source: Own calculations.

5.5.3 Other characteristics of the Slovak SOE sector

Revenues of the largest SOEs in relation to GDP

Table 5.39 provides data on the relationship of the value of ORs of the SOEs from the Top 100 and Top 20 compared to the value of the nominal GDP of Slovakia in selected years. The importance of Slovak SOEs as measured by these indicators is at a moderate level. There were decreases in these values between 2009 and 2013, but later these indicators slightly increased.

SOEs in selected industries

SOEs are relatively widespread in selected industries of the Slovak economy. They dominate in energy, railway and postal sectors. They are also present in

Table 5.40 Estimated share of SOEs in selected industries of the Slovak economy, 2018

Oil and gas	*Energy*	*Railways*	*Postal sector*	*Telecomm.*	*Banking sector*	*SS-I*
2	4	3	3	0	1	2.17

Source: Own estimation according to the rules given in Section 3.3.2.

Table 5.41 FSOEs in the Top 100 of the Slovak companies

	2009	*2013*	*2018*
Number	5	6	6
Share in ORs (%)	13.0	18.5	11.2
Share in TAs (%)	16.9	25.5	24.5

Source: As in Table 5.35.

oil and gas and banking industries. Such sectoral structure is quite common in post-communist economies. Our estimations for selected industries are presented in Table 5.40.

Listed SOEs

Out of 13 Slovak SOEs from the Top 100 non-financial companies in 2018, none was a listed company.

5.5.4 FSOEs in Slovakia

In 2018, there were six FSOEs in the Top 100 non-financial companies. In the Top 20, there were two FSOEs. The largest of them was Slovnaft, which ranked third on the list in 2018 and is controlled by the Hungarian MOL. The share of FSOEs in all categories is high. Data on FSOEs in the Slovakian economy are presented in Table 5.41.

5.5.5 Summary

The share of SOEs in the group of the largest Slovak enterprises in the Top 100 is at a rather high level, close to 25%, while in the Top 20, it is half as high. In the analysed period, the share of SOEs decreased significantly. Of the 13 SOEs in the Top 100, 9 are fully owned by the state. There was only one SOE in the Top 10. The share of the largest SOE in the revenues of all SOEs from the Top 100 group is 19.3%. There is no concentration of SOEs in the Top 20 and there are no minority SOEs – see Table 5.42.

Table 5.42 Share ratios for the Slovak economy

Share ratio	*2009*	*2013*	*2018*
SS-100 (%)	32.5	26.2	24.1
SS-20 (%)	25.5	15.7	12.3
CS-20	0.79	0.6	0.51
miS-100 (%)	0	0	0

Source: Own calculations.

6 Aggregate and comparative data and their analysis

H. Christiansen is right claiming that "comparisons across countries are complicated by the fact definitions of state-owned enterprises differ significantly" (2013, 9). This is especially the case when - as the Organisation for Economic Co-operation and Development (OECD) does in its reports - the source of information on SOEs is the data officially provided by governments, as we wrote in Section 3.2. In such cases, it is extremely difficult to keep the uniformity of the definitional approach, which results in limited data comparability, both between countries and over time. We have tried to avoid this weakness of empirical studies on SOEs in our analyses, as the data we use, in its essence, come from one source and have been standardised with the utmost care according to the procedure described in Section 3.2.2.

This chapter covers the aggregate and comparative results of the research, referring mainly to the four distinguished groups of countries. The first group consists of 32 world's largest economies (WLEs) by nominal GDP. In this group, two smaller ones are recognised: 19 developed market economies (DMEs) and 13 emerging market economies (EMEs). The fourth group consists of six post-communist economies (PCEs), members of the EU. The Polish economy appears twice - as the only one - in our lists: in the WLE (EME) group as well as in the PCE group. The details of this division, somewhat arbitrary, are presented in Section 3.4.2.

The chapter consists of four parts. In the first part, we examine the shares in the economy, significance and types of SOEs in 2018. In the second, we present and analyse the sectoral distribution of the largest SOEs. In the third, we demonstrate the set of the largest SOEs from our research. In the fourth, we analyse the changes in the shares and types of SOEs between 2009 and 2018 in the economies and groups of economies under review. Here we also present the results of our original analysis of the shares of SOEs in the sets of the world's largest companies (Fortune Global 500).

DOI: 10.4324/9781003244462-7

6.1 SOEs in 2018 – cross-country analysis

6.1.1 Share of SOEs in the economy

In the analysis, we use two basic indicators, defined in detail in Section 3.3, that characterise the share (or, to put it differently - the scope) of state-owned enterprises (SOEs) in the set of the 100 largest non-financial domestic companies (Top 100). These indicators, referring both to the aggregate data for the distinguished groups of countries (as average values) and to cross-country comparisons, are:

- SS-100 - the share of SOEs in the Top 100 set,
- Rev-100/GDP - the ratio of the sum of operating revenues (ORs) of SOEs from the Top 100 set to GDP.

We also use the number of SOEs or average numbers of SOEs in the Top 100 (Top 50 and Top 20).

In 2018, the average share of SOEs in the Top 100 set of non-financial companies in the analysed 32 world's largest economies (WLEs), as measured by the SS-100 index, was 27.4%. The average share of SOEs in 19 developed market economies (DMEs) was 14.1%, and in 13 emerging market economies (EMEs) as high as 46.7%, so over three times more. The average share of SOEs in six post-communist economies (PCEs) was 29.1%. The average ratio of ORs of SOEs from the Top 100 sets to nominal GDP, as measured by the Rev-100/GDP ratio for the 32 WLEs, was 12.9%. In this case, the differences between the distinguished groups of countries were somewhat smaller than for the SS-100 index.

In the 32 sets of the Top 100 non-financial companies from the WLEs under review (among 3,200 companies), there were 476 SOEs, which is 14.9%. The difference between DMEs and EMEs was significant, almost threefold. In the group of the analysed 1,900 companies from the DME Top 100 sets, there were only 162 SOEs (8.5%), while in the group of 1,300 companies of

Table 6.1 Share of SOEs in the groups of countries (average value in the group, %), 2018

	WLEs			*PCEs*
	Total	DMEs	EMEs	
SS-100	27.4	14.1	46.7	29.1
Rev-100/GDP	12.9	8.6	19.1	11.0
Number of SOEs in the Top 100	14.9	8.5	24.2	12.7
Number of SOEs in the Top 50	16.4	8.6	27.7	16.0

Source: Own calculation based on the Orbis data and other data.

EMEs, there were as many as 314 SOEs (24.2%). In the PCE group, among the 600 largest companies, there were 76 SOEs (12.7%).

A summary of figures that characterise the shares of SOEs in the distinguished groups of countries is presented in Table 6.1. Major differences can be observed between DMEs and EMEs in all analysed characteristics. In turn, the values of the indicators for PCEs were in between those for DMEs and EMEs.

Table 6.2 presents the set of ten WLEs with the highest (left side) and lowest (right side) shares of SOEs measured with the SS-100 index, and Table 6.3 is a summary of the shares of SOEs for PCEs.

Among the ten countries with the highest share of SOEs, exceeding 40%, there are eight EMEs and two DMEs (Norway and Italy), while among the ten countries with the lowest share of SOEs, there are only DMEs. In the five countries listed in the right-hand part of Table 6.2, the share of SOEs is less than 2.5% - it can be described as negligible. The shares of SOEs in PCEs are between 20% and 30%, except for Poland, where the share of SOEs is roughly double that of the other PCEs.

Tables 6.4 and 6.5 contain data on the second measure of the SOE share in the economy, i.e. the ratio of ORs of all Top 100 SOEs to GDP. As above, Table 6.4 lists ten countries with the highest (left side) and ten countries with the lowest (right side) value of the Rev-100/GDP ratio, and Table 6.5 contains data on the PCE group.

The right-hand part of Table 6.4, containing the set of countries with the lowest Rev-100/GDP ratio value, is not very different from the right-hand part of Table 6.2, containing the set of countries with the lowest SS-100 index value - nine countries reappear in both sets but in different orders. The value

Table 6.2 WLEs with the highest (left side) and lowest (right side) share of SOEs in the Top 100, 2018 (%)

Country	*SS-100*	*Group*	*Country*	*SS-100*	*Group*
China	85.9	EME	US	0.6	DME
Saudi Arabia	85.3	EME	Australia	2.2	DME
Russia	59.6	EME	Netherlands	2.3	DME
Indonesia	57.0	EME	Ireland	2.3	DME
Egypt	50.6	EME	UK	2.3	DME
Poland	49.6	EME	Spain	5.0	DME
Norway	48.4	DME	Canada	7.4	DME
Italy	47.4	DME	Japan	7.9	DME
Thailand	46.5	EME	Belgium	8.5	DME
India	40.7	EME	Switzerland	9.4	DME

Source: As in Table 6.1.

of the Rev-100/GDP ratio for six countries, all from the DME group, is less than 2.5 - the share of SOEs in these countries can be described as negligible.

For the left-hand part, the similarity to Table 6.2 concerning the SS-100 index is smaller. Only seven countries are repeated. In the group of ten countries with the highest Rev-100/GDP value, there are admittedly three EMEs in the top positions, but in total there are five EMEs and five DMEs.

China, the unquestionable leader of most sets concerning the share of SOEs in the economy, ranks only third on this list. This is because the value of the revenues of the entire Top 100 group, dominated by SOEs, is relatively small (around 42%) in relation to the GDP of China. While in the case of Thailand, for example, which has a similar Rev-100/GDP ratio with a much

Table 6.3 Share of SOEs in the Top 100 in PCEs (%), 2018

Country	*SS-100*
Poland	49.6
Hungary	29.0
Czech Republic	26.9
Bulgaria	24.2
Slovakia	24.1
Romania	20.6

Source: As in Table 6.1.

Table 6.4 WLEs with the highest (left side) and lowest (right side) Rev-100/GDP value, 2018 (%)

Country	*Rev-100/GDP*	*Group*	*Country*	*Rev-100/GDP*	*Group*
Saudi Arabia	58.9	EME	US	0.3	DME
Thailand	35.0	EME	UK	0.6	DME
China	34.9	EME	Australia	0.9	DME
Norway	34.6	DME	Spain	1.9	DME
Russia	26.5	EME	Canada	2.0	DME
Singapore	18.9	DME	Ireland	2.5	DME
France	18.5	DME	Netherlands	3.0	DME
Poland	16.5	EME	Argentina	3.5	EME
Italy	14.4	DME	Japan	4.9	DME
Taiwan	14.0	DME	Belgium	5.4	DME

Source: As in Table 6.1.

lower share of SOEs in the Top 100, the revenues of the entire Top 100 group account for as much as 85% of the GDP. The value of the Rev-100/GDP ratio depends on both the size of revenue shares of SOEs in the Top 100 and the ratio of the sum of revenues of the companies in and outside the Top 100.

Tables 6.6 and 6.7, with a similar layout as above, contain data on the number of SOEs in the Top 100 and Top 50 for the countries under review. The predominance of China over other countries is striking. The similarity between the set of countries from the left-hand part of Table 6.6 and the set in

Table 6.5 Rev-100/GDP ratio value for PCEs, 2018, (%)

Country	*Rev-100/GDP*
Hungary	22.5
Poland	16.5
Slovakia	8.6
Bulgaria	7.7
Czech Republic	7.2
Romania	3.7

Source: As in Table 6.1.

Table 6.6 WLEs with the highest (left side) and lowest (right side) numbers of SOEs in the sets of the largest enterprises, 2018

No. of SOEs in the Top 100		*No. of SOEs in the Top 50*		*No. of SOEs in the Top 100*		*No. of SOEs in the Top 50*	
China	78	China	40	US	1	UK	0
Egypt	37	Egypt	19	UK	2	US Australia Netherlands	1
Russia	33	Russia	17	Mexico	3		
India	32	Saudi Arabia India Poland	16	Australia Netherlands	4	Mexico	2
Saudi Arabia	22						
Thailand	21			Japan	5	Spain Belgium Japan	3
Poland	20	Indonesia	13	Ireland Spain	6		
Indonesia	19	France Italy Thailand	11				
Norway Turkey	18			Argentina Canada Korea Singapore	7	Argentina Canada Germany Korea Switzerland	4

Source: As in Table 6.1.

Table 6.7 Number of SOEs in the sets of the largest enterprises in PCEs in 2018

Country	*No. of SOEs in the Top 100*	*No. of SOEs in the Top 50*
Poland	20	16
Hungary	13	10
Slovakia	13	9
Romania	12	7
Czech Republic	9	6
Bulgaria	9	6

Source: As in Table 6.1.

the left-hand part of Table 6.2 is very high, with nine countries reappearing in both the Top 100 and the Top 50.

6.1.2 Significance of SOEs

By significance of SOEs we understand - generally speaking - the share of SOEs in the narrow groups of the largest domestic companies, i.e. in the Top 20 and Top 10. This share can be measured by three different indicators defined in Section 3.3 - SS-20, Rev-20/GDP, CS-20. The data on the number of SOEs in the Top 20 and Top 10 is also used in the analysis. A summary of figures that characterise the significance of SOEs in the distinguished groups of countries is presented in Table 6.8.

Table 6.8 Characteristics of the significance of SOEs in the groups of countries, 2018

	WLEs			*PCEs*
	Total	*DMEs*	*EMEs*	
SS-20*	31.9	15.3	56.2	35.4
Rev-20/GDP*	9.7	5.6	15.8	7.8
Total number of SOEs in the Top 20	129	38	91	25
Number of SOEs in the Top 20*	4.0	2.0	7.0	4.2
Total number of SOEs in the Top 10	79	22	57	12
Number of SOEs in the Top 10*	2.5	1.2	4.4	2.0
CS-20*	0.93	0.72	1.23	1.01

* Average value in the group (%).

Source: As in Table 6.1.

Table 6.9 Countries with the highest SS-20 value (for PCEs - all countries), 2018

DMEs	*SS-20*	*EMEs*	*SS-20*	*PCEs*	*SS-20*
Norway	66.0	China	94.9	Poland	67.3
Italy	64.1	Saudi Arabia	92.7	Hungary	46.1
France	37.7	Indonesia	73.3	Czech Republic	33.3
Austria	31.6	Russia	67.8	Bulgaria	26.3
Taiwan	17.4	Poland	67.3	Slovakia	12.3
Sweden	16.1	Egypt	60.4	Romania	4.1
Germany	12.7	Thailand	54.3		
Japan	11.3	Brazil	49.4		
Korea	11.2	India	42.7		
Switzerland	7.3	South Africa	35.9		

Source: As in Table 6.1.

As before, considerable differences between DMEs and EMEs (especially for SS-20 and the number of SOEs in the Top 10) are noticeable, and the values of the indicators for PCEs are again in between DMEs and EMEs. There are only 22 SOEs in 19 DME Top 10 sets (so among 190 companies), while there are as many as 57 SOEs in 13 EME Top 10 sets (130 companies). The values of the CS-20 index show that the concentration of SOEs in the Top 20 in the EME group is 70% higher than in the DME group.

Table 6.9 lists the countries with the highest value of the SS-20 index (for PCEs - all countries). It should be noted that in five WLEs (with the lowest share of SOEs in the economy - as can be seen in Table 6.2) – Australia, Ireland, the Netherlands, the UK, the US – there are no SOEs in the Top 20, so the SS-20 index equals zero.

As with the SS-100 index, China and Saudi Arabia dominate heavily, with the SS-20 index exceeding 90%. Indonesia, Russia, Poland, Egypt and Thailand from the EME group show a very high value of this index, over 50%. This is also true for two countries from the DME group - Norway and Italy. For the EME group, Argentina has the lowest value of the index - yet, relatively high, being 23.1, while in the DME group, alongside five countries with the index of zero, another three countries (Belgium, Singapore, Spain) have the index lower than five. In the case of the PCE group, the high index value, next to Poland, is for Hungary, while the SS-20 index for Romania is 11 times lower than for Hungary and 16 times lower than for Poland.

The second important indicator in this sphere is the number of SOEs in the Top 20. Table 6.9 lists the countries with the largest number of SOEs in the Top 20 for DMEs and EMEs, as well as the number of SOEs in the Top 20 for PCEs.

Table 6.10 Countries with the highest number of SOEs in the Top 20 (for PCEs - all countries), 2018

DMEs	*No. of SOEs*	*EMEs*	*No. of SOEs*	*PCEs*	*No. of SOEs*
Italy	7	China	18	Poland	9
France	6	Russia	10	Hungary	5
Norway	5	Egypt	9	Slovakia	4
Germany	3	Poland	9	Bulgaria	3
Taiwan	3	Thailand	9	Czech Republic	3
Austria	2	Saudi Arabia	8	Romania	1
Japan	2	India	7		
Korea	2	Indonesia	7		
Sweden	2	South Africa	4		
Switzerland	2	Brazil, Turkey	3		

Source: As in Table 6.1.

The distribution of countries with the highest number of SOEs in the Top 20 is similar to the distribution by other share ratios. The DME group is led by three countries – Italy, France and Norway – while in the EME group, eight countries stand out: China, Russia, Egypt, Poland, Thailand, Saudi Arabia, India, Indonesia.

In 2018, in the sets of the Top 10 non-financial companies in the analysed 37 counties, SOEs were missing from as many as 10 DMEs: Australia, Belgium, Canada, Ireland, the Netherlands, Singapore, Spain, Switzerland, the UK, the US, as well as Romania from the PCE group. In contrast, there were no such cases in the EME group. In turn, the largest number of SOEs in the Top 10 was in China (9), followed by Russia, Saudi Arabia (7), Indonesia, Poland (6), Italy (5), Egypt, France, India, Italy, Thailand (4). In the remaining PCEs (except Poland), the number of SOEs in the Top 10 was one or two.

A list of WLEs with the highest value of the CS-20 index is presented in Table 6.11 (we take into account only the countries with at least two SOEs in the Top 20).

The high position of Japan and Mexico results from the fact that relatively few SOEs in these countries are concentrated in the Top 10 set. In the case of the PCE group, the highest values of the CS-20 index were for Hungary and Poland. The CS-20 index for China is only 1.11 - although the number of SOEs in the Top 20 is very high, a very large group of SOEs is distributed relatively evenly across the Top 100 set.

Table 6.11 WLEs with the highest values of the concentration index, 2018

Country	*CS-20*
Thailand	1.46
South Africa	1.45
Japan	1.43
Italy	1.41
Norway	1.36
Mexico	1.35
Brazil	1.33
Indonesia	1.29
Argentina	1.20
France	1.20

Source: As in Table 6.1.

6.1.3 Types of SOEs

According to the definitions and division presented in Section 3.2.1, we distinguish two basic SOE types: majority and minority SOEs. Among majority SOEs, we distinguish 100% state-owned SOEs (fully owned or complete SOEs, central SOEs (CSOEs)). Additionally, we distinguish those SOEs whose shares are listed on stock exchanges - listed SOEs (LSOEs) (we provide a more detailed analysis of listed SOEs in the economies under review in Section 7.1). Table 6.12 presents data on the types of SOEs in the groups of countries.

Table 6.12 Types of SOEs (number and percentage share) in the analysed groups of countries, 2018

	WLEs						*PCEs*	
	Total		*DMEs*		*EMEs*			
	No.	*%*	*No.*	*%*	*No.*	*%*	*No.*	*%*
Number of SOEs	476	100.0	162	100.0	314	100.0	76	100.0
Majority SOEs	394	82.8	123	75.9	271	86.3	67	88.1
CSOEs	216	45.4	83	51.2	133	42.4	47	61.8
Others	178	37.4	40	24.7	138	43.9	20	26.3
Minority SOEs	82	17.2	39	24.1	43	13.7	9	11.9
LSOEs	231	48.5	67	41.4	164	52.2	19	25.0

Source: As in Table 6.1.

Table 6.13 Countries with the highest number of majority SOEs (left side) and CSOEs (right side) in the Top 100, 2018

Country	*No. of maSOEs*	*% of SOEs*	*Group*	*Country*	*No. of CSOEs*	*% of SOEs*	*Group*
China	71	91.0	EME	China	32	41.0	EME
Egypt	33	89.2	EME	Egypt	16	43.2	EME
India	31	96.9	EME	Russia	15	45.5	EME
Russia	29	87.9	EME	Turkey	15	83.3	EME
Indonesia	19	100.0	EME	Norway	13	72.2	DME
Norway	16	88.9	DME	India	12	37.5	EME
Thailand	16	76.2	EME	Hungary	10	76.9	PCE
Turkey	16	88.9	EME	Poland	9	45.0	EME
Poland	15	75.0	EME	Bulgaria	9	100.0	PCE
Austria	14	87.5	DME	Slovakia	9	69.2	PCE

Source: As in Table 6.1.

There are majority SOEs, including "complete" SOEs, in all 37 analysed economies. In five countries (Australia, Bulgaria, Mexico, the UK, the US), all SOEs from the Top 100 set are CSOEs. In this case, the differences between country groups are smaller than previously, with the greatest differences occurring in the case of minority SOEs. The list of countries with the highest number of majority SOEs and CSOEs is presented in Table 6.13.

In six DMEs (Australia, Belgium, Ireland, Korea, the UK, the US) and four EMEs (Argentina, India, Indonesia, Mexico), there were no minority SOEs in the Top 100. A similar situation occurred in three PCEs (Bulgaria, the Czech Republic, Slovakia). In turn, the average share of minority SOEs was almost twice as high in DMEs as in EMEs. Table 6.14 lists the countries with the highest number and share of minority SOEs (measured by the miS-100 index - see Section 3.3.1) in the 37 economies analysed.

The case of Saudi Arabia is symptomatic. The country has as many as nine minority SOEs (41%), while their share measured by the miS-100 index is only 7.3%. The reason for this is the very large share (around 75%) in the SOE group of the petrochemical giant Saudi Aramco, which in 2018 was fully owned by the government. The opposite situation is in Germany - the number of minority SOEs is low, while their share is high, which results from the existence of two large SOEs with minority state shareholdings - Deutsche Telekom and Deutsche Post.

6.2 Sectoral analysis of SOEs surveyed

The analysis consists of three parts. In the first one, we present the sectoral characteristics of the largest SOE (one) and three largest SOEs in the studied economies in 2018. In the second, we analyse the shares of SOEs in the six specific industries, defined as strategic (selection and description of these industries - see Section 3.3.2). In the third, we compare some of our data on the presence of SOEs in the strategic industries with similar data from 50 years ago.

Table 6.14 Countries with the highest number of minority SOEs (left side) and the highest miS-100 index value (right side)

Country	*No.*	*Group*	*Country*	*miS-100*	*Group*
Italy	9	DME	Italy	69.7	DME
Saudi Arabia	9	EME	Germany	63.7	DME
France	8	DME	France	57.9	DME
China	7	EME	Japan	57.0	DME
Thailand	5	EME	Hungary	54.7	PCE
Poland	5	EME	Poland	40.1	EME
Taiwan	4	EME	Singapore	37.9	DME
Egypt	4	EME	Turkey	37.2	EME
Russia	4	DME	Austria	35.9	DME
			South Africa	31.9	EME

Source: As in Table 6.1.

Table 6.15 The sector of the country's largest SOE by country groups, 2018

	WLEs			*PCEs*
	Total	*DMEs*	*EMEs*	
Oil & gas	16	5	11	2
Energy	5	5	–	4
Post & telecomm.	6	6	–	–
Transport	2	1	1	–
Other	3	2	1	–
Total	32	19	13	6

Source: As in Table 6.1.

Table 6.16 Industry distribution of the country's three largest SOEs, 2018

	WLEs				*PCEs*
	Total	*in %*	*DMEs*	*EMEs*	
Energy	25	26.0	17	8	9
Oil & gas	25	26.0	6	19	7
Transport	17	17.7	13	4	2
Post & telecomm.	15	15.6	14	1	–
Metal/mining	4	4.2	2	2	–
Other	10	10.5	5	5	–
Total	96	100.0	57	39	18

Source: As in Table 6.1.

Among the 32 WLEs analysed, in as many as 16 cases, i.e. half, the largest SOEs belonged to the oil & gas sector. In six cases, it was the post & telecommunications sector, and in five energy. Among the six PCEs analysed, in four cases it was the "energy" sector and in two oil & gas. Table 6.15 contains information on the largest SOEs for the country groups studied.

The situation is slightly different when we consider the three largest SOEs from each country. In this case, the transport industry is significant. In total, over 85% of the largest SOEs belong to four core sectors: oil & gas, energy, post & telecommunications, transport - Table 6.16.

More than half of the largest SOEs in 32 WLEs operate in two industries: oil & gas and energy. Almost 35% of SOEs operate in the next two industries (transport and post & telecommunications). All other industries are of marginal importance.

The next subject of the analysis is to estimate the presence (position) of SOEs in each country in the six specific industries, described as strategic (for details, see Section 3.3.2). We determine the scope of SOEs' presence in each industry using an indexed scale of 0–4 (4 - monopolistic or near-monopolistic position, 3 - dominant position, exceeding 50%, 2 - significant position, around 15–50%, 1 - low position, around 5–15%, 0 - no or negligible presence). Table 6.17 contains average values, showing the estimated presence of SOEs in the analysed industries for the selected groups of countries.

Three sectors - energy, railways and postal sector - definitely stand out in terms of the SOE presence, both in the WLE group and in the other three subgroups of countries. The lowest presence of SOEs is in the telecommunications industry, and this is true for all country groups (in the PCE group, there are virtually no SOEs operating in this industry). Significant differences between DMEs and EMEs exist in the oil & gas and in the banking sector.

Table 6.18 lists the countries with the highest and lowest average presence of SOEs in six strategic industries. We use the SS-I indicator, defined in

Section 3.3.2 (the arithmetic mean of the SOE share indicators in six strategic industries).

In eight countries listed in the left-hand part of Table 6.18, the SS-I indicator is at least "3", i.e. the share of SOEs is dominant or monopolistic. Among these countries, two are DMEs - Norway and Taiwan – and the rest are EMEs. In turn, among the ten countries with the lowest value of the SS-I indicator, as many as nine are DMEs. Mexico is an exception.

Table 6.17 The average value of the SOE presence index in the six selected industries, 2018

		WLEs			*PCEs*
		Total	*DMEs*	*EMEs*	
1	Oil & gas	1.68	0.80	3.00	2.00
2	Energy	2.66	2.32	3.15	3.00
3	Railways	2.81	2.50	3.23	3.17
4	Postal sector	2.68	2.71	2.64	2.67
5	Telecomm.	1.38	1.42	1.31	0
6	Banking sector	1.63	1.11	2.38	0.83
Average		2.14	1.81	2.63	1.95

Source: Own estimation.

Table 6.18 Countries with the highest (left side) and lowest (right side) presence of SOEs in six strategic industries (estimate), 2018

Country	*SS-I*	*Group*	*Country*	*SS-I*	*Group*
China	3.83	EME	UK	0.50	DME
Saudi Arabia	3.33	EME	US	0.67	DME
Norway	3.17	DME	Australia	1.00	DME
Russia	3.17	EME	Canada	1.17	DME
India	3.00	EME	Netherlands	1.17	DME
Indonesia	3.00	EME	Spain	1.17	DME
Taiwan	3.00	DME	Mexico	1.50	EME
Thailand	3.00	EME	Ireland	1.67	DME
Egypt	2.83	EME	Germany	1.83	DME
Poland, Switzerland	2.33	EME DME	Japan	1.83	DME

Source: Own estimation.

The last part of the sectoral analysis involves the comparison of our estimates of the SOE presence in strategic industries (for 2018) with a similar estimate made exactly 40 years ago in a book edited by P. Toninelli (2000, p. 275). Table 6.19 presents - using an analogous scale (0, 1, 2, 3, 4) - the 1978 and 2018 estimates for five industries (all, for which comparable data exist - the estimates for the "banking sector" were missing in the book edited by P. Toninelli).

The data in the table shows that in all countries (within the industries analysed) and in all industries (within the countries analysed), in 1978–2018, a very significant decrease in the presence of SOEs has been noted, over 40% on average. Of the 18 countries analysed, the largest decrease, by over 50%, occurred in the UK, the Netherlands, Spain, Australia, Mexico. In turn, the smallest decrease, around 18%–30%, occurred in Japan, Korea, India, Belgium and Switzerland.

By sector, the shares of SOEs declined the most in telecommunications (by over 70%) followed by oil & gas (over 57%).The smallest decrease in the shares of SOEs occurred in the energy sector (by only 17%).

6.3 Country's largest SOEs and world's largest SOEs in 2018

In 2018, in 14 out of 32 WLEs, the largest SOE (by ORs) was also the largest domestic company. This was the case in 3 (Austria, Italy, Norway) out of 19 DMEs and as many as 11 (Argentina, Brazil, China, Egypt, Indonesia, Mexico, Poland, Russia, Saudi Arabia, South Africa, Thailand) out of 13 EMEs and 2 PCEs (Hungary, Poland). In five countries, the three largest non-financial companies are SOEs (China, Indonesia, Italy, Norway, Saudi Arabia), and in the next four countries, the Top 5 largest non-financial companies include at least three SOEs (India, Poland, Russia, Thailand).

In several cases, the largest SOE and, at the same time, the largest domestic company was several times larger (in terms of generated ORs) than the second-largest SOE on the Top 100 list. This was the case in Egypt (Egyptian General Petroleum - 7 times) and Saudi Arabia (Saudi Aramco - 7.8 times), which means that the impact of that one company on the total share of SOEs is decisive. Table 6.20 provides more detailed data on this subject.

Chinese SOEs have an overwhelming predominance in the group of the world's largest non-financial SOEs. Out of the 100 world's largest SOEs (by OR) in 2018, as many as 64 were Chinese companies. The next country, France, had seven SOEs in the world's Top 100, followed by India (four), Germany, Italy, Japan, Russia (three each). There were 12 Chinese companies in the set of the 20 world's largest SOEs. The share of ORs of Chinese SOEs in the ORs of the entire Top 100 SOE group was also 64%.

Table 6.21 lists 25 largest SOEs from China, while non-Chinese ones are listed in Table 6.22. There is a striking difference in the industry allocation of companies in both tables. There are 12 industries in the Chinese

Table 6.19 Comparison of estimates of the SOE presence in strategic industries in 1978 and 2018

No.	*Country*	*Oil & gas*		*Energy*		*Railways*		*Postal*		*Telecomm.*		$\sum$ *1978*	$\sum$ *2018*	*Change %*
		1978	*2018*	*1978*	*2018*	*1978*	*2018*	*1978*	*2018*	*1978*	*2018*			
1	Australia	2	0	4	2	4	1	4	3	4	0	18	6	−66.7
2	Austria	4	3	4	4	4	3	4	3	4	0	20	13	−35.0
3	Belgium	2	0	1	2	4	3	4	3	4	3	15	11	−26.7
4	Brazil	4	3	4	3	4	1	4	3	4	0	20	10	−50.0
5	Canada	0	0	4	3	3	1	4	3	1	0	12	7	−41.7
6	France	4	0	4	3	4	3	4	3	4	3	20	12	−40.0
7	Germany	2	0	3	1	4	3	4	3	4	3	17	10	−41.2
8	Netherlands	3	1	3	2	4	3	4	0	4	0	18	6	−66.7
9	India	4	4	4	3	4	4	4	3	4	1	20	15	−25.0
10	Italy	4	3	3	3	4	3	4	3	4	0	19	12	−36.8
11	Japan	0	0	0	2	3	1	4	3	4	3	11	9	−18.2
12	Korea	0	2	3	4	4	3	4	3	4	0	15	12	−20.0
13	Mexico	4	3	4	4	4	0	4	2	4	0	20	9	−55.0
14	Spain	3	0	0	0	4	3	4	3	4	0	15	6	−60.0
15	Sweden	4	0	2	3	4	3	4	3	4	3	18	12	−33.3
16	Switzerland	4	1	4	3	4	4	4	3	4	3	20	14	−30.0
17	UK	3	0	4	0	4	2	4	0	4	0	19	2	−89.5
18	US	0	0	1	1	1	0	4	2	0	0	6	3	−50.0
In total		47	20	52	43	67	41	72	46	65	19	303	169	−44.2
Change 2018/1978 in %		−57.4		−17.3		−38.8		−36.1		−70.8		−44.2		

Source: Own estimation, Toninelli 2000, p. 275.

Table 6.20 Countries in the WLE group with the highest (left side) and lowest (right side) shares of OR of the largest SOEs in the entire group of SOEs from the Top 100[a], 2018

Country	*Share in %*	*Group*	*Country*	*Share in %*	*Group*
Saudi Arabia	76.5	EME	China	8.7	EME
Mexico	75.5	EME	France	16.8	DME
Argentina	67.0	EME	India	22.6	EME
Egypt	59.2	EME	Belgium	24.8	DME
Brazil	56.2	EME	Russia	27.0	EME
Netherlands	52.9	DME	Turkey	27.2	EME
Norway	52.9	DME	Switzerland	27.6	DME
Korea	51.1	DME	South Africa	28.8	EME
Indonesia	50.5	EME	Italy	29.2	DME
Japan	45.2	DME	Poland	30.6	EME

[a]Countries with at least 3 SOEs in the Top 100.
Source: As in Table 6.1.

SOE group, while there are 6 in the other group. The largest Chinese SOEs are much larger than those outside China. In total, their ORs amount to €2,706 billion, and the sum of total assets is €4,564 billion, while these values for non-Chinese SOEs are €1,918 billion and €3,162 billion, respectively. Among the 25 largest Chinese SOEs, as many as 15 are complete SOEs, while among the non-Chinese SOEs, only five are complete SOEs.

6.4 Changes in the presence of SOEs in the global economy from 2009 to 2018

6.4.1 Basic data for the analysed country groups

One of the main research objectives of this book is to determine the changes in the presence of SOEs in the global economy after the financial crisis of 2008–2009. The basic synthetic indicator used for this purpose is the SS-100 index. We also analyse other indicators and characteristics concerning the share of SOEs in the economy. As in the previous sections, the analysis covers the group of 32 WLEs, distinguished groups of economies, and individual countries.

The data in Table 6.23 clearly show that between 2009 and 2018, the SS-100 index as well as - which must be strongly emphasised - all other

Table 6.21 25 largest Chinese SOEs by the value of ORs,[a] 2018

No.	*No. Top 100*	*Name of SOE*	*Industry*	*OR (bill. €)*	*TA (bill. €)*	*State shares (%)*
1	1	Sinopec	Oil & gas	369.4	202.9	68.3
2	3	State Grid	Energy	303.4	499.8	100.0
3	4	Petrochina	Oil & gas	299.9	309.9	80.9
4	5	China State Constr. Eng.	Construction	150.8	237.3	59.6
5	6	Saic Motor	Automotive	114.5	99.8	79.9
6	9	China Mobile Comm.	Post & telecomm.	97.9	223.0	72.5
7	10	China State Railway	Transport	97.6	1019.0	100.0
8	12	China Railway Group (CREC)	Construction	94.6	120.1	50.7
9	13	China Railway Constr.	Construction	92.5	117.0	51.1
10	14	China National Offshore Oil	Oil & gas	87.7	155.0	100.0
11	16	Dongfeng Motor	Automotive	79.1	57.8	59.6
12	17	China FAW Group	Automotive	78.1	58.0	100.0
13	23	China Resources	Other	74.8	185.9	100.0
14	24	Sinochem	Chemicals	74.1	59.8	100.0
15	25	China Comm. Construction	Construction	73.3	174.1	63.8
16	26	China Post Group	Post & telecomm.	71.8	1250.0	100.0
17	27	Energy Investment	Energy	71.6	226.8	100.0
18	29	China Southern Power Grid	Energy	67.9	103.9	100.0
19	31	China Minmetals	Metals	66.8	114.3	100.0
20	37	Norinco	Defence	59.8	50.9	100.0
21	38	Cofco	Agribusiness	59.5	71.5	100.0
22	39	Tewoo	Mining/metals	58.3	33.4	100.0
23	41	China Baowu Steel	Metals	57.4	89.6	100.0
24	42	Aviation Industry Corp. of China	Aerospace	57.2	120.6	100.0
25	46	Guangzhou Automobile Industry	Automotive	48.1	37.2	100.0
				2706.1	4563.6	

[a] Based on our data. Non-financial companies only.
Source: As in Table 6.1.

Table 6.22 25 world's largest SOEs (non-Chinese) by the value of ORs,[a] 2018

No.	*No. Top 100*	*Name of SOE*	*Country*	*Industry*	*OR (bill. €)*	*TA (bill. €)*	*State shares (%)*
1	2	Saudi Aramco	Saudi Arabia	Oil & gas	309.6	346.6	100.0
2	7	Gazprom	Russia	Oil & gas	104.9	262.0	50.1
3	8	Rosneft	Russia	Oil & gas	103.6	165.5	50.1
4	11	NTT	Japan	Post & telecomm.	95.3	178.9	42.4
5	15	Petrobras	Brazil	Oil & gas	83.5	193.9	50.3
6	18	Deutsche Telekom	Germany	Post & telecomm.	76.9	145.4	31.9
7	19	Eni	Italy	Oil & gas	76.9	118.4	30.1
8	20	Petroleos Mexicanos	Mexico	Oil & gas	76.4	92.1	100.0
9	21	Électricité de	France	Energy	76.0	283.3	83.8
10	22	Enel	Italy	Energy	75.3	165.4	23.6
11	28	Equinor	Norway	Oil & gas	69.5	98.3	67.0
12	30	Indian Oil	India	Oil & gas	67.8	43.1	72.9
13	31	Engie	France	Energy	65.6	153.7	34.9
14	32	PTT	Thailand	Oil & gas	63.1	63.4	58.9
15	33	Deutsche Post	Germany	Post & telecomm.	62.9	50.5	21.0
16	34	USPS	USA	Post & telecomm.	61.8	23.2	100.0
17	35	Airbus	France	Aerospace	60.1	66.7	10.0[b]
18	40	Renault	France	Automotive	57.4	115.0	15.0
19	43	Oil & Natural Gas	India	Oil & gas	54.3	63.8	85.6
20	44	Tokyo Electric Power	Japan	Energy	50.9	102.4	54.7
21	45	Petramina	Indonesia	Oil & gas	50.6	56.5	100.0
22	48	Korea Electric Power	Korea	Energy	47.4	144.7	58.3
23	49	Deutsche Bahn	Germany	Transport	46.4	58.5	100.0
24	54	Orange	France	Post & telecomm.	42.0	96.6	29.5
25	56	Saudi Basic Industr.	Saudi Arabia	Chemicals	39.7	74.5	70.0
					1917.9	3162.2	

[a] Based on our data. Non-financial companies only.
[b] In addition, significant shares of other governments.
Source: As in Table 6.1.

indicators that characterise the share of SOEs declined significantly for the core group of the 32 WLEs in our research.

It is - in our opinion - a rather unexpected result, contradicting the views that exist in the literature about the increasing importance of SOEs in the economy in the last several years. This issue is examined further in Section 6.4.3.

Table 6.24 contains similar data to Table 6.23, but for the three distinguished groups of countries.

The key findings of our research, presented in Table 6.23 and 6.24, lead to the following conclusions:

1 Between 2009 and 2018, in the 32 WLEs as a whole, all indicators concerning the share and significance of SOEs declined. The basic SS-100 index decreased by 4.5% and the SS-20 index by 5.9%. The total number of SOEs in the analysed sets and the number of listed SOEs decreased slightly. The quantitative indicators of the presence of SOEs in the narrow sets (Top 20 and Top 10) of the largest domestic companies, as well as the concentration of SOEs in the Top 20, have also decreased significantly, by more than 10%. By far the most significant decrease, by over 20%, was in the SOEs' ORs to GDP ratios.
2 In the case of three distinguished groups of countries, the situation is less obvious and the differences between the groups are substantial. In the DME group, all basic share ratios decreased significantly (by over

Table 6.23 Changes in various indicators concerning SOEs for the group of 32 WLEs, 2009–2018

No.	*Indicator*	*2009*	*2018*	*Change in %*
1	SS-100 (%)	28.7	27.4	−4.5
2	SS-20 (%)	33.9	31.9	−5.9
3	Rev-100/GDP (%)	16.4	12.9	−21.3
4	Rev-20/GDP (%)	13.7	9.7	−29.2
5	Number of SOEs in the Top 100	483	476	−1.5
6	Number of SOEs in the Top 50	281	262	−6.8
7	Number of SOEs in the Top 20	145	129	−11.0
8	Number of SOEs in the Top 10	88	79	−10.2
9	CS-20	1.07	0.93	−13.1
10	Number of CSOEs	225	216	−4.0
11	Number of miSOEs	83	82	−1.2
12	Number of LSOEs	246	231	−6.1

Source: As in Table 6.1.

Table 6.24 Changes in various indicators concerning SOEs for the groups of countries, 2009–2018

No.	*Indicator*	*DMEs*			*EMEs*			*PCEs*		
		2009	*2018*	*Change in %*	*2009*	*2018*	*Change in %*	*2009*	*2018*	*Change in %*
1	SS-100 (%)	16.3	14.1	−13.5	46.9	46.7	−0.4	28.9	29.1	+0.7
2	SS-20 (%)	18.8	15.3	−18.6	56.0	56.2	+0.4	34.8	35.4	+1.7
3	Rev-100/GDP (%)	11.0	8.6	−21.8	25.1	19.1	−23.9	10.6	11.0	+3.8
4	Rev-20/GDP (%)	7.5	5.6	−25.3	22.8	15.8	−30.7	7.6	7.8	+2.6
5	No. of SOEs in the Top 100	178	162	−9.0	305	314	+3.0	83	76	−8.4
6	No. of SOEs in the Top 50	101	82	−18.8	180	180	0	59	54	−8.5
7	No. of SOEs in the Top 20	51	38	−25.5	94	91	−3.2	30	25	−16.7
8	No. of SOEs in the Top 10	28	22	−21.4	60	57	−5.0	13	12	−7.7
9	CS-20	0.97	0.72	−25.8	1.20	1.23	+2.5	1.13	1.10	2.7
10	Number of CSOEs	102	83	−18.6	123	133	+8.1	60	47	−21.7
11	Number of miSOEs	36	39	+8.3	46	43	−6.5	8	9	+12.5
12	Number of LSOEs	66	67	+1.5	180	164	−8.9	13	19	+46.2

Source: As in Table 6.1.

10%) or very significantly (by over 20%), only the number of SOEs decreased slightly less, by 9%. The basic SS-100 index decreased by 13.5% and the SS-20 index by as much as 18.6%. The SOE ORs to GDP ratios decreased by over 20%. There was a marked decrease in the number of CSOEs, while the number of miSOEs increased, although to a lesser extent. The concentration of SOEs in the Top 20 fell significantly.

3 In the EME group, both share indices, SS-100 and SS-20, were virtually unchanged. In turn, the Rev-100/GDP and Rev-20/GDP ratios decreased very significantly, much more than in the case of DMEs. This is probably due to the fact that a group of smaller companies, outside the Top 100, generally dominated by private companies, grew much faster in this group of countries than the SOE sector from the Top 100. The number of SOEs in the Top 100 in EMEs in the analysed period increased a little, while the number of SOEs in the Top 10 and Top 20 decreased slightly. But the concentration of SOEs in the Top 20 slightly increased. It seems surprising that the number of CSOEs increased quite significantly, while the number of LSOEs decreased.
4 In the PCE group, the situation is most diverse, although it must be taken into account that the results for this only six-element group are distorted by a very large (2–3 times) increase in all share ratios for Hungary, due to the nationalisation of the largest Hungarian company MOL in 2011. The SS-100 index and the SS-20 index practically did not change in the period under review, while the number of SOEs in all analysed sets decreased. Inversely to the EME group, the number of LSOEs markedly increased while the number of CSOEs markedly decreased.

6.4.2 Data for selected countries and specific groups of countries

To begin with, Table 6.25 presents a list of countries with the greatest changes in the numbers of SOEs in the Top 100 during the period under review.

Table 6.26 lists the countries with the greatest changes - increases and decreases in the SS-100 index between 2009 and 2018. Only the countries where the share of SOEs in 2018 exceeded 5% are considered. In the countries with a negligible share of SOEs, even very small nominal fluctuations, within a statistical error, imperceptible on the scale of the economy, translate into significant percentage changes (an example is the UK, where the SS-100 index increased from 1.1 to 2.3, so 109%).

The extraordinary increase in the SS-100 index in Argentina was due, as we mentioned, to a one-off event - the nationalisation of the petrochemical giant YPF in 2012. A similar phenomenon in South Africa was most likely due to the relatively higher revenue growth of SOEs, compared to private companies. In Mexico, the situation was the opposite - Petroleos Mexicanos (Pemex), which accounts for the vast majority of SOEs' revenues in this country, experienced revenue growth, but to a lesser extent than private companies (Pemex noted a drop on the Fortune Global 500 list as well, from 64 to 95 position). A very serious decline in the shares of SOEs, noted in Sweden and Singapore, and other developed countries, is a part of a broader trend of de-statisation in these countries over the past 30 years.

As far as the PCE group is concerned, the extraordinary increase in the shares of SOEs, by almost 100%, was recorded in Hungary due to the nationalisation of a large petrochemical company MOL in 2011. Poland recorded an

Table 6.25 Countries with the greatest increase (left side) and decrease (right side) in the number SOEs between 2009 and 2018

Country	*Group*	*Change in SOEs*	*Country*	*Group*	*Change in SOEs*
Thailand	EME	+6	Norway	DME	−6
China	EME	+5	Switzerland	DME	−5
Belgium	DME	+4	Bulgaria	PCE	−5
Egypt	EME	+4	Singapore	DME	−4
Italy	DME	+3	Russia	EME	−4
Hungary	PCE	+3	Indonesia	EME	−4
Japan	DME	+2	Australia	DME	−3

Source: As in Table 6.1.

Table 6.26 WLEs with the utmost increase or decrease in the SS-100 index (2009–2018)

Country	*SS-100 change in %*	*Group*	*Country*	*SS-100 change in %*	*Group*
Argentina	183.8	EME	Sweden	−35.7	DME
South Africa	58.7	EME	Singapore	−25.6	DME
Egypt	18.2	EME	Mexico	−25.5	EME
Japan	17.9	DME	Germany	−20.6	DME
Poland	9.0	EME	Taiwan	−20.5	DME
Russia	7.2	EME	Austria	−20.1	DME
Italy	6.8	DME	Canada	−20.0	DME
Korea	6.2	DME	Brazil	−15.5	EME
Belgium	4.9	DME	France	−13.9	DME
Indonesia	2.7	EME	India	−13.2	EME

Source: As in Table 6.1.

increase of 9%, and other countries' decreases - Romania and Slovakia – was very significant, of over 25%, and for Bulgaria and the Czech Republic it was minor, around 10%.

Among the 37 countries analysed, the number of SOEs in the Top 100 between 2009 and 2018 increased in 11 countries, decreased in 14 countries and remained unchanged in 7 countries. The largest increase in the number of SOEs occurred in Thailand (6), China (5), Belgium and Egypt (4 each). The largest decrease in the number of SOEs was recorded in Norway (6), Switzerland (5), Indonesia, Russia, Singapore (4 each).

There is an interesting situation regarding the number of SOEs in the Top 20, i.e. among the largest and most significant companies in each country. During the period under review, it increased in only six countries, while it decreased in as many as 15 countries and remained unchanged in 16 countries. Significant increases occurred only in Russia (3) and Saudi Arabia (2). In turn, the largest decreases were recorded in Austria, India, Romania (4) and Brazil, Ireland, Turkey (2).

There were no SOEs in the Top 20 in two countries (Australia, the UK) in both 2009 and 2018. Further three countries (Ireland, the Netherlands, the US) had SOEs in 2009 but missed them in 2018. In Spain, on the other hand, the situation was the opposite - no SOEs in 2008 and one SOE in 2018.

In the case of the Rev-100/GPD ratio, the decreases cover many more countries. Of the 37 countries analysed, an increase in the ratio occurred in six countries between 2009 and 2018, with significant increases only in Hungary (13.4 pp) and Argentina (2.1 pp), the countries where the largest domestic companies were nationalised. In Belgium, Japan, Russia and Spain the increase was negligible, less than 1 pp, and therefore within a statistical error. In turn, the Rev-100/GPD decrease occurred in as many as 31 countries. Of the PCE group, Bulgaria (3.6 pp) and the Czech Republic (2.9 pp) recorded the largest falls. The countries with the largest decrease in the ratio for the DME and EME groups are shown in Table 6.27.

It should be noted that a significant decline in the Rev-100/GPD ratio, and so the relative importance of the largest SOEs in the economy, occurred in several countries with a traditionally very large share of SOEs: Norway and Austria from the DME group and Saudi Arabia, India, Indonesia, Thailand from the EME group. Lower but noticeable decreases occurred also in Italy, France, Brazil, Egypt and Poland. For the two remaining countries with a large or very large share of SOEs, the ratio remained virtually unchanged (for China it decreased from 35.0 to 34.9, and for Russia it increased from 26.2 to 26.5). In the case of Saudi Arabia, the large decline was due to the fact that the revenue growth rate of Saudi Aramco, the company with a profound influence on the revenues of the entire SOE group, was less than the Saudi GDP growth rate.

The last table in this section (Table 6.28) shows the changes in the shares of SOEs between 2009 and 2018 for two specific groups of countries. The first group consists of 12 WLEs (by nominal GDP in 2018 - the US, China,

Table 6.27 Countries with the largest decrease in the Rev-100/GPD ratio (2009–2018), percentage points

DMEs	*Decrease in Rev-100/GPD*	*EMEs*	*Decrease in Rev-100/GPD*
Singapore	−9.5	Saudi Arabia	−13.5
Sweden	−8.7	South Africa	−8.0
Norway	−6.1	India	−7.8
Austria	−4.0	Indonesia	−3.7
Netherlands	3.7	Thailand	−3.4
Switzerland	−2.6	Brazil	−3.0
Taiwan	−2.2	Egypt	−2.4
Ireland	−2.0	Mexico	−2.1
Italy	−1.6	Poland	−1.3
France	−1.4	Turkey	−0.8

Source: As in Table 6.1.

Japan, Germany, the UK, France, India, Italy, Brazil, Korea, Canada, Russia) and the second of 22 OECD (Organisation for Economic Co-operation and Development) countries (for which the figures are available). Additionally, we analyse the two WLEs, the US and China, separately in Table 6.28.

The average SS-100 index value for both groups of 12 WLEs and 22 OECD countries decreased markedly (by 6% and by 6.7%) between 2009 and 2018. In the group of 12 WLEs, the index value decreased for seven countries and increased for five countries. A similar situation occurred with the SS-20 index. The average Rev-100/GDP ratio decreased to a greater extent, by 10.9% (in absolute values by 1.4 pp). The ratio decreased for 10 WLEs and increased for only two. The number of SOEs decreased significantly in the OECD countries – from 136 to 122.

The comparison of the status and changes in the shares of SOEs in the US and China shows fundamental, even drastic differences in this respect for each indicator analysed.

6.4.3 Verification of the hypothesis on the return of SOEs

In Section 1.5, while analysing the condition and situation of the SOE sector in the world economy over the last several years, we pointed to views emerging in the economic literature that can be described as the hypothesis on the return of SOEs. This hypothesis assumes that after the financial crisis of 2008–2009, a sustained increase in the scope and importance of SOEs

Table 6.28 Changes in selected indicators on SOEs for selected groups of countries and countries

Country	*SS-100 (%)*			*SS-20 (%)*			*Rev-100/GDP*			*Number of SOEs*		
	2009	*2018*	*Change in %*	*2009*	*2018*	*Change in %*	*2009*	*2018*	*Change*	*2009*	*2018*	*Change*
12 WLEs	30.2	28.4	−6.0	35.4	33.1	−6.5	12.8	11.4	−1.4	216	217	+1
22 OECD	19.4	18.1	−6.7	23.3	21.5	−7.7	9.9	8.7	−1.2	136	122	−14
US	3.3	0.6	−81.8	6.3	0	-	1.2	0.3	−0.9	2	1	−1
China	92.1	85.9	−6.7	94.4	94.9	0.5	35.0	34.9	−0.1	73	78	+5

Source: As in Table 6.1.

in the global economy and an increase in state ownership activity could be observed. While the statements about the importance of SOEs, their role and their actual functions in the economic system are difficult to verify empirically, quantitative changes relating to the presence of SOEs are relatively easily and unquestionably verifiable.

In light of the findings of our empirical research presented in Tables 6.23 and 6.24, there are no indications to support the hypothesis on the "return of SOEs" in quantitative terms in the global economy. Between 2008 and 2019, the shares of SOEs in the significant group of WLEs, as well as in the vast majority of domestic economies, declined markedly.

In order to counter the argument that perhaps the increase in the presence of SOEs in the economy was transitory and occurred immediately after the financial crisis, we prepared a similar data set as above for the period 2009–2013. Table 6.29 provides data on this subject.

Just like in the 2009–2018 period (Table 6.23), all indicators characterising the share of SOEs in the economy also decreased for the 2009–2013 period. And, again, as before, the greatest changes were in the Rev-20/GDP ratio and the Top 10 and Top 20 sets, in the narrow group of the largest companies.

In the comprehensive OECD report published in 2018, with many interesting data and insights on contemporary SOEs, the authors write: "The presence of SOEs in the global economy has grown strongly in recent years. Today they account for over a fifth of the world's largest enterprises as opposed to ten years ago where only one or two SOEs could be found at the top of the league table" (OECD 2018, p. 4). In this short quotation, besides the justified first part of the second sentence, there are two fundamental errors, also frequently repeated by other authors.

Indeed, it is true that SOEs now account for about one-fifth of the world's largest companies. The results of our research on the group of the 32 WLEs

Table 6.29 Changes in various indicators on SOEs for the group of 32 WLEs, 2009–2013

No.	*Indicator*	*2009*	*2013*	*Change in %*
1	SS-100 (%)	28.7	28.4	−1.04
2	SS-20 (%)	33.9	33.2	−2.06
3	Rev-100/GDP (%)	16.4	15.2	−4.87
4	Rev-20/GDP (%)	13.7	12.4	−9.48
5	Number of SOEs in the Top 100	483	469	−2.89
6	Number of SOEs in the Top 50	281	275	−2.13
7	Number of SOEs in the Top 20	145	135	−6.89
8	Number of SOEs in the Top 10	88	82	−6.82

Source: As in Table 6.1.

(Table 6.8) show that the average numerical share of SOEs in the Top 20 sets is 20.2%, with the key point being the deep variation in the shares of SOEs in various country groups. In turn, a simple analysis of the group of the world's largest SOEs, presented below, also generally supports the above statement.

Yet, it is not true that "the presence of SOEs in the global economy has grown strongly in recent years". According to the results of our research, the presence of SOEs in the global economy has decreased markedly between 2009 and 2018 and slightly less between 2009 and 2013. Similar conclusions, although with a stipulation concerning China, emerge from the analysis of the group of the world's largest SOEs. Actually, it is not true that ten years ago there were more SOEs "at the top of the league table" than there are today, as we demonstrate below.

Using a method identical to that described in Section 3.3, we identified SOEs in the large group of the world's largest companies, included in the Fortune Global 500 list.[1] We made a distinction between SOEs from DMEs, EMEs and China. Treating China separately seems fully justified methodologically due to the huge share of Chinese SOEs in the Fortune Global 500 list. The findings of our analysis are presented in Table 6.30.

It is true that between 2009 and 2018 the number of SOEs in the Fortune Global 500 list increased by 38 SOEs, but the number of Chinese SOEs

Table 6.30 Various characteristics of SOEs from the Fortune Global 500 (revenues in billion $)

No.		*2009*	*2013*	*2018*	*Change 2009–2018 in %*
1	No. of SOEs	102	141	140	37.3
2	No. of SOEs - China	40	82	89	122.5
3	No. of SOEs except China	62	59	51	−17.7
4	No. of SOEs - EME except China	18	24	20	11.1
5	No. of SOEs - DME	44	35	31	−29.5
6	Share of China's SOEs (%)	39.2	58.2	63.6	62.2
7	Revenues of SOEs	4988	9178	9873	97.9
8	Revenues of SOEs - China	1800	5261	6405	255.8
9	Revenues of SOEs - except China	3188	3917	3468	8.8
10	Revenues of SOEs - DME	2355	2298	1991	−15.5
11	Revenues of SOEs - EME except China	833	1619	1477	77.3
12	Share of Chinese SOEs in revenues of SOEs	36.1	57.3	65.1	80.3
13	Revenues of non-SOEs from the Top 500	18097	21880	22793	25.9
14	Revenues of all Top 500	23085	31058	32666	41.5

Source: Own calculations.

increased by as many as 49, so the number of SOEs from other countries decreased by 11, thus by more than 17%. When considering the total revenues of SOEs, the situation is analogous. The revenues of Chinese SOEs increased by as much as 55.8%, while the revenues of non-Chinese SOEs by only 8.8% (so de facto they decreased, as the table includes values at current prices).

The extraordinarily rapid growth of Chinese SOEs between 2009 and 2018 can be seen even more clearly among the Top 100 largest companies from the Fortune Global 500 list. The number of Chinese SOEs quadrupled in this group, and their total revenues increased even more. In turn, the number of non-Chinese SOEs dropped by almost a third, and their revenues at current prices fell by 15%.

The analysis of the data of the Fortune Global 500 in both tables leads to a similar conclusion we formulated based on the analysis of our data - after the financial crisis of 2008–2009, the return of SOEs did not occur on a global scale. The number of SOEs has admittedly increased markedly but this was solely due to the increase in the number of Chinese entities. At the same time, what is important, the shares of Chinese SOEs did not increase at all within the Chinese economy; on the contrary, the SS-100 index for China decreased from 92.1 to 85.9 in our research between 2009 and 2018. In turn, the share of the Chinese economy in the global economy increased remarkably (according to the IMF – International Monetary Fund) data, between 2010 and 2018, the GDP (nominal) for China grew by 163%, for the US by 42% and for Germany by only 16%). Since the Chinese economy, especially in the group of the largest companies, is strongly dominated by SOEs, as if "in the

Table 6.31 Various characteristics of SOEs from the Top 100 companies on the Fortune Global 500 (revenues in billion $)

No.		*2009*	*2013*	*2018*	*Change 2009–2018 in %*
1	No. of SOEs	24	33	33	37.5
2	No. of SOEs - China	5	14	20	300.0
3	No. of SOEs except China	19	19	13	−31.6
4	No. of SOEs - EME except China	4	8	5	25.0
5	No. of SOEs - DME	15	11	8	−46.7
6	Revenues of SOEs	2529	4556	4781	89.0
7	Revenues of SOEs - China	679	2392	3212	473.0
8	Revenues of SOEs - except China	1850	2164	1569	−15.2
9	Revenues of SOEs - DME	1492	1219	809	−45.8
10	Revenues of SOEs - EME except China	358	945	760	112.3

Source: Own calculation.

passing", the numbers and shares of SOEs in the global economy increased as well, which is reflected in the data contained in the Fortune Global 500. In this sense, the observed increases in the number and shares of SOEs in the Fortune Global 500 are not due to the return of SOEs globally but are a simple consequence of China's changing position in the global economy. An analysis conducted for the 100 largest non-financial companies included in the Fortune Global 500 showed similar results (Table 6.31).

6.5 Summary and conclusions

The chapter presents the aggregate (distinguished country groups) and comparative (cross-country analysis) key findings of our empirical research. The results concerned the condition of SOEs in the world in 2018 and the changes that occurred in this field between 2009 and 2018. The main conclusions of the research are as follows:

1 The average share of SOEs in the Top 100 of the analysed 32 WLEs, as measured by the SS-100 index (the arithmetic mean of the shares by ORs and by total assets), was over 27% in 2018. The share as measured by the number of SOEs in the Top 100 and Top 50 sets and by the Rev-100/GDP ratio was lower, around 15%.
2 In all dimensions analysed, there are fundamental, profound differences between the share of SOEs in DMEs and EMEs. The basic share ratio - the SS-100 index - was 46.7 for EMEs and was more than three times higher than for DMEs (14.1). A similar difference occurs for the share of SOEs in numbers. The values of share ratios for PCEs were close to the average values for the whole WLE group.
3 In two EMEs, China and Saudi Arabia, the share of SOEs in the economy, as measured by the SS-100 index, can be described as very large (85.9% and 85.3%, respectively), and in the next seven EMEs - as large, exceeding 35% (Russia, Indonesia, Egypt, Poland, Thailand, India, Brazil). In turn, among DMEs, there were only two countries with a large share of SOEs (Norway - 48.4% and Italy - 47.4%), and in the next two, the share of SOEs can be described as significant (France - 31.5%, Austria - 31.4%).
4 In five DMEs out of the 32 WLEs studied, the share of SOEs was less than 2.5% and therefore negligible (the US, Australia, the Netherlands, Ireland, the UK) and in the next five - Spain, Canada, Japan, Belgium, Switzerland - it was low, less than 10%. Within the EME group, Argentina had the lowest share of SOEs of 19.1%. In the PCE group - apart from Poland, mentioned above - in all other countries, the share of SOEs was 20%–30%.
5 In the case of the Rev-100/GDP ratio, which is primarily useful for analyses of changes in SOEs over time, the differences between DMEs and EMEs were somewhat smaller. It is worth noting that seven DMEs (the US, the UK, Australia, Spain, Canada, Ireland, the Netherlands) had very low values of this indicator, not exceeding 3%.

6 When it comes to the number of SOEs in the Top 100 and Top 50, China is the undisputed leader (78 and 40 SOEs, respectively), followed in both cases by the same countries - Egypt, Russia, India and Saudi Arabia. In contrast, the countries with the fewest SOEs are the US, the UK, Australia, the Netherlands, Mexico.[2]

7 In the case of the Top 20, i.e. the narrow set of the largest (and most important) domestic companies, the average share of SOEs as measured by the SS-20 index in the group of the 32 WLEs exceeded 30%, while the difference between DMEs and EMEs was more than 3.5 times. For the share of SOEs by number, the situation is similar, and for the Top 10 set, the difference between DMEs and EMEs was even greater, 3.8 times. The PCE group showed shares similar to the overall WLE group.

8 As with the SS-100 index, two countries, China and Saudi Arabia, had a very high SS-20 index value of over 90%, and another seven countries had a high value of over 50%: Indonesia, Russia, Poland, Norway, Italy, Egypt and Thailand. In five DMEs – Australia, Ireland, the Netherlands, the UK, the US – there were no SOEs in the Top 20.

9 Of the 476 SOEs present in 2018 in the Top 100 lists from 32 WLEs, as many as 394, i.e. 82.7%, were majority SOEs (of which 216, i.e. 45.4%, were complete SOEs) and 82 (17.2%) were minority SOEs; 231 SOEs (48.5% of all SOEs) were listed companies, 1/3 of them with minority state shareholdings but controlled by governments. The differences between DMEs and EMEs, as well as PCEs, were moderate, with proportionately fewer minority SOEs in the EME group (13.7%, compared to 24.1% in DMEs), and there were relatively fewer listed SOEs in the PCE group than in DMEs and EMEs.

10 The sectoral distribution of SOEs in all countries analysed (we considered the three largest SOEs from each country) shows a very strong dominance of four industries: energy, oil and gas, transport, post and telecommunications. In contrast, a comparative analysis of the estimates of the presence of SOEs in five strategic industries in 18 countries between 1978 and 2018 shows that all analysed countries and all industries experienced a significant decline in the presence of SOEs over this period.

11 The set of the world's largest SOEs is very much dominated by Chinese companies. The largest SOE (by ORs) in the world in 2018 was, according to our calculations, the Chinese petrochemical giant Sinopec, followed by Saudi Aramco, also in the oil & gas sector. There were as many as 64 Chinese entities in the Top 100 world's largest SOEs. Their revenues accounted for 63.5% of the revenues of the entire set and their total assets accounted for 61.8%. There were six Chinese SOEs in the Top 10 world's largest SOEs.

12 All share ratios of SOEs decreased between 2009 and 2018 in the group of the 32 WLEs analysed. The basic SS-100 index dropped by 4.5% from 28.7 to 27.4. The SS-20 index decreased slightly more, by 5.9% (from 33.9 to 31.9). The total number of SOEs in the 32 Top 100 sets decreased

from 483 to 476 (1.5%) and the number of SOEs in the Top 20 sets decreased significantly from 88 to 79 (by 11%).

13 In DMEs, between 2009 and 2018, all share characteristics of SOEs decreased considerably (from about 10% to about 25%). In EMEs the situation was different. The SS-100 and SS-20 indices remained virtually unchanged, as did the number of SOEs. In contrast, the Rev-100/GDP and Rev-20/GDP ratios decreased surprisingly significantly (23.9% and 30.7%). This means that in the EME group between 2009 and 2018 SOEs retained their strong position in the Top 100 sets, while the share (and therefore the importance) of these largest SOEs in the economy decreased significantly. An explanation may be the faster growth and development of smaller companies outside the Top 100, generally more privately owned.

14 Our findings on the decline in the shares of SOEs in the world economy in the period after the 2008–2009 financial crisis lead to the conclusion that the hypothesis on the return of SOEs is negated. This is also confirmed by the analysis of the presence of SOEs on the lists of the world's largest companies (Fortune Global 500). The reported increase in the number and shares of SOEs (as measured by revenues) is the sole result of the very rapid development of the Chinese economy, dominated by SOEs, during this period. Globally, except in China, both the number of SOEs and the shares of SOEs in the Fortune Global 500 (and even more so in the Fortune Global 100) declined significantly.

Notes

1 The authors of the Fortune Global 500 list distinguish companies in which governments have majority (more than 50%) ownership stakes. Our analysis aimed to identify all SOEs in the list, thus also the companies that are controlled by governments through minority ownership or indirectly. The Fortune Global 500 list includes also, unlike our data set, financial entities.

2 The situation in Mexico is unusual. The SS-100 index for Mexico is quite high at 23.7, while there are only three SOEs in the Top 100, including the Mexico's largest company Petroleos Mexicanos and the energy conglomerate Comision Federal De Electricidad (CFE), fourth on the Top 100 list.

Bibliography

Christiansen, H. (2013). *Balancing Commercial and Non-commercial Priorities of State-owned Enterprises* (No. 6). OECD Corporate Governance Working Papers. Paris: OECD Publishing.

Galambos, L. (2000). State-Owned Enterprises in a Hostile Environment: The U.S. Experience. In P. A. Toninelli (Ed.), *The Rise and Fall of State-owned Enterprise in the Western World*. Cambridge: Cambridge University Press.

OECD. (2018). *Ownership and Governance of State-Owned Enterprises: A Compendium of National Practices*. Paris: OECD Publishing.

Toninelli, P. M. (Ed.). (2000). *The Rise and Fall of State-owned Enterprise in the Western World*. Cambridge: Cambridge University Press.WW

7 Selected problems of SOE presence in the economy in light of our findings

The final chapter of the book presents and analyses selected issues related to the presence of state-owned enterprises in the contemporary economy. Each part is a study of a different issue referring to the empirical results presented in the previous chapters. The first part focuses on the scope and share of listed SOEs among the largest non-financial companies in 37 selected economies. In the second part, a similar analysis is conducted with respect to foreign SOEs. In the last part of the chapter, a statistical and econometric analysis is conducted to examine the relationships between the scope of SOEs and the socio-economic system, including the institutional environment of each country. The countries under review have been classified into five groups and the shares of SOEs in their economies were related to the various socio-economic measures.

7.1 Listed state-owned enterprises

7.1.1 Introductory remarks

As we wrote in Chapter 1, in the last few decades, entities with mixed state-private ownership, whose shares are listed on stock exchanges and which are de facto controlled by one of the shareholders - the state owner - have appeared and become increasingly common in the economies of many countries around the world. Nowadays, such listed companies - hereinafter referred to as "listed SOEs (LSOEs)[1]" (i.e. listed state-owned enterprises) - are found in a significant number of stock exchanges in a great many countries of the world. The reasons for the emergence of LSOEs varied. These were incomplete privatisations (reluctant privatisations, so changing the ownership structure without losing state control), rescue (usually temporary) nationalisations of private entities in crisis situations or, eventually, acquisitions of parts of shares in private companies with state funds, both wealth and pension funds. This last case is not always associated with gaining control of the company by the government (so the creation of a LSOE), as these funds are essentially passive investors.

DOI: 10.4324/9781003244462-8

Various issues related to the functioning of LSOEs have been considered quite extensively in the economic literature in recent years. Many authors write about the hybrid nature of LSOEs, which, on the one hand, like all listed companies, are entities operating on the market, but, on the other, as all SOEs, are a particular type of government-dependent entities (Bruton et al. 2015; Vining & Laurin, 2020). This area of research also includes the issues of leveraging control over LSOEs by the state shareholder, e.g. through golden shares or special provisions in the companies' articles of association (Pargendler, 2011; Baltowski, 2017). There are relatively broad streams of research on the effectiveness of LSOEs, its relation with the ownership structure and the origins of companies (Lin et al., 2009; Arocena & Oliveros, 2012; Kabaciński et al., 2020) but also on the governance of LSOEs and the issues of state ownership control organisation, also in terms of maintaining competitive neutrality (OECD, 2012; Milhaupt & Pargendler 2017).

A very large portion of these studies and analyses concerns Chinese LSOEs (e.g. Yu, 2013; Lin et al., 2020; Wei, 2021), which is justified given the position of Chinese companies among the world's most important LSOEs (discussed further below). There are also studies on the presence of LSOEs in specific stock exchanges, such as the Brazilian (Musacchio & Lazzarini, 2014), Russian (Abramov et al., 2017) and Polish exchanges (Baltowski, 2017; Baltowski & Kwiatkowski, 2018). There are, however, few studies for several countries from one particular region (e.g. Carney & Child, 2013, for the East Asian countries; Milhaupt & Pargendler, 2017, for eight selected countries).

The primary source of comparative data on a global scale concerning the scope and ownership structure of listed companies is the OECD (Organisation for Economic Co-operation and Development) 2019 report *Owners of the World's Listed Companies*. It contains the results of various analyses of almost 41,000 listed companies from 54 countries. The report distinguishes five categories of shareholders (owners) of listed companies, including the "public sector", which "includes direct ownership by central governments, local governments, public pension funds, state-owned enterprises and sovereign wealth funds" (De la Cruz et al., 2019, p. 9).

According to the results of this study, among the world's 10,000 largest listed companies, the "public sector" holds above 50% of the shares in almost 800 companies. In addition, in 1,140 companies the public sector holds between 10% and 50% of the shares (p. 26). Thus, in total, the "public sector" holds significant stakes in almost 20% of companies. The majority of these are direct government holdings, with almost 1/4 holdings through sovereign wealth funds, and, to a lesser extent, holdings through public pension funds and by other SOEs.

Our analysis of LSOEs in the global economy, presented in the following section, differs fundamentally from the analysis in the OECD report, which mainly covers the data on the value (capitalisation size) of shares held by different types of owners, including the owner referred to as the "public sector". Our analysis focuses on specific LSOEs, i.e. listed companies actually controlled by governments. From the OECD report, it is possible to get an answer to the question of what is the value of public equity in listed companies in different countries (both in absolute and in relative terms). Our analysis seeks to determine what portion of listed companies - in terms of both numbers and size - is controlled by governments in individual countries. Obviously, as throughout the book, at the basic level, the analysis is limited to the LSOEs from the 100 largest companies in each of the 37 countries under review. In the final section, we also extend the analysis to companies outside this group.

7.1.2 Condition and characteristics of LSOEs in the group of 37 economies analysed

In the analysed Top 100 lists from 37 countries for 2018, using the methods described in Section 3.2, we found 239 LSOEs, which is 6.5% of all analysed companies and 44.9% of SOEs, the set of which included 532 entities. In 2009, there were slightly more LSOEs – 250 in the Top 100 lists, representing 46.0% of the 544 domestic SOEs.

Detailed data on LSOEs in the 32 world's largest economies (WLEs) and the distinguished groups of countries for 2009 and 2018 are provided in Tables 7.1 and 7.2. It should be noted that in 2009 among the 37 economies analysed, there were no LSOEs in nine: five developed market economies (DMEs) (Australia, Canada, Ireland, the Netherlands, the UK), two emerging market economies (EMEs) (Argentina, Mexico) and two post-communist economies (PCEs) (Bulgaria, Slovakia). In 2018, there were no LSOEs in eight countries: five DMEs (Australia, Ireland, the Netherlands, the UK, the US), one EME (Mexico) and two PCEs (Bulgaria, Slovakia).

Table 7.1 Values of various characteristics and indicators concerning LSOEs for the group of the 32 WLEs, 2009–2018

	2009	*2018*	*Change in %*
No. of LSOEs	245	231	–5.7
OR-LSOEs (bill. €)	2467.0	4839.9	96.2
TA-LSOEs (bill. €)	3951.3	7771.2	96.7
No. of LSOEs/No. of SOEs (%)	50.7	48.5	–4.3
OR-LSOEs/OR-SOEs (%)	60.6	60.7	0.2
TA-LSOEs/TA-SOEs (%)	53.9	49.8	–7.6
OR-LSOEs/GDP (%)	6.7	7.3	8.9

OR-LSOEs – the sum of OR values of all LSOEs in the studied group.
TA-LSOEs – the sum of TA values of all LSOEs in the studied group.
OR-SOEs – the sum of OR values of all SOEs in the studied group.
TA-SOEs – the sum of TA values of all SOEs in the studied group.
Source: Own calculations.

The characteristics and indicators concerning LSOEs in the WLE group changed little over the period analysed. The number of LSOEs declined, but both operating revenues (ORs) and total assets (TAs) of LSOEs grew slightly faster than the same characteristics of the entire group of the 32 WLEs. The relations of the various characteristics of LSOEs to SOEs remained roughly similar. They show that LSOEs represent, in terms of both numbers and values, about half of all SOEs.

Table 7.2 provides analogous characteristics and indicators on LSOEs in the distinguished country groups over the period analysed.

In the case of developed countries, the number of LSOEs remained the same, while in the case of emerging markets, it decreased slightly, but the share changes were not significant. In turn, in the case of PCEs, a marked increase in all characteristics and indicators concerning LSOEs was recorded. The very large increase in ORs and TAs of LSOEs in the EME group is due to the increase in Chinese LSOEs, as we explain further.

Table 7.3 lists the countries with the highest number of LSOEs and the highest total value of ORs of LSOEs.

The 11 economies with the highest number of LSOEs include 9 EMEs and 2 DMEs. The situation is different when it comes to the ORs of LSOEs (right-hand part of the table) - there are six EMEs and five DMEs in the leading group. The position of Chinese LSOEs is specific. Their number

Table 7.2 Values of various characteristics and indicators concerning LSOEs for the distinguished country groups, 2009–2018

	WLEs						*PCEs*		
	DMEs			*EMEs*					
	2009	*2018*	*Change in %*	*2009*	*2018*	*Change in %*	*2009*	*2018*	*Change in %*
No. of LSOEs	67	67	0	178	164	−7.9	11	19	72.7
OR-LSOEs (bill. €)	1116.9	1326.4	18.8	1350.2	3513.5	160.2	45.2	97.9	116.6
TA-LSOEs (bill. €)	1992.9	2687.8	34.9	1958.4	5083.5	159.6	66.7	139.3	108.6
No. of LSOEs/ No. of SOEs (%)	37.6	41.4	10.1	58.4	54.5	−6.7	13.6	25.0	83.8
OR-LSOEs/ OR-SOEs (%)	71.8	71.3	−0.7	54.5	58.1	6.6	48.5	64.4	32.8
TA-LSOEs/ TA-SOEs (%)	66.2	67.0	1.2	46.4	44.4	−4.3	41.1	55.0	33.8

Source: As in Table 7.1.

represents more than 27% of all LSOEs from EMEs, while the value of their ORs represents more than 70% of the ORs of all LSOEs from the EME group and more than 51% of the ORs of LSOEs from the group of the 37 economies analysed.

Table 7.4 lists the countries with the greatest change in the number of LSOEs between 2009 and 2018.

A very marked decrease in the number of LSOEs in China, with a simultaneous increase in the number of SOEs in that country (from 73 to 78), is due, in our opinion, to two reasons. First, it is a result of a change in

Table 7.3 Countries with the highest number of LSOEs (left side) and the highest value of ORs of LSOEs (right side), 2018

Country	*Group*	*No. of LSOEs*	*A*	*Country*	*Group*	*OR (billion €)*	*B*
China	EME	45	57.7	China	EME	2476.5	58.4
India	EME	18	56.3	France	DME	387.8	85.9
Russia	EME	17	51.5	Russia	EME	310.9	80.5
Egypt	EME	16	43.2	India	EME	234.3	78.2
Saudi Arabia	EME	16	72.7	Italy	DME	212.0	80.5
Brazil	EME	12	85.6	Japan	DME	195.4	92.6
Italy	DME	12	68.8	Germany	DME	170.4	72.7
Indonesia	EME	11	57.9	Brazil	EME	143.0	96.4
Poland	EME	11	55.0	Norway	DME	110.4	84.1
France	DME	10	71.4	Thailand	EME	109.4	70.6
Thailand	EME	10	47.6	Saudi Arabia	EME	88.7	21.9

A – percentage share of LSOEs in the total number of SOEs in the Top 100.
B – percentage share of LSOEs in ORs of all SOEs in the Top 100.
Source: As in Table 7.1.

Table 7.4 Countries with the greatest change in the number of LSOEs against the change in the number of SOEs between 2009 and 2018

Country	*2009*	*2018*	*LSOEs change*	*SOEs change*
Poland	6	11	+5	–2
Thailand	7	10	+3	+6
Italy	9	12	+3	+3
Spain	1	3	+2	+1
Romania	3	5	+2	–5
Austria	6	4	–2	0
Russia	19	17	–2	–3
Singapore	7	5	–2	–4
Egypt	20	16	–4	+4
China	59	45	–14	+5

Source: As in Table 7.1.

the general economic policy towards the largest companies, involving the extension of state control over them. Second, it is a result of very large Chinese non-financial companies with 100% state ownership entering into the Top 100, pushing relatively smaller companies with mixed state-private capital off the list. Similar processes seem to have taken place in Egypt.

The opposite situation occurs in the case of two PCEs, i.e. Poland and Romania - the increase in the number of LSOEs occurs with the decrease in the number of SOEs. In the case of Poland, the increase in LSOEs results from several reluctant privatisations of very large SOEs during this period. It is likely that in the case of Romania the reason is similar.

Table 7.5 contains data on minority listed SOEs (miLSOEs), so the companies with mixed capital that are controlled by governments, even though they hold only minority stakes. Obviously, the control in such cases is smaller than in SOEs with 100% or majority government ownership. At the same time, the dependence on the market and the need to operate more transparently are greater.

Noticeable differences can be seen between the EME group and the other two groups. In the EME group, miLSOEs represent less than a quarter of LSOEs, in the DME group more than a half and in the PCE group exactly a half. In the case of miLSOEs in terms of ORs, the difference is even more pronounced. This is because in the four large EMEs (so with the revenues of SOEs on average higher than in other EMEs) the number of majority LSOEs is far greater than the number of miLSOEs - China: 37 vs. 7, India: 17 vs. 1, Russia: 13 vs. 4, Indonesia: 11 vs. 0. This means that the governments of these countries accept to transfer only a certain part of control powers over state-private companies to the markets.

Table 7.6 lists the countries with the highest number and highest total ORs of miLSOEs.

In the case of miLSOEs, the situation is different than for the entire set of LSOEs. There are as many as six DMEs in the right-hand part of the table, with two countries from the DME group, France and Italy, leading. China, on the other hand, shows an exceptionally small share of the ORs of miSOEs in the ORs of all LSOEs (only 7 out of 45 Chinese LSOEs are miLSOEs).

Table 7.5 Minority LSOEs in the entire set of LSOEs, 2018

	WLEs			*PCEs*
	Total	*DMEs*	*EMEs*	
No. of LSOEs	231	67	164	19
No. of miLSOEs	76	36	40	8
No. of miLSOEs /No. of LSOEs (%)	32.9	53.7	24.4	50.0
OR-miLSOEs /OR-LSOEs (%)	27.6	66.0	10.3	58.6
Change in miLSOEs 2008–2018	+2	+2	0	+5

Source: As in Table 7.1.

Table 7.6 List of countries with the highest number (left side) and highest total revenues (right side) of miLSOEs

Country	*Group*	*mi LSOEs*	*A (%)*	*Country*	*Group*	*OR (bill. €)*	*B (%)*
Saudi Arabia	EME	9	56.3	France	DME	307.2	79.2
Italy	DME	8	66.7	Italy	DME	191.2	90.2
France	DME	8	80.0	China	EME	176.5	7.1
China	EME	7	15.6	Germany	DME	149.3	87.6
Poland	EME	5	45.5	Japan	DME	112.8	57.7
Taiwan	DME	4	66.7	Poland	EME	38.6	55.6
Russia	EME	4	23.5	Brazil	EME	34.2	23.9
Germany	DME	3	75.0	Russia	EME	33.9	10.9
Egypt	EME	3	18.8	Norway	DME	27.5	24.9
Brazil	EME	3	25.0	Austria	DME	23.2	76.7
Thailand	EME	3	30.0	Taiwan	EME	21.7	74.5
South Africa	EME	3	75.0	South Africa	EME	20.7	88.8

A – percentage share of LSOEs in the total number of SOEs in the Top 100.
B – percentage share of LSOEs in ORs of all SOEs in the Top 100.
Source: As in Table 7.1.

Table 7.7 Sectoral distribution of listed SOEs, 2018

Industry	*WLEs*			*PCEs*
	Total	*DMEs*	*EMEs*	
Energy	45	20	25	8
Oil & gas	25	6	19	6
Chemicals	23	0	23	2
Post & telecomm.	23	14	9	0
Metals	21	4	17	1
Transport	21	8	13	1
Construction	12	1	11	0
Aerospace/defence	8	4	4	0
Machinery & equipment	8	2	6	0
Trade	8	0	8	0
Automotive	7	1	6	0
Food, tobacco	7	2	5	0
Mining	7	0	7	1
Water & sewage	4	1	3	0
Others	12	4	8	0
In total	231	67	164	19

Source: As in Table 7.1.

Table 7.7 shows the sectoral distribution of LSOEs in 2018 in the set of the 37 economies under review.

When compared to the list showing the industries of the three largest SOEs from each country (Table 6.16), quite fundamental differences can be noted.

First, the sectoral diversity of LSOEs is much greater than that of the largest SOEs, which particularly applies to the EME group. Second, alongside industries, where the participation of SOEs is traditionally significant (energy, oil & gas, post & telecommunications, transport), industries such as chemicals, metals, construction are strongly represented.

Table 7.8 lists the 20 largest LSOEs by ORs in 2018.

Four Chinese LSOEs are leading the table, with eight in the entire Top 20 set. In terms of market capitalisation, the value of Chinese LSOEs represents 47% of the capitalisation value of the entire Top 20 set, and their ORs represent 57% of the ORs of the entire set. The presented set includes 15 majority LSOEs (including all Chinese) and 5 miLSOEs.

Table 7.8 20 world's largest LSOEs[a] by the value of ORs, 2018

No.	*Name of the SOE*	*Country*	*Industry*	*OR (bill. €)*	*TA (bill. €)*	*Capitalisation (bill. €)*	*State shares (%)*
1	Sinopec	China	Oil & gas	369.4	202.9	92.2	68.3
2	Petrochina	China	Oil & gas	299.9	310.0	173.5	80.9
3	China State Constr. Eng.	China	Construction	150.8	237.3	35.8	59.6
4	Saic Motor	China	Automotive	114.5	99.8	45.0	79.9
5	Gazprom	Russia	Oil & gas	104.2	261.6	52.3	51.1
6	Rosneft	Russia	Oil & gas	103.6	165.5	63.1	51.1
7	China Mobile Comm.	China	Post & telecomm.	97.9	223.0	172.6	72.5
8	NTT	Japan	Post & telecomm.	95.3	178.9	70.0	42.4
9	China Railway Group (CREC)	China	Transport	94.5	120.1	21.2	50.7
10	China Railway Constr.	China	Construction	92.5	117.0	19.9	51.1
11	Petrobras	Brazil	Oil & gas	83.5	193.9	79.7	50.3
12	Eni	Italy	Oil & gas	76.9	118.4	54.6	30.1
13	Deutsche Telekom	Germany	Post & telecomm.	76.9	145.4	69.3	31.9
14	Électricité de France	France	Energy	76.0	283.2	38.3	83.8
15	Enel	Italy	Energy	75.3	165.4	55.1	23.6
16	China Comm. Constr.	China	Construction	73.3	174.1	25.2	63.8
17	Equinor	Norway	Oil & gas	69.5	98.3	67.8	67.0
18	Indian Oil	India	Oil & gas	67.8	43.1	19.1	72.9
19	Engie	France	Energy	65.6	153.7	31.6	34.9
20	PTT	Malaysia	Oil & gas	63.1	63.4	58.9	38.2

a Based on our data. Non-financial companies only.
Source: As in Table 7.1.

At the end of this part of the analysis, we will present the results of our research, which aimed to determine the scope of the presence of listed SOEs on selected global stock exchanges. We considered 16 stock exchanges from 16 countries (8 from the DME group and 8 from the EME group) where the share of SOEs is relatively high. We analysed the presence of LSOEs distinguished on the basis of the criterion of government corporate control, both non-financial and financial, in the main stock indices in these countries in 2009 and 2018. When there were more than 30 companies in the main index, the calculations included the 30 companies with the largest capitalisation; when there were 30 or fewer companies, the calculation included all the companies from the index. We also determined the share of LSOEs in the capitalisation of the studied group of listed companies in each country. All data show the status at the end of the relevant year - Tables 7.9 and 7.10.

The results of the analysis are not surprising. The list, drawn up according to the share of LSOEs in capitalisation in 2018, is headed by the three DMEs with the largest share of SOEs in the economy (apart from Norway, not included in the analysis). There is a clear decrease in the number of LSOEs (from 33 to 28, i.e. by 15%) between 2009 and 2018. Of the eight countries, only the Italian stock exchange saw an increase in the number of LSOEs. The average share of LSOEs in the capitalisation of the stock indices analysed also fell, by more than 25%. The shares dropped for seven stock exchanges, while in the case of one, the share increased slightly.

Table 7.9 Some characteristics of the presence of LSOEs on the stock exchanges of selected countries from the DME group

Country	*Index name*	*2009*			*2018*			*Change in capitalisation share (%)*
		No. of LSOEs	*Share in number (%)*	*Capitalisation share (%)*	*No. of LSOEs*	*Share in number (%)*	*Capitalisation share (%)*	
Italy	FTSE MIB	8	26.7	41.3	10	33.3	41.5	0.6
Austria	ATX[a]	7	35.0	45.0	4	20.0	31.0	–31.0
France	CAC 40	5	16.7	21.4	5	16.7	14.8	–31.2
Japan	TOPIX 100	3	10.0	13.7	3	10.0	12.7	–7.2
Germany	DAX 30	4	13.3	9.6	2	6.7	9.3	–3.1
Sweden	OMX 30	2	6.7	21.0	1	3.3	4.5	–78.7
Korea	KOSPI	3	10.0	7.5	2	6.7	4.0	–46.4
Switzerland	SMI[a]	1	5.0	2.7	1	5.0	2.5	–9.5

a The index includes 20 companies.
Source: own compilation based on stock exchange data and other sources.

Table 7.10 Some characteristics of the presence of LSOEs on the stock exchanges of selected countries from the EME group

	Index name	*2009*			*2018*			*Change in capitalisation share (%)*
		No. of LSOEs	*Share in number (%)*	*Capitalisation share (%)*	*No. of LSOEs*	*Share in number (%)*	*Capitalisation share (%)*	
China	CSI 300	27	90.0	94.4	25	83.3	87.4	–7.4
Poland	WIG 20[a]	5	25.0	47.3	12	60.0	70.8	49.8
Saudi Arabia	TASI	14	46.7	62.8	14	46.7	68.6	9.7
Russia	RTS	12	40.0	62.0	13	43.3	50.6	–18.4
Brazil	Ibovespa	7	23.3	48.6	7	23.3	34.3	–29.4
Egypt	EGX 30	3	10.0	16.6	7	23.3	25.8	55.1
Turkey	BIST-30	3	10.0	10.9	5	16.7	20.1	83.3
India	NIFTY 50	8	26.7	32.1	8	26.7	17.8	–44.7

a The index includes 20 companies.
Source: own compilation based on stock exchange data and other sources.

In the EME group, the situation is more diverse. The number of LSOEs increased significantly in the years under review (from 79 to 91, i.e. by 15%), while the average share of LSOEs by capitalisation did not change. The share of LSOEs in capitalisation increased in four countries and also decreased in four. The share of LSOEs in the capitalisation of the main stock index in countries such as China, Saudi Arabia and Russia is very high, close to the share of SOEs in the economy. These results of our analysis are close to those presented by T.J. Putniņš (2020, p. 215): "state-backed companies account for 80% of the value of China's stock market and 62% of Russia's".

In India, on the other hand, the share of LSOEs in capitalisation is quite low, which is evidence of the relatively strong private sector in the country. The situation in Poland is symptomatic, where the number of LSOEs increased from 5 to 12 and the share in capitalisation from 47.3% to over 70%. This is due, as we mentioned earlier, to several reluctant privatisations of large energy and financial companies carried out during the period under review.

7.2 Foreign SOEs

7.2.1 Introductory remarks

The term "multinational state-owned enterprises" (or "state-owned multinational companies" – SOMNCs) used in the economic literature means "independent firms with direct ownership by the state that have value adding activities outside its home country. These value adding activities can be production facilities or sales subsidiaries, or purchasing subsidiaries or design or R&D centres" (Cuervo-Cazurra et al., 2014, p. 925). This definition, thus, distinguishes the SOEs that have internationalised, i.e. operate outside their country of origin. Because SOEs always perform both economic and non-economic functions, as we wrote in Chapter 2, SOMNCs often become tools of political or geopolitical expansion for some states,[2] which, in turn, provokes reactions of other states. An example of this type of reaction is the "Statement Regarding Investment by Foreign State-Owned Enterprises" (https://www.ic.gc.ca/eic/site/ica-lic.nsf/eng/lk81147.html) issued by the government of Canada in 2012. It highlighted the risks associated with the investments of foreign SOEs (FSOEs), which are "inherently susceptible to foreign government influence that may be inconsistent with Canadian national industrial and economic objectives". Similar restrictions on the activities of entities controlled by foreign governments (sometimes in the form of a so-called "national interest test") also exist, for example, in Australia and Russia (UNCTAD 2019, p. 94).

The comprehensive monograph *State-Owned Multinationals: Governments in Global Business* (Cuervo-Cazurra, 2018), published a few years ago, exhaustively presents and analyses various aspects of the theory and principles of operation of SOMNCs, as well as their role in the modern globalised economy. The international strategies of SOMNCs are brilliantly presented in the paper by Estrin et al. (2021). Similar issues, although more in practical than theoretical terms, are analysed in the OECD report entitled *State-Owned Enterprises as Global Competitors. A Challenge or an Opportunity?* (OECD 2016). When it comes to databases on SOMNCs, the most comprehensive and widely used source is the UNCTAD's *World Investment Report*.

The subject of the analysis below is not SOMNCs, i.e. large internationalised companies controlled by governments, but individual foreign elements (subsidiaries) of SOMNCs. Sometimes the term "a state-owned enterprise's foreign affiliate (SOE's-FA)" is used in the literature for these types of entities. Such companies can be considered FSOEs from the point of view of a given economy. The academic literature on FSOEs in the global economy is not extensive. It focuses more on the strategy of SOEs' internationalisation rather than the scale and scope of FSOEs and mostly concerns Chinese FSOEs (Wei, Nguyen 2017; Meyer et al. 2018). The problem of foreign investments of SOEs from the EU countries in the EU countries in both quantitative and qualitative terms is analysed by Szarzec et al. (2021).

The primary objective of our analysis is to determine the scope, position and significance of FSOEs, as elements of SOMNCs, in the host countries studied, i.e. in a large group of the WLEs and five PCEs. Such a research objective is obviously not accidental. First, the database we have created, described in Chapter 3, makes it possible to carry out an in-depth, multi-faceted analysis of FSOEs in such scope exactly. Second, this kind of analysis, rare in world literature, seems cognitively sensible. Using the verified figures for 37 countries, we show both the scope of the presence and different characteristics of FSOEs in the group of economies studied and the changes that have occurred in this area between 2009 and 2018. The results of our quantitative analysis can make an important contribution to further qualitative research on the international expansion of SOMNCs.

7.2.2 Condition and characteristics of FSOEs in the group of 37 economies analysed

In the analysed Top 100 lists from 37 countries for 2018, using the methods described in Chapter 3, we found 161 FSOEs, which is 4.4% of all analysed companies. This is a significant number, as it amounts to more than 30% of the domestic SOEs, of which there were 532 in the analysed set. In 2009, there were 143 FSOEs on the Top 100 lists, representing 26.3% of the 544 domestic SOEs. Adding up the number of SOEs and FSOEs, it can be concluded that the number of government-controlled entities in the group of the largest companies from 37 countries in 2009 was 687 (18.6%) and in 2018 it was 693 (18.7%).

Detailed data on FSOEs among the 32 WLEs and in the distinguished country groups in 2009 and 2018 are provided in Tables 7.11 and 7.12. It should be noted that in 2009, among the 332 economies under review, FSOEs were absent from three DMEs (France, Taiwan, the US) and two EMEs (China, India). In 2018, FSOEs were missing from two DMEs (Canada, Taiwan) and three EMEs (China, India, Mexico).

A slight increase in most of the characteristics and indicators concerning FSOEs in the WLE group can be seen over the period analysed. The ORs of FSOEs increased by more than 105%, while the ORs of companies in the Top 100 of the entire WLE group increased by 75% during this period. For TAs, the increments for the FSOE group and the entire WLE group were similar. There was a significant increase in the number of FSOEs relative to

Table 7.11 Values of various characteristics and indicators concerning FSOEs for the group of 32 WLEs, 2009–2018

	2009	*2018*	*Change in %*
No. of FSOEs	117	130	11.1
OR-FSOEs (bill. €)	555.3	1137.7	105.7
TA-FSOEs (bill. €)	569.3	1040.8	82.8
No. of FSOEs/No. of SOEs (%)	26.3	30.3	15.2
OR-FSOEs/OR-SOEs (%)	13.6	14.3	5.1
TA-FSOEs/TA-SOEs (%)	7.8	6.7	–14.1
OR-FSOEs/GDP (%)	1.52	1.72	13.2

OR-FSOEs - the sum of ORs of all FSOEs in the studied group.
TA-FSOEs - the sum of TAs of all FSOEs in the studied group.
OR-SOEs - the sum of OR values of all SOEs in the studied group.
TA-SOEs - the sum of TA values of all SOEs in the studied group.
Source: Own calculations.

the number of SOEs, as well as in the ratio of ORs of FSOEs to GDP. The ratio of ORs of FSOEs to ORs of SOEs increased slightly and a similar ratio for TAs decreased. This may mean that the observed increase in FSOEs is mainly in "lighter" industries, such as trade or services.

Table 7.12 provides analogous characteristics and indicators concerning FSOEs for the distinguished country groups.

In the DME group, all characteristics and indicators concerning FSOEs increased significantly during the period under review. In 2018, the number of FSOEs in this group was more than 60% of the number of SOEs and their OR value was more than 55% of the corresponding value for SOEs. For the PCE group, these indicators were slightly lower and for the EME group, they were severely lower - just over 10% for the number and just over 1% for the ORs. This last minimum value is mainly due to the fact that China and India, countries with very high values of the ORs of SOEs, lacked FSOEs in the Top 100.

Table 7.13 is a comparison of the shares of FSOEs and SOEs in the country groups analysed. The parameter defined as the "Share of FSOEs" was calculated analogously to the SS-100 index for SOEs, i.e. as the average of the shares of FSOEs in the Top 100 by ORs and TAs in percentages.

As before, there are very large differences between the distinguished country groups. In the DME and PCE group, the share of FSOEs is close to 30% of the share of SOEs, while in the EME group, it is almost seven times lower.

Table 7.12 Values of various characteristics and indicators concerning FSOEs for the distinguished country groups, 2009–2018

	WLEs						*PCEs*		
	DMEs			*EMEs*					
	2009	*2018*	*Change in %*	*2009*	*2018*	*Change in %*	*2009*	*2018*	*Change in %*
No. of FSOEs	87	98	12.6	30	32	6.7	29	36	24.1
OR-FSOEs (bill. €)	474.4	1025.6	116.2	56.1	68.9	22.8	31.4	50.7	61.5
TA-FSOEs (bill. €)	461.2	901.0	95.4	77.6	97.1	25.1	34.0	52.1	53.2
No. of FSOEs/ No. of SOEs (%)	48.9	60.5	23.7	9.8	10.2	4.1	35.0	47.4	35.4
OR-FSOEs/ OR-SOEs (%)	30.5	55.2	81.0	2.3	1.1	–52.2	33.7	33.3	–1.2
OR-FSOEs/ GDP (%)	1.8	2.4	33.3	0.6	0.3	–50.0	4.2	4.1	–2.4

Source: As in Table 7.1.

Table 7.13 Comparison of average shares of SOEs and FSOEs in the Top 100, 2018

	WLEs			*PCEs*
	Total	*DMEs*	*EMEs*	
SS-100	27.4	14.1	46.7	29.1
Share of FSOEs	3.3	4.2	2.0	8.3
Share of FSOEs/SS-100 (%)	12.1	29.8	4.3	28.5

Source: As in Table 7.1.

Table 7.14 Countries with the highest values of some characteristics on FSOEs, 2018

Country	*Group*	*A*	*Country*	*Group*	B	*Country*	*Group*	C
Singapore	DME	14	Germany	DME	195.9	Japan	DME	152.1
Netherlands	DME	11	Singapore	DME	194.1	Netherlands	DME	146.4
Australia	DME	10	UK	DME	127.1	Spain	DME	85.9
Romania	PCE	9	Netherlands	DME	107.0	Germany	DME	72.5
UK	DME	8	Japan	DME	92.9	UK	DME	71.3
Spain	DME	7	Spain	DME	62.7	US	DME	63.3
Italy	DME	7	US	DME	37.8	Australia	DME	62.1
Brazil	EME	7	Italy	DME	37.2	Belgium	DME	52.0
Bulgaria	PCE	7	Australia	DME	34.7	Ireland	DME	41.2
			Ireland	DME	31.5	Singapore	DME	35.5

A - number of FSOEs.
B - the sum of ORs of FSOEs (billion €).
C - the sum of TAs of FSOEs (billion €).
Source: As in Table 7.1.

Table 7.14 lists the countries with the highest number of FSOEs in the Top 100, the highest total value of ORs of FSOEs and the highest total value of TAs of FSOEs in 2018.

The list covering the number of FSOEs, in addition to the dominant DMEs, includes two countries from the PCE group (Romania and Bulgaria) and one country from the EME group - Brazil. The other two lists include only DME countries, especially those with a small share of domestic SOEs in the economy. The data in the middle part of the table confirm the previous research findings that among the EU countries "The most attractive countries for investment [of SOEs] are the United Kingdom [...], Germany and the Netherlands" (Szarzec et al. 2021).

Table 7.15 lists host countries with the highest and lowest value of the ratio of ORs of FSOEs to the ORs of SOEs.

In the left-hand part of the table, there are as many as eight DMEs and two PCEs. In several countries with very low levels of domestic SOEs (the

Table 7.15 Countries with the highest (left side) and lowest (right side) values of the ratio of ORs of FSOEs and ORs of SOEs (%), 2018

Country	*Group*	*OR of FSOEs/ OR of SOEs*	*Country*	*Group*	*OR of FSOEs/ OR of SOEs*
UK	DME	883.2	France	DME	1.0
Netherlands	DME	444.0	Saudi Arabia	EME	1.9
Ireland	DME	380.5	Russia	EME	2.9
Singapore	DME	314.6	Indonesia	EME	3.4
Australia	DME	311.2	Thailand	EME	4.3
Spain	DME	261.1	Argentina	EME	6.4
Romania	PCE	243.3	Norway	DME	7.4
Slovakia	PCE	113.6	Poland	EME	8.8
Germany	DME	83.6	Turkey	EME	11.9
Belgium	DME	72.9	Egypt	EME	12.2

Source: As in Table 7.1.

UK, the Netherlands, Ireland, Australia, Spain), the share of FSOEs is relatively high. The right-hand part of the table is dominated by EMEs. It also includes two DMEs, including France, a country with a high share of domestic SOEs and an extremely low share of FSOEs (one company from Russia). All economies in the right-hand part of the table are characterised by very large or large shares of domestic SOEs. There is a spectacular difference between the UK (at the top of the left-hand part of the table) and France (at the top of the right-hand part of the table) - two highly developed European countries.

Table 7.16 shows the countries with the highest and lowest values of another indicator - the ratio of ORs of FSOEs and GDP. This indicator can be seen as a measure of the importance of FSOEs in the national economy.

At the top of the left-hand part of the table, there are the two countries with the highest number of FSOEs - Singapore and the Netherlands, while three PCEs - Slovakia, Romania and the Czech Republic - also hold high positions. The right-hand part of the table is dominated by EMEs, although the top two positions are occupied by two DMEs - aforementioned France and the US, where there is also one FSOE (from Germany).

The situation in Singapore is symptomatic, where the ORs of FSOEs are more than three times higher than the revenues of domestic SOEs and their value is almost 60% of the national GDP. As many as 84% of these ORs (and 87% of the corresponding TAs) are attributable to nine Chinese FSOEs. It can, therefore, be argued that the economy of Singapore is as if colonised by the SOE from China. There has been a fundamental increase in the share of ORs of Chinese FSOEs during the period under review - from 59% in 2009 to 84% in 2018.

Table 7.17 provides data on the sectoral distribution of FSOEs in both analysed years. The sectoral distribution is somewhat different from the one for SOEs. Although industries typical of state ownership (oil & gas, energy, post & telecommunications) top the table in both years, two other industries - machinery & equipment and chemicals - also have a significant position.

Tables 7.17 and 7.18 contain data on the countries of origin of FSOEs. In this case, of course, the list of countries goes beyond the set of the 37 surveyed economies. Table 7.18 contains data on the various characteristics of the countries of origin of FSOEs.

Two countries - China and France - top all three lists of the countries of origin of FSOEs, by a significant margin. Both countries are characterised by

Table 7.16 Countries with the highest (left side) and lowest (right side) values of the ratio of ORs of FSOEs and GDP (%), 2018

Country	*Group*	*OR of FSOEs/ GDP*	*Country*	*Group*	*OR of FSOEs/ GDP*
Singapore	DME	59.5	France	DME	0.2
Netherlands	DME	13.4	US	DME	0.2
Slovakia	PCE	9.7	Argentina	EME	0.2
Ireland	DME	9.4	Indonesia	EME	0.4
Romania	PCE	9.1	Turkey	EME	0.7
Germany	DME	5.7	Russia	EME	0.8
UK	DME	5.1	Brazil	EME	1.1
Spain	DME	5.0	Saudi Arabia	EME	1.1
Czech Republic	PCE	4.2	Poland	EME	1.5
Austria	DME	4.1	Thailand	EME	1.5

Source: As in Table 7.1.

Table 7.17 Sectoral distribution of FSOEs, 2009, 2018

	Number of LSOEs	
	2009	*2018*
Oil & gas	41	45
Energy	25	35
Post & telecomm.	23	22
Machinery & equipment	24	15
Chemicals	11	14
Transport	5	13
Agribusiness	7	8
Other	7	9
In total	143	161

Source: As in Table 7.1.

a high share of SOEs and a very low (France) or zero (China) share of FSOEs in their economies. The sets include three countries outside the 32 WLEs (the United Arab Emirates, Finland, Qatar), all with a large share of SOEs in the economy.

Interesting findings emerge from comparing the changes in the number of FSOEs by country of origin between 2009 and 2018. These changes - in different directions - generally were not large, around 1–2 entities, while the change for China was enormous - from 13 FSOEs in 2009 to 32 in 2018. The ORs of FSOEs of Chinese origin increased almost sixfold during this period (from €51.8 billion to €304.5 billion). While in 2009, the ORs of FSOEs of Chinese origin accounted for about 9% of the ORs of all FSOEs, in 2018, it was as much as 27%.

Table 7.19 shows the geographical distribution of FSOEs from the countries with the highest number of them.

Table 7.18 Countries of origin of FSOEs with the highest values of some characteristics concerning FSOEs, 2018

Country	*Group*	*A*	*Country*	*Group*	*B*	*Country*	*Group*	*C*
China	EME	32	China	EME	304.5	France	DME	352.2
France	DME	29	France	DME	225.1	China	EME	134.3
Italy	DME	15	Finland	DME	86.0	Italy	DME	90.7
UAE	EME	9	Saudi Arabia	EME	74.8	Germany	DME	76.9
Austria	DME	9	UAE	EME	57.5	Saudi Arabia	EME	62.8
Germany	DME	8	Italy	DME	52.8	Brazil	EME	54.9
Japan	DME	8	Germany	DME	46.7	Finland	DME	52.0
Saudi Arabia	EME	5	Sweden	DME	41.8	Qatar	EME	49.1
Russia	EME	5	Qatar	EME	30.1	UAE	EME	44.9
			Norway	DME	29.3	Singapore	DME	19.7

A - number of FSOEs.
B - the sum of ORs of FSOEs (billion €).
C - the sum of TAs of FSOEs (billion €).
Source: As in Table 7.1.

Table 7.19 Host countries for the FSOEs with the highest number of FSOEs, 2018

Country of origin	*No. of FSOEs*	*No. of host countries*	*Host country with the highest number of FSOEs*
China	32	14	Singapore - 9, Australia - 4, UK - 4, Brazil - 3
France	29	17	Belgium - 3, Italy - 3, Netherlands - 3, Romania - 3
Italy	15	9	Brazil - 3, Spain - 3

Source: As in Table 7.1.

The 32 FSOEs of Chinese origin operate in 14 countries around the world, including 16 FSOEs in 11 European countries. Of the 29 FSOEs of French origin, as many as 23 operate in various European countries.

We conclude our analysis by presenting (Table 7.20) a list of the 20 largest FSOEs in the 37 economies analysed by ORs.

It is important to note that, on average, FSOEs were significantly smaller than SOEs - in 2018, the average OR in the FSOE group was €4.76 billion, which was three times less than in the SOEs group (€15.0 billion). In the case of TAs, the difference was 4.5 times.

For about half of the companies in the list, a very large difference between the OR value and the TA value is noticeable. This is most likely due to the fact that FSOEs are largely trading companies whose business is to deliver home country products to the market of the host country and not to undertake manufacturing activities in the host country.

Table 7.20 List of the 20 largest (by ORs) FSOEs[a], 2018

No.	*Name of the SOE*	*Industry*	*OR (bill. €)*	*TA (bill. €)*	*Host country*	*Home country*
1	Nissan Motor	Automotive	92.9	152.1	Japan	France
2	Uniper	Energy	84.5	50.6	Germany	Finland
3	Vattenfall Energy Trad.	Energy	38.0	4.8	Germany	Sweden
4	T-Mobile US	Post & telecomm.	37.8	63.3	US	Germany
5	CNOOC Trading	Oil & gas	36.2	1.8	Singapore	China
6	Sinochem Internat. Oil	Chemicals	32.4	2.0	Singapore	China
7	Petrochina Internat.	Oil & gas	30.2	6.9	Singapore	China
8	Sinochem Internat. Oil	Chemicals	29.2	2.0	UK	China
9	Petroineos Trading	Oil & gas	26.7	3.0	UK	China
10	Statkraft Markets	Energy	25.6	1.6	Germany	Norway
11	Comp. Espanola De Petrol.	Oil & gas	24.8	13.2	Spain	UAE
12	Aramco Overseas.	Oil & gas	24.6	24.1	Netherlands	Saudi Arabia
13	Unipec UK	Oil & gas	24.3	1.7	UK	China
14	SABIC International	Oil & gas	24.3	19.1	Netherlands	Saudi Arabia
15	Endesa	Energy	20.2	31.7	Spain	Italy
16	S-Oil Corporation	Oil & gas	19.9	12.5	Korea	Saudi Arabia
17	TenneT TSO	Energy	19.1	6.1	Germany	Netherlands
18	Wingas	Oil & gas	18.2	2.4	Germany	Russia
19	China Aviation Oil	Oil & gas	18.0	1.4	Singapore	China
20	Petrobras Global Trad.	Oil & gas	15.0	54.9	Netherlands	Brazil

a Based on our data. Non-financial companies only.
Source: As in Table 7.1.

7.3 Econometric and cluster analysis[3]

7.3.1 Introductory remarks

At the end of our deliberations, we will present the results of a statistical-econometric analysis of the relationships between indicators describing the state's ownership stake in the business sector (share ratios) and indicators characterising the "environment of SOEs", i.e. the socio-economic system and the institutional environment. Because this problem, which is very important in itself, goes beyond the basic objectives of the book, and because of the volume requirements of the book, we limit ourselves only to a summary presentation of the issue.

We focus our attention on the impact of the environment on share ratios but some of the results obtained are ambiguous as to the basic direction of the relationship. The study used three groups of variables (109 indicators in total):

1 Indicators characterising state ownership share (all share ratios of SOEs used in the book): SS-100, SS-20, Rev-100/GDP, Rev-20/GDP, CS-20, number of SOEs in the Top 100, Top 50, Top 20, Top 10, number of central SOEs (CSOEs), number of miSOEs, number of LSOEs, SS-I. The SS-I indicator was only available for 2018 and all other indicators were defined for 2009 and 2018. We have also introduced indicators describing the dynamics (change between 2009 and 2018) of the listed share ratios.
2 Quantitative indicators characterising the socio-economic system: Nominal GDP per capita (GDP-PC), HDI, national debt to GDP ratio (ND-GDP), national debt per capita (ND-PC), all for the years 2009 and 2018 and, additionally, indicators describing the dynamics (change between 2009 and 2018) of the listed quantitative indicators.
3 Indicators characterising the quality of the country's institutional system, also for the years 2009 and 2018, and, separately, indicators of their dynamics. This group of indicators consisted of two subgroups:
   A Worldwide Governance Indicators (WGI) by the World Bank (focusing on institutional aspects of the economy): Voice and Accountability, Political Stability No Violence, Government Effectiveness, Regulatory Quality, Rule of Law, Control of Corruption and the Score of WGI – a variable we created (the arithmetic mean of the above six indicators – S-WGI),
   B Index of Economic Freedom (IEF) by the Heritage Foundation (focusing on legal regulations and other determinants of economic freedom) and its component indicators describing freedom in 12 core areas: Property Rights, Judicial Effectiveness, Government Integrity, Tax Burden, Government Spending, Fiscal Health, Business Freedom, Labour Freedom, Monetary Freedom, Trade Freedom, Investment Freedom, Financial Freedom.

A detailed description of the WGI indicators is included in http://www.govindicators.org/ and the IEF indicators in https://www.heritage.org/index/

To gain an insight into general statistical relationships and possibly to select variables for deeper research, a Pearson correlation analysis of the above-mentioned indicators was carried out for three sets:

1 All economies studied, i.e. 32 WLEs and 5 PCEs,
2 The set of 19 DMEs,
3 The set of 13 EMEs and 5 PCEs.

The PCE set was too small for a separate analysis, and – as it turned out – its combination with the EME set did not significantly affect the outcome of the study.

The analysis showed that:

1 The variables describing state ownership involvement are highly correlated with each other, so most of them can be excluded from further analysis. This particularly applied to the variables describing the numerical share of SOEs in individual "Tops", which gave almost identical correlation coefficients with the variables of groups 2 and 3.
2 The variables describing state ownership dynamics correlate poorly with "environment" variables, so they can also be generally omitted from the in-depth analysis. To a large extent, this also applied to variables describing the dynamics of the "environment".
3 Variables expressing volumes in relation to GDP tended to have a poor or negligible correlation with other variables, so they were excluded from further analyses.

7.3.2 Basic correlations and conclusions

Table 7.21 shows the results of the correlation analysis for the set of the 37 studied economies for the most important selected indicators. Analogous tables, with the same indicators, were made for the other two sets.

The correlation analysis produced some interesting results:

1 There is a very large difference between the number of significant correlations (at the level of at least 0.05) between the set of 37 economies and the other two sets. For the whole set, statistically significant correlations were 7–10 times more frequent than in the other two sets of economies under review.
2 For the set of 37 economies, the analysis showed a strong negative correlation (with high significance levels) of the basic share ratios of SOEs for 2018 (SS-100, SS-20, Top 100) with qualitative indicators – HDI, S-WGI and S-IEF – as well as GDP-PC with a positive correlation with dynamics of public debt per capita. It can be argued that this is a result

Table 7.21 Pearson correlation for the set of the 37 countries analysed

	SS-100 _2018	*SS-20 _2018*	*Rev-100 _2018*	*Rev-20 _2018*	*CS-20 _2018*	*Top 100 _2018*	*Top 50 _2018*	*Top 20 _2018*	*Top 10 _2018*	*SI*
GDP-PC_2018	–.506**	–.496**	–.183	-.217	–.491**	–.401*	–.478**	–.502**	–.476**	–.340*
HDI_2018	–.551**	–.542**	–.211	-.222	–.427**	–.515**	–.528**	–.541**	–.490**	–.445**
D-GDP_2018	–.241	–.207	–.251	-.274	–.058	–.154	–.170	–.149	–.212	–.262
ND-PC_2018	–.503**	–.484**	–.273	-.314	–.375*	–.395*	–.443**	–.444**	–.440**	–.421**
S-WGI_2018	–.663**	–.635**	–.356*	-.390*	–.436**	–.537**	–.591**	–.606**	–.613**	–.479**
S-IEF_2018	–.632**	–.618**	–.303	–.347*	–.495**	–.526**	–.574**	–.580**	–.580**	–.481**
HDI_Dyn	.519**	.464**	.331*	.279	.282	.587**	.584**	.527**	.530**	.528**
GDP-PC_Dyn	.386*	.324	.361*	.230	.022	.582**	.554**	.503**	.398*	.474**
ND-PC_Dyn	.270	.190	.175	.090	–.140	.456**	.428**	.357*	.249	.202

* Correlation is significant at the 0.05 level (2-tailed).
** Correlation is significant at the 0.01 level (2-tailed).
Source: Own calculations.

consistent with the liberal view on the economy – a better economy and better institutional environment, as well as greater economic freedom, is accompanied by a lower share of SOEs and therefore lower state influence on the economy.

3. At the same time, a strong positive correlation was found between several indicators describing the scope of the SOE sector (Top 100...etc. and SS-I) and indicators of growth and socio-economic development (HDI_Dyn and GDP-PC_Dyn). This is probably a manifestation of the dependencies in EMEs and PCEs described below.
4. For the set of 19 DMEs, the analysis showed a fairly significant correlation (negative) only for the S-IEF indicator. This seems to be an interesting result as it means that in the case of highly developed countries, the degree of state ownership involvement in the business sector is primarily related to the extent of economic freedom (in various dimensions). However, in general, the scope of SOEs shows no relationship with either the level of socio-economic development of the country or the quality of the institutional setup.
5. For the set of 18 EMEs + PCEs, the results of the analysis were quite surprising. A relationship (positive) between some variables describing the SOE sector (mainly quantitative: Top-100, Top-50 and Top-20) and the dynamics of socio-economic indicators, such as HDI, GDP per capita and public debt per capita, was demonstrated. Contrary to expectations, only one indicator correlates (also positively but with a not very high level of significance) with WGI and IEF: the presence of SOEs in strategic sectors – SS-I. This means that, in general, it can be presumed that countries in this group with higher dynamics of socio-economic processes also have a larger state sector. The question – why this is so – remains open.

Interestingly, the study for the set of 37 countries showed that the score of WGI (the arithmetic mean) was the only one to exhibit a significant negative correlation with all 10 SOEs (for eight indicators at the 0.01 level, 2-tailed and 2 indicators at the 0.05 level, 2-tailed). Figure 7.1 illustrates the strongest correlation recorded, i.e. the score of WGI and SS-100.

7.3.3 Regression analysis

A multiple linear regression analysis was performed to explain how the value of the dependent variables (share ratios of SOEs) is affected by the independent variables (indicators characterising the socio-economic system and indicators characterising the quality of the country's institutional system).

Three dependent variables were used, selected based on the correlation analysis: SS-100 in 2018, change (dynamics) in SS-100 from 2009 to 2018, SS-I. When it comes to independent variables, all the previously mentioned indicators for 2018 from the second and third groups were used. Additionally,

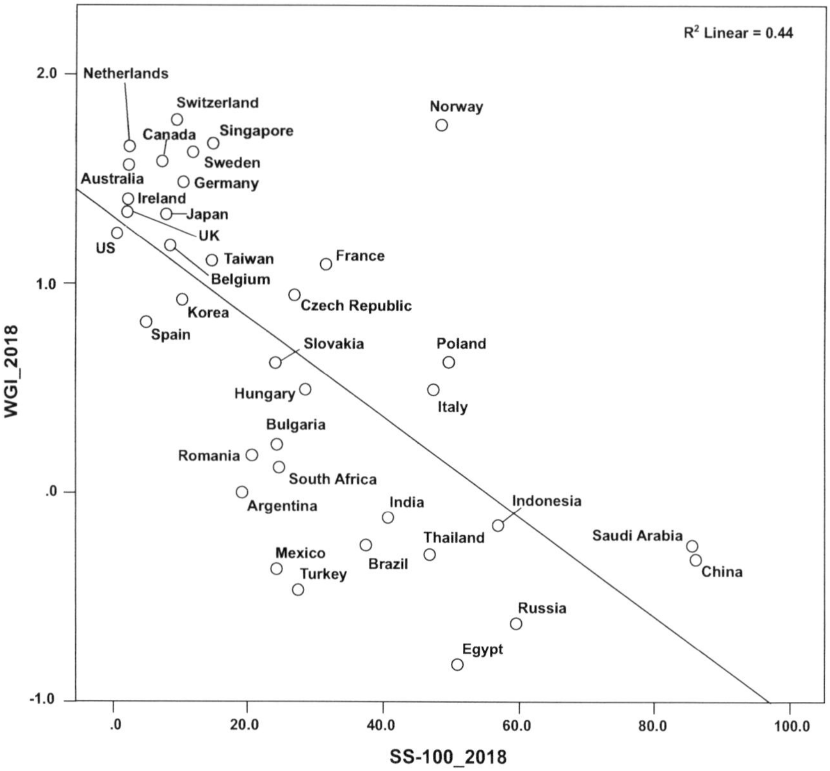

Figure 7.1 Score of WGI and SS-100 in 2018.
Source: Own calculations.

three indicators were used describing the membership of each of the three sets of countries studied. A stepwise analysis method was applied.

The results of the study can be summarised as follows:

1 In the set of 37 countries, the IEF Investment Freedom variable proved to be the strongest predictor (with a negative correlation) for the SS-100 and SS-I variables (explaining more than half of the variance). Additionally, models were built for the SS-100 taking into account (according to decreasing importance) WGI Voice and Accountability, IEF Government Spending and IEF Trade Freedom. Together they explain more than 3/4 of the variance, which is a lot. The SS-100 dynamics index performed poorly, the only predictor being IEF Investment Freedom with a low significance of Adjusted R Square (just 0.136).
2 In the set of DMEs, the only predictor (also negative) for the SS-100 turned out to be IEF Financial Freedom, with just over 1/3 of the

variance explained. In the case of the SS-I indicator, the IEF Fiscal Health indicator was also almost equally important, together explaining almost 2/3 of the variance. The analysis for the SS-100 dynamics could not be carried out – there were no relevant correlations.

3 In the set of EMEs + PCEs the picture was quite different. For SS-100, WGI Voice and Accountability turned out to be the most important predictor (over half of the variance), followed by IEF Government Integrity in the second place and IEF Investment Freedom in the third. A model including all three indicators explains more than 3/4 of the variance. For the SS-I variable, IEF Investment Freedom turned out to be the most important predictor (as much as over 2/3 of the variance); in addition, the programme selected models that also included WGI Voice and Accountability and WGI Rule of Law. Together this explains as much as over 4/5 of the variance. The dynamics of SS-100 turned out to be to some extent positively dependent (about 1/4 of the explained variance) on the size of public debt relative to GDP.

Overall, the results of the regression analysis confirmed and further highlighted the observations made during the correlation analysis. The indicators concerning the quality of governance and economic freedoms as explanations for the shares of SOEs in the economy within the set of 37 countries are far more relevant than the indicators describing the socio-economic situation in both quantitative and qualitative terms. However, the situation is different within the two separate smaller sets, i.e. DMEs and EMEs + PCEs.

In the DME set, the size of the SOE sector does not really depend on the indicators of the environment, especially the institutional determinants of the quality of governance. All of the observed correlations, which are relatively weak, relate only to the restrictions on economic freedom. It even seems that the correlation found may be reversed in terms of cause and effect: it is the larger sector of SOEs, especially in strategic sectors, that leads to certain restrictions on economic freedom. To confirm this hypothesis, an additional analysis would need to be conducted in which the dependent variables would be the indicators of economic freedom and the predictors would be the indicators of the scope of the SOE sector.

In the EME + PCE group, on the other hand, indicators relating to the quality of governance come to the fore – and perhaps this points primarily to a direct cause-and-effect relation: in this group of countries the SOE sector is larger and more important where there are problems with democratic mechanisms, transparency of politicians' and governments' actions, rule of law, corruption, etc. This situation results in limiting economic freedom, above all when it comes to investing – expanding state, as Barbara Błaszczyk (2017) puts it, "crowds out" private investments. This applies particularly to strategic sectors. Moreover, it is only in this group that a relationship between the change in the size of the SOE sector and the economic situation can be observed: the SOE sector is more likely to increase in more indebted

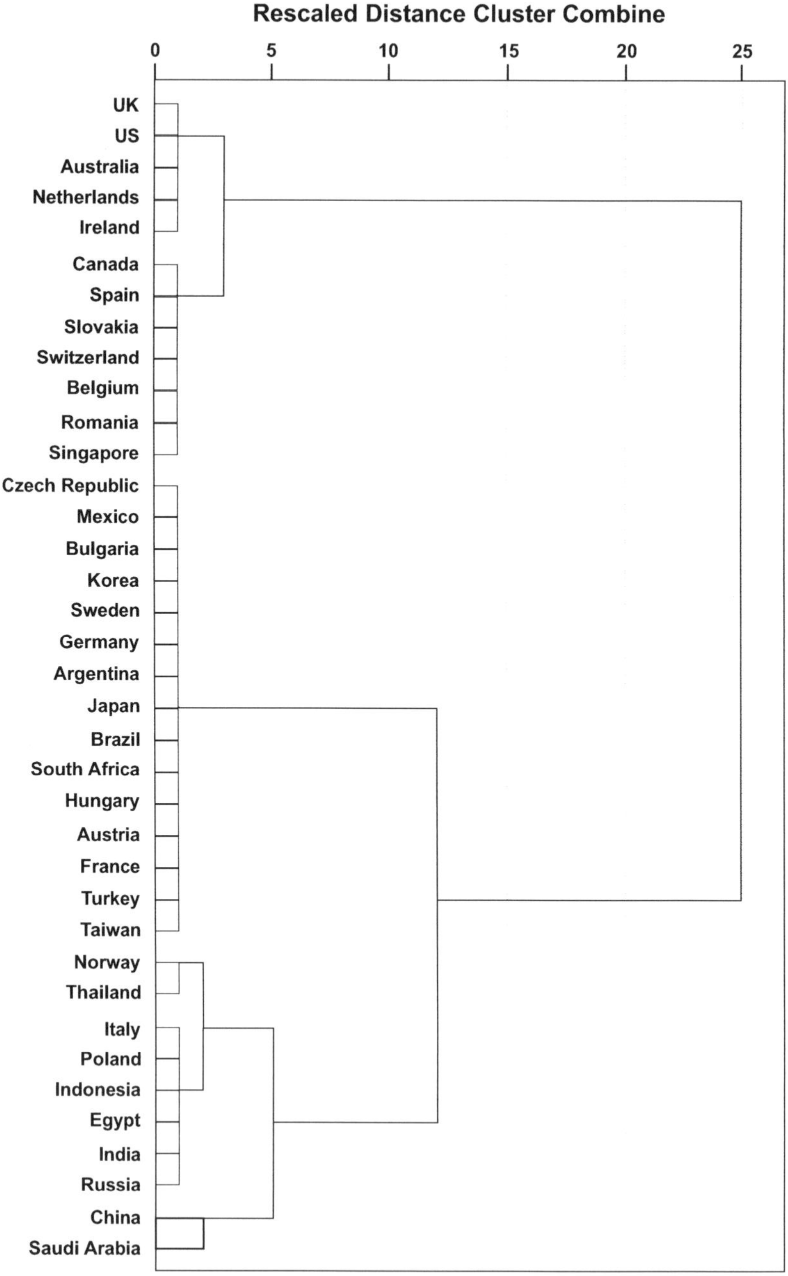

Figure 7.2 Results of the hierarchical cluster analysis for the group of 37 countries surveyed.

Source: Own calculations.

economies. It is not clear what is the cause and what is the effect. Perhaps it is the growth of the SOE sector that is causing more debt. Deciphering the direction of this relationship would also require a deeper analysis.

7.3.4 Cluster analysis

Based on the data characterising the share of the SOE sector in the economy, a cluster analysis was conducted to group the 37 economies studied. Using the results of the correlation analysis, five indicators for 2018 – SS-100, SS-20, Rev-100/GDP, number of SOEs in Top-100, SS-I – were selected for the analysis. The results are presented in Figure 7.2.

Table 7.22 Countries with very high and high shares of SOEs

No.	*Country*	*Group*	*SS-100*	*No. of SOEs*	*SS-I*
Very high share of SOEs					
1	China	EME	85.9	78	3.83
2	Saudi Arabia	EME	85.3	22	3.33
High share of SOEs					
1	Russia	EME	59.6	33	3.17
2	Indonesia	EME	57.0	19	3.00
3	Egypt	EME	50.6	37	2.83
4	Poland	EME/PCE	49.6	20	2.33
5	Norway	DME	48.4	18	3.17
6	Italy	DME	47.4	16	2.17
7	Thailand	EME	46.5	32	3.00
8	India	EME	40.7	21	3.00

Source: Own calculations.

Table 7.23 Countries with an average share of SOEs

No.	*Country*	*Group*	*SS-100*	*No. of SOEs*	*SS-I*
1	Brazil	EME	37.1	14	2.17
2	France	DME	31.5	14	2.17
3	Austria	DME	31.4	16	2.17
4	Hungary	PCE	29.0	13	2.17
5	Turkey	EME	27.4	18	2.00
6	Czech Republic	PCE	26.9	9	1.50
7	South Africa	EME	24.6	10	2.17
8	Bulgaria	PCE	24.2	9	1.67
9	Mexico	EME	23.7	3	1.50
10	Argentina	EME	19.3	7	2.17
11	Taiwan	DME	14.7	9	3.00
12	Sweden	DME	14.6	11	2.00
13	Germany	DME	10.4	8	1.83
14	Korea	DME	10.3	7	2.00
15	Japan	DME	7.9	5	1.83

Source: Own calculations.

Table 7.24 Countries with a low share of SOEs

No.	Country	Group	SS-100	No. of SOEs	SS-I
1	Slovakia	PCE	24.1	13	2.17
2	Romania	PCE	20.6	12	1.83
3	Singapore	DME	11.9	7	2.00
4	Switzerland	DME	9.4	11	2.33
5	Belgium	DME	8.5	10	2.17
6	Canada	DME	7.4	7	1.17
7	Spain	DME	5.0	6	1.17

Source: Own calculations.

Table 7.25 Countries with a very low share of SOEs

No.	Country	Group	SS-100	No. of SOEs	SS-I
1	Ireland	DME	2.3	6	1.50
2	Netherlands	DME	2.3	4	1.17
3	UK	DME	2.3	2	0.50
4	Australia	DME	2.2	4	1.00
5	US	DME	0.6	1	0.67

Source: Own calculations.

The results of the cluster analysis confirm our earlier intuitions. The studied set of 37 economies can be divided into five groups of countries based on the share of SOEs in the Top 100 non-financial companies – (Table 7.22-7.24). Two other important indicators – number of SOEs in the Top 100 and SS-I – are also included.

7.4 Summary and conclusions

1. Listed SOEs, government-controlled mixed-ownership entities whose stocks are listed on stock exchanges, represent a very large, almost 50%, share of the world's largest SOEs. They are found in 29 out of the 37 economies analysed. There are no LSOEs in five DMEs (Australia, Ireland, the Netherlands, the UK, the US), one EME (Mexico) and two PCEs (Bulgaria, Slovakia), i.e. countries with a low share of SOEs in the economy. The countries with the relatively largest number and greatest importance of LSOEs include both EMEs (China, Russia, India, Brazil) and DMEs (Italy, France).
2. Between 2009 and 2018, the number of LSOEs in the DME group remained unchanged (67) and in the EME group, it decreased by 14 (from 178 to 164), while the number of LSOEs in China decreased by exactly the same number (from 59 to 45). The reason for this may be the increasing control of the Chinese government over SOEs in recent years and the faster increase in the number of very large Chinese SOEs with

100% state ownership than that of listed companies with mixed capital. In the PCE group, the number of SOEs grew from 11 to 19, mainly in Poland and Romania.

3 In the set of 231 LSOEs from WLEs in 2018, there were 76 (almost 33%) miLSOEs, i.e. companies actually controlled by governments holding minority ownership stakes. There were significant differences here between the groups of countries analysed. In DMEs, miLSOEs accounted for 54% of all LSOEs, in PCEs for 50% and EMEs for only 24%.

4 In the case of several EMEs, the share of LSOEs in the capitalisation of national stock exchanges (among the 30 largest listed companies) was very significant in 2018. In China, it was 87%, in Poland 71%, in Saudi Arabia 69% and in Russia 51%. Among DMEs, the Milan (42%), Vienna (31%) and Paris (15%) stock exchanges showed the highest share of LSOEs in capitalisation.

5 In the 2018 Top 100 lists from 37 countries, we found 161 FSOEs, i.e. entities controlled directly or indirectly by foreign governments. There were no FSOEs in two DMEs (Canada, Taiwan) and three EMEs (China, India, Mexico). In turn, most FSOEs were in countries with a low share of domestic SOEs – Singapore, the Netherlands, Australia, Romania and the UK.

6 In terms of the country of origin of FSOEs, two countries are by far the leaders – China (32 entities) and France (29 entities). Both countries are characterised by a high share of domestic SOEs and a very low (France) or zero (China) share of FSOEs in their economies. The sets of FSOEs' countries of origin include three countries outside the 32 WLEs (the United Arab Emirates, Finland, Qatar), all with large shares of SOEs in their economies.

7 Between 2009 and 2019, the number of FSOEs in the 37 economies studied increased by 13%, mainly in PCEs and DMEs. In the EME group (except Poland), it remained unchanged. Changes in the number of FSOEs by country of origin were small, except for China, where the change was significant – from 13 FSOEs in 2009 to 32 nine years later. The ORs of FSOEs of Chinese origin increased almost sixfold during this period (from €51.8 billion to €304.5 billion). This is a clear sign of the increasing expansion of China's SOEs outside the country.

8 In the last part of the book, an abbreviated statistical-econometric analysis was conducted to examine the relationships between the socio-economic system and institutional environment of each country and the scope of SOEs. Detailed conclusions are presented in Section 7.3. The analysis confirmed the main notion emerging from our research regarding the fundamental diversity of SOEs in the analysed countries and country groups. This diversity manifests itself primarily not in the quantitative dimension but the dimension of the functions and roles of SOEs in the economic system.

9 A correlation analysis, further confirmed by a linear regression analysis, showed radically different significant relationships between indicators

characterising the scope of SOEs and indicators characterising the "environment" of SOEs within the two sets of economies studied – the set of 19 DMEs and the set consisting of 13 EMEs and 5 PCEs. In the DME set, the size of the SOE sector does not really depend on the indicators of the environment, especially the institutional determinants of the quality of governance. In turn, in the EME + PCE set, the SOE sector is larger and more important where problems with democratic mechanisms, transparency of politicians' and governments' actions, rule of law, corruption, etc., occur.

10 Using five basic indicators describing the shares of SOEs in the economy in 2018 (SS-100, SS-20, Rev-100/GDP, number of SOEs in the Top 100, SS-I), a cluster analysis was conducted. Its results made it possible to divide the examined set of 37 economies into five groups – countries with a very high (2), high (8), average (15), low (7) and very low (5) share of SOEs in the economy.

Notes

1 Sometimes for LSOEs the term "hybrid SOEs" is used in the literature (Vining & Laurin, 2020, p. 413).

2 This view is perfectly illustrated in a recent article with the telling title: China's State-Owned Enterprises: Instruments of Its Foreign Strategy? (Nie, 2021).

3 Section 3.3 owes much to the substantive assistance of Professor Piotr Kozarzewski.

Bibliography

Abramov, A., Radygin, A., & Chernova, M. (2017). State-Owned Enterprises in the Russian Market: Ownership Structure and Their Role in the Economy. *Russian Journal of Economics*, *3*(1), 1–23.

Arocena, P., & Oliveros, D. (2012). The Efficiency of State-Owned and Privatized Firms: Does Ownership Make a Difference? *International Journal of Production Economics*, *140*(1), 457–465.

Baltowski, M. (2017). Więcej władzy niż własności – Skarb Państwa jako szczególny inwestor na GPW w Warszawie [More Control Than Ownership: State as a Specific Investor on Warsaw Stock Exchange]. *Studia Ekonomiczne*, 1(92), 27–45.

Baltowski, M., & Kwiatkowski, G. (2018). *Przedsiębiorstwa państwowe we współczesnej gospodarce* [State-Owned Enterprises in the Modern Economy]. Warszawa: WN PWN.

Blaszczyk, B. (2017). Privatization Reversal and Crowding Out the Private Business. Polish Examples. *3rd SVOC International Conference 'The Role of State in Varieties of Capitalism', CEU, Budapest, December* 1.

Bruton, G. D., Peng, M. W., Ahlstrom, D., Stan, C., & Xu, K. (2015). State-Owned Enterprises Around the World as Hybrid Organizations. *Academy of Management Perspectives*, *29*(1), 92–114.

Carney, R. W., & Child, T. B. (2013). Changes to the Ownership and Control of East Asian Corporations Between 1996 and 2008: The Primacy of Politics. *Journal of Financial Economics*, *107*(2), 494–513.

Cuervo-Cazurra, A. (Ed.). (2018). *State-Owned Multinationals: Governments in Global Business*. Cham: Palgrave MacMillan.

Cuervo-Cazurra, A., Inkpen, A., Musacchio, A., & Ramaswamy, K. (2014). Governments as Owners: State-Owned Multinational Companies. *Journal of International Business Studies, 45*(8), 919–942.

De La Cruz, A., Medina, A., & Tang, Y. (2019). *Owners of the World's Listed Companies*. OECD Capital Market Series. Paris: OECD.

Estrin, S., Li, J., & Shapiro, D. M. (2021). State-Owned Multinational Enterprises: Theory, Performance, and Impact. In K. Mellahi, K. Meyer, R. Narula, I. Surdu, & A. Verbeke (Eds.), *The Oxford Handbook of International Business Strategy*. Oxford: Oxford University Press.

Kabaciński, B., Kubiak, J., & Szarzec, K. (2020). Do State-Owned Enterprises Underperform Compared to Privately Owned Companies? An Examination of the Largest Polish Enterprises. *Emerging Markets Finance and Trade, 56*(13), 3174.

Lin, C., Ma, Y., & Su, D. (2009). Corporate Governance and Firm Efficiency: Evidence from China's Publicly Listed Firms. *Managerial and Decision Economics, 30*(3), 193–209.

Lin, K. J., Lu, X., Zhang, J., & Zheng, Y. (2020). State-Owned Enterprises in China: A Review of 40 Years of Research and Practice. *China Journal of Accounting Research, 13*(1), 31–55.

Meyer, K. E., Ding, Y., Li, J., & Zhang, H. (2018). Overcoming Distrust: How State-Owned Enterprises Adapt Their Foreign Entries to Institutional Pressures Abroad. In A. Cuervo-Cazurra (Ed.), *State-Owned Multinationals*. Cham: Palgrave MacMillan.

Milhaupt, C. J., & Pargendler, M. (2017). Governance Challenges of Listed State-Owned Enterprises Around the World: National Experiences and a Framework for Reform. *Cornell International Law Journal, 50*(3), 473.

Musacchio, A., & Lazzarini, S. G. (2014). *Reinventing State Capitalism: Leviathan in Business, Brazil and Beyond*. Cambridge, MA: Harvard University Press.

Nie, W. (2021). China's State-Owned Enterprises: Instruments of Its Foreign Strategy? *Journal of Contemporary China*. https://www.tandfonline.com/action/showCitFormats?doi=10.1080%2F10670564.2021.1966897&area=0000000000000001

OECD. (2012). *Competitive Neutrality: Maintaining a Level Playing Field Between Public and Private Business*. Paris: OECD Publishing.

OECD. (2016). *State-Owned Enterprises as Global Competitors: A Challenge or an Opportunity?* Paris: OECD Publishing.

Pargendler, M. (2011). State Ownership and Corporate Governance. *Fordham L. Rev., 80*, 2917.

Putniņš, T. J. (2020). State-Owned Enterprises and the Public Mission: A Multidimensional Lens. In L. Bernier, M. Florio, & P. Bance (Eds.), *The Routledge Handbook of State-Owned Enterprises*. London; New York: Routledge.

Szarzec, K., Nowara, W., & Totleben, B. (2021). State-Owned Enterprises as Foreign Direct Investors: Insights from EU Countries. *Post-Communist Economies, 33*(5), 517–540.

UNCTAD. (2019). *World Investment Report 2019*. United Nations Conference on Trade and Development (UNCTAD) World Investment Report (WIR). New York: United Nations Publications.

Vining, A., & Laurin, C. (2020). State-Owned Enterprise Hybrids. In L. Bernier, M. Florio, & P. Bance (Eds.), *The Routledge Handbook of State-Owned Enterprises*. London; New York: Routledge.

Wei, C. (2021). State Ownership and Target Setting: Evidence from Publicly Listed Companies in China. *Contemporary Accounting Research*, *38*(3), 1925.

Wei, Z., & Nguyen, Q. T. (2017). Subsidiary Strategy of Emerging Market Multinationals: A Home Country Institutional Perspective. *International Business Review*, *26*(5), 1009–1021.

Yu, M. (2013). State Ownership and Firm Performance: Empirical Evidence from Chinese Listed Companies. *China Journal of Accounting Research*, *6*(2), 75–87.

Final remarks

The main objective of the analysis in the book was to determine the place and structure (in terms of size, type, geography, industry, etc.) of state-owned enterprises (SOEs) in the global economy, as well as changes in this area after the 2008–2009 financial crisis. We have also considered - mainly in light of the results of our research - some important issues related to the existence of SOEs - their origin, functions and relationship with the state owner. Our empirical research included 32 world's largest economies, divided into developed market economies (DMEs) and emerging markets economies (EMEs) and an additional five post-communist economies (PCEs) and it was based on several methodological assumptions, presented in detail in Chapter 3, two of which are the most important. The first assumption is that the set of companies studied is narrowed down to the 100 largest non-financial companies from each country. The second is that SOEs are distinguished from the analysed sets following a special individualised procedure, according to the criterion of actual – direct or indirect – control of the government over a given enterprise.

Detailed conclusions of the analysis are presented at the end of each chapter (except for Chapters 4 and 5 which contain country-specific figures). Here, we will try to formulate four general conclusions related to the phenomenon of SOEs in the contemporary economy. They derive mainly from the analysis in the book, but also draw on the authors' previous studies on SOEs and the findings of other researchers.

Global diversity of SOEs

The basic, striking conclusion is that the scope and consequently the economic importance of SOEs is highly diversified globally. This diversity is particularly evident when dividing the set of the world's largest economies into DMEs and EMEs and occurs in virtually every area examined - the number of SOEs in the Top 100, the number of SOEs in the narrow Top 20, the share of SOEs in the operating revenues and total assets of the groups examined, the ratio of SOEs' revenues to GDP. The differences between DMEs and EMEs, analysed in detail in Chapter 6, are best illustrated by the comparison of the two largest and most important economies in the world today – the US and China,

DOI: 10.4324/9781003244462-9

referred to in the Introduction. In the former, there are few SOEs present, and their economic importance is marginal. In the second their presence is enormous and their role in the economy is just as significant.

The scope of SOEs is diversified not only in the EMEs-DMEs dimension but also within the DME group. While in the EME group all countries studied show either a very high or a high presence of SOEs, this is not the case in the DME group. Among DMEs, there are countries with a relatively large share of SOEs but also countries with a negligible share. Of the 19 DMEs analysed, four clearly stand out from the others in terms of the scope of SOEs - Norway, Italy, France and Austria. When we compare these four countries with another four DMEs - Sweden, Spain, Germany, the Netherlands - which are very similar to them in terms of their size, level of development and quality of life, the difference between the presence of SOEs and their importance in these two small groups is striking. We identified 64 SOEs in the first group of four countries and 29 SOEs in the second. In the former group, the average share of SOEs in the Top 100 (as measured by the SS-100 index) was 39.7%, and in the latter group only 8.1%. When comparing a narrow set of the largest companies (Top 20), the differences between these groups are even more pronounced – in the number of SOEs 20 vs. 6 and in the share of SOEs 50% vs. 8%.

However, despite these fundamental differences when it comes to the scope of SOEs, there are no differences, at least no radical ones, between the two groups of countries in terms of the level of economic development or quality of life. The econometric analysis carried out in Section 7.3 confirms this observation. Both in the cross section of DMEs-EMEs and especially within the DME group, there are no clear correlations between the scope of SOEs in the country (shares of SOEs in the economy) and indicators characterising the level and dynamics of development or the level of social welfare.

A fundamental question then arises: how to explain this peculiar insensitivity, or at least low sensitivity, of the quality of the economic system (level of economic development or level of welfare) to the scale and extent of the presence of SOEs in the economy? Is the scope of SOEs irrelevant? There seems to be no single and easy answer to these questions, as it is different for highly developed countries with well-established institutional systems and the rule of law, and different for developing countries, usually with flawed democracies, weak institutions and authoritarian tendencies of governments. Indeed, it is not the quantitative parameters – the scale, range or scope of SOEs – that constitute important factors differentiating economies globally, but the qualitative parameters, primarily the range of functions performed by SOEs in the economy.

Functional diversity of SOEs on a global scale

The differentiation between SOEs in DMEs, i.e. the de facto developed countries of the West, and SOEs in EMEs, i.e. mainly the countries once referred to as the Third World, becomes fully evident when we name the

SOEs in these two groups of countries – allowing for some idealisation – using two different terms, according to their actual function and place in the economy. In fact, SOEs in the DME group and SOEs in the EME group are two different elements of the economic system; they differ in many dimensions. This view, fundamental in light of the results of our research, is generally insufficiently taken into account in analyses of SOEs.

SOEs in the DME group can be described as "public enterprises", where a public enterprise is a common good belonging indirectly to all citizens. It is an element of national wealth that is looked after by the government. The purpose of the public enterprise is to perform various socially useful functions, mainly of an economic nature, often resulting from an established historical legacy. Although usually the efficiency of public enterprises does not match that of private entities, they operate under clearly defined rules and are subject to democratic control procedures.

SOEs in the EME group can be described as "government enterprises", where a government enterprise is an economic entity owned by the government or, more broadly, by the party in power. It is a form of political spoils accruing to the current state authorities and their actual ownership. The purpose of the government enterprise is to carry out functions assigned directly by the government. The range of these functions is relatively wide, as we wrote in Section 2.3. It covers both economic and non-economic functions, including predatory functions, which means treating such entities as sources of political rent. The efficiency of government enterprises, in general, does not have to be lower than that of similar private enterprises. However, this is generally due to various kinds of privileges obtained from the government-owner or the government-provided monopoly position in the market.

It must be taken into account that the greater the scope of SOEs in the economy, greater the possibility and greater the temptation to assign various functions, not only economic ones, to these entities. However, while in countries such as Norway or France, for example, this temptation is strongly constrained by systemic rules and institutional maturity, in countries such as China, Russia and Egypt such constraints do not exist and certainly do not work in practice.

There is a kind of substitution when choosing how to carry out different economic policy tasks – they can be carried out either through regulatory or through ownership tools. In the case of DMEs, the choice of ownership tools is usually associated with greater social losses (costs) than the choice of regulatory tools, as a result of the aforementioned higher – in general – operational efficiency of private-owned enterprises (POEs) compared to SOEs. This efficiency premium may be a result of the rule of law. In contrast, in countries like China, private companies are also subject to arbitrary interventions and that makes the difference between them and the state companies less sharp. Because of this efficiency premium in DMEs, economic policy tasks are most often carried out using regulatory tools, by means of creating conditions for the proper functioning of private enterprises.

For EMEs the situation is different. From the point of view of political power, the time horizon for which is often not limited by the end of the parliamentary term in this group of countries, the choice of regulatory tools, targeting mainly POEs, would lead to a reduction in the potential area of political rent extraction. However, when the state acts as an owner, the opportunities for political rent extraction increase; additional sources of rent are also created. The political benefits of those in power (including the material benefits of clients designated by authorities) associated with the functioning of SOEs are more important than the social losses resulting from the lower economic efficiency of SOEs.

It must be added that for many EMEs, the choice of ownership economic policy tools seems not only more beneficial from the point of view of interests of the authorities, but also easier to carry out. SOEs, presented in the political narrative as national, domestic capital, amid social fears of globalisation can be treated as a kind of counterbalance to large foreign corporations.

The problem of the "return of SOEs" and the increasing importance of Chinese SOEs in the world

The results of our research did not confirm suggestions, formulated after the 2008–2009 crisis, of a "return of state-owned enterprises", and thus of a general increase in the scope and significance of SOEs in the global economy. Between 2009 and 2018, as many as 21 of the 32 largest economies saw a decline in the shares of SOEs (as measured by the SS-100 index), while an increase in the shares of SOEs occurred in only 11 economies. On average, the SS-100 index decreased from 28.2% to 27.4%. The total number of SOEs in the economies under review also decreased from 483 to 476, as well as all other aggregate SOE share ratios. We examined this issue in detail in Section 6.4.

These figures seem to stand in contradiction – apparent, as it turns out – to the analysis of the presence of SOEs on the global lists of major companies, most notably the Fortune Global 500 (Fortune Global 500 also features financial entities not included in our research). Indeed, an analysis of the Fortune Global 500 lists, carried out for the period 2006–2020, which is longer than the period we have adopted, using a method analogous to that applied in our research (i.e. based on distinguishing SOEs using the criterion of actual government control), shows a very clear increase in the number of SOEs during this period – from 71 to 141, almost twofold. While SOEs accounted for 14.2% of the Fortune Global 500 companies in 2006, it was 28.2% in 2020. The significant increase in the number of SOEs in the set of the world's largest companies is undeniable. However, do these elementary data prove that "the return of state-owned enterprises" has occurred? In our view - no. The data illustrated in Figure C.1 support this statement.

The data clearly show that the increase in the number of SOEs on the Fortune Global 500 lists is solely due to the increase in the number of SOEs in China. Globally, except in China, the number of SOEs on the Fortune

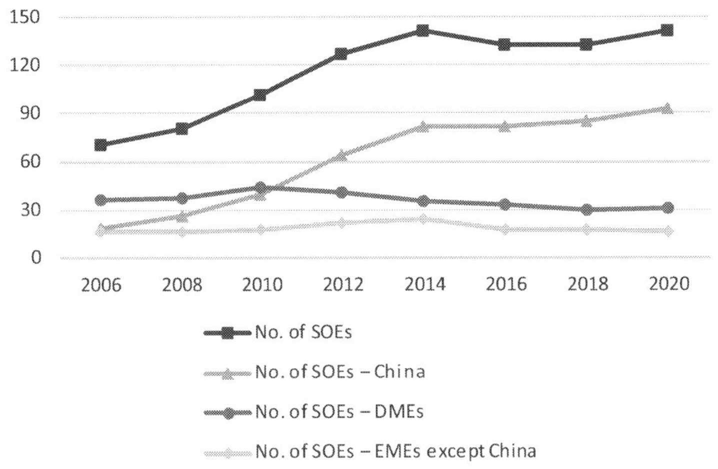

Figure C.1 Changes in the number of SOEs in the Fortune Global 500 in different country groups.
Source: Own calculations.

Global 500 lists decreased from 52 to 48 between 2006 and 2020 (on the Fortune Global 100, the decrease in SOEs was even greater). What is important, within the Chinese economy, is that SOEs have not gained importance at all – our calculations show that within the Chinese economy between 2009 and 2018, the share of the largest SOEs, as measured by the SS-100 index, declined quite markedly (from 92.1% to 85.9%). The Chinese nominal GDP grew by 245% over this period, while the GDP of the EME group (except China) grew by 88% and of the DMEs group by only 57%. The Chinese economy has been growing much faster than other economies in recent years. The consequence of this is that Chinese SOEs, which have been present in the economy of this country for years, are entering the set of largest companies in the world.

It must still be noted that the number of SOEs on the Fortune Global 500 lists has hardly changed since 2014. The steady increase in the number of Chinese SOEs is counterbalanced by the decrease in the number of SOEs in both DMEs and EMEs except China.

In our opinion, although the "hypothesis of the return of state-owned enterprises" is not correct in a quantitative sense, there is a grain of truth in it. Namely, the importance of state ownership policy within economic policy has clearly been increasing in recent years, and the range of functions of SOEs, especially non-economic ones, has been expanding in many countries. This is particularly evident in the group of EMEs, ranging from China through Russia, Indonesia, Brazil, Egypt to Poland. While the phenomenon of using SOEs as a tool of government influence on the economy is measurable, its empirical verification is very complicated. Nevertheless, the observation of the functioning of SOEs in many countries of the world over a longer period entitles us to formulate – in the form of a hypothesis – the opinions expressed above.

Implications for economic theory

In our view Peng et al. (2016) correctly identified two principal reasons why the place and role of SOEs in economic theory, especially in theories of the firm, are of minor importance. First, these theories generally assume that companies maximise profit or shareholder value in the market, which is often problematic in the case of SOEs. Thus, there was no reason to include SOEs in these theories. Additionally, the vast majority of modern economic theories were developed in the US and other Anglo-Saxon countries, "which historically do not have a sizable SOE sector", as we mentioned above. Moreover, the authors point out that the existence of SOEs somewhat contradicts axiological assumptions concerning economic theories developed in the West: "the ideological nature of the debate on state ownership has resulted in the difficulties of incorporating SOEs into theories of the firm. Some scholars have framed the debate as socialism versus capitalism, which has made it politically and ideologically difficult for Western scholars to openly advocate the potential merits of SOEs, especially in post-war decades".

There is a third reason, important in our view, for the reluctant attitude of the economic science towards SOEs. The existence of SOEs distorts the image of economics as a field of science capable of formulating universal laws and distinct from other sciences. Since the time of D. Ricardo, theoretical economists have been trying to find and formulate universal laws, i.e. laws that are general enough to cover the widest possible range of human economic activity. In the case of research on SOEs, this is difficult, if not impossible. The empirical analysis of the phenomenon of SOEs at the level of the global economy, and not just the economies of the "Western World", presented in this book, points to the fundamental ontological diversity of SOEs on a global scale, concerning the types and kinds of SOEs, as well as their purposes and functions in the economic system, the rules of operation and their relationship with the state owner. Thus, the results of synthesising research are unsatisfactory and lead to the observation that the description of the behaviour of economic entities, the principles and the effects of their operation, always underlying the economic theory, must have – at least partly – a contextual character. Consequently, economics appears not as a universal science but as a science that studies and solves problems in a given place and time. There is not and cannot be a single and coherent economic theory which, given the scale of the diversity of both the scope and consequently the significance of SOEs, would find a single universal and coherent framework and explanation of the phenomenon of SOEs in the contemporary economy.

In addition, economists studying SOEs and their place in the economic system must take into account the fact that they perform not only economic functions, but – in many countries – a strongly combined range of non-economic functions, mainly political and social (as discussed in more detail in Chapter 2), and that SOEs are, in essence, not only economic entities but often constituting elements of the state. This makes the traditional research perspective of economic science insufficient to properly recognise and understand the place and role of SOEs, as well as the principles of their functioning in the economy. An institutional perspective is needed, as well as a political and sociological one, which requires breaking the barrier of specialisation typical of modern science.

If we want to understand what SOEs are, what functions they perform or what principles they operate on in the contemporary global economy, we must give up looking for general, universal truths and theories. In this case, theoretical idealisation would imply the need for simplifications that blur the natural, multi-faceted diversity of SOEs. We need to analyse SOEs contextually, here and now, in economies at a certain level of development, in a certain political system and institutional environment, with certain economic and social or sometimes geopolitical objectives. The picture we get gives specific, detailed knowledge, but at the same time, it is incoherent, patchwork, making it impossible to formulate generalisations and universally applicable laws. This can leave researchers feeling unsatisfied or even disappointed. But, in our view, this state of affairs should be accepted with humility – this is simply the way the modern economic world is, diverse and inconsistent.

Bibliography

Peng, M. W., Bruton, G. D., Stan, C. V., & Huang, Y. (2016). Theories of the (state-owned) firm. *Asia Pacific Journal of Management*, *33*(2), 293–317.

Index

Note: **Bold** page numbers refer to tables and page numbers followed by "n" denote endnotes.